Democracy
in an Age
of Corporate
Colonization

SUNY series in Speech Communication
Dudley D. Cahn, Jr., editor

DEMOCRACY IN AN AGE OF CORPORATE COLONIZATION

Developments in Communication
and the Politics of Everyday Life

Stanley A. Deetz

STATE UNIVERSITY OF NEW YORK PRESS

Published by
State University of New York Press, Albany

© 1992   State University of New York

Printed in the United States of America

For information, address State University of New York Press,
90 State Street, Suite 700, Albany NY 12207

Production by Dana Foote
Marketing by Dana E. Yanulavich

Library of Congress Cataloging-in-Publication Data

Deetz, Stanley.
    Democracy in an age of corporate colonization : developments in
communication and the politics of everyday life / Stanley A. Deetz.
      p.   cm. — (SUNY series in speech communication)
    Includes bibliographical references and index.
    ISBN 0–7914-0863–9 (alk. paper) . — ISBN 0–7914-0864–7 (pbk. :
alk. paper)
    1. Management—Employee participation. 2. Industry—Social
aspects. 3. Communication in organizations. 4. Organizational
behavior. I. Title. II. Series.
HD5650.D43   1992
302.3'5—dc20
                                                      90–26171
                                                      CIP

10 9 8 7 6 5 4 3 2 1

For My Parents,
Oscar and Gloria

CONTENTS

Democracy in the United States, and perhaps the world, has reached an important juncture. While much of the world struggles for democracy in state political processes, meaningful public democracy is gradually disappearing in the great state democracies. In its place has arisen the most effective system of control in human history. On most counts, the corporate organization has become the most central institution in modern society. Everything from personal identity and use of natural resources to definitions of value and distribution of goods and services has increasingly come under corporate control. The extent of the modern corporate encroachment into nonwork and noneconomic sectors of life and its domination of other institutions might properly be called a new colonizing activity—a colonization of public decision making and of the everyday life world. Commercial organizations make decisions for the public, but rarely are these decisions grounded in democratic processes. Management is more often about control than about democratic decision making. Further, this corporate control and elite decision making do not rest on an open public consent, but on a consent manufactured in the workplace, reproduced in routine everyday practices, and hidden by the assumption of an open contractual relation. The price of the antidemocratic character of corporate control is more difficult for individuals to understand and respond to than excesses of the state. While the state's power is exercised primarily through restriction, corporate organizations provide "disciplinary" structures embodied in routines and technologies that appear enabling and apolitical.

The inadequacy of concepts of democracy for commanding a public interest in the corporate domination of public decision making rests largely in an obsolete understanding of communication processes and power relations. For most people, issues of democracy, representation, freedom of speech, and censorship regard the relation of individuals and groups to the government. Unfortunately the practice of democracy is limited to occasional political processes in elections and meetings. The politics and potential democracy vested in everyday life practices is rarely a focal concern. And yet it is in the day-to-day processes of living and forming collective responses that democracy either exists and makes a difference or control is exercised most deeply. Democracy is about a society's practices in reaching decisions rather than simply its means of selecting officials, otherwise state democracy becomes merely an alibi and disguise for inadequate public participation.

This work reclaims a deeper conception of political democracy through looking at the production of personal identity and joint decisions within the corporate context. This is accomplished through a reconception of the communication process in relation to the production of meaning, personal identity, and knowledge, followed by an in-depth investigation of modern corporate organizations in relation to democracy in everyday life. In bringing these issues together, this work (1) develops a conception of communication analysis appropriate for the politics of everyday life, (2) demonstrates the specific discursive processes by which meaning domination happens within commercial corporations, and (3) uses a moral, communication-based conception of democracy to critique current practices and suggest alternative ones.

This work is primarily intended for professionals and scholars interested in communication theory, organizational studies, management science, and political processes in the United States. But owing to the political and social issues the work raises, I have tried to keep the work accessible to a wider audience. Technical terms have been kept to a minimum, and I have tried to explain references to contemporary debates in social philosophy in ways that keep the issues clear to those unfamiliar with these literatures. While the book demonstrates the critical significance of communication-based analyses and explanations of social processes, the issues raised are of interdisciplinary importance. The book could be used in upper level undergraduate and graduate courses in communication theory, organizational studies, management theory, cultural studies of organizations, political theory, social philosophy, sociology of work, and American studies.

The book builds on several of my earlier attempts to deal with these issues, some of which are appropriately acknowledged here. Portions of chapter 5 are adapted from my essay "Interpretive Research in Communication," *Journal of Communication Inquiry* 3 (1977): 53–69. Sections of chapter 7 are revised from my essay "Reclaiming the Subject Matter as a Basis for Ethics and Effectiveness in Interpersonal Communication," *Communication Quarterly* 38 (1990): 226–43. Chapter 8 was developed from the first portion of an essay published with Dennis Mumby, "Reclaiming the Critical Tradition in Organizational Communication Studies," in *Communication Yearbook 13*, edited by Jim Anderson (Sage Publications, 1990), 18–47. And finally, small portions of chapters 5 and 10 first appeared in my essay "Representation of Interests and the New Communication Technologies," in *Communication and the Culture of Technology*, edited by M. Medhurst, A. Gonzalez, and T. Peterson (Washington State University Press, 1990), 43–62.

Special thanks for help in completing this manuscript are due to many. Portions of the manuscript were written while I was on a visiting appointment at Arizona State University. I wish to thank Chuck Bantz for help in securing resources and for many valuable discussions while there. The Department of Communication at Rutgers University provided important resources and release time throughout the writing process. Several individuals helped greatly in the development of the analysis and the final manuscript. I wish to thank Dennis Mumby, Charles Conrad, Michael Huspek, series editor Dudley Cahn, and three anonymous reviewers for SUNY Press for their reading, comments, and discussions regarding the manuscript. Bill Gordon, Teresa Harrison, Jim Taylor, Mats Alvesson, Hugh Willmott, and Linda Putnam also read the manuscript and provided important evaluations. Brittin Skelton, Karen Brooks, Christine Rodier, and Jane McCardell provided much needed help as research assistants. And finally, Karen Mahon, my best friend among other things, provided care, love, support, and help at all the right times. My gratitude for the help, as well as for the reminder that there is much more to life than work and books, is only partially expressed in a formal statement like this. The constantly rekindled tension of the appeal of many good things has made each moment a blessing.

Stanley Deetz
October, 1990

A scholarly work has meaning by its relation to intellectual traditions as well as by the statement it attempts to make. The task is always to interpret and contribute to a way of thinking by addressing theoretical questions as well as immediate practical ones. This work cuts across a set of modern theoretical concerns and primarily tries to stake out a position rather than to explicate the work of others. This makes it even more important to situate the work in relation to contemporary theoretical debates. I do this at the outset to relieve (or appropriately situate) the anxieties of the professional scholar, and to avoid criticism for being insensitive to critical differences. In making a pointed statement, I wish in no way to deprecate the mass of works that have carefully explicated the modern social philosophies coming primarily from Europe and the critical differences among them. But equally valuable is the desire to ask what these works say together in contrast to the operant philosophies of everyday people. In this introduction I wish to place the work that follows in the muddy conflictual field of contemporary social philosophy as well as in relation to the practices of everyday life. The reader more interested in the social issues the work addresses might simply choose to begin with chapter 1.

Two fundamental changes have taken place in modern society, one ideational and the other structural and material. First, the basic conception of the relationships among the individual, the external world, and social relations has changed, thus making the understanding of communicative practices central to modern analysis and necessitating a different view of communication. Communication studies have gradually become freed from psychological reductionism and have come to pay attention to the processes by which meaning is produced rather than simply those by which it is transmitted.

Greater understanding of the social construction of the individual, meaning, and knowledge is commonplace, but the implications remain to be worked out. Central to this is a politics of meaning, experience, and sensuality—a politics of everyday life. Such a politics reclaims democracy as a continuous life practice of joint decision making against the reduction to free expression and representational governance. Numerous scholars have taken these concerns seriously in the analysis of state control and mass media, but in the rush to study repressive mechanisms, media, and technologies, most have missed what I consider to be a more significant second change.

The modern corporation has emerged as the central form of working relations and as the dominant institution in society. In achieving dominance, the commercial corporation has eclipsed the state, family, residential community, and moral community. This shadowing has hidden or suppressed important historical conflicts among competing institutional demands. Corporate practices prevade modern life by providing personal identity, structuring time and experience, influencing education and knowledge production, and directing entertainment and news production. The modern corporation operates on a web of what Foucault has called "disciplinary structures." The consent manufactured and the routines reproduced by corporate disciplinary power stretch deeper into life and are more difficult for individuals to understand and respond to than control provided by a "sovereign" power. The "rationalization" and "normalization" of corporate experience provides cover for forms of arbitrary domination through systematically distorted expression, suppressed conflict, and dominant articulations of experience. With the growth of such systems, the potential of corporations to represent their various stakeholders and contribute to the general welfare must be questioned. With the growth of corporate influence outside of the corporate site and the reduction of political questions to economic ones, the public becomes fragmented, recollected only by temporary images, and the possibility of meaningful public decision making appears progressively less likely. Significantly, commercial corporations, even in the democratic states, do not operate with democratic principles. The inequitable distribution of political, economic, and social power supports a narrow and distorted system of interest development and representation.

While these are worldwide changes fed in part by the growth of multinational corporate units, they are instantiated differently in different cultural contexts. This work will only consider the democracy of everyday life and corporate development within the United States. Although this excludes consideration of global features, the choice allows the work to focus on local examples in more detail. The U.S. corporate model, however, impacts on all cultural groups in the world and is a principal player in the development of a world political as well as economic order. The tragedy is that the Eastern European nations may lose their democracy to external corporate structures almost as soon as they gain it from external state ones. Insight into the structures of U.S. corporate practices can be extended into more general implications for other societies as they engage in their own developmental processes.

The theme driving this work is quite simple. Corporate organizations make most decisions regarding the use of resources, the development of technologies, the products available, and the working relations among people. Organizational decisions, products, and practices have major effects on human development. Anything that influences the continued formation or deformation of the human character has ethical implications. While no one is in a position to define the social good or what the human character ultimately should be like, the full representation of differing people and their interests would seem to be fundamental to ethical choices regarding development. *Representation, communication,* and *morality* become mutually defining terms. The desire for a stronger everyday democracy is deeply shared in different forms in modern society but remains to be implemented for lack of clear conception and alternative practices. I do not agree with the postmodernist claim that there can be no public and that all moral democratic impulses are by necessity disguised dominations or nostalgia for a past. But the public often has no opportunity for expression and genuine decision making, and what have passed for "moral" understandings are often opposed to further democratization. The modern enlightenment project based upon reason and technology may well be dead, and with it the liberal ideals and utopian visions it spawned. But this need not be seen as simply dumping us into a reactive amoral postmodern reality. Perhaps it better lays the foundation for a new age of responsibility and, most importantly, *insightful responsiveness.*

Let me be clear from the outset that reclaiming a democratic ideal can not become a hope for some past social arrangement that was somehow more fair or pure than our own. From

the Greek denial of citizenship for women and slaves to contemporary silencing and marginalization of different groups of
citizens, democracy has always been partial (incomplete and
favoring some) and often used as a cover for privilege and domination. But the criticism leveled at the Greeks, as well as more
modern versions, is still driven by a vague, historically situated
hope of greater democracy. If we trash the concept of democracy along with the liberal humanism that underpins its modern
form and justification, I fear that we will not have gained a new
era of freedom but will have lost a powerful and evocative
hope. Every critique of privilege need not evoke a conception
of an ideal state without arbitrary privileges, but can be a principled practice to give the voiceless a voice. It is neither an
ancient nor a modern-enlightenment form of democracy that
this work hopes to reclaim. It is not a specific ideal to be
encouraged or implemented. Democracy is a critical, incomplete, tension-filled motive/motif, a fiction that compels
against the reality of privilege. The task of each age is to understand the privileges and dominations of its time and to broaden
the reaches of participation.

Current social and organizational practices frequently limit
the development of moral democratic understanding at the
same time as they limit representation. Consequently we have
arbitrarily skewed human development, and the processes of
development have been hidden from public awareness. Normative guidance helps isolate limitations on representation, providing a means of critiquing certain practices and enabling more
ethical practice. While competing norms may be advanced,
norms based in communication and democracy do not define *a
priori* how we should develop, but promote conflict and discussion where various power configurations have closed them
down. The issues advanced here cannot be reduced to corporate
(that is, managerial) social responsibility or to worker participation in decision making. Processes of determination of the social
good, decisions as to who should participate, and the nature of
meaningful participation require a deeper look at democracy
and communication. Ultimately such concerns demand that the
modern corporation be considered as the new site of public decision making rather than as limited and protected by an imaginary link to older, small, private businesses.

In a capitalist society, private owners have the right to have
their property and profit interests represented. But in a democratic society, we recognize that other groups and interests are

equally invested in the corporation and have their own rights of representation. Management could be seen as a legitimate coordinating function whereby conflict among these various interests could be brought to the fore and innovative responses could be formulated. Unfortunately, the *managerialism* practiced in the modern corporation has failed on both economic and representational grounds. With managerialism, certain interests are arbitrarily privileged, the process of reaching decisions is distorted, and meaningful conflicts are suppressed. And finally, managerialism's arbitrary authority relations demean the human character.

The early portion of this work proposes a conception of democratic communication that can provide a more productive and interesting way of discussing power and the production and representation of human interests in corporate decision making. Most current conceptions of democratic communication focus on freedom of expression and the open marketplace of ideas. Articulating democracy through such conceptions tends to portray democracy merely as an expression of self-interests rather than as a form of social relations that aims simultaneously at developmental individualization and the collective good. American pragmatists such as James, Mead, and most clearly Dewey understood these issues and provided a more useful conception of democracy, but they were limited by an emphasis on reflective consciousness and an inadequate conception of language. And much of their analysis has been lost through the years.

More recent European works have, of course, recovered the interest of these works and provided new developments and political sensitivities. Writers like Gadamer, Habermas, Baudrillard, Bourdieu, Lyotard, and Foucault have produced works that can be used to produce or recollect a conception of communication as participation in the construction of identity, knowledge, and meaning, even while the later few strongly deny the value of modern liberal democracy. They all work in very different directions, but together they create a way of thinking about communication in which the nature and potential problems of communicative practices change. I have chosen to focus on what can be said in common from these works rather than explicating their differences. Such a move will offend some. For example, suggesting a latent political practice in Foucault analysis that is complementary to Habermas's work has been much debated. I do it tentatively here, but it is still troublesome. But showing how such contrary analyses can work together hardly diminishes their difference. Rather I hope to reveal a stream with many forces that provide many new channels to cut, cross, and bridge.

The current work is a result of several years of attempting to come to grips with central concerns regarding communication and contemporary social theory. These concerns are presented as a group of problematic issues with suggestions as to how they might be approached. These issues grow out of a tradition of work that differs greatly from most communication research in the United States. There are many reasons for the choice of traditions and many paths that might have been taken to coming to formulate these central issues. This work reflects my own realization of what I take to be an important moment in human history. With Foucault, though for different reasons, the personal motives arise as a continued struggle to understand the events of 1968. The analysis itself bears little relation to the specific issues and events of that time. Rather than looking back, this work hopes to focus the struggle for democracy in the 1990s. My personal path adds context to the work itself as a presentation of one way a generation tries to be responsive and responsible to the issues of its age.

By the 1960s the functionalists' domination of communication studies in United States was so complete that any critical analysis of the social consequences of existing communication conceptions and practices was nearly impossible. Conceptions of meaning based in reductionist psychology, concern with control and system integration, fragmented empirical observations, and preoccupation with transmission conspired together to make impossible a rich theoretical understanding of the social historical nature of modern communication practice. The weaknesses of such a position are developed clearly in the more recently published debates about critical and administrative research. They need no development here. The costs of such weaknesses become increasingly clear with the emergence of expanded computer-assisted communication technologies and accompanying policy issues. Attempts to reform this tradition with new concepts, in most cases, either provided technical solutions within the dominant conception (e.g., feedback loops and mediational processes), reaffirmed existing assumptions (e.g., focus on receiver interpretive processes), or generated no systematic development or research (e.g., process conceptions). As I will argue later, both the conceptual weakness and the social issues of the day required a return to fundamental issues of communication, social existence, and social development.

Against this backdrop, as a doctoral student in the early seventies, I, like many, was taken by the so-called "linguistic turn" in philosophy. As a result, much of my early work was an attempt to understand the manners in which language and communication could serve as guiding philosophical issues in the same way that mind and consciousness had been to the generation before. This interest led to a master's thesis exploring speech-act theory and a doctoral dissertation that developed implications of Heidegger's and Gadamer's work for communication theory. This path lead to research concerned with the social construction of knowledge and meaning, focusing especially on the methods one might use to study these processes. In doing this work I became preoccupied with the inequality of representation in knowledge and meaning construction and with the concept of power. These issues led me to the German critical theorists and finally to various contemporary French authors, especially Foucault.

The debt to Habermas's work in particular will be apparent. Habermas provides several important points of departure for the development of an adequate theory of communication. Significantly, he has developed a theory of interests that simultaneously accounts for social historical development and the individual's subjective experience. Further, he was able to show how a moral political stance could be grounded in the communicative structures of natural communication communities. But the project here is still quite distinct from his. His theory of communication is still largely a reproduction model growing partly from his utilization of analyses in sociology, philosophy of language, and argumentation rather than careful consideration of natural interaction systems. The critiques of his work, focusing on intellectual elitism and hence problems with the universality of his universal pragmatics and his restrictive negative account of power, have to be taken seriously. And his emphasis on consensus formation leaves out the equally important task of reclaiming dissent and conflict as a necessary first, as well as continual move to keep any consensus (no matter how legitimate in formation) from becoming dominant and suppressing emerging conflict.

Habermas himself presented what I take to be a more productive project than the critical philosophical one he pursued. As he suggested: "We can try to assess the empirical usefulness of formal-pragmatic insights. For this purpose, there are above all three relevant areas of research: the explanation of pathological patterns of communication, the evolution of the foundations of sociocultural forms of life, and the ontogenesis of capabilities for action" (1984, 139). Habermas rejects such an alternative primarily owing to the sheer volume of work that would have to be done in each area. If we take away Habermas's desire for a universal foundation, and limit the study to a specific context, the project becomes more feasible. In looking at pathological communication systems, their formation, and the remaining action possibilities, I wish here to accept much of Habermas's ideal speech situation as a moral process but to the end of recovering and sustaining difference and conflict rather than to produce a new more legitimate consensus.

Perhaps the project is best conceptualized in Dreyfus and Rabinow's (1986) terms of "social maturity." This would combine a Germanic philosophical concern with critical reason and Foucault's interpretive analytics. Social maturity would enable us

> (1) to describe and interpret our current practices so as to understand what aspects of our modernity we have to accept as inescapable; (2) to characterize the sense, diffusely manifest in the practices of some epochs that in some pervasive way things have gone awry...; (3) to articulate further a widely shared sense that the promise of the enlightenment has yet to be fulfilled; (4) to go beyond thinkers and anti-thinkers in taking a stand toward the present that does not legislate universal norms but encourages conflicts of interpretation; (5) and to go beyond Foucault in rhetorically strengthening the postenlightenment practices that are positive, such as many of our technological, legal and medical advantages, and in identifying and preserving pre-enlightenment practices which have so far escaped rationalization and normalization. (Dreyfus and Rabinow 1986, 120–21).

Such a project requires an examination of the corporate organization as a key institution in which such concerns are played out. This work is a beginning.

The first two chapters of the book look at the place of the corporation in the politics of everyday life. Through reviewing its structural form and relation to the state, family, education, and mass media, the corporation is shown as the central modern institution. Further, it is shown as having significant effects on the quality of life, political and conceptual activity, and the contemporary production of meaning. Finally, it is shown that while the corporation could be a public democratic site, it is protected from answering to its various publics while it colonizes their perceptions, thoughts, feelings, and actions.

Chapters 3, 4, and 5 develop the connection between conceptions of communication and the advancement of participatory democracy. Initially this requires a consideration of the role of theorizing in the production of a democratic consciousness and practice. Second, the historical relations among social needs, the conception of communication, and the issue of participation is investigated. This leads to a discussion of the emergence of a political understanding of experience and identity situated in a philosophy of language and communication.

Chapters 6 and 7 then develop a formal-pragmatic theory of communication in relation to the moral claim of democracy. The interest is not in reconstructing the universal conditions for communicative action per se, but in proposing a formal-pragmatic theory as a partial but heuristic device for guiding and evaluating communication practice within contemporary social conditions. As such, the conception serves as a both normative and descriptive theory, providing an account of expressive systems including technologically assisted ones, and a guide for policy decisions. Habermas provides an important angle on this concern, but one that is better seen as a moment in larger, more complex analyses. Both Gadamer's ontology of understanding and Foucault's discursive structures provide conflicting but necessary alternative moments. Here, the corporation will be considered as a potential site of pathological communicative practices exemplifying the general forms of discursive closure and systematic distortion common to the modern age. These practices may be considered pathological to the extent that (1) they violate normative standards already held by members of a democratic society, (2) they endanger the survival of the human and other species, and (3) they pose arbitrary limits on the development of individualization and the realization of collective good.

Chapters 8 and 9 propose the corporate institution as an essential sociohistorical location (or site in the anthropological sense) in which to examine communicative practice. This focuses on the historical development of the corporation within the rationalization of the Western life world. The corporation is to be understood as an institution that both epitomizes the advanced development of instrumental-reason domination and privileges particular groups and interests. Both lead to hidden, suppressed conflict. The rise of *managerialism* provides a dominated and repressed politics of everyday life based in the desire for control and the translation of all of life into a power-and-money code. The development of the modern corporate form has provided economic well-being and opportunity for most. But even the most beneficial growth leads to ecological and human costs if its tendencies toward systematically distorted development are left unmediated and unchecked.

Chapters 10 and 11 provide the detailed analysis of how power, control, and systematic distortion exist in the modern corporation. The initial focus is on the character of disciplinary power. The concern is with how the politically loaded construction of perception, categories of people, knowledge, and personal identity become invisible in practices of standardization and normalization. Self-surveillance, forms of knowledge, accounting, data collection, and communication technologies will each be investigated to demonstrate their political effects. This analysis is then extended through examining the active processes of producing consent and reproducing these political constructions. Discussion will consider the production of images, language use, narratives, and cultural management as active, if hidden, strategic political actions.

Finally, chapter 12 considers alternative structures and processes of communication that focus resistance to domination and reclaim meaningful conflict. There is no desire here to propose how to do it right or to design a new organizational form; rather, the interest is in providing perpetual critique and constant reclaiming of openness to the future. In contrast to the technological futurists and seekers of excellence, this work may appear more filled with dismay than hope. But hope, faith, and optimism for a future drive this work. The hope is neither revolutionary nor utopian. Change comes in the responsive moment. It is in the momentary, daily, and commonplace decisions within organizations that a more responsible practice happens. The modern corporate form has been developed and inculcated over a rather lengthy period of time. It has fingers in every aspect of modern life. By necessity, its meaningful change will follow a long developmental curve, but that should not keep us from starting.

The social construction of order *and* change has been a primary theme of the twentieth century. When reading various descriptions of our time, we appear caught between seeing social control as mounting and denying freedom and seeing modern life as fragmented, groundless, and without center. Both can be true. The point can neither be to claim a new center—a new modernity—nor to promote a postmodern fragmentation. The development of a productive tension between new mutually formed centers *and* the perpetual critique of them becomes our task.

But for better or worse, this new form of life will not be simply forged by the fires of the great intellectual traditions that got us here, for they struggle to sustain themselves in our time. Such a new life will be tentatively pounded out by everyday choices of the people who go to work every day. The choices of and for the future cannot be worked out in advance but are momentary and continuous. In our ordinary roles as everyday folk, we seem to understand that claims to Truth and utopian dreams are fictions used to control us, a lesson we often forget in our specialized roles as scientists and scholars. But it is also in the everyday that we are least aware of the forces of power and complicity that direct, limit, and distort the formative practical choices of life. The everyday penetration into the basis of social order is partial at best. And everyday personal freedom and social cynicism frequently obscure and support existing forces of control and advantage. I write as an academic with the tools, theories, and all-too-often pedantic tone that accompany that. I cannot deny the various privileges that come with the role, including the time to reflect critically and hopefully penetrate aspects of social order that others must take for granted.

I share with others the frustration of not always knowing where to start or what is of value. With all the simple and obvious transcendent groundings no longer supportable or understood as merely the handmaidens of vested political interests, what can guide such choices and critical analysis? How can we lose the pretense of authority, theoretical purity, and privilege and yet gain the advantages of complex modern theoretical analytics? How do we maintain a partnership in two communities, to open a more productive dialogue about everyday practice and to enhance the rigor of theoretical development? Writing between the obvious groups risks leaving each unhappy. Writing with conviction risks being rejected as dogmatic or elitist. I seek to be bold, though I hope not unfair. I hope to stake a claim for an arena of discussion, and trust others will set the boundaries. Dreyfus and Rabinow (1986) attribute to Foucault what every modern work, including this one, aspires to: "There is a kind of ethical and intellectual integrity which, while vigorously opposing justifications of one's own actions in terms of religion, law, science or philosophical grounding, nonetheless seeks to produce a new ethical form of life which foregrounds imagination, lucidity, humour, disciplined thought and practical wisdom" (121). I hope to contribute in that tradition.

CHAPTER 1

Corporate Colonization of the Life World

> If the corporation is not to defeat democracy, then democracy must defeat the corporation—which is to say that the curbing of monopoly and the transformation of corporatism is a political, not an economic, task. Democracy proclaims the priority of the political over the economic; the modern corporation rebuts that claim by its very existence. [L]iberal democracy is too vulnerable—its citizens too passive and its ideas of freedom and individualism too illusory—to recognize, let alone do battle with, the mammoth modern corporation that has assumed the identity and ideology of the traditional family firm.
> (Benjamin Barber 1984, 257)

Barber is one of the more recent of numerous authors over the past one hundred years who have been concerned with the growth of organizational bureaucracies and corporate power. From the beginning of the industrial revolution and accompanying bureaucratic growth, social scientists have shared with workers, elected representatives, and the general public various concerns with the transformation of work, power relations, and democracy. Many descriptions have been exaggerated and most of the extreme predictions have not come to fruition, yet the social transformations, while more innocent and quiet, have been great.

As we look back on these writings, we have to be as interested in the effects of these writings on decisions that were made and what has actually come to pass as we are with their predictive accuracy. Images from these writings have directed attention to aspects of our world that were overlooked in their naturalness and helped produce knowledge that could not have been produced in their absence. Our future is not just to be predicted, it is also to be produced. What is and what ought to be are carefully intertwined in every observation and produced in every decision. Our images and conceptions can lead us as well as mislead us; they can lead and enable us to see, or they can substitute for being in touch with the world. The fear that comes with the fallibility of our conceptions should lead us to be not more cautious but more bold. The lesson of our age is that there is no instant truth, no instant rationality, no instant morality, no *a priori* certainty (R. Bernstein 1984). Ironically, the new Western package is the old-fashioned kind. Indeed truth, rationality, morality, and certainty are to be worked out through conflicting expressions by real people in real communication communities growing and passing with those same communities (Apel 1972). Fallibility is understood again as the opening for discussion rather than as the reason for reserve and silence. As Charles Sanders Peirce was fond of saying, what is one to do with a great idea but to run with it, to follow it to its end. Others will always pull us back. I propose at the outset a new debate regarding the nature of the corporate workplace and democracy, a debate fostered more by hope of a better future than by condemnation of the present or fear of an impending crisis. Hopefully, the absence of crisis potential and the lack of promise for quick answers will leave a space for discussion rather than subtract from the critical nature of the discussion.

Corporations and Democracy: The Feudal Analogue

A variety of writers have identified a number of concerns for the nation-state and democracy itself with the rapid development of the significance of major national and transnational corporations. The most extreme image they have produced is that of a new age in world development. The analogy central to this image is that of a new feudalism (Mirow and Maurer 1982; Schiller 1989; Williams 1983). The extreme version of the image is something like this:

The transnational organizations are structured as a new feudal system with a handful of lords who are constantly at war.

The battles are civil and courtly owing to kinship ties through cross-directorates, international cartels, and common social and educational circles. The wars transpire as takeovers and mergers, since it is the control of information and workers, rather than land, that is contested. The boundaries of the lords' corporations are best represented by lines of authority and constraints on information flow. Employee obedience to those in power supersedes any private romantic loyalty to church, family, community, or nation-state. The employee is first a resource, never a citizen. While the ongoing wars are psychologically costly to this mass of corporate workers, the largely benevolent lord offers support in terms of retraining and relocation payments, through paid physical and mental health plans, through maintaining a pleasant work environment with integrated cultural practices and values, and through the openness of the system so that anyone might him- or herself become a lord (at least hypothetically). Although they are often unpleasant and disruptive, the wars make grand media tales of warriors and intrigue and clearly appear far less costly than the old tension and property wars of the nation-state system, which had become harmful to regularized commerce.

The nation-states retain importance by maintaining a forum for resolution of boundary conflicts and by promoting stable work environments by legislating fair practices and regulation. Further, the state assures stable market conditions and provides a well-trained labor force. Through participation in elections, people feel secure and protected and feel that state policing action is legitimate. Occasionally the national state bureaucracy interferes with corporate action by restricting data flow or protecting less advantaged segments of society (often those hurt in corporate wars), but generally it provides the necessary regulation for corporate development and successful commerce. State power is constantly limited by the fear of big government and the threat of centralized state control of thought and information. The corporate form delivered the consumer goods, and the pro-growth attitudes sustained the ever higher desire for consumption.

It is small wonder that life is generally so integrated and harmonious. Children are born in corporate hospitals environmentally structured with corporate values of rationality and routine, go to corporate sites with their parents to participate in corporate-run daycare, and from there go to schools where they primarily learn positive work-related skills and attitudes. In

addition, most transnationals own their own publishing houses, magazines, newspapers, movie studios, radio stations, and
television networks,which provide the bulk of the information,
news, and entertainment in each society in the world.

Of course, this is an extreme version of the contemporary
situation. But the elements of truth are responsible for the bodily felt urge to refute the account, to "yes, but" it, or to assure
ourselves that things are okay. Without debating the accuracy
of this view or making value judgments about the goodness or
harm of such a potential or real situation, clearly even the most
conservative reformation of the account raises questions about
the changing nature or even viability of democracy. If we look
closer at this story, democracy is left a funny role. Decision
making that affects the general public happens in three realms:
the legislative body, the administrative/regulatory/policing
bureaucracy, and the corporate. Yet only the legislative body
has elected representation. The modern corporation is the most
protected from direct public control, and it is there that most
decisions are made.

If the feudal account has any validity, our old history lessons
lead us to wonder about a historical cycle where a new concept
of democracy might become the issue. The imagination runs
with dumping data in the bay (probably letting viruses eat it),
magnets on computer disks, and cries of "no takeover, no profit
sharing, no movement of operations without representation."
Surely statements of the inalienable right to meaningful work,
protection of native cultures, and freedom of community and
nation-state allegiance cannot be far behind. Clear differences
can be demonstrated between the corporate and feudal world
systems, but the corporation looks far more like a feudal system
than the small family business, an image that is often used to
stop discussion of alternate systems of administration.

The imagination sets a kind of anchor point. The descriptions and issues raised by such images deserve a careful assessment. It is not enough to grant some truth to each point of
view on the issues; differences reflect the need for greater specification of "under what circumstances" or examination of the
warrants for claims made. Most of this volume will develop
conceptions that enable a meaningful account and discussion
of corporations and democracy in the modern context; this
requires a reformed discussion of what politics and democracy
are all about and the nature and effects of the emergence of the
modern corporate form. In doing so, it raises questions about

the processes of communication in a democracy and internal to corporations. In the end, developmental processes are explored in light of their contribution to the representation of human interests. I will start with a specification of the issues involved.

The Centrality of the Corporate Institution

The extreme image is partially right. In many respects the corporate sector has become the primary institution in modern society, overshadowing the state in controlling and directing of individual lives and influencing collective social development. Workplace values and practices extend into nonwork life through time structuring, educational content, economic distributions, product development, and creation of needs. Modern corporations affect society by both their products and their income distribution but also by the practices internal to them. This is to suggest not a simple or unidirectional effect, but a critical way of pulling together social forces and providing a particular "circuit" of power (Clegg 1989).

Major national and international corporations have frequently, wittingly and unwittingly, replaced religious, familial, educational, and community institutions in the production of meaning, personal identity, values, knowledge, and reasoning. Rather than each sector having competing demands worked out in floating day-to-day decision making, corporate ideology and practices form a relatively harmonious hierarchical integration largely through distorting the expression of competing needs located in other institutions and suppressing the potential conflicts. In such a fixed mechanical integration, translations and calculations in steering media such as power and money replace discussion and compromise as the primary modes of integration. With such institutional domination in place, every other institution subsidizes or pays its dues for the integration given by the corporation structure, and by so doing reduces its own institutional role. The state developed for public good interprets that as the need for order and economic growth. The family that provided values and identity transforms that to emotional support and standard of living. The educational institution that fostered autonomy and critical thought trains for occupational success.

The extent of the modern corporate encroachment into nonwork life and transformation of other institutions might properly be called a "colonizing" activity—a colonization of the life world (Habermas 1984, 1987). As will become clear, much of this "colonization" is organic rather than merely mechanical and has arisen along the line of extension of dominant existing values and practices. Everyday language has gradually become commercialized, private control of media and places of expression has been extended and centralized, education has become increasingly professionalized and focused on job skills, and women have added to a less expensive and more highly trained work force. In many respects the modern corporation has been the benefactor rather than initiator of such social changes. But the corporate sector has also been active in getting favorable legislation passed to extend corporate power and control. The corporate world's fear of what was seen as a liberal press and antibusiness sentiment on campuses has contributed to huge expenditures on public relations, greater educational involvement, and the purchase of most mass communication capacities. None of this has been trivial, and significant shifts in institutional relations have resulted.

The Eclipse of the State

Much has been written during the past decade on the complex changing relationships between business organizations and the state largely as a result of the new communication systems and technologies (Braman 1989; Schiller 1986; Wallerstein 1980). Business organizations have become the primary institution in many societies, perhaps even in the United States. Part of this is a result of sheer economic power. The United States is one of a handful of nations with gross national products larger than the gross product of several international corporations. Deeply involved with the growth of the multinationals have been issues of accountability and effects on nations' economies and public policies. As Morgan (1986) summarized:

> Many modern organizations are larger and more powerful than nation-states; but, unlike nation-states, they are often not accountable to anyone but themselves. For example, recent research has suggested that the activities of many multinationals, particularly those operating from the United States, are highly centralized, their foreign subsidiaries being tightly controlled through policies, rules, and regulations set by headquar-

ters. The subsidiaries have to report on a regular basis (often weekly), and their staffs are often allowed very little influence on key decisions affecting the subsidiary. The resources of the multinationals are also usually managed in a way that creates dependency rather than local autonomy (302).

But structure, as well as size and power, is the issue. In the historically "less planned" economies, the state's power is exercised primarily through restriction and crude guidance through taxation and environmental protection, while corporate organizations are empowered to make most decisions as to technological development, utilization of resources, and working relations among people. As will be shown, such a situation is likely to grow, since the state lacks the ability and resources to collect independent data, to engage in large-scale monitoring, and to generate large-scale value consensus, *even if* it desired to create values different from those instituted by corporate organizations (Votaw and Sethi 1973). Clearly, even the "planned" economies as well as the traditional societies of the world gradually had to develop a market orientation as they opened up to international commerce (Evans 1989). The point here is not to present a nostalgic claim for a strong nation-state or national allegiance, any more than it is to make a claim for a return to the primacy of any other institution. We should recognize, however, that the modern corporation is a significant site of public decision making, perhaps more significant than the state. Any conception of politics that restricts political analysis to governance by the state misses the operant politics of modern society. Certainly federal officials have not been unaware of the change. Even *Newsweek* (Clift 1990) recently featured an article entitled "They're Crying in the Capital: Washington Discovers its Global Irrelevance," outlining the sense of loss of state importance (though focusing on the absence of press attention rather than the absence of power). Clearly the sense of relevancy changes with wars and international tensions. But the trend toward an invisible regulatory mechanism and corporate-run public decisions seems clear.

The State Subsidy of Corporations.   The growing corporate domination of social decision making is not simply a result of the separation of the public from the private or of a minimalist view of government. In the United States, the federal government actively supports and promotes corporate interests. Or as

Gandy (1982) would most completely argue, the government and press are essentially corporate "subsidies." For example, the regulation of bandwidth in radio broadcasting promotes commercial stability and allows competing corporations to fight the economic battle in the FCC rather than in the more costly marketplace (Streeter 1989). The United States executive-branch decisions to support market-regulated, rather than socially regulated, transnational data flows shows a procorporate growth position not shared by most other nations, who may be more vulnerable and use different criteria (Schiller 1989; Gandy 1982). Even state agencies such as social welfare, hospitals, job (re)training centers, and schools perform important procorporation political functions such as disposing with troublesome social problems, defining notions of health and safety, legitimating societal patterns of inegalitarian treatment and domination, and preparing people for future corporate needs. Such "subsidies" appear natural, necessary and appropriate. Clearly, at root, the enlightenment transformations left the state as the *"guarantor of society's progress"* (Donzelot 1988, 395). Global competitiveness and increased material goods are seen as state responsibilities fulfilled by the promotion of corporate interests. As Luke (1989) claimed, "Private-sector firms have teamed up with the blessing of public-sector state agencies to regulate the consumption of goods and services of private individuals in the privacy of their own homes as part of a larger public interest of constant economic growth" (98). In this strange logic, the state becomes the most powerful promotor of commercial organizations as the means of fulfilling its public obligation.

Although governmental bureaucracies, like corporate ones, are complex, multifaceted, and often filled with contradictions, the directions seem clear. Corporations support a minimalist government in regard to social planning and social decisions, and a big and active government for the promotion of corporate autonomy and commercially based decision making. Public decisions rest more and more in the economic rather than in the political sphere. The extent of the corporate desire to reduce potential public-criteria competition was clear in a National Commission report on private/public sector interaction in the information area. Schiller (1989) summarized the issue: "Industry in this case challenged the right of the public sector (government, libraries, public universities, etc.) to engage in *any* informational activities the industry regarded as its own province" (80). Be it postal service, retirement funds, road construction, or information, the corporate sector aims at taking as its own any area of service where profit (subsidized or not) can be made and relegating only unprofitable services to the state (which, as a side effect, further demonstrates the inefficiency of publicly run services).

Democracy is threatened as governments give far more governance power and public decision making to the commercial sector. Mirow and Maurer (1982) document the tremendous power and effects multinationals can have on societies around the world. Such organizations pose threats to all democracies. As Morgan (1986) expressed well, contradictions "arise when strong authoritarian powers like the multinationals are allowed to exist in democratic states. For they are in a position to make complete nonsense out of the democratic process, obliging governments to be more responsive to corporate interests than to those of the people who elected them" (304). The concern is not primarily that such activities are often exploitative and that income is shifted to the hands of a few, but that certain groups have the "capacity to control the ends toward which the vast resources of large organizations are directed" (Perrow 1979, 14). Multinationals, however, are not the only powerful force, and it is not just the outcome of major public issues that is at stake. Authoritarian structures eat at democracy in the moment-to-moment processes of everyday life. Such issues will be taken up later.

Corporate Forms of Power. Significantly, the issues involved are deeper and more complex than simply a shift in power from the state to the corporation and a change in the site of public decisions. The type of power being exercised, the manner of its deployment, and the form of decision making are different. Foucault (1980a) argued that the idea of a sovereign, legitimate state passed away some time ago. In some sense, the rise of democracy itself noted a shifting, floating sovereign with power widely dispersed in the society. Certainly the state exists and has its effects, but to a great extent its existence misguides our attention as it conceals the actual procedures of power and the operant sites of decision making. Foucault (1980b, 83ff.) argued that the predominant discussions of power treat it in relation to sovereign rights and that power has a juridico-discursive character. Primarily, power is conceptualized as restrictive of freedom; hence questions about the right or necessity by which a rule made acquire central importance. The rule of law is not only restrictive but restricted. Its extension must always be justified over and against the power and rights of the individual.

The state as a social force arose in a historical process. The historical development of the state as a public entity centralized and exhausted all institutional legal claims on the individual except for those obligations that the individual freely and contractually enters into as a private person, e.g., working for a corporation and abiding by its rules, or tithing at a church. Such a centralization seemed necessitated by the conflicting demands of numerous dense and entangled prestate powers of conflicting lords and the church. The corporation appears to inherit a similar function at this historical point. This is partly a result of the construction of the postmodern person and emerging conceptual weaknesses in state coordination.

With the schematization of state power in juridical form, the logic of law, taboo, and censorship appears as a normal extension of the conception of power in different aspects of life. "Confronted by a power that is law, the subject who is constituted as subject—who is 'subjected'—is he who obeys. To the formal homogeneity of power in these various instances corresponds the general form of submission in the one who is constrained by it—whether the individual in question is the subject opposite the monarch, the citizen opposite the state, the child opposite the parent, or the disciple opposite the master. A legislative power on one side, and an obedient subject on the other" (Foucault 1980b, 85). Strong state power becomes intolerable because it restricts freedom and does so visibly, the visibility extending to discussions of state control or restrictions on the discussion of control. The breakdown of the oppressive governments in Eastern Europe is the most recent example of that. Such a conception effectively hides or draws attention away from the "devious and supple mechanism of power" that characterizes most of the advanced democracies in the Western world, a power that "is tolerable only on condition that it mask a substantial part of itself" (Foucault 1980b, 86). Control and influence are actually dispersed into norms and standard practices as products of moral, medical, sexual, and psychological regulation—what Foucault called "discipline." This topic will be developed later, but in general, power thus is not dispersed in modern society to citizens who argue and vote and determine the politics of central government, but is spread out through lines of conformity, commonsense observations, and determination of propriety.

"Disciplinary power" poses a new set of questions regarding freedom, representation, and democracy. What can we say, then, of this power that is so masked, a power that normalizes experience rather than provides norms for action, a power that is not up for election, a power that escapes democracy? And given the fragmentation of power sites and the conflict of pulls from competing institutions in the postmodern context, how does the corporation arise as a new center providing the same coordination and relief of tension that the state arose to replace (and suppress) in its time? What is of interest is not so much the powerlessness of the state that presumably represents the will of the people, but the organization of these innumerable sites of disciplinary power through the modern corporation and the complicity of the state in these hidden power relations. The modern corporate power is not monolithic but more like a web that has sites or nodes of decision and control (Clegg 1989). The control knits together practices and decisions of institutions and individuals in everyday life, providing what Laclau and Mouffe (1985) described as a "sutured" totality. Contemporary society is not so much organized around a dominant worldview, a grand narrative, or integrative consensual processes, as tied together through partial stories and numerous mechanisms of coordination. Such effects are at once centralized and dispersed, and analysis must move between centered to decentered concepts of the locus of control. The state is not the only institution increasingly residing in the shadow of corporate organization. The family and community, educational institutions, and the mass media all feel the effects.

The Corporate Structuring of Community and Family

Corporate work practices have transformed the family and community both subjectively and materially. Elias (1973; see Dégot 1987) has provided the most complete description of the development of "industrial civility" whereby values of restraint of personal feelings, good manners, and time structuring move from their development as important aspects of organizational efficiency to being extended into society as a whole (see also Lefebvre 1968). This analysis is in many ways simply a more sensitive and detailed treatment of the historical move Weber (1978; Habermas 1984) examined in the development of the methodical way of life from the Protestant work ethic. Clearly, over time the family and community have lost their primary institutional functions to a variety of secondary institutions. As Luke (1989) argues, "The family system necessarily has been dismantled from without as professional experts in areas of health care, childbirth, nutrition, education, fashion, morality, elder care, shelter, leisure, and mortuary and funeral services expropriated these functions from the family, where they had been provided naturally as use value, to return them in exchange as commodified goods and services" (108). To be sure, life has been materially enriched by these transformations. The new institutional arrangements, however, enable greater and often unnecessary standardization and most importantly greater control by powerful groups like corporations. Some of this control is direct, but often the family members actively seek guidance. Definitions of health, safety, and lifestyle are strongly influenced by organized societal messages. Although competition and conflict exists among these messages, the degree of competition is less than that possible within individual families in cultural communities. Variety is reduced. Freedom of definition has been neither gained nor lost in these changes, but the site of domination has changed.

Further, the family and community have changed their basic relations to the work experience. Increasingly each is structured around the demands of the workplace. Needs internal to each unit are reordered where possible for the minimal intrusion into worklife. Moving, choice of living community, and timing of children are increasingly tied to work rather than to kinship and community ties (Berger and Berger 1983). Child-rearing practices change with different work arrangements. With industrialization, at least one parent left the home for work, and the child's skill learning became partially separated from that parent. The emergence of two-career families and the creation of daycare extended the separation. Certainly such changes arise at the intersection of corporate and other forces in society. For example, take the following statistics: 85 percent of all U.S. households with children have working mothers (Shreve 1987); many if not most working parents, particularly single ones, express significant amounts of guilt regarding the lack of child-rearing involvement (L. Harris 1987); and since 1973 the average number of hours in the work week has risen from 40 to nearly 50, while weekly leisure hours have decreased from 26 to about 15 (Harris 1987). Whether this has been *initiated* by corporate practices or not, work extends more deeply into the family, people feel the extension, and corporate practices are intertwined with such changes (see Lambert 1990).

Corporate choices will make a difference in the speed and character of such changes and in how people adapt to them. The question is how much the total community will participate in the choices and how much certain segments of the corporate world will make those choices for the community. How deeply, even if benevolently, will corporate influence extend?

The degree of potential tension between work and family has been widely discussed in the debates over the so-called "mommy track" (Schwartz 1989). Clearly the current realities of business require work commitment and continuity, both of which often conflict with the responsibility for children. Clearly increasing numbers of women (and men) are willing to forego children for their careers. This is an interesting modern shift in site of identity and the nature and structure of "home." The discussion also points up the "invisibility" of the "daddy track" and the often-unquestioned compromises men make— and men's inability, often, to articulate and perform their non-career roles (Hall 1990). Much of the discussion of these issues, as well as discussion of women's corporate experiences in general, has carried a peculiar utopian optimism (Blum and Smith 1988). The attempt has often been to submerge the tension through holding out certainty that women (and men) can have it all. The "have it all" reasoning denies the institutional competition and the check that each institution places on the unrestricted growth of other ones.

For example, in what many would call an "enlightened" move, many corporations have developed daycare centers for working parents. Clearly this has provided many working mothers an equal opportunity for advancement. But such a move has another side. The preference for daycare internal to the corporation presumably supports individual and corporate productivity, but it does so in a way that changes the traditional family–workplace relation. In this way, the conflict between their competing needs is realigned and appears less conflictual (Martin 1990). Flextime, in contrast, recognizes the family as having equal competing needs and forces the corporation to bend to its demands; it does not transform the family into an inconvenience to be minimized. The choice could have been to shift the burden away from the family and individual and require new principles of work organization—a choice that is rarely thought of and lacks a place where it can be voiced. The order of corporate work structure appears to increasingly dominate.

In increasing numbers, children begin life in corporate hospitals with their particular orders and structures, and then go to the workplace with the parents to grow up in the structure and orders of the workday. Further, children usually do not enter the work area and learn the parents' trades and their subjective relations to work; rather, they enter the more anonymous and autonomous daycare world with its own objective orders, structure, and reconstructed value relations. Corporate daycare is unlikely to teach the communal and home values that would have been taught by the grandparent in traditional society or by parents in a more modern one. In fact, if daycare centers were to explicitly teach values, many people would object to this as an invasion of the prerogatives of the private (!) home; yet the "neutral" corporate values of order, particular routines, and orientations to industry are instituted with each moment. Again, the point is not to send the parent home or do away with daycare, but to understand the current situation and open discussion on the society's interest in the structure of work life and its intrusions (see Lambert 1990).

The tendency to move from a family- and community-centered identity to a corporate one passes with little notice. Job mobility connected to geographic mobility creates a type of person who is homeless in a quite specific sort of way. Identity becomes connected to what is stable rather than what is changing, the company or career rather than site community. Quite clearly many people structure the family and home as a place of emotional support and recreation to better enable them to sustain their organizational lives, rather than go to work to sustain their families, wherein one's central identity lies (Kanter 1977). People seem to willingly give their most rested, alert, chemical-free portion of the day to work rather than to family and community, though clearly there are groups that resist. Several social changes have been misunderstood largely because of the neutrality ascribed to corporate life. As women left the home for careers, they presumably gained a measure of autonomy and self-determination. In many respects, the woman was freed from being defined in regard to her husband and his career, but her autonomy is illusionary, because she became defined in terms of her corporate role. Rather than the autonomy of identity being achieved, the origin of identity was changed—and this change is often more paternal and constraining of her identity than the institutional definition she was freed from. The point is not to prefer the former, but to distinguish real movement toward autonomy and self-determination from an illusion of such movement that supports certain interests.

Friendship patterns and community development are of course affected along with the family. The greater the work identity, the less the development of community ties and solidarity. Particularly the mobility fostered in the modern workplace has predictable effects. Many companies discourage employees from becoming tied to their home communities, because such ties make mobility more difficult. Even the nature of houses built and bought is influenced. Homes that are presumed easy to resell are preferred over custom or individualized construction. The first item in the description of the proud new "home" is its resale potential. Such motivation produces homes that are normalized and routinized, with costs to individual expression, lifestyle diversity, and aesthetics. Neighborhoods are more homogenized than stable. Investments made in people are reduced to those at work, since only those are likely to have lasting qualities or value. Noncommitment and replaceability reduce the tension of attachment, expectations, and separation of people and place of residence.

Corporate Education In and Out of the Workplace

Corporate growth is felt not only in the family and community, but also, deeply, in the secondary socialization and learning environments, principally schools and training centers. Classical education was preparation for one's role in the state either as "statesman" or citizen; modern education is primarily a training ground for assuming occupational roles (Geiger 1980). This is not to attribute motives or direct effort to organizations. The shift in function is better attributed to the shared values and legitimacy granted to the corporate institution. But such values and legitimacy are produced and reproduced in micropractices including communication both within and outside of the corporation and with corporate influence (see Bourdieu and Passeron 1977; Bowles and Gintis 1976). The extension of such values to the educational process seems necessary and rational when one assumes the very commodity structure and view of knowledge that is fostered by the corporate experience. As the definition of success becomes monetary and singular, the educational system seems more naturally an extension of corporate training. The tremendous amount of material given to school systems by corporations each year far exceeds what is given, or would ever be permitted to be given, by political or religious groups. But in nearly every case these materials are clearly political, probably religious, and certainly value laden.

As Bourdieu and Passeron (1977) argued, all pedagogic activities are potentially "symbolic violence" since they are "the imposition of a cultural arbitrary by an arbitrary power" (5). By this they mean that individuals and groups have meanings imposed on them. These meanings have no privilege except that acquired from the apparent legitimacy of their provider, a legitimacy derived primarily from the hidden exercise of power relations. Education can produce and reproduce the schemes of perception, thought, appreciation, and action preferred by the groups on whose behalf it is carried out (35). The point is not to end education, but to more clearly understand on whose behalf it is carried out. The admission of the arbitrary nature of such schemes draws our attention to the arbitrary power relations sustaining them and helps us identify where and when they might be changed. As will become clearer in the discussion of the politics of everyday life, such things as community control of school rarely touch the more basic and important power relations. Corporations have a number of clear, though not clearly justified, political advantages in these power relations.

The rather strange linguistic attribution of realness to the work world and abstraction to the educational one, inscribed in everyday talk and work experiences, performs clear political functions. The conception initially functioned to protect experienced but nondegreed managers from the postwar expansion of scientific expertise and college education by providing for a contrary form of knowledge and expertise; it became a criticism of paternalistic and outdated higher education; and it functions today to privilege certain types of knowledge and learning, most importantly to privilege the corporate experience. Rarely do such terms as *practical* or *real* signify anything other than employment concerns, even though the community and family are filled with practical and real needs.

The modern advantage is not just one of content and justification, each centered on employment issues, but primarily one of the relation of person to knowledge. The conception of knowledge, grades, and degrees as objects to be acquired reproduces a specific type of instrumental orientation—definitions substitute for concepts, textbooks for treatises, and research reports for theories. Students are led to *master* the subject matter, rather than to encounter or surrender to (properly to understand) subject matter that draws students out of and beyond themselves to new insights and new relations to the world. Conceptions of effective education and accountability schemes further hide the value premises involved and make their collective examination more difficult and seemingly unnecessary. Learning contracts and competency-based education, for example, may provide educational benefits, but they have the side effects of defining the learner, knowledge, and the act of learning in a particular manner. In each case these align extraordinarily well with corporate knowledge practices. Misgeld (1985) provided a useful analysis of the way research in instructional technologies and training dovetail with corporate goals. Says Misgeld:

> Thus education is entirely assimilated to training. Research and training have in common that they do not require self-initiated insight into the purposes of the research or of the training program. They require that the interests in self-generated insight be put aside. The risk-burdened enterprise of critical self-reflection is replaced by a program for the avoidance of conflict and uncertainty. This is why behaviorally organized reform of instructional practice places much emphasis on evaluation (93).

Again the issue is not to glorify some past (which probably did not exist) as some defending liberal arts do. Given possible competing relations among kinds of knowledge and understanding, the lack of competition and the potential effects on the relation of social institutions must be noted. For example, it becomes unclear whether students today "really" write less well because of the emphasis on noncorporate literature and creative expression or simply write too well for corporate work. I am not suggesting a new answer, but pointing out that the question is not being widely raised. Education today lacks a theory of culture and society and a conception of its place in them and instead it moves between tradition and the marketplace, which involves a conflict for sure, but one unlikely to raise discussion of collective goals. Much has been made of declining math scores, but schools fail to a much larger degree to develop taste in either the elitist concept of high culture or in the more basic concept of rendering judgments on goodness and beauty.

The increasing use of textbooks participates in value extension and domination. Textbooks are seldom controversial in themselves and tend to be written in ways that skirt major theoretical divisions, particularly critical and more radical forces (McHoul 1986). The market-driven economy of text production most often results in the broadest (though often lowest) possible denominator rather than in stirring books. And this market orientation "teaches" the dominant interest, market-oriented learning. Ethnocentricism is common in texts (van Dijk 1989), but most of the ethnocentricism happens in subtle glorifications of certain lifestyles, certain types of technological developments, and certain work ethics. The tone of neutrality and certainty enforce a sense that this should be learned, and excludes critical reflection and alternatives. The lack of an authorial voice, except for a faceless expert, hides the concept of point of view, and controversy, much as the corporate report does. Leading conceptions of educational process and testing emphasize memorization, clear objectives, and making the process of "learning" easier, and thus they require texts that enable efficiency and require little effort from teachers or students. Computer-assisted texts like *Supertext* further extend the efficiency-driven "finding what is known about the topic" rather than the development of an argument or means of understanding. Learning to read slowly and critically is discouraged by boldface print, internal summaries, and providing the interpretation for the reader. Many texts today look much like *USA Today*, cater to the same audience, and carry the same duality of "U.S." and "us"—a homogenous reader and a collective author. "Learning" hence often becomes an inconvenience to quickly moving ahead. The lesson is clear. Learning should be quick and easy. Careful learning is costly and to be avoided. This metalesson of books and schooling of antieducation intersects with many compatible forces in modern society aiding and perpetuated by a particular corporate form.

Not only have the content and process of education taken on a corporate orientation, but corporations have become much more directly involved in the process of education. Corporations today spend as much on training and educational programs as society does on all of its four-year and graduate education combined (Eurich and Boyer 1985). Corporate facilities for education far exceed their public counterparts in quality. And most postgraduate education is conducted either by corporations or in community colleges with instruction often drawn from the cor-

porate ranks. Such educational programs actively teach corporate values and avoid historical analyses and the liberal arts. The
historical development of these modern corporate centers of
education probably differs little in character or in nobility of
motive from the earlier development of church- and, later, publicly sponsored education. The singularity of value orientation
and the ability to direct massive resources, however, become
more of an issue as both church- and publicly sponsored educational institutions become more dependent on corporate financ-
ing and focus their curricula for the work world (Evangelauf
1985, 1987). The blurring of the differences between the public
and the corporate by the domination of the corporate and the
consequent loss of competing voices is significant.

Culture, Inc.: Media Entertainment and News

Further, the institutional relations between mass-media institutions and other corporate institutions contribute to the preeminence of the corporation as a social institution. The older pat-
tern of diverse, largely privately owned media organizations has
changed to centralized corporate ownership. In the 1980s
alone, the number of corporations that controlled half or more
of the media business declined from over 50 to under 25
(Bagdikian 1990). As Schiller (1989) reports: "A prediction
made in the mid-1980s that by 1995 almost 90 percent of all
communication facilities (including newspapers, broadcast outlets, cable systems, telephone lines, relays, and satellites) would
be in the hands of fifteen companies is close to realization well
before that date" (35). We would probably be greatly concerned
if an institution like the church or state came to dominate the
media, but such an eighteenth-century mindset fails to account
for the actual institutional alignment today. How would people
feel if the govenment or church produced a "commercial" (or
propaganda, depending on the institution of concern) every
ten to fifteen minutes on the television and had primary say
over the programming? We know something of that, because
we know moments in history when such domination was
accepted *and* when it was rejected. We would feel oppressed if
billboards had pictures of national leaders on them with
encouraging statements, even if we were in agreement with the
message. And we would be deeply concerned about such a
dominance even if we agreed with the political or religious
message. But why not with billboards depicting people drink-

ing beer and defining every aspect of value and lifestyle? The recent outcry of the artistic community over possible NEH judgments on the appropriateness of artistic expression and the possibility of new censorship must be a concern for us all. But commercial influence and indeed virtual censorship has been many times more extreme, yet it passes with occasional reference. Dominance is dominance; the question is who should be the master and when should we be outraged or have a say.

How deeply ownership patterns affect the content of media is a matter of dispute. Moreover, the issue is one of not only ownership effects but the effects on decisions, because they are made within a corporate context. How diligently will a reporter pursue a story reflecting negatively on the parent company? When does reporting become whistle-blowing? What happens when news programs have to show a profit? And how does media education handle the modern social context? The merging of reporting and public relations training in many journalism programs is merely an institutional representation of larger social forces and changes (Becker, Fruit, and Caudill 1987). The lines have long been blurred with pseudoevents and press releases, but the connections are now deeper and connected to structural lines of authority rather than to cozy arrangements. All information today, whether news, entertainment, or commercial, has to be considered as sponsored information. Such changes can hardly be seen as innocent. Rarely do journalism and radio or television programs include course-work on covering business decisions, and such reporting when discussed focuses on producing business news rather than on being the public watchdog.

The media clearly have effects on the public's relation to corporations and the work experience. As Turow (1984, 1989) argued, mass-media "models depict conduct by people and institutions along with the consequences of the conduct. Doing that, the models (a) convey rules guiding the allocation of resources for society's educational, leisure, medical, economic, media, military, and governmental activities (that is, they depict principles of institutional order); and (b) they illustrate preferred ways to employ those resources (that is, they depict styles of production and consumption)" (1989, 454–55). Many recent studies of media have demonstrated the ways that media function in cultural production. Gans (1979) and Tuchman (1978) have shown how standard media "frames" structure the content and presentation of news, thereby providing a concept of human responsibility, "objective" accounts of events, and particular conceptions of the causal relations among events. The routine and daily reports of such things as the Dow Jones Industrial Average remind people of the importance of the health of the economy, and the absence of any equivalent index of the arts or healthcare hide their importance. Gitlin (1980) and S. Hall (1977, 1985), through use of Gramsci's concept of "hegemony," penetrated even deeper into the processes by which consensus is engineered through media. Media messages elaborate ideology into common sense and everyday practices by reproducing social conflict in terms derived from the dominant ideology. The media might well be described as the principal "ideological management industry" (Carey 1987). Certainly it is possible within existing routines to produce "oppositional" or diverse views, but it is difficult and largely not accomplished (Eliasoph 1988). The responsibility for diversity can even be taken on by the message receiver (Steiner 1988), but the outside perspective of the viewer must somehow be accounted for. Clearly the media has an agenda and, equally clearly, such dominant values align well with corporate interests (see Gandy 1982; Ganley and Ganley 1989). In the United States such a closure can be seen in the propagation of corporate forms and managerial decisional prerogatives in the name of efficiency, effectiveness, and economic growth.

Adequate evidence exists for a procorporate attitude in news content as well as in commercials and entertainment content (Rachlin 1988). As Gans (1979) demonstrated, news presents a rather consistent image of responsible capitalism. Primarily it presents "an optimistic faith in the good society, [that] businessmen and women will compete with each other in order to create increased prosperity for all, but that they will refrain from unreasonable profits and gross exploitation of workers or consumers" (Gans 1979, 46). Such an analysis preceded the conservative media move of the '80s and the massive corporate buyout. Even a casual observer would say that the perspective is stronger today.

Entertainment and commercials, in addition, clearly structure the need for products and for the corporations that produce them. The issue is not just that the media tend to support particular images of happiness based on having consumer goods and hence people buy according to created needs, though that has to be an issue (Ewen 1976). The larger issue is that by establishing the having of consumer goods as *the* social good, corporations are valued more highly, because they are the institution that provides them. The criteria for and evidence of the corporate contribution are presented at the same time. If, for example, the message day after day was one of working in the community or spending time with the family, the judgment of the relative effectiveness of the corporation in helping accomplish social good would be greatly reduced.

Even before modern ownership patterns, the media rarely played the "watchdog" in regard to business with the concern and vigor it directed to the government, whether the issue was a scandal, pay increases, private lives, or inefficiency. The picture produced for the past several years was that of an inactive (except in their sex lives), overpaid, corrupt, inefficient government of officials contrasted with an efficient, action-oriented, hard-working corporate manager who occasionally pursued profit too vigorously. For example, legislative salary raises are pursued with great skepticism, while much larger expenses paid by the public, due to the size of corporate salaries, are rarely discussed. Recently, *Business Week* ("Where U.S. CEOs Have Foreign Rivals Beat,"1990) reported the following in a small column (reproduced here in full):

> American top executives are continuing to outdistance their competitors overseas in at least one area: their compensation packages. According to a recent worldwide survey by Towers Perrin Forster and Crosby, the typical U.S. chief executive officer of a company with annual sales of $250 million earns about $543,000 a year in salary, bonuses, incentives, benefits, and perks.
>
> That's over 50% more than the $352,000 earned by a similar Japanese executive, and 90% more than the total compensation of around $287,000 received by German and British CEOs. It's also more than four times the compensation of a typical Korean top executive.
>
> In purchasing-power terms, American top executives come out even further ahead. TPF&C estimates that the typical U.S. CEO in their survey can buy three times as much in his [sic] home country as a similar Japanese executive and about twice as much as a German.

Few stories appeared in either the broadcast or print media reporting or discussing such a finding. Three months later similar statistics from TPF&C were reported on page 48 (!) of the New York Times Business Supplement, followed by even starker ones. The CEOs from top U.S. companies who had held their jobs for seventeen years or more changed from earning 24 times the after-tax pay of the average U.S. manufacturing worker from 1973 to 1975 to earning 157 times their pay from 1987 to 1989 while the average tax rate of CEOs declined from 50 to 28 percent and the average worker's tax rate increased from 20 to 21 percent (Crystal 1990). The performances of the companies studied were no better than average during the time period. Why not a series of front-page stories on such startling findings? Can we accept the alibi that "the dog that bites the man is not newsworthy"? Hardly not. The potential congressional raise (an old story) in 1989 from $80,000 to $125,000 was major news for over a month. This is only one instance. Corporate managerial self-interest in new office space and takeovers are rarely reported in their actual cost to the corporation or society (Friend and Lang 1988; Weidenbaum 1988). Some business scandals are reported in investigative reporting programs, but the difficulty in getting "proprietary" information and the presumed complexity of corporate decision making lends itself to unclear and messy stories or simple scapegoats. More often than not, when a corporation shows a lack of social responsibility or illegal action, the government is faulted for insufficient surveillance or action. Hence corporate irresponsibility demonstrates governmental failure. A clear set of values is presented as "objective" reporting.

Gans (1979) provided a more specific, vivid example that demonstrates the more general tolerance for business corruption and inefficiency and that reveals more of the processes by which bias is subtly inserted in the news. Says Gans: "The January 2, 1978, issue of *Time* included a three-page critique of governmental bureaucracy, entitled 'Rage Over Rising Regulation: To Autocratic Bureaucrats, Nothing Succeeds Like Excess'; but a business-section story reporting that General Motors had sent refunds to the purchasers of Oldsmobiles equipped with Chevrolet engines was only one column long and was headed 'End of the Great Engine Flap'." As Gans concluded, "Actually, the news often fails to notice that corporations and other large private agencies are also bureaucracies given to red tape" (46).

Perhaps the most significant example of this was the savings and loan scandal. Society will pay tens, perhaps hundreds, of billions for the bailout of corporate irresponsibility on the part of both lenders and borrowers. The press was late in investigating the events—except for some local papers, it never commanded the news time equal to its importance—and in many national reports the Federal government received the primary blame owing to insufficient regulatory surveillance. Clearly, if the press had been more diligent or responsible in reporting during the industry's eight-year "suicidal spree," intervention might have happened (Hume 1990). As Hume (1990) asked, "Why did the well-paid, well-educated, and constitutionally protected press corps miss the savings and loan scandal, which is the most expensive debacle in U.S. history?" The story was "too complicated and boring to interest mainstream journalists. Regulatory changes—such as accounting tricks and reduced capital requirements that helped paper over the first phase of the savings and loan crises in the early 1980's—weren't big news" (Hume 1990). Even Hume, whose analysis is one of the few public explanations of why the press failed in its self-professed role, seems far too ready to accept commercial and value explanations without condemning or even critically examining them. The commercial pressure for exciting news protects the commercial corporate enterprise. What other commercial pressures might exist? And what values remain hidden that protect the corporate world from serious examination?

No meaningful forum exists for the equivalent presentation of alternative perspectives. Congress requires that broadcasters serve the "public interest," and the Fairness Doctrine requires that opposing views be aired on controversy, but the media largely "define public interests" and "controversy." As Williams (1977) argued, any definition of public interest "depends, finally, on a consensus version of 'public' or 'national' interest: a consensus which is first assumed and then vigorously practised, rather than a consensus which has been arrived at and made subject to open review" (39). While few suggest any simple direct effects from media messages, the collective influence of media on cultural beliefs and values appears without question (see Chesebro 1984). The force of such studies is augmented by data on media usage showing that the average person spends 4 to 6 hours a day receiving media messages (and 8 to 10 hours receiving other corporate messages at work). The sun rises and sets with corporate messages. Where is the space between?

Corporate Effects on the Quality of Life

The corporate work environment has significant effects on the "quality of life" experienced by the individual, the family, and the community. We are past the active period of quality-of-life research of the late 1960s and 1970s, but most of the issues documented then still exist. One might well ask where all of that work went. The work experience influences the physical and mental health and longevity of the worker and family members. Much of this work is summarized by Alvesson (1987a). Clearly the growth of economic well-being has not led to an equivalent growth in mental and physical health (Deetz 1979). All of these not only influence work and productivity but also affect the family and members of the wider society.

We all have a vested interest in the work conditions of each corporation. Although this social interest has been partially fulfilled by increased worker-safety regulation, rarely does regulation cover anything beyond direct physical harms. For example, the recent merger-and-takeover mania not only had economic costs to the society but had great psychological costs, and since mergers fail about two-thirds of the time, they generated a second round of social costs (Geber 1987). But never was the effect on employees seriously addressed. Environmental impact statements are required for opening new plants, but we have no equivalent "people impact statements" for human costs of corporate changes.

Karasek (1981) has done a good job of addressing the questions about mental health and accompanying physical disorders. In his work he found that both workload and lack of opportunity to make decisions correlated highly with symptoms of depression such as exhaustion, difficulty in waking in the morning, nervousness, sleep difficulties, and anxiety. Even in their more conservative analysis, Katz and Kahn (1978) concluded that negative work experiences are associated with "more general negative affects—feelings of depression, irritation and anxiety. These in turn are associated with somatic symptoms" (607). Alvesson (1987a, 59) used Gardell's work to summarize work conditions that tend to be unhealthy:

- Authoritarian and detailed supervision
- Tasks characterized by severe restriction with respect to the individual's possibilities of utilizing the resources in an all around manner
- A production system that places little demand on the individual to contribute knowledge, responsibility, and initiative
- Few possibilities for the individual to exercise influence on planning or organization of the job

- Tasks that deprive the individual of self-determination of work rate and working methods
- Tasks that permit few or no human contacts during work

Understanding these relations, many companies have initiated job-enrichment and worker-participation programs—programs that have great social significance beyond productivity increases. Sashkin (1986, 1984) reviewed the various works on participative management and concluded that nonparticipative jobs lead to psychological dysfunctions and, in the long term, physical disabilities. On the basis of this he could conclude that the issues are more moral than economic in character. It is wrong to knowingly do physical and psychological harm to others. Proclaimed ignorance or using other alibis only excuse once. The continuation of autocratic practices is a social health issue. The corporate effect on the quality of life is great. Understanding these effects is part of a modern understanding of corporations and provides one basis for greater public involvement in the content of the work experience.

Workplace Effects on Thinking and State Democracy

The workplace is a site of learning. This should be no surprise. Thinking routines and social practices utilized over and over again, day after day, gradually influence the way one thinks. Pateman's (1970) extensive review of democratic theory and decision-making structures supported the argument that work resting on undemocratic authority socializes people into passivity and political apathy. Golembiewski (1989) concurs: "Organizational members can learn some awkward lessons from bureaucratic structures, and those powerful learnings may be transferred to feelings about personal potency, political efficacy, and social participation in broader social/political spheres" (221). He continues later: "Our broad life-experiences powerfully influence political behavior. Moreover, a hardy representative democratic consciousness is poorly served by incongruent organizational practices. Organizations are powerful molders and reinforcers of attitudes and behaviors—arguably the most persisting and powerful. Hence the growing paradox of conceptually pairing representative democracy with organizational structures and practices that are neutral to, if not negative about, the consciousness required for representative democracy" (495). Empirical evidence (Elden 1981; Woodman et al. 1985) continues to support correlations between types of decisional structures and varying amounts of personal autonomy and social participation outside of the workplace. Generally, having control over one's work increases the motivation to take up participatory opportunities in other settings. Practices and attitudes from the workplace function to further undermine the quality and legitimacy of the public decisional process. Voting and public participation in societies with authoritarian work structures tend to be diminished in a number of ways.

Less work has been done to explore the ways in which thinking patterns indigenous to corporations become reproduced in more general life contexts. Do authoritarian work structures foster authoritarian home practices? Do work environments lead some workers to be more dependent on authorities and less on experience and data? To what extent does the working experience affect one's assumptions about forms of knowledge, use of evidence, and preferences for data types? The lack of research is partially due to a lack of theoretically grounded concepts of forms of reasoning and detailed analyses of actual decisional processes. Researchers such as Mitroff (1983) outline thinking styles, and testing has been done using the Myers-Brigs instrument. But I know of no work correlating style preferences in specific organizations with the use of such styles outside the work context. Gilligan (1982; also Belenky et al. 1986) has carefully outlined differences between male and female reasoning processes. Women clearly come to (or are trained to) perform dominant male forms of communication, and it is likely they utilize them outside the work context.

That no effects result from eight hours of focused work every day and massive corporate training programs appears to be more difficult to imagine than that there are significant effects. As Alvesson (1987a) concluded from the research on work experience and family life: "[T]he influence of working life on the parents may reasonably be supposed to affect parents' way of relating to their children" (222). It is likely that authoritarian work structures create more authoritarian childrearing practices. And there is growing evidence that the modern corporate experience enhances or creates addictive personalities and codependency relational patterns at home (Schaef and Fassel 1988). The authoritative/submissive response style appears to be built into the modern corporation and reproduced in other institutional settings.

Deinstitutionalization and Colonization of the Life World

The issue of concern here is not simply the emerging corporate dominance over other institutions and its effects on knowledge, reasoning processes, and everyday life. If that were the case, the debate would primarily concern the relative values of different forms of thought and ways of making life decisions. Corporations are a different type of social institution from the family and community, particularly regarding the production of meaning and identity. They offer a secondary, reconstructed set of meanings rather than primary "life world" ones. As the identity- and meaning-giving functions of the family and community are eroded, the individual becomes centralized as the site of meaning. As Berger and Kellner (1965), following Gehlen, argued: "As the old institutional stabilities are lost, modern man is forced to turn to various new modes of structuring his life. These are characterized by 'subjectivism' on the personal level, in which man tries to find the ordering principles within himself, and on the social level by constantly changing interpretive schemata (such as those carried by the mass media), which supply a tenuous support for the individual's efforts to come to terms with his world" (17). (Today the analysis would more clearly include women.) Lyotard's (1984) work has been the most bold presentation of this "postmodern" condition. In his view, contemporary individuals as subjects are cut adrift from the metanarratives of history that previously functioned to produce identity and give meaning. Instead people today have fleeting identities created by fragments of knowledge and meaning. They are bewildered, bemused, betrayed, or schizophrenic—lost in the fragments and living on borrowed identities. In such a condition there is a momentary rush and "ecstasy" of freedom and unconstrained expressionism (Baudrillard 1983a), but also the feeling of "lack" and fear become articulated as the desire for the next fix. The fragmented subject is not without political purpose or effects. Such a subject is easier to control and cannot generate a sustained critical stance.

This ongoing process, which has been called "deinstitutionalization," is further reflected in the various literatures discussing contemporary narcissism in the growth of self-help and New Age literature (Lasch, 1978; Berger, Berger, and Kellner 1973). As Sennett (1977) argued, the concern with intersubjective experience, substantive events, and public processes has given way to the centrality of the personal and subjective. Certainly, within several literatures there is a growing feeling that the growth of chemical and dysfunctional relational dependencies is an unfortunate means of coping with a fragmented postmodern age (Bellah et al. 1985). The "drug crisis" is not just a problem of production, distribution, and consumption of illegal substances (with violence as an outgrowth), but is more centrally the growth of a desire or "need" for drugs.

The outgrowth of the deinstitutionalization process is the loss of trust and commitment to institutions, making collective planning difficult. The loss of legitimacy in institutions reduces trust in institutional constraints, reduces voluntary compliance, and makes explicit guidelines more critical. The lack of general compliance and inconsistency of enforcement in turn feed greater motivation and legitimacy difficulties. Not surprisingly, personal motivation becomes attached to the immediate and tangible, and corporations turn to management by objectives. No group has simply, or with clear forethought, constructed such a condition, but it is not without direction, strategic acts that advance it, and groups that benefit from it.

Deinstitutionalization and the fostering of individualism reflect weakened primary meaning-giving institutions and lead to the development of more specialized secondary institutions to fulfill their functions. Support from friends can be replaced by a therapist; child rearing can take place in daycare; community value-education can be replaced by value-clarification exercises in schools. As different forces in society, including corporate practices themselves, lead to the erosion of stable production of meaning and identity in the home and community, the corporation becomes ever more central in the process of coordinating individual activity (Ziehe and Stubenrauch 1982). Corporate management and organizational communication researchers seem to be implicitly aware of the significance of this central meaning function. Alvesson (1987a, 187ff.; 1987b) has carefully demonstrated how corporate culture studies have been utilized to provide integration and reduce the crisis potential. Important questions are raised in these analyses regarding personal identity, social knowledge, and structures of meaning and the relation of corporations to other institutions in their collective production. In some sense corporate organizations have realized their institutional role that Selznick (1949) and others (W. Scott 1987) in the "institutional" school claim they have shirked. For better or worse, corporate organizations are in the "meaning" business and are concerned with the subjective as well as objective conditions of work. Like a modern thermostat, they control climate. The inability of the society to provide unified meaning systems or to maintain external control mechanisms leads to the development of institutions to teach individuals to control themselves. These selves, however, are produced selves, products of what Habermas (1984, 1987) called "inner colonization."

But there is a catch. Corporations provide meaning around a more narrow set of human needs than primary institutions and lack community participation in their construction. Corporate integration and motivational systems are based either on a technological futurism, in which all social problems merely require more advanced technological management, or a reaffirmation of the profit motive and fulfillment of personal interests. The strength of these depends at first glance on one's point of view. Habermas (1984, 1987) has become the most powerful critic of either futurism or a monetary steering mechanism as adequate for social development. Habermas argued that as bureaucratic institutions grow, language-based, life world institutions that provide consensual understanding are overloaded by the need for ever more system coordination. As they fail, they are supplemented by the development of system-steering media that coordinate through the use of instrumental values like money and power. Once set in motion, the process creates further domination by bureaucratic systems, which leads to increased motivation and legitimacy problems. Habermas (1975) shows the cycle is both endless and a crisis.

Most basic to his analysis is the historical emergence of "rationalization." In the progressive "liberation" from traditional values and institutions, efficiency and effectiveness become the primary criteria for the evaluation in all of life. This is not to claim a distinct new age or to hold that past forms of reasoning are gone. Competing forms of reasoning and discourses do coexist but not as equals. As will be detailed later, technical/scientific/instrumental reasoning processes have become privileged; others have been marginalized (Fischer 1990). Such domination creates a two-sided problem: one regarding the formation of self-identity and the conception of self-interest, and another regarding the social opportunity for the expression of self-identity and self-interest. Alvesson (1987a) has done an excellent job of showing how this reasoning form dominates organizations, but he has not extended the analysis into the actual communicative practices by which the domination happens. Clearly an earlier balance between a focus on productivity in work and the pressure of maintaining family, community, and religious commitments created a balance and useful tension that breaks down as the corporation strengthens and the others weaken. Although he is far more conservative in his analysis, Berger (1986) would agree with Habermas and other critical theorists that the family and religion are necessary "balancing institutions" for modern capitalism's self-destructive characteristics of hyperindividualism and alienation. Many would argue that without the communal benefits of more traditional institutions, modern society would self-destruct. Social problems of substance abuse and narcissism (the socially disapproved and approved responses) and corporate problems of absenteeism, carelessness, loss of professional ethics, sabotage, and excessive careerism are often considered symptoms of alienation and crisis potential.

The crisis account is certainly noteworthy, but the situation raises interesting questions even if inner colonization and crisis are questioned. One could argue that from both an ecological and a humane standpoint the greatest potential fear comes from the lack of crisis potential, for a crisis would at least evoke public concern and discussion. The greater fear may be that integration mechanisms will destroy the natural environment and narrow the human character—Foucault's (1977) more dismal "carceral" society. The very phenomena that some would accept as symptoms of crisis could be read as a peculiar discourse of resistance. Unfortunately, as resistance it is destructive to the resisting subject and extends the production of the control mechanism being resisted.

Such a position makes clearer the place and importance of reclaiming space for public discussion and choice at the various sites of decision. As the meaning function of corporate institutions becomes greater, the public interest in, and perhaps right to participate in, workplace design and decisions becomes greater. There are many "owners" or "stakeholders" of modern corporations. There are owners of labor, expertise, resources, and public good as well investors. And there is no clear reason why one type of owner should be privileged, especially in the meaning and identity business. We need to consider in depth what type of "business" this is, who the moral claimants are, how privilege is organized, and what the possible democratic responses are.

CHAPTER 2

Communication and the Politics of Everyday Life

> In our society...a formal instrumental orga-
> nization does not merely use the activities of
> its members. The organization also delin-
> eates what are considered to be official
> appropriate standards of welfare, joint val-
> ues, incentives, and penalties. These concep-
> tions expand a mere participation contract
> into a definition of the participants' nature
> of social being. These implicit images form
> an important element of the values which
> every organization sustains, regardless of its
> efficiency or impersonality. Built right into
> the social arrangements of an organization,
> then, is a thoroughly embracing conception
> of the member—and not merely a concep-
> tion of him *qua* member, but, behind this a
> conception of him *qua* human being.
> (Erving Goffman 1959, 164)

Postenlightenment conceptions of democracy and communication have focused on individual freedom and representation in
regard to the state and "public" decisions. Contemporary conceptions of first-amendment rights, through discussions of
equal access to various technologies and media, elaborate and
extend these early conceptions. Democracy as a concern has
remained primarily tied to state political processes, with communication serving as a supportive vehicle in creating the
"informed public" and fostering the marketplace of ideas. The
electoral process and information relevant to the electoral process are often conceptualized as more central to the democratic

process than information that influences everyday decisions. As many would argue, democracy is historically more linked to election day than to everyday life.

The mass focus on election-day politics grants legitimacy to contemporary social arrangements and channels social conflicts into forms of resolution, thus enabling certain social choices and suppressing other conflicts and alternative social choices. As Jamieson (1984) argued regarding the significance of political advertising,

> Political advertising legitimizes our political institutions by affirming that change is possible within the political system.... Advertising channels discontent into avenues provided by the government and acts as a safety valve for pressures that might otherwise turn against the system to demand substantial modification.... The contest they reflect is over who should be elected, not over whether there should be an election. The very existence of the contest suggests that there is a choice, that the voter's selection of one candidate over the other will make a difference. (452–53)

Advertising hardly stands alone. News media, social groups, and education all affirm the critical significance of electoral democracy, that its conflict can reflect the basic conflicts in a society and that it can lead to meaningful changes. The attention to this process, however, directs attention away from other political processes.

One does not have to diminish the significance of elections in the least to still say that the focus on expression and election rather than on socially produced conceptions and decisions provides a remarkably narrow democracy. With the democracy-as-election conception, democratic communication is frequently little more than the handmaid of the representation of private interests, rather than intrinsic to the development of community and collective choice (Barber 1984). In the modern domination of economic over political thought, democracy has come to look far more like capitalism than capitalism like democracy. The media tends to strongly reinforce the reduction of democracy to capitalism. This is vividly seen in the general equation of political freedom and market ecomony in the reporting of the events in Eastern Europe. In this reduction, the voter becomes merely a special type of consumer, and Madison Avenue runs the election campaigns. Conceptions of communication, meaning, and identity further articulate these basic relations. Power differences in the creation of meaning and identity and in access to information and communication channels often pass with relatively less public attention than the fear of censorship and rights of self-expression. The right of expression appears more central than the right to be informed or to have an effect.

The idea was hardly new, but during the 1960s the general society, as well as communication scholars, began to adopt a conception of the politics of everyday life. Educational institutions, the workplace, the family, and the media were examined with regard to how they represented different group and individual interests in their decisions. The very concept of what was the "public" in many respects shifted. Many authors started to take seriously the attempt to reclaim a public sphere where the *polis* would be more than a "nexus of behavioral modes" managed toward affirmation rather than consensus (Habermas 1973, 269; see also Dallmayr 1984a). Questions of the social distribution of power and influence, particularly in regard to expression opportunities and effects on the social construction of meaning and personal identity, became important, even if they often remained obscured and ill-conceived. The new political battle became one over the content of the subjective world, not just its expression or human behavior. As the feminists most clearly expressed it, "The personal is political." Or as Baudrillard (1975) perhaps best captured the change, the issues were no longer attributed to economic distributions and speaking opportunities within the existing mode of representation, but became a fight against the monopoly of the "code" itself. Concern shifted to alternative codes and the manner in which the presumption of "free" and autonomous expression itself suppresses alternative representations and hides that monopoly. The primary force of domination could not be seen as economic exploitation with false consciousness providing its alibi but was conceptualized as the imposition of particular manners of world, self, and other production. And significantly, analysis began to focus on systems that developed the subjects' active complicity in producing and reproducing domination. Democratic communication in these terms must be about the formation of knowledge, experience, and identity, not merely their expression.

Evolving from this concern, communication scholars during the past decade have begun to focus on the politics of meaning in regard to both state politics and everyday-life institutions. Theories of the media have revived the distinction between critical and administrative research, while the development of "cultural studies" has focused attention on the role of media in culture production (Hall 1989). Recent studies have begun to investigate in more detail the specific communication processes through which mass-distributed messages have an impact (van Dijk 1989). Though less developed, critical studies of corporate organizations have worked out new conceptions of power in organizational discourse and demonstrated the processes through which meaning domination is sustained and extended (see, for example, Mumby 1987, 1988). As the brief analysis in chapter 1 suggested, the rise of the social power of the modern corporation and the corporate intrusion into other institutions has focused a need for an investigation of communication and the politics of meaning within the corporate site.

The social distribution of power and influence, particularly in regard to expression opportunities and effects on the social construction of meaning and personal identity, should be a central communication question in a democratic society. Such a question is clearly a political one. The concept of the politics of meaning and identity construction, however, is obscured in modern society through linguistic and social forces. To make clearer the political dimension of everyday life, Foucault's previously mentioned distinction between *sovereign* and *disciplinary* "political" power may help. From such a conception, the political significance of corporate domination becomes clearer.

Initially for the sake of easy identification, I will designate such distinctions as uppercase-*P* Politics and lowercase-*p* politics. Lowercase-*p* politics is the ordinary notion of politics that we learn in school. It is the politics of presidential elections, debates over policies, and decision making. It is the giving of information and having influence in the explicit, direct sense of persuasion and control. This conception of politics derives from the issues Foucault developed as involved in sovereign power. Capital-*P* Politics is less easily understood and discussed but can be clarified by Foucault's concept of disciplinary power. As Foucault (1980a, b) argued, "disciplinary" power is hidden and dispersed. In fact, the extent of its domination is "tolerable only on the condition that it masks a substantial part of itself. Its success is proportional to its ability to hide itself" (Foucault 1980b, 86). This Politics exists in social formations, institutional forms, the distinctions made by language, and the particular technologies available. This is the Politics of consensus and consent rather than direct influence (see Lukes 1974; Jameson 1981). For example, the greatest censorship comes in what is never thought of and in the forces that make some things unthinkable, rather than in restrictions on what can be printed. Disciplinary power escapes the world of political process—the making of policies and laws—and returns to colonize that world with principles of normalcy and self-evidence.

Authority and strategic influence (politics) clearly exist in modern organizations (Pettigrew 1973; Mintzberg 1983). No one needs to be told that corporations are political. Unfortunately, this knowledge misdirects attention. Individuals believe that they can gain such power and "beat" the game. The "winning" is shallow, clearly false, and ultimately destructive. The cynicism denies self-development, leads to decisions opposed to community development and mutual benefit, and fosters the production of deeper forms of control. The individual understands neither the nature nor the deployment of power. Most corporate power is invisibly exercised in the "free" decisions of those influenced. If control is *in* the personal experience, the perceptions, the knowledge and premises for decisions, then there is no need for explicit control. In this way, consent is always the hidden side of power. In corporate organizations, despite all the discussions of forms of power, managers only manage by the willfull consent of the managed (see Burawoy 1979; Deetz and Mumby 1990). No organization is powerful enough to regulate the behaviors of its employees, any more than a state could enforce its laws without organized consent. The organization of consent, rather than the organization of power, is central to understanding Politics. And even beyond consent, modern systems define routines and subject identities that "normalize" the chooser as well as the chosen. This is the Politics of the background practices of everyday life.

The Search for a Meaningful Public Sphere

Anglo-American conceptions of political democracy have historically depended on a particular conception of the routine practices of everyday life and a historical split between the public and private spheres. Both of these made good sense in their historical context but have interesting new meanings today. A few examples help show the meaning of these changes. Eighteenth- and early nineteenth-century political activity was more than metaphorically tied to the marketplace. It was in the routine practice of shopping that a public place and forum were created. In many respects the soapbox provided the quintessential image of democracy at its best. Even more so than the town meeting, the marketplace provided the place of unrestrained free speech and democratic influence. But shopping and the marketplace have changed. Today the shopping mall is a privately owned space. Many states allow large shopping malls to post signs that explicitly prohibit public meetings, solicitation, and advocacy (Schiller 1989). All first-amendment rights are to be left at the door. While the airport remains public, the public apology for those actualizing their rights is clear for all to see. The concept of democracy has not kept up. But democracy is not revived by simply reclaiming public spaces or even by engendering a renewed mode of public decision making as suggested by Habermas (1973, 1974) in his insightful and important analysis of the loss of the public. The routine of modern life establishes information gathering and thought formation elsewhere.

Many would argue that the public forum of today is the airwaves and perhaps the growing computer networks (Arterton 1987). But the forum here is hardly any more open than the modern marketplace (Elliott 1986; Murdock and Golding 1989). Access here, and thus capacity as well as freedom of speech, is largely limited to news reporters and to those able to buy air time. What is the point of free speech if the significant forums for expression are unavailable? The "protest" as a modern public expression is totally mediated and demonstrates rather than challenges the structural issue. Certainly this has been a significant social concern for the past thirty years. Dennis, Gilmore, and Glasser (1989), for example, have done much recently to identify ways in which citizens can define meaningful forums for expression. But the access issue is a small part of the modern puzzle regarding democracy. A quick look at the public/private distinction opens the question in a more productive way.

The public/private distinction is Politically significant in the way in which it defines the place for political discussions and protects aspects of life from state intrusion. The separation of church and state is perhaps the most discussed implication of the distinction. The clear liberal value comes in protecting religious and value expressions from state regulation. But the Religious Right is partially correct in claiming that the modern consequence is different from this. In effect the distinction has produced religion and even morality as a private matter and restricted public discussion of certain types of value questions. Religious value discussions are removed from the public forum. Secular values dominate by having no private protection *or* public exclusion. Potential conflict between religious and secular values is suppressed or displaced by discussions regarding the relation of church and state. The problem is not the separation between the state and the civil social realm. Such a separation is important. But as Held (1987) argued, we need a "double democratization," an "interdependent transformation of both the state and civil society" (283).

Significantly, the private/public distinction situates the workplace as an extension of private property conceptually, and often legally, outside the province of democratic theory. This, of course, has been the subject of much debate and poses a number of significant issues. Clearly, however, "the process of democratization has not even begun to scratch the surface of...big business and public administration" (Bobbio 1987, 57). Many of the issues are internal to the corporate context (see Ezorsky 1987). What data can a corporation properly collect about an employee? What criteria can be utilized in employment decisions? What are employee rights regarding free expression and opposition to corporate policy to both internal and external audiences? To what extent are political democratic processes applicable to corporate decisions? Such questions are extremely important if the argument is accepted that significant social decisions are made by corporations rather than governments. If this is accepted, the shop floor and corporate conference rooms may be more significant potential "public" forums than modern media. Thus, decisional structures and access to expression forums in the workplace are critical. The public/private distinction protects such questions from serious examination.

The potential questions are larger than simply those internal to corporations. The question of who should own and control the means of communication has been an issue from the beginning of the development of mass communication capabilities. As the media have become more central and the technologies more sophisticated, the issue has been bigger but essentially already answered. The corporate development and ownership of communication means, data bases, and mediation networks is largely beyond question (Schiller 1989). Even talk of information systems as public utilities has waned in recent years. For example, a recent *New York Times* article (Markoff

1989) headlined the access issue inherent in the expensive home installation of optical fibers, yet the discussion did not raise the political issues of private control of the means of public communication. But these new systems give the capacity to intrude into the old private realm in ways unimagined by the most extreme despotic traditional government, and normal safeguards are absent. If either the church or the state were to own and dominate the means of communication, fears of propaganda and censorship would lead to both a prudent receiver and a means of broader representation. Yet media commericals are treated as a normal part of commerce and various entertainment biases essential to profitability. There is little discussion of the possibility of equal-time counterconsumerism commercials or the possibility that society might be better if television programs were not as entertaining. High viewership is not necessarily a public good, nor does it lead to a well-informed public. The argument that the public should have the right to view what it desires without the imposition of taste judgment would be more powerful if wide selections were available and if different interests had the means to produce alternatives and competitively market them. Corporate-sponsored "public" television at best provides a partial option.

The legal status of corporations and their continuing definition as "persons" through court rulings creates a growing limitation of the "public" space. Since the late nineteenth century, corporations have been granted "due process" protection as a "person" under the Fourteenth Amendment. Schiller (1989) accurately demonstrates that the impact of this is to free the corporation from public accountability "except under the most limited and circumscribed conditions" (47). Such a ruling made sense in the nineteenth century, but the type of corporation protected was not the type of corporation that was to rise soon thereafter (Sklar 1988). With recent court rulings, principally the *Bellotti* case, corporate First Amendment rights have been greatly extended (Miller 1981; Vibbert 1990). But the marketplace ideal assumed basic expression equality between participants. Although the corporation is given rights like those of an individual, the individual is not given the expression power of the corporation. The "right" of the listener to hear everything that is worth hearing gets little attention owing to the emphasis on everyone having a right of speech (Bollinger 1984). Business leaders may debate whether corporations should exercise their freedom of speech "rights" (Hatano 1984), but the legitimacy of that right appears increasingly taken for granted. The concept of the "open" marketplace is lost to both the private capture of the public places of expression and to the corporate domination of expression in the remaining public sphere. To an outsider it might seem strange that corporate rights as "persons" were growing at the same time that the Equal Rights Amendment for women and women's control over their own bodies were failing.

The argument here is not for public ownership. Rather I wish to initially show the changing character of the public sphere and the extent to which the corporate institution and its values enjoy an advantage over legitimate competing institutions and individuals. The point is not to favor another institution but to investigate redefining a public space and begin discussion of how other voices can be given a legitimate speaking turn. The conception of equal access to communication media based on marketplace democracy was always structurally weak. The enclosure of the public place and the conception of the corporation as a person are merely natural consequences of private interest *politics* in a *Politically* constituted arena. A new conception of democracy is needed to meaningfully discuss these issues as not just an issue of voice but as one of representation in public meaning formation and decision making. As will become clearer as this analysis proceeds, the marketplace root conception is part of the difficulty.

The constant attention to the media in relation to democracy is a focus on the various amplification of the voices in the marketplace. Perhaps the workplace, rather than marketplace, is the more critical site of public decision making and the media are better seen as an extension of decisions at work. The critical concern with the media of authors as diverse as Schiller (1989) and S. Hall (1989) has been with the role of mass media in cultural production. The fear of these authors is that media messages, even while mediated through active listener thought-processes, strongly affect the production of identity and meaning and hence can distort the listener's ability to participate in public political process. The excess of concern with communication in media over the workplace has no good foundation. While listeners demonstrate complicity in the media-supported meaning domination, media messages are still publicly produced and publicly displayed to each listener. In this sense they can be publicly discussed and evaluated, thus helping the listener in meaning production. Despite the legitimacy of concern with the media, the erosion of a democratic consciousness can be more extreme in the workplace, since the workplace member more actively and privately engages in the production and reproduction of systems of domination that are hidden from public scrutiny.

Organizations Embody and Represent Competing Human Interests

Corporate organizations are potential political sites in both the upper- and lowercase-*p* sense. They serve a place where different values and forms of knowledge and different groups' interests are articulated and embodied in decisions, structures, and practices. As institutions, they provide meaning and identity. Decisions are made within them that affect the public good and different segments of society. Yet except in the narrow sense of personal interests, issues of politics and political democracy are rarely raised there. For many, the capitalist economic model (whether or not this model resembles the modern corporate form) assures the freedom that is for many the backbone of democracy. But in what ways is the modern employee meaningfully "free," and where is the democracy this freedom provides? The freedom is frequently reduced to the right to leave (assuming that is even realistic), but the right to leave does not make the workplace any more free or democratic for those who stay.

Despite the general impact and collective interest in corporate decisions, most corporate organizations have remained largely totalitarian in form, even (or especially) in the great state democracies. Perhaps one of the more interesting questions of the day is why people so willingly consent to and support this degree of control, which no modern state has seemed to be able to accomplish through its exercise of power. For most people today, issues of democracy, representation, freedom of speech, and censorship concern the relations of individuals and groups to the government. Although such liberal ideas arose in response to the power of the state, they tend to be quite conservative and to support systems of domination as corporations become the primary policy and regulatory body. As Edwards (1979, 22) argued: "Concerns of the workplace intersect directly with larger scale issues, for the great contradiction in bureaucratic control [founded on rationality] is its implicit tyranny. Workers are treated fairly within the rules, but they have no say in establishing the rules."

During the 1970s both state and federal legislation increased the rights and protection of employees (Aram and Salipante 1981). This ranges from safety and "right to know" protection to attempts to enact due-process procedures. Ewing (1983) has demonstrated that most of these procedures only consider relatively extreme or acute situations such as discrimination, sexual harassment, or job termination. Not only do these miss much of the daily practice of organizations, but they lacked continued development in the 1980s.

Organizational processes and products fulfill certain human needs. These needs can be described as the interests, or "stake," that stockholders, managers, workers, consumers, suppliers, and the wider society have in the organization (Abrahamsson 1977; Dahrendorf 1959; March and Simon 1958). Beyond these work-related distinctions, interest differences can often be demonstrated along gender and racial lines. Organizational structures, communication and decision systems, technologies, and work design influence the representation and fulfillment of different human interests. People produce organizations, but people are not all equal in their abilities to produce or reproduce organizations that fulfill their interests. Organizations are thus never politically neutral. Managerial groups are clearly privileged in decision making. Other groups exercise only occasional and usually reactive influences and often are represented only as economic commodities or "costs." Later chapters will demonstrate that the advantages given to management are based on neither rational nor open consensual value foundations, nor are they simply acquired through management's own strategic attempts. They are produced historically and actively reproduced through discursive practices in corporations themselves. Managerial advantage and prerogative take place through economic-based structures *and* systems of discursive monopoly. In the modern corporation such an advantage is not so much conceptualized as a right or as legitimate, as unproblematically reproduced in routines and discourse. As such this privilege is treated as natural and neutral. The presumed neutrality makes understanding the Political nature of organizations more difficult. Order, efficiency, and effectiveness as values aid the reproduction of advantages already vested in an organizational form (Jehenson 1984). Concepts of organizational effectiveness tend to hide possible discussion of whose goals should be sought and how much each goal should count (Keeley 1984; Cameron and Whetten 1983).

Clearly the worker and the general society have interests in work that are only partially and indirectly shared by management and owners. These include the quality of the work experience and work environment, mental health and safety, the skill and intellectual development of the worker, the carryover of thinking patterns and modes of action to social and political life, and the production of personal and social identity. Organizational life could be a site of political struggle as different groups try to realize their own interests, but the conflicts there are often routinized, thereby evoking standard mechanisms for resolution and reproducing presumed natural tensions (i.e., between workers and management). Even more basically, the work site could be considered a polysemic environment where the production of individual and group interests could itself be seen as an end product (or temporary resting place) in a basic conflictual process defining personal and group identity and the development and articulation of interests. Such potential conflicts are even more completely suppressed in normalization of conception, identity formation, and nondecisional practices. The production of the conflicts that exist and the lack of other equally plausible ones does not signify false consciousness as much as a type of discursive closure. The possible development of these interests and the subsequent tension between them is often suppressed in organizational practices and discourse through representational marginalization, reduction of alternative interests to economic costs, socialization of members, and the shift of responsibility to the individual.

Known power differences often lead to inequitable interest representation, but power differences are sometimes quite subtle. Different stakeholders are not always in positions to analyze their own interests, owing to the lack of adequate undistorted information or insight into fundamental processes. Both stockholders and workers can be disadvantaged by particular accounting practices and the withholding of information (Ansari and Euske 1987; Hopwood 1987). Further, the presence of ideology in the external social world or at the workplace, perpetuated through legitimation and socialization processes, can indicate the inability of certain or even all groups to carefully understand or assess the implicit values carried in their everyday practices, linguistic forms, and perceptual experiences. And even more basically, even if they could be assessed, the individual doing the assessing is a product of prior social processes. As Lukes (1974) argued, the interior itself is contestable: "Man's wants themselves may be a product of a system which works against their interests, and in such cases, relates the latter to what they would want and prefer, were they able to make the choice" (34). Under such conditions, power relations are best represented as a system of domination, since the empirical manifestation is that of free consent and reproduction of structures that work against competitive practices and fulfillment of the variety of interests. With such a view, what are taken as legitimate consensual processes are evidence more often of domination and suppressed conflict than of free choice and agreement. Ideological critique alone, however, is not sufficient to account for the full nature of this domination. Ideological compliance and failure to understand self-interest does not account for the frequent situations where compliance and consent are results of clear member understanding of the material conditions for their success. As Przeworski (1980) argued, the desire to live well provides a pressure toward active participation in the corporate system. In many workers' minds, corporations have delivered the goods, and workers receive a necessary and even desired standard of living for their participation. Who is to speak better than they of the quality of the trade-offs that they have made? The same interpretation could be made of Burawoy's (1979) description of the "making out" game. In his analysis, the organization of "making-the-rate" provides predictability, security, and favorable relations even though the worker is co-opted. The worker is not living an illusion or failing to accomplish interests. The more deeply these systems are probed, the clearer it is that the individual is making "rational" decisions. But in making rational, aware decisions, the worker is perpetuating a structure of advantage, one of self- *and* corporate advantage. But the identities and decisions structured here are not *Politically* neutral. They participate in the construction of a future in which there is a larger stake. The decisions lack an open democratic character not because the calculus or calculations are distorted, but because the human character and needs are specified in advance rather than being developed in response to complex situations. The lack of conflict in these "self-referential systems" precludes discussion and mutual determination of this future. A noncontestable decision has already been made.

With such a view, consensual processes exhibit less evidence of free choice and agreement than of suppressed conflict.

As will be developed, the choice is conceptual as well as empirical. From a conceptual standpoint, the researcher's choice to see an organization as consensual and integrated or conflictual and having potential suppressed conflict is based on whether the researcher wishes to advance management or describe the relation of the many interests (Young 1989). The empirical account requires investigation of structures of decision making and communicative practices in specific sites. Theoretically guided empirical analysis is essential.

Both the rising and passing of the concept of organizations as rational instruments for goal accomplishment hide goal and value conflict. Weber (1972) saw in his treatment of the rise of bureaucracy the potential liberation from traditional authority and community-held beliefs. In the new institutional arrangement, scientific knowledge and rules based in reason could replace older and less efficient systems of control. But he also saw the possibility of the "iron cage," of instrumental rationality and the divison of labor turning the organization into a machine dehumanizing the very creature who produced it. The potential tension between technical and humane interests has continued to reemerge in various forms in Western industrial development—scientific management versus human relations, studies of quality and meaning of life, and now cultural studies. It is also seen over and over again as Western work processes are assumed by tradition-based cultures (Evans 1989). What Weber could not foresee as well was the eventual expansion of order, instrumental rationality, and the "methodic way of life" into personal life scripts. Bureaucracy was to become a site of individualistic, self-interested, managerial careerism, where reason was to become connected to upward mobility rather than bureaucratic rules. The "new age" instrumentally planned and ordered life would come to coexist with bureaucratic rationality and finally subvert it.

My concern is not managerial domination, but the corporate development of the obedient, normalized mind and body, which are held up against equally legitimate but unthought alternatives. The interest here is in describing the ways by which managers and workers both become obedient in their own structurally prescribed manners (Burrell 1988, 227). While managers and sometimes owners gain in these structures, the force that drives them is not those gains. Rather they are driven by a set of practices and routines that constitutes identities and experiences. In doing so they provide unproblematic asymmetries, privilege particular forms of knowledge, and locate expertise in some and not others. Thus, they instantiate inclusions and exclusions in decisional processes. The path I begin here and believe must be extended in research is to reclaim conflicting experiences through describing the practices and routines by which alternatives are disregarded or rendered invisible. The understanding of the processes by which value conflict becomes suppressed and certain forms of reasoning and interests become privileged requires an investigation into the politics of meaning, language, and personal identity.

The Discursive Politics of Knowledge and Identity

The politics of identity and identity representation may be the deepest and most suppressed struggle in the workplace, and hence the "site" where domination and responsive agency are most difficult to unravel. Conceptions that place experience within individuals, present language as a transparent representation, and treat communication as if it were simply a transmission process, make it difficult to carefully describe these processes. My position here differs greatly from this. As will be discussed in detail later, each individual exists with produced identities placed in an already meaningful world. The psychological subject with experiences, and the presumed objective world to be described, arise out of a set of discursive practices that constitute the subject and produce a world of distinguished objects. The historical nature of language is not such that a word stands in the place of an absent, to-be-recalled object. Rather, language holds forth the historically developed dimensions of interests, the lines along which things will be distinguished. Language holds the possible ways we will engage in the world and produce objects with particular characteristics.

Thus when we consider language from a political point of view within organizations, the interest is not primarily in how different groups use language to accomplish goals, the rationality in language usage, or how the profit motive influences language use. Social groupings and their interests, types of rationality, and the concept of profit are social productions. Each is produced as distinguished from something else. The questions are thus not whether these things exist, have power, or explain organizational behavior, but how they come to exist, coexist, and interrelate in the production and reproduction of corporate organizations and work in the process of potential inner and outer colonization. Such an analysis is further applied to any attempt at explanation. Each explanation, as of market conditions, class interest, social structure, and gender, is produced in a string of larger significations. The display of these interactivities, or in the narrower sense intertextualities, in a communication analysis becomes the goal.

Control in organizations is exercised by both force and consent. In the United States control is extended through force and direct influence, but these practices are not nearly as pervasive or powerful as control by consent and normalization. Foucault's (1980a) analysis of the emergence of "disciplinary" over "sovereign" power, like Habermas's (1987) concern with the development of constitutive rather than regulative steering mechanisms, appears largely accurate in the Western world. Disciplinary power operates by the production of a particular type of person and the normalization of experience and practices. Disciplinary structures are enabling, empowering, *and* restrictive. A full analysis of disciplinary structure would reveal what is made possible and what is marginalized or left out as the strategies develop dominance. Foucault's concepts provide us with a useful analytic for describing domination but little guidance for developing preferable social relations. Perhaps from a theory standpoint we can do no better than that, for how can we escape the "disciplines" that make us what we are or avoid providing simply another historically privileged power configuration? Yet even Foucault made choices of conception and action, and they can be seen as connected to his descriptions (Waltzer 1986). While there is no good reason to simply privilege his or mine, there is no reason to hide an agenda as long as it is recalled as an arguable position rather than an assertion of truth. I believe the critical theorists help much in developing conceptions of preferable social relations.

The path I will begin here and follow throughout the work is to reclaim the opposition to our *norm*-al corporation through revealing the choices perpetuated and the means by which alternatives are disregarded or rendered invisible. I will call these choices "values" to keep it clear that something is always chosen over something else, that affective, cognitive, and behavioral modalities coexist at the moment of the perceptual experience. Clearly, *values* is a laden term and is often used to reference psychological states. But by values I do not mean beliefs or attitudes, something one holds on to. I will use the term *values* in much the same way as Saussure (1974) used the term in looking at systems of differentiation. To value is to differentiate—to act, choose, or desire. To differentiate is to stratify, not by holding the one differentiated thing over the other but by differentiating along this line rather than another. In this sense, "value" is the worthiness of a manner of thinking rather than the worth of a commodity. The use of this conception will become clearer later, but allow me here to preface the development of the analysis of everyday-life politics.

No modern conception of political democracy can deal with expresssion opportunities alone. Neither freedom of speech nor the right to vote has meaning if interests, thoughts, and experience are not formed openly. Otherwise, one is always expressing someone else's experience. Various systems of domination close the open formation of the interior as well as close off expression opportunities and the means for assessing the adequacy of expression as representation of self. As will be shown in chapter 5, every politics of discourse is intertwined with a politics of experience.

The *Politics* of discourse, whether seen in self-expression, interpersonal interaction, or mediated forms, focuses on the dual issues of identity formation and social construction of the world. As a social creature, each individual becomes aware of the self as already in a meaningful world. This entails, in Therborn's (1980) language, a *subjection-qualification*. The individual is *subject* (in the sense of subjected) to an already existing system of meaning, and a subject in the sense of an active choosing agent. *Qualification* describes the double sense of being prepared to or given the ability to perform in certain ways and the limitation of trained incapacities and restrictions. Specific *subject qualifications* can be specified along three lines (Therborn 1980, 18):

1. What exists, and its corollary, what does not exist: that is, who we are, what the world is, what nature, society, men, and women are like. In this way we acquire a sense of identity, become conscious of what is real and true; the visibility of the world is thereby structured by the distribution of spotlights, shadows, and darkness.
2. What is good, right, just, beautiful, attractive, enjoyable, and its opposites. In this way our desires become structured and normalized.

3. What is possible, and impossible; our sense of the
    mutability of our being-in-the-world and the conse-
    quences of change are hereby patterned, and our
    hopes, ambitions, and fears given shape.

This shared consciousness is produced, reproduced and supported by the arrangements of the material world and results in
a consensus and consent, not only with regard to how the
world is but also with regard to how the world should be. This
consensus, expressed in thought and action, shifts control away
from the explicit exercise of power through force and coercion
and places it in the routine practice of everyday life. This control and directed experience under conditions of apparent
agreement hide the fact that the interests of some people are
favored without examination and that communication unwittingly reproduces these conditions. The analysis that will follow builds on Gramsci's (1971) conception of hegemony.
Gramsci, of course, argued that the willing assent of the mass
was engineered through the production of the normalcy of
everyday-life beliefs and practices. Rather than an elite wielding
visible control, "organic intellectuals" (e.g., journalists, teachers, writers) produce a variety of cultural forms that express and
shape values, actions, and meanings and reproduce hidden
forms of domination. The site of hegemony is the myriad of
everyday institutional activities and experiences that culminate
in "common sense," thus hiding the choices made and "mysti-
fying" the interests of dominant groups. Dominant-group definitions of reality, norms, and standards appear as normal rather
than as political and contestable. This part of Gramsci's work is
preserved in Foucault as he develops psychiatrists, doctors, and
wardens as controllers of discourse and providers of definitions
of deviance and normalcy. These expressions of power obviously, though usually unproblematically, support certain ways of
life as normal and others as pathological. Foucault adds to our
understanding by displaying the scattered and conflictual
nature of control and draws our attention to the production of
subject and world intrinsic to shared experience.

The Democratic Interest in Corporations

Compared to studies of the media, relatively few analyses have
focused on the effects of business corporations and their imple-

mentation of communication technologies on cultural production, apart from the most abstract capitalist-reproduction thesis. The work of Gramsci and of the critical theorists has been used, until recently, largely in the critique of the media and the arts in cultural production. Cultural production in the workplace has received far less attention. Foucault also investigated several contemporary institutions, but omitted the modern corporation. But clearly, the corporate context and work experience have unique effects on personal identity and contemporary mass culture, making them potentially far more direct and interesting than media analyses. As the Eastern European countries opened up to democracy, the new leaderships' concerns are less with the "culture industries" and more with industries and their cultures. As East German political leader Hein, (1989) claimed, reflecting on the East German choices of late 1989, "This is our one chance—our first and last. If we fail, we will be devoured by McDonald's" (77). Of course less than a year later, the discussion seemed quaint. The choice had already been made. Amidst the media proclamations of democratic movements, groups of people across the world appear torn between "McWorld" and a new tribalism, neither of which foster much democracy. But moments of choice do exist. And perhaps more importantly, moments don't just come and pass; moments and choices are perpetual. The United States in a less extreme moment must still choose.

The corporate form and corporate decision making raise several moral issues from a democratic communication perspective. Corporations are produced by people to organize resources and talents to accomplish certain ends, but they do not exist in society as simple tool-like instruments of their creators; they are important social institutions. Individual societies certify and foster existence of corporations for the production of social good. Society has a collective interest in the nature and quality of decisions made in organizations, because of the use of resources, effects on the environment and local and general economies, and the need for high-quality products and services. Significantly, corporations do not just produce goods, services, and salaries that differentially affect different members of society. Corporations produce people, public knowledge, and effects on other social institutions. Important questions need to be raised regarding personal identity, social knowledge, structure of meaning, and the relation of corporations to other institutions in their collective production.

Until recently, few in communication studies have raised concerns about equitable social participation in the construction and distribution of knowledge and meaning. Even with this new concern, beyond privacy and honesty, few clear social moral guidelines have been developed to give ethical boundaries to the continued development of communication as an instrument of control. "Fairness" of the means of domination, not domination itself, has been posed as the moral issue. When normative foundations for communication analyses based on issues of participation and democracy have been raised, nearly all have been conceptualized in relation to the state and state politics; hence, they have been of little help in looking at the politics of experience and the production of meaning and knowledge in the context of everyday life in the corporation. Quality-of-life studies have not been alone in trying to explore how the nature and experience of work influences the general sense of social well being. Much of the more recent work has explored how concepts of organizational efficiency and the existence of the managerial prerogative lead to various dislocations and possible distortions in collective decision making and societal development.

Unfortunately, most conceptions of communication in organizations assume the same instrumental reasoning process that favors management and, hence, participate in reproducing this domination. The focus has been largely on message transmission, social influence, and control. Such conceptions aid the perpetualization of domination by particular human reasoning processes and social groups in power. The dominant acceptance of particular social-science methods has added justification to the presumed neutrality of these conceptions and has produced a form of knowledge that has virtually no use other than in extending control and domination. Modern concepts of the nature and social function of "expertise" have further suppressed the potential struggle over appropriate knowledge (Fischer 1990). The communication scholar accepting the corporate focus on efficiency and effectiveness conceptualize conflict itself a cost, further justifying control and forced, one-sided integrations.

Before we can successfully look to the specific communication practices in organizations to raise democratic issues, an adequate conception of democracy and communication must be developed. With such conceptions, we can assess corporate cultures and participatory, as well as more traditional, organizational forms.

CHAPTER 3

The Role of Communication Studies

Perhaps, said the Marchioness, Nature has
reserved the Merit of demonstrating Truth to
the English prisms; that is, to those by whose
means she at first discovered herself.
(Francescon Algarotti 1742, 65)

The focus on the politics of expression rather than the politics of
experience and understanding has been based on inadequate
and politically motivated concepts of communication and
democracy. Neither the inadequacies nor the political motivation have been based on clear foresight or conscious design.
Practical historical solutions to the issues of the time have
stretched over into new contexts and situations and need
reassessment. Trained incapacities, common sense, standard
social recipes, and the natural self-evidence of everyday experience conspire to preclude examination and the reopening of the
plurivocity of human experience. Such examination and
reopening is essential if we are to make decisions regarding our
historically given issues and engage in our self-determination.
Such a reassessment cannot arise from a new philosophical
foundation based in natural rights or from simply making more
empirical observations. As a society, we must choose the nature
of our democracy. As researchers, we must provide the necessary
insight for good social choices, but we cannot do that without
examining the democratic foundations of our own research. Neither natural nor causal or evolutionary models of transformation can redeem us from the inevitability of continued theoretical choices and our moral responsibility to make good choices.

To be meaningful such examination must be theoretically
guided. In saying this, I do not mean to suggest that we can or

should implement simple theoretical solutions to our complex life situation. The failure of utopian and less grand attempts at the "great society" or organizational reform are too obvious and too numerous to need recounting here. Nor am I suggesting that I or anyone else has a clear cross-situational answer. Rather, our community shares ascertainable principles and methods for productive discussion and development that exceed our current practices. It is not in our theory and judgments that we begin, but in our pretheoretical understandings and prejudices.

This chapter begins the development of a theoretical perspective for the analysis of corporations guided by democratic participation. To accomplish this, a conception of theory and research as intrinsically linked to a historical social setting and the development of social good is proposed. Further, I argue for the value of communication as a mode of analysis as well as a phenomenon for analysis. The chapter ends with a discussion of the role of the intellectual in using participative theory to guide the ongoing practices of understanding, critique, and education. From this initial base, subsequent chapters will provide a conception of participation as a pretheoretical normative foundation for acting in and evaluating communication systems.

The Role of Theory

Theory is one of many modern contested terms. The attempt by many to give it a definition, to reduce it to a dead, neutral entity, can be readily grasped as a political maneuver. Theory in popular parlance is treated as abstract and separated from the real world. The development of "positivist" science and elaboration of the hypothetico-deductive model institutionalizes theory as representational of experience. Against this background I wish to claim theory to be an intrinsic part of experience itself.

A theory is a way of seeing and thinking about the world. As such it is better seen as the "lens" one uses in observation than as a "mirror" of nature. Lest the lens metaphor suggests the possible transparency of theory, as if it disappears if it is a good clean lens, recall that the clearest microscope gives us radically different observation than the telescope. Further, if the metaphor suggests the stability of a world only shown differently through different lens, where is the world not seen through some lens? The lens metaphor helps us think productively about theory choice: What do we want to pay attention to? What will help us attend to that? The treatment of observation as if it preceded and could be compared to theoretical accounts, hides the theoretical choice (whether through concept or instrumentation or both) implicit in the observation itself. Hanson (1965) captured well for the natural sciences what seems to be so hard for social scientists and everyday people to accept: all observations are theory-laden. In his metaphor, theory and the external world are like the warp and woof in the fabric called "observation." The woof may typically be the more visible, but the observation cannot exist without the warp. The attempt to talk about one in the absence of the other unravels the total observation, leaving neither the theory nor the world to be of any interest.

The problem with most theories is not that they are wrong or lacking in confirming experiences but that they are irrelevant or misdirect observation, that is, they do not help make the observations that are important to meeting critical goals and needs. Despite popular mythologies, social science theories, whether by everyday people or scholars, are rarely accepted or dismissed because of the data. As Gergen (1978) showed, the major theories that have shaped everyday thinking and definition of social science problems have had very little data. Rather they offered compelling conceptions of central life issues challenging both existing assumptions and the supporting dominant values. This should be no surprise, as Kuhn demonstrated much the same in the natural sciences. For example, hardly a student today can get through college without one or many more presentations of Maslow's hierarchy of needs or Festinger's cognitive dissonance theory. Both were widely taught before the data for either were very good, most instructors don't even know the data or assumptions made in data collection for either, and the support years later for each is very mixed. Human need structures are far more complex than Maslow suggested, and people seek novelty and dissonance as much as they reduce it. There are reasons why certain theories are accepted and not others, but they do not simply consist in the facts. Further, the use of certain theories and even the findings from them are often best explained by popularity cycles, boredom, career needs, and social and economic conditions (Wagner and Gooding 1987).

Gergen (1978) and Rorty (1979) among many have shown

the inadequacy of theories as representational and the hypo-thetico-deductive model as a way of thinking about theory choice. The various assumptions of the preeminence of objec-tive facts, the demand for verification, the goal of universal, temporarily irrelevant findings, and the presumption of the dis-passionate bystander all hide the nature and evaluation of theo-ries (Gergen 1978). Theory does not shape observation, it is part of it. Facts are socially negotiated. Hypothesis testing is largely self-fulfilling over time, since the theory shapes what will be attended to and people respond interactively in testing situa-tions. All findings are historical artifacts both because of theory and because people change over time in part in response to social science reports. The question is only whether we accept the conditions and practices necessary to produce the scientific artifact. Every theory carries the values of a research community that often substitutes its terms and interpretations for those lived by the subject community (Deetz 1973). The modern phi-losophy of science, particularly as practiced in the social sci-ences, overcompensated for the fear of the medieval authority of the church, rhetoric over reason, and the ideological basis of knowledge. In doing so, it became an arbitrary and at times capricious authority producing an ideology itself with its own rhetorical appeal (Schaffer 1989). The greatest problem with a theory is not its being wrong (for that will be discovered) but its misdirecting our collective attention and hindering our assess-ment of where it takes us. Rather than assuming simplistic con-ceptions of science as a fixed answer, the relation of knowledge to the human community is the task to be worked out.

The point here is not to reject hypothesis testing or finding careful methodical ways to distinguish reality-based from imag-inary relations. Such activities, however, need to be comple-mented by a more basic understanding of the relations between theories and the world, relations of power and knowledge, and the relation of theories to real human communities. This is best accomplished by understanding theory as a way of being in the world. Theories are developed and accepted in human commu-nities based on their ability to provide interesting and useful ways of conceptualizing, thinking, and talking about life events. The social-science community and the life world com-munity differ primarily in what they take to be interesting and useful, based on their differences in community standards and in what events they take to be significant. Most often a philoso-phy of science attempts to reconstruct the practices of researchers as if they could be freed from the events of their time, as if we wished that they were freed, and as if everyday people's theories in natural languages have more difficulties than social-science theories in technical languages. More realistically, both everyday-life and social-science conceptions are needed. Everyday people respond to many mythologies, and we have yet to see a life or a society run well based on a social-science theory. This partially explains the double fear of researchers that no one listens to them and that someone might. Rather than beginning with an elitist view of theory, let's start with a reconstruction of everyday life. Eventually this reconstruction will serve as the basis for communication theory, moral democracy, and social science, but here I will start with the fundamental functions of theory.

All creatures develop ways of dealing with practical tasks and problems in their worlds. In that sense they all have theories. They have plans, they make observations, they have an idea of how these observations fit together, and they have a set of activities that follow. This is all we would expect of any theory. Some of them work, others fail. When they work, it is always within certain parameters or domains. Few theories are failures in regard to specific situations, and all theories ultimately fail if applied far enough outside of the specific conditions for which they were developed. Theories thus differ more in the sizes of their domains and the realistic nature of their parameters than in correctness. We all operate day in and day out with flat-earth assumptions. It is only on the occasions when we wish to do things that require another model that we increase the complexity of our thought. In this sense all theories will fail in time, not because of falsity, but because human purposes and environments change.

Abstracting theory from this life context is essential for testing and critical reflection, but in doing so researchers often forget the essential life connection. In this sense, critical reflection and testing are moments in human theorizing, but scientific research and theorizing cannot be reduced to these processes. This may be clearer in an example from Austin (1961) in his analysis of the "representation" problem in language studies. As he reasoned, the question "What is a rat?" differs greatly from the question "What is the meaning of the word 'rat'?" The former treats conception as part of the human act of seeing the world in terms of a specific interest, from a point of view. The latter question removes us from the life context and poses an abstract and universalizing question stripped of the specific domain and practical parameters. Whether the question "What is a rat?" arises as a child's question or as part of a dispute as to whether the creature standing there is one, the focus is outward to the world, to the subject matter. The conception raises new looks, new considerations, further observations, and a relation to the other. The latter question raises the issues of correctness, cleaning up the word, nomenclature committees, and operational definitions. As an analogue, the latter question is about theory, the former is about the world with a theory as the point of view. When thinking about theory these are important complementary questions. Unfortunately, we often contextualize the former in regard to the latter rather than vice versa. When this happens, theory is abstracted from the world rather than intrinsic to our being directed to it. The variable analytic tradition of sequential hypothesis testing, strings of research reports disconnected from their conditions of production, and the "textbook"-style knowledge that results from this, all have this odd quality of being concrete and specific yet only referring back to themselves in their logical interdependence rather than leading to an understanding of the world. C. W. Mills (1959) aptly referred to this as "abstracted empiricism." The more applied and specific such knowledge is made, the further it gets from directing attention to significant features of the outside world and the more tightly interconnected it becomes to its own small imaginary world produced out of itself. The central problem of social science today has always been not its excessive objectivity, but its subjectivity—its inability to escape its own purposes and arbitrary structuring of the world.

The view of theory as representational, as with representational theories of language, is not without motivation. It describes a particular relation of the theorist to the world, one of domination. A domination fostered by fear of nature, fear of the lack of certainty and control. As Levin (1988) explained, following Heidegger: "Re-presentation is the way subjectivity dominates its world, the way subjectivity imposes its will on all that is, all that presences. Re-presentation is therefore aggressive; but it is also a defense, and more specifically, an ego-logical defense, a defense of ego, because it protects the ego's prejudices, stereotypes, and delusions: it protects the ego against the need to be more open; it helps the ego avoid authentic encounters; it blocks perception of otherness and difference" (127). Representational views of theory, as well as the research directed from them, align well with corporate motivations. It is of no surprise that they arise out of the same rational and finally rationalized historical movement.

By investigating the functions of theory in life as it encounters the world, we can arrive at more fruitful ways of thinking about theory. Allow me to suggest three basic functions: *directing attention, organizing experience,* and *enabling useful responses.* Can we see differences that make a difference? Can we form and recognize patterns that specify what things are and how they relate? Can we make choices that not only enable us to survive and fulfill needs but also to create the future we want?

Directing Attention

Attention is largely a trained capacity. While our sense equipment is nature's, or more properly our ancient forebears', theory of what we should be able to detect, our conceptual schemes and sense extensions become the connection to the world of our more immediate history. At the most basic level, theories direct our attention, that is, they guide us to see important details. Plato was certainly right (but for the wrong reasons) that if you didn't know what you were looking for, you wouldn't know when you had found it. Perceptually, this is easy to see. I can recall the first time I looked into a microscope in biology class. The grey mess to me was clearly a mass of cells to the instructor. The eye needed to be trained not so much in seeing but in seeing the differences that mattered, setting the apparatus to be able to have those differences visible. The cell had to be out there, but it also needed to be in here in both setting the right power and noting the key features. Changing theories is like making a gestalt shift; what is figure and what is ground is the issue. Like changing the power of magnification of the microscope, you lose the ability to see certain structures for the sake of seeing others. It is not as if one or the other is the better representation of the "real" thing. Each draws attention to and displays a different structure of potential interest, a different real thing.

Perceptual examples show the basic relation but can be misleading. Let me develop an example that keeps the perceptual experience "constant" but works with the conceptual relation. Let me use a first-grade problem. The teacher presents four boxes. In each there is a picture—of a tree, cat, dog, and squirrel, respectively. The child is asked which one is different. A child worthy of second grade immediately picks the tree. The child knows not only how to divide plants from animals, but also that the plant/animal distinction is the preferred one to apply. The perception is valuational. We know from the outside, however, that the choice is arbitrary and hardly a very interesting way to think about the problem. The squirrel as easily could have been picked if the child had distinguished on the basis of domesticity or things we bought at the store. Or the dog could have been picked because the cat, squirrel, and tree relate in a playful, interactive way. Or the child could have picked the cat since the other three are in the yard. Or any one of them could have been picked based on a having/not having, liking/not liking basis. Each of these is perhaps smarter than the plant/animal distinction. As Foucault (1970) showed in his discussion of a fabled ancient Chinese encyclopedia, the choice is a preference of the system of distinction rather than based on the correct understanding of the nature of the object:

> "Animals are divided into: (a) belonging to the emperor, (b) embalmed, (c) tame, (d) sucking pigs, (e) sirens, (f) fabulous, (g) stray dogs, (h) included in the present classification, (i) frenzied, (j) innumerable, (k) drawn with a fine camelhair brush, (l) et cetera, (m) having just broken the water pitcher, (n) that from a long way off look like flies." In the wonderment of this taxonomy, the thing we apprehend in one great leap, the thing that, by means of a fable, is demonstrated as the exotic charm of another system of thought, is the limitation of our own, the stark impossibility of thinking *that*. (xv)

As will be clear in chapter 5 when the issue of language is taken up directly, the issue is not one of the linguistic/conceptual determination of perception (e.g., how many kinds of snow Eskimos have). Rather the issue is the choice of the distinctions to be used, the differences that matter. Although the reconceptions required of us by the Chinese encyclopedia are perhaps more difficult, no one has any problem working through the reconception of the dog, cat, squirrel, and tree. The question is which is the better frame to use to view the world, rather than the issue of accuracy or truth. Once the system of distinction is "chosen," then questions arise such as should this be classified as an animal, what features distinguish plants and animals, and how should individuals be classified (e.g., which is a virus?). And finally, abstract theories and "empirical" questions and hypotheses can be raised and tested. For example, how many animals are there; and since this is an animal, we expect these behaviors. The problem with starting with a hypothesis tested against the "real" world is that the reason for the quotation marks around *chosen, empirical,* and *real* is lost. The child who circles the tree rarely raises the alternative conceptual distinctions to make the choice, nor do we when presented with the same problem. The issues do not become empirical after we have "decided" to utilize the plant/animal rather than the domestic/wild point of view. They already were. We would smile at the child who when challenged said, "Yeah, we could divide them into categories of domestic and wild, but they're *really* plants and animals." The child's complaint that we are relativists totally misses the point. The presumed real, empirical, and unchosen often misses the value-laden, theory-based observation. Human choices, even if unwittingly made, are key, not the assumed nature of the things themselves. Whether we assume a behaviorist tack or reject it with some humanist view of internal properties, it is choice, not nature, that rules. In his rejection of the humanist critique of behaviorism, Rorty (1981) says:

> If we fail to discern the same virtues in Skinner as in Bohr, it is not because Skinner does not understand his pigeons or his people as well as Bohr understands his particles, but because we are, reasonably enough, suspicious of people who make a business of predicting and controlling other people. We think that these virtues are not appropriate for the situation. We think that there are more important things to find out about people than how to predict and control them, even though there be nothing more important to find out about rocks, and perhaps even pigeons. But once we say that what human beings are *in themselves* suits them to be described in terms which are less apt for prediction and control than Skinner's, we are off down the same garden path as when we say that what atoms are *in themselves* suits them to be described in terms which *are* apt for predication and control. In neither case do we have the slightest idea what "in themselves" means. We are simply expressing a preference for predicting rocks over doing anything else with them, and a preference for doing other things with people over predicting their behavior. (5)

Unfortunately, we have acquired a number of bad habits from the old philosophy of science that lead us away from understanding the importance of theory in directing attention. The metaphysical position that theory provides words to name characteristics of objects in themselves and mirrors fixed relations among objects underestimates the inexhaustible number of things and relations our attention might be directed to see in things and hides the important issues in theory selection. Our simple practices of defining terms operationally or attributionally hides the theoretical construct's function in providing a stable object with presumed fixed attibutes. Rather than questions like "What is communication or information," we should ask questions like "What am I able to see, think, or talk about about if I conceive of them in this way rather than that." Conception rather than definition specifies a point of view, a way of seeing and talking, rather than identifies a domain of objects.

Organizing Experience

Theory not only directs our attention, it also presents our observation as being part of meaningful patterns. The perception of an individual already pulls together past experience with similar people (the lines of relation following the distinctions being utilized) and reaches to anticipate possible actions. Everyday people, like social scientists, are constantly engaged in the process of trying to explain the past and present and trying to predict the future and possible responses to our own actions. But prediction and control, like spiritual and teleological models, account for only part of the available structurings and human interests displayed in patterning. The nature of patterns and types of patterns experienced is potentially very rich. The observation of continuity rather than discontinuity or the seeking of simpler rather than more complex patterns are not simply given in nature but arise out of human orientation to the world (Foucault 1972). Prediction and control should properly be seen as one human motive that is at times privileged over competing motives and organizing schemes that differ greatly from prediction and control.

One of the facets of modern social science is the projection of its own motive to enhance control onto the subjects that it studies. This is perhaps clearest in interpersonal interaction studies. In everyday life, interpersonal relations often show the greatest degree of open negotiation and mutual decision making. Ironically, the usual research emphasis on uncertainty reduction, compliance gaining, and persuasion mirror more the philosophy of science used by the researchers than people I relate to. For example, in the *Handbook of Interpersonal Communication* (Knapp and Miller 1985), trust and warmth are discussed only in relation to influence and compliance, and the words *ethics* and *ethical* appear only twice in 750 pages. The modern focus on uncertainty-reduction theory appears to be based on an assumed fear of difference and the otherness of others, rather than on curiosity, the excitement of novelty, and self-change. (One wonders whether objectifying the other is the cause or result of this assumed fear.) Lannamann (1991) properly identified the dominance of these types of studies as based on a complex set of unexamined values in interpersonal communication research. It is not as if the world cannot be seen this way, not that there aren't everyday people whose experience is organized in ways like this. The universalizing claim of these studies, however, can easily lead to overlooking the full variety of ways people experience the world and, because of the claim of privilege, can influence people to give up other ways of structuring their observations.

Clearly all research is historically situated. People and societies concerned with individualism and control organize experience differently from those interested in the community and fate. Each orientation can produce empirically confirmable structures and orders, but all can be one-sided. Cognitive theorists have been most sensitive to the relation of social-science community orders and everyday orders and tell us much about the various types of ordering relations people have developed and use. Unfortunately, they tend to glorify rule-following reasoning as a metatext for examining and discussing alternatives. While the orders produced may be quite different, the twin themes of differentiation and organization appear to be central to theorizing.

Enabling Useful Responses

Theories in everyday life as well as those in social science have a pragmatic motive. This may often be covered up with a claim of truth or a demonstration of what is, but the choice is always of this truth versus that one, this "what" versus that one. Kelly (1955) demonstrated this clearly from the individual standpoint in his development of the pragmatic basis of personal constructs. Constructs are developed and elaborated in directions that help people accomplish life goals. Institutionalized social science merely extends this individual process. There appears to be little disagreement with this basic motivational frame, though it can be quite complex in practice.

Theoretical conceptions that are useful to one individual or group can be quite detrimental to others. The social choice of theories thus always has to consider questions such as whose goals will count for how much. Consequently, looked at from the perspective of the society, useful responses have to be considered in terms of some conception of social good. Unfortunately, the issue of pragmatics is often read too narrowly both in everyday life and in the social sciences. As will be discussed later, pragmatics as a simple instrumental motive overlooks the competing human desires to overcome their initial subjective motives, to make their own histories toward a richer collective life (Habermas 1971). When theories are considered instrumentally, efficient and effective goal accomplishment would appear to be easily agreed upon as a social good. But not only do such goals have to be assessed from the standpoint of whose goals are accomplished, but efficiency and effectiveness are not themselves goods (Carter and Jackson 1987, 73ff; MacIntyre 1984, 181ff.).

Dewey gives us a better lead on making choices regarding alternative theories. Rorty (1982, 163) phrased his basic questions thus: "What would it be like to believe that? What would happen if I did? What would I be committing myself to?" Such a position does not so much give us an answer to the questions of social good as pose the question of locus and nature of responsibility. Theories about human beings are different from theories about chemicals; they ultimately influence what the subject of the research will become. How we conceptualize and talk about ourselves and others influences what we are and will be. Theories function to produce responses that produce ourselves, our social interactions, our institutions, and our collective future. Theories must be assessed in light of the kind of society we wish to produce. We are concerned with meeting our needs and with doing so in a way that makes us better people. In Rorty's (1979) words: "To say that we become different people, that we ('remake') ourselves as we read more, talk more, and write more, is simply a dramatic way of saying that sentences which become true of us by virtue of such activities are often more important to us than sentences which become true of us when we drink more, earn more, and so on...getting the facts right...is merely propaedeutic to finding new and more interesting ways of expressing ourselves, and thus of coping with the world" (359). All current theories will pass in time. It is not as if they are in error, at least little more or less so than those in the past. They were useful in handling different kinds of human problems, problems we might find ill-formed and even silly, as others will ours. What remains is the human attempt to produce theories that are useful in responding to our own issues. We are struggling to find interesting and useful ways of thinking and talking about our current situations and helping us build the future we want. Such hope is intrinsic to theorizing rather than external to it.

Power and Knowledge

At least since Bacon, most Westerners have believed that knowledge is power, that having or possessing knowledge gives its holder choices and influence. Contemporary thinking has of course totally rearranged such an equation. Foucault (1972, 1980a) in particular has focused attention on the power *in* rather than on the power *of* knowledge. There is a politics *within* the production of knowledge. As Hoy (1986) expressed it: "[T]he relation is such that knowledge is not gained prior to and independent of the use to which it will be put in order to achieve power (whether over nature or over people), but is already a function of human interests and power relations" (129). In this sense, in each society, in each age, there is a regime of truth generated out of a network of power relations. Certain discourses are accepted and made true and mechanisms are developed that enable the distinction between true and false statements. Again, this does not suggest that "truth" is relative in any simple way, for within the constraint of interests and values competing claims can be compared. But what we are interested in making claims about, and the choice of constraints and values in making those claims, are historical choices and are politically charged.

The modern concept of "truth" is a historical product and clearly political. The Greek notion of truth as that which shines forth and compels understanding (as surrendering to it) gives way to something that may be wrestled from nature and captured as a "fact." As Foucault (1980a) has shown so well, the "will-to-truth" is a dominant modern drive and one that more constructs the possibility of elites than elucidates the world. The claim of truth is more often a club than a new insight—a club in the double sense of a big stick that demands acceptance and a group of people who share initiation rites, a special language, and rituals of purification. Against this, the claims of the social sciences can better be seen as one of several competing forms of knowing, where knowing is described as "the ability to act or behave adequately in some particular domain" (Maturana 1988, 60). The focus is then on the basis for determining adequate behavior and the appropriate domains of application. Unfortunately, the modern social sciences try to totalize, to hide their own claims of determining adequate behavior behind mere "truthful" descriptions of behavior. In such a process, they privilege their knowing over competing way of knowing in other domains.

For example, the frequent tension between religious and scientific truth exists at the point where each tries to extend itself into the other's discourse. When science describes what is and religion describes what one should do, they coexist. In contemporary society, science gets in trouble when it tries to empirically derive "oughts," and religion, when it tries to explain empirical reality. The conditions for making a claim to truth differ in each. Knowledge is not so much to be accepted as it is to be explained. This of course is the point of Foucault's genealogy, to explain the conditions constitutive of leading forms of knowledge. This will be taken up again in looking at knowledge in the corporation.

The point here is not to find a way to settle conflicting knowledge claims, nor to degrade truth, but rather to deny privilege by recalling the disciplinary power necessary for any knowledge claim. The knowledge claimed in everyday life—in its institutions of science, commerce, and religion—as well as knowledge about knowledge claims in everyday life are politically loaded. Laying out their driving interests and mechanisms of knowledge production and defense is central to understanding how they work. I hope that it is clear by this point that this work is no exception.

The Value of Communication Theory

A leading goal of this book is to work out a theoretical perspective that leads us to perceive differences that make a difference and organize our perceptions toward making useful social responses. If successful, such a theory should be grounded in the present social-historical context aimed at enhancing useful social responses to contemporary social issues that are themselves partially theoretically constructed. Such a theory is ultimately answerable to real communities of actors rather than universal standards of truth. It also must grow out of that community's struggle to understand and respond to its actual historical context, though it cannot simply end there. In this sense neither a formal reconstructed normative science nor an ethnography of everyday-life theorizing will do (Deetz 1973). A necessary interactivity of social science, researched subjects, and audience community must be assumed.

Contemporary issues of democracy and corporate life are clearly complex. Portions of these issues have been usefully described using economic, sociological, historical, psychological, and technological descriptions. Everyday actors, like social scientists, have tended to be either monist or pluralists in their theorizing, either reducing alternative conceptions to a central driving one (the various "ists") or oscillating between different and often incommensurable perspectives without a conception of how the "elephant" fits together (Albert et al. 1986). Part of the reason for this is the representational theory of knowledge, which treats different means of explanation as if they represented a particular domain of experience, as if there were economic events, psychological events, and so forth. More appropriately, modes of explanation are simply different perspectives on and ways of talking about the same events. Albert et al., (1986) referred to this as enabling the development of a complementary holist perspective whereby different perspectives are different ways of articulating the same complex moment of interconnectedness that gains constancy as an event. In this sense, a holistic perspective draws attention to the complex that can be unpacked along different horizons—the same phenomenon seen in several manners rather than one composed of distinctly different parts or forces. For example, money can be seen as a resource in economic theory, a commodification of value in sociological theory, or information in a communication theory. Personality can be abstracted from a set of communicative behaviors (including test taking) or a cause of communication behaviors (such as giving answers). Voting can be a political act or a communicative one. The question then is not what is this thing, but which way of conceptualizing it and its relations to other events enable the most interesting and socially useful conception. The existence of a reductionist thesis tends to privilege more atomistic explanations over holistic ones, but there is no evidence that such preference is any more than a power move in relation to science's struggle for legitimacy in the nineteenth century (Schaffer 1989). Any such preference should be open to examination.

Different social-science disciplines arose at points when certain social conditions posed problem, or sets of issues for which current approaches could not provide useful conceptions (Foucault 1970). Psychology could not exist without a concern with nonspiritual hidden causes and could not be sustained without the development of an individualistic point of view and the desire to predict and control individual behavior. Modern economics required an exchange theory of value, and sociology required urbanization and the breakdown of community structures.

Modern social conditions have lead both scholars and everyday people to pose communication questions. This does not so much foster an *academic* discipline (for the institutionalized study of communication primarily engages in psychological explanations) nor a new domain of phenomena (though mass media are somewhat new), but more so a way of thinking about and conceptualizing social issues—a discipline.[1] Such a change can be readily evidenced in several academic disciplines. For example, literary studies have gradually come to be understood in communication terms. This contrasts with understanding mass communication in literary terms, as was done at the turn of the century. The so-called linguistic turn in philosophy identified the community of natural-language users as more central than consciousness as the site of knowledge and understanding. Communication explanations growing out of this stretch widely into critical theory, ordinary-language philosophy, and structuralist and poststructuralist thought. The popular discussion of an "information" society and concern with communication media, technologies, access, and language policies represent real if often ill-conceived changes in a public discourse. The gradual replacement of immediate experience with mediated ones produces a new realm of symbolic events, organized public perception, and increased interest in the interactional dimensions of personal experience. The substantive event is somewhere else by someone's account and disappears behind more and more levels of reports—checked and reinforced by more stories.

The alignment of new material technologies, organizational structures, linguistic and symbolic forms, rapid individual life changes, new interactional places and constraints, and the need for constant social negotiation of the premises for collective decisions enable and call for a new way of thinking. Each certainly can and will be explained in economic, technological, and psychological terms, but the conditions make possible an interesting discussion by conceptualizing each of these from a communication perspective. What we have today in Foucault's terms is a new *problematization.*

But what does it mean to discuss psychology, economics, and sociology in communication terms rather than explain communication in psychological, economic, or sociological terms? Certainly communication as meaning transmission or self-expression offers little. A communication perspective denotes here the primacy of the system of interaction as "textual" in several areas: the production of personal identity, the meaning of individual behavior, the formation of social structure, and the determination of value (for a similar development, see Pearce 1989, 23–31). Such a position is consistent with Baudrillard's (1981) more fully developed argument that every commodity signifies. This includes material texts, objects, behaviors, and technologies. This is not to claim that everything is communication (a domain problem of nonexclusion). Certainly Baudrillard has been accused of being unable to distinguish the food from the menu, the materiality of objects as signs and the materiality of language texts as signs (Clarke 1988). Such a problem does not arise if communication is understood as one of the several perspectives through which everything can be viewed, that among other ways everything can be seen in its communicative constitution and communicative function. Each has costs and advantages. A communication perspective gives unique and interesting insights into today's issues.

A communication explanation is structural and multidimensional, producing unity and discontinuity. Watzlawick, Beavin, and Jackson (1967) clearly demonstrated such a position in their treatment of the family interaction system. The individual personality is not fixed but is produced in the family system and fulfills functions unique to that system. A produced personality may influence the formation and function of a new system, but the causal direction of relation between personality and interaction systems is a choice. More properly, the individual is seen as one of many sites of agency, each having limited but real effects and all effects being interactive. Kristeva (1984; Moi 1986) from a very different theoretical perspective concluded much the same about the production of identity and subjectivity. She goes on, however, to show that the decision to position a unified subject (the psychological subject) as first cause of experience performs a political function to hide power relations in the construction of identity and experience. One of the most significant products of the past century is the production of the psychological subject and consequent explanatory devices (Henriques, et al. 1984; Shotter and Gergen 1989; Radford 1990). Reproblematizing this political relation ultimately leads to a preference for a structural communication explanation over competing ones. This will become clearer in chapters 4 and 5. Space here does not permit the similar consideration of structuration (Giddens 1979, 1984) as a communication account of social structure or the discursive quality of economic resources.

The justification for a communication perspective, however, cannot consist in demonstrating its possibility or its historical presence; rather, theories with a communication perspective can be developed that raise and give insight into significant social issues. This position promises not an ultimate cause and delineation of causal forces but descriptions of the various forms of interactivities, the processes by which the elements produce, are produced and reproduce structural configurations. For example, in examining the modern corporation, the presence of a "free" psychological subject is critical to new forms of control. Neither the production of this subject nor the forms of control can be merely assumed as existing and causal; they can be described through particular structural configurations. To work this through, I return to the issue of community-based social good, only now in the context of a communication perspective.

The Role of the Intellectual

This chapter has focused on the role of communication theory in analysis of democracy within a politics of everyday life. I have juxtaposed concepts from hermeneutics, critical theory, and Foucault. I hope to have shown a common movement within the works, gaining something of the power from each without totally losing the tensions among them, a set of tensions I think we have to live with. I see this as more complementary than integrative or pluralistic. The tension and the complementarity can be revealed one more time here. As we move into the analysis of language and experience and finally to the description of life in (and out of) the modern corporation, what is the appropriate role of the intellectual? I say role of the intellectual rather than role of theory or research, since it is individuals alone and in concert who act and are responsible. And the terms *researcher* and *scholar* are too detached and implicitly privileged for their use to be anything other than a hidden power move. Intellectual here is to simply mean anyone who systematically reflects on life's experiences.

Traditional critical thought has attributed a leading role to the intellectual. Enlightenment for Kant (1965) was "emancipation of man from a state of self-incurred tutelage, of incapacity to use his intelligence without external guidance. Such a state of tutelage I call 'self-imposed' if it is due, not to the lack of intelligence but to lack of courage or determination to use one's own intelligence without the help of a teacher. *Sapere aude!* Dare to use your intelligence! This is the battle-cry of the enlightenment" (177). Democracy was recovered in enlightenment and is preserved and expanded in a transformed enlightenment impulse today. Democracy is to be understood in opposition to new forms of tutelage and advanced by research and education that fosters autonomy and participation, though these, like democracy, must be understood in light of contemporary conceptions of identity and experience. As Misgeld (1985) expressed well, "The notion of emancipation that has emerged from Enlightenment thought has a practical meaning: It requires the removal of force and suffering caused by ignorance and the persistence of traditional authority, unshaken by new possibilities of knowledge. But the Enlightenment has enthroned a conception of reason and of method that can be interpreted as a new form of domination, subjecting societal members to new modes of regimentation" (80). In this regard, the works of Gramsci (1971) and Adorno and Horkheimer (1972) perhaps set the tone of the most aggressive role for the intellectual. The intellectual vanguard could make possible the intellectual progress of the general society through conceptual and philosophical elaboration of ideas that could enlighten and lead revolutionary change. Habermas in his several works has provided a more restricted conception of cultural criticism along the lines of the Enlightenment ideal of self-understanding, reclaimed public space, and reasoned discourse.

Foucault is far more cautious and gives a less clear role to the intellectual. As Smart (in Hoy 1986) presented Foucault's awkwardness with the role of the intellectual, "It is argued that events have shown that the masses do not lack for knowledge, the problem is that their local and popular forms of knowledge have been steadily discredited, disqualified, or rendered illegitimate by the very institutions and effects of power associated with the prevailing 'regime of truth' within which the modern intellectual operates" (165). The modern intellectual lacks any basis for a "universal" role as the conscience of the collectivity, and as a "specialist" often engages in privileging systems of expertise growing out of conceptions of universal or objective truth. In Foucault's view Habermas tries to recover "truth" from domination, but it is the "will to truth" rather than any particular group's domination that leads modern repression. As Foucault (1980a) argued, the option is not that of "emancipating truth from every system of power...but of detaching the power of truth from the forms of hegemony, social, economic, and cultural, within which it operates at the present time" (133).

But clearly Foucault is a modern intellectual driven to study institutions of repression,and he actively participated in acts directed toward social change (Waltzer 1986). Foucault's objection to the critical tradition might well be centered more on the language of truth and privilege than on the reluctance to take a position based on careful analysis. Habermas (1983, in Hoy 1986) can perhaps interestingly, if we bracket correctness, argue that a will to knowledge provides a reformed enlightenment drive in Foucault's work when it is detached from the will to truth. It is from this, what I take to be productive, tension between tentativeness and commitment, that we can describe an appropriate role. This is a role with three moments. I will call them *insight* ("hermeneutic understanding" in the critical tradition, "archaeology" to Foucault), *critique* ("genealogy" to Foucault, "deconstruction" to the poststructuralists), and *education* (in Dewey's sense; *conscientização* in the critical tradition).

Insight: Hermeneutic Understanding and the Archaeology of Knowledge

Everyday knowledge and scientific research are produced out of a set of interrelated structures that are both present in them and extend in an implicative web. Most of the time social members as well as traditional researchers take for granted this knowledge and the formed nature of objects and events. "Insight" denotes the process of seeing into the manners by which this knowledge and the objective character of objects and events are formed and sustained. The term recalls the hermeneutic understanding of language as disclosive and opening a field of consideration rather than the representational view of language that undergrids knowledge as truth claims. Insight can properly be called the leading edge of human thought. It is structured along the line of the powerful exemplar rather than the mass of data. Insight is both the process of producing a unity of interest in the data—of knowing what data to collect and how it fits together—and understanding the conditions for such a unity.

Insight is a type of practical knowing, a seeing what is important. Insight, as suggested in the more general look at communication, is not into individuals, situations, or their meanings but of the systems of relations that make such meaning possible (Deetz 1973, 1982). Foucault (1970) described his archaeology as "an inquiry whose aim is to rediscover on what basis knowledge and theory became possible; within what space of order knowledge was constituted; on the basis of what historical *a priori,* and in the element of what positivity, ideas could appear, sciences could be established, experience be reflected in philosophies, rationalities be formed, only, perhaps, to dissolve and vanish soon afterwards" (xxi–xxii). In this sense most ethnographies and cultural studies are at most a first step in a much larger analysis. Particular persons and situations are artifacts used to understand the system of meanings through which particular persons and situations are composed and connected to the larger sociocultural context. The aim here is, of course, more narrow than Foucault's. As the focus turns to the corporation, questions are raised as to the structures whereby corporations are constituted and how particular kinds of knowledge and members are constructed and sustained.

Insight in both a hermeneutic and an archaeological sense detaches knowledge from the ahistorical "truth" claim and reopens a consideration of its formation, thereby reframing knowledge and providing choices that previously were hidden by the accepted knowledge, standard practices, and existing concepts. The production of insight establishes the possibility of competing discourses through the recovery of conflict and choice. Without such insight members remain in a sense victims of meaning structures that were developed in response to past situations and perpetuated in their talk and actions. Although as Giddens (1979) argued, all cultural members have some degree of "discursive penetration"—that is, some insight into the structural properties of knowledge production—they are unlikely to enlarge the penetration on their own, due to practical restrictions and various mechanisms of discursive closure. The intellectual is free of some of these constraints and, while not privileged, is capable of the distantiation necessary for claiming counterdiscourses within particular sites of production.

Critique: Deconstruction and the Genealogy of Knowledge

Political, economic, and community forces and individual interests are inscribed in organizational arrangements, in social relations, and in every perception. As Frost (1980), following Habermas, suggests, these inscribed interests result in blockages, repressions, and distorted communication. Meaning structures are filled with privileged interests, and it is from these that perceptions of objects and events are formed. It is not sufficient to describe these as naturally occurring; they arise historically and arbitrarily advantage certain groups. A normative foundation for communication can help draw our attention to both describe and criticize such systems. Chapter 6 will provide a conception of participation as such a normative ideal. The participative ideal does not so much give a norm or criterion for evaluation as provide a set of interests and analytic foci for acting upon them, a way of thinking about these systems. Grossberg (1984) described the task as to "describe (and intervene in) the way messages are produced by, inserted into, and function within the everyday lives of concrete human beings so as to reproduce and transform structures of power and domination" (393).

In recognizing the need to go beyond neutral descriptions, Foucault presented a "genealogy" to complement his archaeology. Orders are selected, controlled, and distributed within societies along lines of strategy and advantage. Foucault used the term *apparatus* to denote the heterogeneous forces that direct the presence of certain constitutive conditions. This will be considered in detail in chapter 10, but an initial statement here helps focus the role of the intellectual. As Foucault (1980b) described it: "[T]he apparatus is essentially of a *strategic* nature, which means assuming that it is a matter of a certain manipulation or relation of forces, either developing them in a particular direction, blocking them, stabilizing them, utilizing them, etc.

The apparatus is thus always inscribed in the play of power, but it is also always linked to certain coordinates of knowledge which issue from it but, to an equal degree, condition it" (196). Insight into these strategies and understanding them to be deployments of power, is itself a strategy toward recovering alternative practices and marginalized alternative meanings. Knowledge is an important part of this relation, for the apparatus both produces knowledge and is extended and sustained by it. Produced knowledge can guide participation or domination. Thus the critique of everyday dominations must always include a critique of the social science, the management science, that accompanies it.

The Derridian conception of "deconstruction" can also be seen as a form of critique. Deconstruction shows the manner of historical privilege and recalls the equivocality, the many voices, the alternative texts that become the hidden background for the centered one. The movement of science as the positive production of knowlege, and communication as the transmission of it, share the privileging of the speaker and the known and produce a centered text, the dominance of a particular unity or point of view over others. The unity appears innocent as a consensus. Deconstruction reopens the equivocal in the certain. As Culler (1983) put it, "[D]econstruction is not a theory that defines meaning in order to tell you how to find it. As a critical undoing of the hierarchical oppositions on which theories depend, it demonstrates the difficulty of any theory that would define meaning in a univocal way: as what the author intends, what conventions determine, what a reader experiences" (131). In the broader terms of this work, deconstruction denies the univocal products of the intellectual, the result of methods and procedures, and common sense of the public and in its place opens the movements in and between them.

Critique thus is directed at the conventions and structures of social orders and the forms of knowledge and privileged understanding that are complicit with such orders. Critique itself operates as part of a participative communicative act, the act of reopening effective communication to productive conversation.

Education: Concept Formation, Resistance, and Conscientização

Education is the natural counterpart to insight and critique. It can easily be claimed that critical writings in both the enlightenment and postenlightenment traditions have placed too much attention on awareness and understanding and not enough on enabling alternative responses. The implicit faith that if people knew what they wanted and were aware of the system of constraints, they would then know how to act differently, has little basis. Those who hold out for revolutionary change miss the implications of domination by disciplinary rather than sovereign power. Meaningful change is in the micropractices at the innumerable sites of control. Communication education must be involved in the production and distribution of a kind of political competence. Following Simonds (1989), political competence in modern society means "not just access to information but access to the entire range of skills required to decode, encode, interpret, reflect upon, appraise, contextualize, integrate, and arrive at decisions respecting that information" (198). Clearly, as we have seen around the world, increased literacy is more threatening to autocratic rule than an uncensored press. Literacy in the modern complex corporation and regarding complex communication systems and technologies is itself a complex phenomenon. The concern is not just that people get wrong or biased information (the propagation of false consciousness), but that they lack the resources to assess what they have. And more importantly, they do not understand the modern means by which control is exerted, particularly in the corporate context.

Freire (1970) has provided the most stirring discussion of the role of education to open cultural development. While much of his social theory was caught in the Marxism of his day and the immediate political realities of Brazil, his conception of conscientização locates a meaningful role for intellectuals in the construction of human agents—i.e., subjects who choose to make their own history. Many researchers today conceptualize and teach their subjects to be objects, known and acted upon, but objects can be taught to be subjects who know and act. The point is then not to produce a new theory of domination as knowledge, but producing ways of seeing and thinking and contexts for action in which groups can express themselves and act.

Thus the movement toward greater participation and democracy is not accomplished by rational arguments and the display of systems of domination alone, but also by helping to create responses to the current situation. Members of the everyday community have learned their concepts, practices, and skills over a lengthy period of time. Learning competing discourses, embracing conflict, and participating in decision making are skills to be learned. But interaction skills are only part of the matrix. Developing technologies for participation and skills in using technologies and communication media are important parts of the democratizing effort.

Further, the intellectual is not a teacher in any standard sense. We do not know a lot about participation, and we certainly do not know the contours of the sites as well as everyday participants. The role Freire (1970) ascribed is more appropriate to the need to combine research with education: "We must never merely discourse on the present situation, must never provide the people with programs which have little or nothing to do with their own preoccupations, doubts, hopes, and fears.... It is not our role to speak to the people about our own view of the world, not to attempt to impose that view on them, but rather to dialogue with the people about their view and ours" (85). Unfortunately it is not they who are not ready to talk with us, it is we who are often not yet ready.

Despite the power in various social formations, there is always resistance and opportunity for difference and change. Local resistance often fails, owing to trained incapacities, inadequate concepts, and unknown structural constraints. The final goal is the formation of new concepts and practices for social members and researchers that enhance understanding of organizational life. Living and working in organizations is a practical activity for organizational members. Particularly for new members and ones in new roles, but also for all others, there exists a need to know how things get done in the organization, how to avoid unpleasant outcomes, how to recognize critical features, and so forth. The choices in the everyday context require a type of *practical consciousness,* or adequate knowledge, as suggested by Giddens (1979, 1984, 1989) or *phronesis* (practical wisdom) as suggested by Gadamer (1975). Certainly the modern intellectual can aid the production of this. Concepts developed by the academic community need not be privileged to give voice to concerns and understanding that have not been brought to discourse in everyday contexts. Such concepts can be generative, and thus can question and reconstitute social experience (see Gergen 1978; Giddens 1989). To fulfill this function our concepts must be recovered from operational and textbook definitions and reconnected to ways of seeing and thinking about the world.

In the dialectics of the situation and the talk of individuals with different perspectives, the emergence of new ways of talking becomes possible. Such a process both enhances the natural language of corporate members and leads to the development of new concepts to direct the attention of the research community. I believe that this can be accomplished along the lines of progressive differentiation and individualization (suggested by Habermas 1984) without falling into the traps of preferring certain differentiations or advancing individualism. Conceptual development is important for the participation conception of communication as a foundation for political democracy in the modern context.

Notes

1. The academic discipline representing communication studies has struggled to define itself in terms of a domain that often reflects either message variables or fascination with mass media and communication technologies. But it has failed to make a significant social contribution or gain much scholarly distinction because as a whole it has never developed a mode of explanation. It only extends or applies the work of other academic disciplines. Especially the conceptual domination exercised by the Michigan State school of thought has glorified psychological explanations and a philosophy of science grounded in control. Hence, research in social influence has dominated everything from interpersonal to mass communication studies and looks surprisingly like the rhetorical studies it hoped to replace (see Berger and Chaffee 1987). Certainly competing voices have developed, especially in the last decade. It remains to be seen whether communication studies will take communication as seriously as do departments of English, philosophy, sociology, and even accounting (see chapter 10).

CHAPTER 4

The Historical Relation of Communication and Democracy

> Democracy is not an alternative to other
> principles of associated life. It is the idea of
> community life itself...a name for a life of
> free and enriching communion.
> (John Dewey 1927, 148, 184)

Communication and democracy are intrinsically interrelated in social science and everyday life. As democracy seems to be dominated by expressionism and representation of self and group interests, everyday life and social science research are dominated by linear conceptions of the communication process. Despite the scholarly conceptions withstanding, the conduit metaphor for communication is thoroughly taken for granted in institutional structures and everyday thinking about communication (Reddy 1979; Axley 1984). This is no accident, for it aligns well with the liberal enlightenment conception of democracy and "fortuitously" well with dominant power structures. It in turn helps reproduce such a conception of democracy and those power relations. The authority of such a conception rests primarily in its self-evidence and naturalness, but if we take a historical look, its interrelatedness with social issues and problems rather than its natural existence becomes evident. In a historical look, current conceptions both make more sense and can be more thoroughly seen as constructions.

There are many histories of modern communication conceptions (for review see Rowland 1988; Robinson 1988). Many of these historical accounts are really reconstructed intellectual histories, in the sense that they are reconstructions of changing concepts developed by theorists at different points in history (Peters

1986). The primary impact of most histories has been to demonstrate conceptual continuity among theories leading to the present. They show theoretical problems that have arisen and the attempt to revise theories to deal with them. Most of these have a pre-Kuhnian view of scientific development, even when they speak of paradigmatic change. Primarily these works speak of changing focuses but still see the problems with which theories must deal in a puzzle-solving way. The emphasis is on continuity. Theories of the past are often seen as simply less developed versions of current perspectives on the same problems. Basic relations of communication to cultural notions of the world or social existence are rarely explored. And nearly all these attempts are elite centered. Other than through works like those of Foucault (1970) and Gebser (1985), most histories offer little idea of how *everyday* people understood the communication process at different times. The point here is not to produce another history or even to give a detailed account of the forgotten communication conceptions of the people on the streets. Rather I hope to structure a way of thinking about the issues in developing a conception of the communication process. Space will leave the analysis superficial (and open to detailed corrections, I'm sure), but a historical characterization can function like an ideal type to provide an interpretive frame for considering both elite and common conceptions. The point is actually to reclaim a tension or conflict in conception suppressed in each affirmative historical account of the nature of the communication process.

Communication theories reside at different nodes of historical interconnectedness. Theories of communication and theories of democracy are simply two different ways of looking at this conjuncture. Voting can be seen as a highly mediated and constrained communication act or communication can be seen as simply the means of expressing political preference. Each theory is a way of looking at the juxtaposition of social, political, economic, and historical forces. My attempt here is to ground democracy in communication rather than to conceptualize communication in terms of democracy. So the focus will be on the historical place of communication conceptions, though by the end it should be clear that the outcome would have been the same if we had proceeded in the other direction.

Communication theories at each historical moment have arisen as practical solutions to dominant historical social problems. While these may be reconstructed as a form of intellectual history, they are better understood as conceptions emerging as each society attempts to reflect upon its problems and produce solutions. In this sense, as fundamental social problems change, we expect fundamental shifts in the concept of communication. The theories are better understood in their relations to technological developments, worldviews, and other conceptualizations of their times than in relation across time to other theories of communication. Each age clearly does draw on the resources of past conceptions, but as one would build with the stones hewn for a former but now useless building. In this way, we can see more clearly the ruptures in theory across time that have been covered up in historical reconstruction. Communication theory as an everyday life conception and practice is an attempt to answer fundamental problems of the day. But like any solution to everyday problems, theories are not politically neutral. They embody and represent political struggle (though often quiet and suppressed) regarding the problem and retain the "winning" group's understanding of the nature of human association, knowledge, and power.

The modern so-called linguistic turn in philosophy, which has represented a shift in conceptions of human experience and sociability, is not a matter of insight but is interconnected with a change in institutions, the growth of the "information society," and urbanization. It is a political as well as practical response. As a new configuration it both presents a solution and creates part of the historical problem. But looking a little further, we can easily ask why modern society is referred to as the "information" rather than communication society and why it is information theory rather than the linguistic turn that is addressed on the streets. The problems that a society addresses are not fixed, but some are privileged and others diminished. Inequitable speaking opportunities is as significant a problem as data storage and retrieval, and the lack of physical touching is as serious as network systems, yet research attention is not given equally to each of these concerns. Although development of these issues and choices are beyond the scope of this work, an overview of communication concepts in historical context suggests a way of thinking through these issues.

Participation and Effectiveness as Fundamental Communication Goals

Fundamental conceptions of the relations of communication to truth, power, the external world, and the internal world are different at different historical periods, and historical communication theories are largely incommensurable. Yet they can be displayed as answering certain recurring human concerns even though in decisively different ways. All conceptions of communication share with the community a dual concern with *participation* and with *effective presentation*. This seems equally true whether we look at scientific communication, the politics of the state, or corporations (Sless, in press). Historical theories of communication when looking at truth, ethos, reason, arguments, and so forth, are simply radically different elaborations on the fundamental answer to these two issues. Types of communication theories and even historical periods might be identified by whether participation or effectiveness is the central term and which is the background one.

Let me characterize these two fundamental issues more clearly. *Participation* deals with who in a society or group has a right to contribute to the formation of meaning and the decisions of the group—which individuals have access to the various systems and structures of communication and can they articulate their own needs and desires within them. *Effectiveness* concerns the value of communicative acts as a means to accomplish ends—how meaning is transferred and how control through communication is accomplished. Each historical theory of communication attends to each issue but in different ways. One issue or the other can dominate at different historical times. Each resolution is an attempt to solve the practical problem of the day but is never free from the politics of the time.

Participation and Effectiveness as Historical Concerns

Without a doubt, early Greek writings set the stage for most of the intellectual writings on communication to follow. Forgetting for a moment the full complexity of Athenian society, at root Athenian Greek considerations of communication included conceptions of both effectiveness and participation. Unfortunately, this duality is often forgotten in the everyday view. Aristotle's *Rhetoric* is often simply presented as about influence, and the attention is given to effectiveness—how to employ the available means of persuasion to influence others in different social forums. This basic textbook reading of Aristotle is probably based more on politically guided misunderstanding than on intention. This recurring view often forgets to mention that the

Greek conception of effectiveness presumed a model of participation to be already in place. We don't have to be too charitable to Aristotle or overly simplistic to suggest that, even at this late stage in Athenian democracy, training in rhetoric was not primarily to give one an advantage over others, as perhaps Plato's view of the Sophists suggests. The point was to enable all citizens (from which they excluded women and slaves) to contribute effectively within the public forum to enable truth itself to emerge. In this sense rhetoric was intended to be in support of the dialectic of truth, not in opposition to it (Valesio 1980). In fact, Aristotle could write about rhetoric in the way he did only because of the presumption of a dialectic based on participation and a forum for participation firmly established in the society. The social problem he addressed was not effective presentation of truth but how to make truth effective. The Athenians, were concerned with effectiveness as a means of promoting greater equalization of participation so that the optimal conditions for the emergence of truth would be present. While we can easily call the Athenian system a flawed democracy in its exclusion of women and slaves (as well as for many other reasons), we can still see its interest in a participatory process. Properly we must ask about both the nature of participation as well as who is allowed to participate. And although we today easily see both as inherently flawed, we cannot deny the central role given to the issue of participation.[1]

If we take this as a point of departure, it is easy to see that at another point in history we could have an emphasis on effectiveness that does not have this presumption of participation, hence the meaning of Aristotle's work would be quite different. Valesio (1980) demonstrated, for example, how rhetoric at different moments of history has been treated as opposed to dialectic, rather than as its handmaiden. Such an opposition can be used to degrade rhetoric, as in the anti-rhetoric period of the Renaissance, or to free it from a responsibility to truth, as in the modern period (see Valesio 1980, 41ff.).

The ordinary modern treatment of Athenian communication theory is thus often distorted by the emphasis on effective self-presentation rather than participation for social good and truth. But the received history is even more one-sided than this. Most histories trace the development of communication theory through the rhetorical tradition where the effectiveness justification is easier, rather than through other political and social writings. Aristotle's writings on friendship and conversa-

tion raise the everyday-life and participation issues more clearly, but they are rarely discussed. The elite in elite activities, and
the speaker in persuasive activities, provide the starting point
and the continuity for the modern politics of communication
theory. The choice of Athens as an origin for communication
theory and democracy is of course itself politically charged. The
pre-Socratics' emphasis on the call of truth, community production, and the centrality of language as logos was already
partially commoditized and personalized by Aristotle (Heidegger 1961). The Sophists that Plato railed against had already
moved from a participatory tradition that preceded them. The
claim here is not for a new or better origin, but to understand
that history and origin are always produced from a present vantage point and are politically charged (Schudson 1989).

This is clear in the Roman appropriation of Aristotle's conception of rhetoric. The concern there with rhetorical effectiveness focused on personal gain and political control rather than
the participatory emergence of truth. The central effective concern was with representation of one's point of view or opinion
in the senate or public forum. A concept of participation was
still present. There were reasonably clear guidelines regarding
who could participate in what ways. The conception of participation here was not an essential part of communication itself
but an external social condition. Quintilian's emphasis on the
good person was necessitated by the lack of the Greek concept
of truth in relation to expression, for if one acquires a position
of influence through one's communicative ability, one's moral
condition as a human being is critical. The administrative view,
as opposed to representative or presentative views of expression, becomes central. Legitimacy becomes an issue of authority rather than communicative process.

Much of Western history can be characterized in terms of
this Roman appropriation rather than in terms of any of the
Greek models of communication. Whether it was the pope
through direct connection with God or the divine right of the
king, the concept of public communication was no longer in
service of the dialectic but was now in terms of effectiveness.
Participation was presumed to be a right that one acquired outside of communication. And participation was largely limited
to specific groups of individuals who had this externally
grounded right. Communication remained primarily a tool for
the advancement of personal positions (though this advancement was considered rightful and for the good of the commu-

nity). Certainly the Roman view matches well with concepts of communication used in corporations today.

The most significant historical break from the Catholic/ Roman conception came with the enlightenment and the rekindled interest in Greek thought. As the enlightenment advanced in different areas of life, changes in the conception of communication were evidenced across areas. From the standpoint of communication, the Protestant reformation signals the end of the church and king as primary speakers. The reformation opened up a concept of communicative religious participation. If the individual can have a direct relationship with God and have the power to read the scriptures, the individual becomes a participant in religious process in a new way. Salvation, hence, no longer came through the pope or the church but rather through one's private communicative relationship with God. The development of a position of anti-rhetoric signaled an end to courtly social propriety and the initiation of modern individualism and the confessional poem. The processes of rationalization conceptually removed positive concern with tradition, authority, and rhetoric from science.

Enlightenment conceptions were gradually extended to the political process. In the most extreme forms, the French and American Revolutions, the relationship between the human being and the state was transformed. The concept of sovereignty gave way to a concept of participation as the central legitimizing force. In this regard, the most significant aspect of the French and American Revolutions was the institutionalization of representative government and the formation of new models of communication in the political process. The right to vote is, hence, a new concept of communication, the right to have a say about political matters.

These changes utilized the Greek conceptions of communication but were clearly not the same. The new transcendent was not truth and the nature of the world but the nature and rights of the individual to use reason to reach *a* rather than *the,* truth. The new notions of truth, of course, were not necessarily better, but they worked to fulfill new motives to break from traditional authority and to control nature. As they liberated, they also destroyed a way of being interconnected to others and nature. A new concept of participation brought with it a new emphasis on effective speech. Neither communal truth nor rightful administration, but expression of position and gaining a following were the problems to be addressed.

When we trace the development of communication theory subsequent to this time, we see, particularly in the Populist movement within the United States, the popularity of training in public speaking as an attempt to build the possibility of the everyday person speaking. This training was linked to the ability to contribute to the political process. The development of journalism, and mass communication and eventually the full development of the concept of objectivity in science and news is grounded in the desire for an enlightened, well-informed individual to enhance participation in political processes.

The development demonstrated a turn from participation issues to effectiveness concerns, but it is not the same reversal seen during the Roman revision of Greek communication theory. The primary issue became the establishment of participation through a concern with effectiveness. Effectiveness was the manner in which this participation could take place. This of course differs from the Roman conception of control through effectiveness. The concept is still different from the Greeks with their concern with truth. It is the individual's position to be advanced rather than to disappear behind the emerging truth. Truth was something that some could possess and subsequently express, hence external to the communication process rather than intrinsic to it.

The Twentieth-Century Institutionalization of Communication Studies

Throughout the early part of the twentieth century, in the public sphere we see the continuation of concern with free speech and public participation with a simultaneous development of greater means of control through communication. The personalized "voice" developed in the rights of political expression became *amplified* first in public speaking and even further in the expansion of the press and forms of telecommunication. Gaining an audience for one's truth replaced the discursive production of truth in political discussion. The movement of the population from the farm to the urban areas and the creation of the "mass" also raised concerns about the future of democracy. Dewey and several in the "Chicago school" of sociology focused on the creation of a new sense of community. Dewey's conception of democracy as a way of being in community rather than simply a form of government provided a focused value orientation to social science research. Social science was to promote the creation and development of democracy. Growing fears of information inequality stimulated debates regarding mass media as public utilities. Developments in public education and public libraries that had been initiated in the nineteenth century took on even greater focus and development. But the concept of being informed directed most decisions rather than enhanced decision making. Even for Dewey, the concern for developing systems of integration and control within a society with a "weak state" was critical within modern democracy. In fact the two could not be separated (Hamilton and Sutton 1989). The liberal ideal, that widespread public information aided by an enlightened elite would lead to positive social development, directed conceptions of effective communication systems as essential to wider participation.

Although in most analysis the growth of communication media was seen as a good in providing public information and social integration, there were also growing fears of possible dysfunctions, particularly of mass entertainment, and manipulations of the public mind. The rise of Hitler in Germany focused the fear that, through propaganda, communication systems developed for participation could be used for control and could undermine individuals' possibilities for meaningful participation in the political process.

The institutionalization of communication study in the United States emerged in this schizophrenic environment. Peters (1986) productively utilized Weber's conception of "prophet" and "priests" to describe the transformation. If Dewey can be seen as the prophet providing a morally guided vision of the universe as a meaningful totality, the "priests" would transform this vision into doctrine, rituals, standard conceptions and practices, and leadership roles. Unfortunately, the moral foundation would be lost in the translation. Social science and its elite would provide the instrumentalities, but severed from democratic values. The drive for theory and research, focused on administration, control, and effectiveness, was great. As corporations became larger, the need for communication systems expanded, and as the communication technologies became available, corporate expansion increased (Chandler 1977). The focus on leadership and public-speaking training evidenced the desire and possibility of upward mobility of those who could take control. Both personal advancement and corporate expansion became more dependent on communication systems and skills and less dependent on traditional elements (such as class) and money (though class and money could go a long way in providing communication control). The mass media greatly expanded the possibilities of advertising, public relations, and other commercial applications.

The fear of control through communication, and the desire for commercial expansion of control, directed theories and research to regard communication in models of effect rather than participation. Research would both ascertain how real the fear should be and extend the administrative capacity for control (Tomaselli and Louw 1989). Lazersfeld (1969) generally gets credit for providing the conception that could allow each to exist and structure a research agenda. A thesis of mediated effects could argue, on the one hand, that the media need not be controlled, since their impact is mediated through traditional institutions and decision processes, and on the other hand that corporations and governments should allocate massive resources to change the public's mind. Such a solution would later enable advertisers to spend billions of dollars to promote products to children and to argue that the content of programming has little effect on children's behavior. From a research standpoint, the solution enabled an isomorphism in studies designed to protect the public from persuasion and those used to enhance it. The presumed balanced view hides the fact that both were studying communication from an effectiveness perspective and concepts of participation were left out. In many respects Lazersfeld was the ideal impetus and symbol for the transformation in institutionalized communication analysis. As an avowed positivist Lazersfeld made a clear distinction between research and social values, and as a recent immigrant he had little sense of the everyday communal democracy in place in the United States. From his standpoint, democracy was already established as a political reality, and the problem was only to provide stability, integration, and growth.

The continental tradition in communication was developing at the same time. The concern there with cultural impact and the social formation of meaning, rather than effects of messages, provided a partial participatory model. Adorno's work, in particular, was available but had little impact until considerably later (see Ferment in the Field 1983). The *Authoritarian Personality* was the most widely read of Adorno's works and the meaning of the essays there could be seen as placing responsibility on the individual rather than focusing on communication process. And, ironically, Adorno's concern with the cultural effects of mass media was read as smug, elitist, and European. Such attributions could lead him to be seen as antidemocratic rather than as providing for renewed communal participation.

Not only did the focus of communication studies change, but so too did the presumed relation of communication to knowledge. The conception of knowledge as publicly contestable from a variety of points of view passed to an elitist certification of right or objective knowledge. The development of an asocial conception of knowledge and of a representational theory of language worked together in this transformation. In the increasingly rationalized world, knowledge was conceptualized as produced by a privileged method. The positivity of knowledge was simultaneously a quest for certainty and a process by which conflicts over knowledge claims could be resolved. The effect was an attempt to prevent culture-specific values from entering into knowledge claims and thus remove politics from knowledge. The success of the attempt can be seen in defining an autonomous realm for science freed from the political constraints of the day. The attempt, of course, failed as a philosophy of science, in regard both to being value-free and to being free from a community, but the conceptual legacy remained in scientific and everyday conceptions of methodological determinism (Apel 1972, 1979a). The solution to the practical problem for human development in one period becomes the problem in the next.

Communication study was affected in several ways. A clear fact/fiction distinction was important to separate news from entertainment and editorial commentary. News as objective could serve the well-informed citizen and thus aid the political process without itself being political. The view of language as representational argued that while everyday language is value-laden, it could be brought to approximate the language of science through operational definition and many related principles best exemplified by teachings in general semantics. The possibility of a realm of everyday discourse based in fact could cleanse discussion from inferences and value-laden political dimensions. No theory of language has appealed to either society or communication researchers as thoroughly. The modern realization that conceptions of facts, objectivity, and representational language are inevitably heavily value-laden and politically loaded has been slow to sink into everyday life and communication studies (Dallmayr 1984b). As useful as they were in overcoming traditional myths and authorities, representation conceptions provided limited conceptions of the political, communication, and democracy.

The focus of communication analysis throughout the first half of the twentieth century regarded primarily mass media and the political process. The possibility of participation seemed self-evident if speech freed from censorship were granted and the individual had access to appropriate information. When we consider the "nonpolitical" realms of life, little concern with communication or participation can be seen. Neither the church, the family, nor the educational system seemed to gain any sustained democratization. As communities grew into cities, town meetings and other forms of participation declined. The most drastic changes can be seen in the workplace. The development of industrialization and the rapid growth in the size of corporations can be seen as reducing most individuals' communicative participation and power in decision making. As traditional authority relations disappeared, the loss of relationship with the decision maker and control by routine and machine removed the possibility of negotiation. Conflicts between owners and workers in the various labor movements in the United States were rarely advanced at the level of political participation. The primary structure was that of an economic conflict based on interest differences rather than participation for common good. Only occasionally were questions raised concerning the owners' right to control the place of work. Even where the control issues were raised, especially around issues of state ownership, the actual practices of management and the communication patterns in the place of work remained fundamentally unchanged. This was clearly true in the United States and Western Europe and was equally clear with postrevolutionary Soviet Union organizational forms with Lenin's implementation of scientific management principles.

The free-speech/marketplace-of-ideas perspective, effectiveness models of communication, privacy and individualism as the conception of the individual, and a positivist representational view of language and knowledge together set a context for meaning domination hidden as reasonable and democratic. Effectiveness models of communication are present in the vast majority of communication studies and are largely accepted as self-evident by the public, then and now. Fact/fiction/value distinctions, objectivity, and the representational view of language are virtually everyone's basic operating equipment. But it is precisely these that have to be rethought.

Participation and Making the Personal Political

The conflicts centering in the sixties in many ways evidenced the public's at times naïve attempt to understand and deal with the political implications of these conceptions as well as the beginning of academic reconsideration. While the various experiences of the sixties can be characterized in a number of different ways—for example, in the United States as dissent against the Vietnam war—they had a clear communication theme not limited to the United States or its policies. A set of issues seemed to arise almost spontaneously worldwide. The international issues were clearly more significant than specific local or national ones. As Wallerstein (1989) has claimed: "As an event, 1968 has long since ended. However it was one of the great, formative events in the history of our modern world-system, the kind we call watershed events. This means that the cultural-ideological realities of that world-system have been definitely changed by the event, itself the crystallization of certain long-existing structural trends within the operation of the system" (431). The international issues surrounded language, the nature of experience, and personal and cultural identity. The sixties functioned to focus change in the nonpolitical aspects of life much as the French and American Revolutions did regarding the political aspects of life. It was a process of revolt around issues of participation in nonstate political processes.

Metaphorically, the sixties can be characterized as the revolt of the listener. The concept of "listener" can be used to designate members of the society who were presumably passive and silent (silenced), who received messages, who were acted upon, who accepted the identity that someone else gave them, and who spoke someone else's meanings. This included students, women, blacks, workers, and various colonized peoples. It was these segments that demanded a speaking turn. As Baudrillard (1975) carefully demonstrated:

> Hence there is a major role for students, youth who are disqualified in advance, voluntarily or not, as well as all types of social groups, of regional communities, ethnic or linguistic, because...they fall into marginality....

Excluded from the game, their revolt henceforth aims
at the rules of the game.... The black revolt aims at race
as a code, at a level much more radical than economic
exploitation. The revolt of women aims at the code that
makes the feminine a non-marked term. The youth
revolt aims at the extremity of a process of racist discrimination in which it has no right to speak. The same
holds for all those social groups that fall under the
structural bar of repression, of relegation to a place
where they lose their meaning. This position of revolt is
no longer that of economically exploited; it aims less at
the extortion of surplus value than at the imposition of
the code, which inscribes the present strategy of social
domination. (134–35)

Clearly such social movements were different from those of the
past. They did not serve primarily to give social groups more
power or a bigger piece of the action. They were largely not
about distribution. Ultimately, they were in Habermas's sense
"fragmentary pieces of civil society working to retain independent identities and autonomy on the periphery of institutional
state/corporate structures" (Luke 1989, 215). Such movements
were about the protection of a life world outside the reaches of
the colonization, a space for a protected interior. They were
often noninstrumental in their attempts to oppose a form of
rationality and instrumental reasoning. Their challenge arose
from their disregard, disdain, and playfulness. In this sense
they were often more reactionary than revolutionary.

In the United States this is seen in the Berkeley Free Speech
Movement as a start of the student protests. As the movement
emerged in other places, the theme remained as one of self-
determination as opposed to control by parents and parental
educational institutions. Unlike early adolescent rebellions or
student dissension regarding campus rules, the focus was not
on what could and could not be done but rather on who has
the right to say. This of course included education curriculum,
lifestyle, body identity, and the construction of meaning.

The same basic issues arose in the black community emerging from the civil rights movement. While the civil rights
movement focused primarily on the political process, the development of the concept of "Black Power" focused on self-determination of identity and the cultural articulation of that identity in a realm outside the political arena. The women's move-

ment followed a somewhat different path but came to the same issues. Suffrage had not led to significant changes in social life. In the sixties the women's movement likewise turned to the politics of the family, the workplace, and identity itself. The issue was, of course, primarily trying to find a self-determined female identity (a woman's voice) and to create a forum for its articulation.

White male workers, like students, women, and blacks, were underrepresented in the process of meaning production but did not initially pick up on the theme of participation. This was especially true in the United States. White male Workers largely accepted the "code," if not necessarily their share of the rewards within it. Participatory management programs nearly all followed economic motives rather than political ones. Occasionally a different theme was heard. But generally, even with the growth of attitudes of "entitlement" (Mason 1982), job enrichment rather than control often served as the critical impulse. This is not to say that meaningful reforms did not emerge out of the popularity of quality-of-life studies, only that these did not foster a worker consciousness. Much of the reason for this can be located in internal communication processes, which will be discussed later.

The New Problem of Expression

Social theorists were not absent in the everyday working-out of a new conception of person, experience, and politics. Many of the "darlings" of the sixties, Marcuse (1964) for example, provided what became the slogans of the age but only partially anticipated and structured the emerging response. The theoretical writings of the sixties and early seventies, such as those of Baudrillard, Derrida, Lacan, and Foucault, developed the concept of voice and the politics of meaning to provide a reconstructed understanding of what had already happened in the public consciousness. Ironically, as their works have developed and in most ways have further rejected the self-evident subject and the various elitisms, they have become increasingly elitist. The thematization of power and the political nature of moral decisions have often further justified a self-interested public mind, rather than provided a way out of it. This current work takes the more hopeful position that the descriptive power of these works can be reconnected to a latent public drive for collective self-determination.

Even before the theoretical writings, the various groups of the sixties had already understood the issue of participation in linguistic terms. Since these groups had only participated marginally in the historical development of language and verbal expression systems, they were obviously at a disadvantage in self-understanding, let alone expression of their own meanings. Each group glorified nonverbal expression and moments of silence, though often without clear political awareness. The presumption was that there were other forms of expression that might better be utilized to express the meanings experienced as so hard to conceptualize in the white, adult male linguistic system. Reason itself was suspect, given its association with the dominant trend of Western rationalization. The value-free purity of science was open to full question. The recognition of the irrationality of the rational, however, led not to a new focus on the processes of reason but more often to a return to the personal and mystical. It is perhaps because of this that the movement would only expand democracy in limited ways.

The rising concern with participation was not focused only upon self expression. Properly it might better be cast as a politics of experience, of sensuality itself. These politics were not philosophically worked out, but there was an awareness of the social production of perception, a social production of what the body was allowed to feel. Unfortunately, this was also cast in individualistic, personal ways, as the individual pitted against the social (Laing 1967), so that the social was left outside of experience rather than protrayed as needing reform. Rather than a political reform of democracy, its basic conditions of individual self-interest were reproduced. Ultimately, the attempted (at least conceptually revered) individuality would be reduced to highly administered forms of permissive and possessive individalism where even personal growth and leisure could create major industries.

Several recent writings have followed the attempt to reduce the issues of the sixties to the glorification of youth and self-expressionism. In most of these the outcome has been used to reconceptualize the intent. For example, Meyrowitz (1985) in his popular account argued that television brought the "backstage" (in Goffman's sense) into view. Children were able to see that parents negotiated behind the scene to produce the public front, hence the self-evidence and certainty of the parental voice were lost. Apart from whether television can be said to be the cause, Meyrowitz's contention, that this has led to a spoiled and eventually disenchanted segment of the population, misses far too much. Clearly the backstage became public and came to be understood as where all the action is, but the youth culture was only one of several groups that became interested in the negotiation of the rules of the game rather than competing within them. Further, to read these movements as mere self-expression rather than as a renewed attempt at a new participative community misses the communal drive in them (even though the media portrayed them as self-indulgent and they may have become that). And most importantly, to treat the modern dissatisfaction as one of simply having failed to acquire the self-desired material possessions, overlooks an equally likely thesis that the modern dismay and even depression comes from not a lost youth but an inability to participate even as adults.

The Impact on Communication Conceptions

The sudden societal concern in the sixties and early seventies with expanded concepts and practices of participation placed great strain on existing communication theories. Most theories assumed the existence of an underlying value and meaning consensus, with communication theory focusing on the transmission of these existing meanings. With expanded participation and conflict over fundamental meanings, theories of transmission and control are of little help. The focus must be on negotiation and the transactional creation of meaning and subsequent consensus. The growth of nonverbal and interpersonal communication classes and discussion of a "process view" of communication all showed the influence of social experience on the academic study of communication issues. Many of the early attempts to reform communication theory turned to humanistic psychology and personalized the concept of meaning. The result of this was to hide even further the nature of the social production of individual experience and undermine the power of communication to rebuild a participatory community. Claims of authenticity became "jargonistic" and stimulated their own subservience to long-dominant meaning structures (Adorno 1973; Jacoby 1975). "Receiver views" complicated the effects model by placing meaning in the receiver rather than in the speaker, but did little to focus attention on meaning production. These views further psychologized the communication process and made social criticism more difficult, since listeners presumably created their own demise (Schiller 1989, 59). Ultimately, the attempt in the sixties to reform authority-based communication processes turned to humanistic psychology and ended by prizing self-expression over collective decisions (Adorno 1973). The Donahue show becomes the modern survivor as it champions expressions protected from examination in their display (Carbaugh 1988). The Dewey-based open classroom collapsed to a place of self-expressionism and advocacy of self-interest rather than a place where democracy and community could be learned. In the media world, Meyrowitz's reconstruction reproduces itself.

Somewhat more successful was the development of a systems conception arising from family research (Bateson 1972; Watzlawick, Beavin, and Jackson 1967; Pearce and Cronen 1980). Here the focus could be on the reciprocal production of meaning with useful insight into the production of identity and social responsibility. While this work will aid my analysis later, this work in itself has not developed a theory of society with an understanding of the relations among interpersonal systems and their social and historical contexts. Neither humanistic psychology nor systems theory could deal with the structural determination of power in the society, and consequently neither could provide help in understanding the more fundamental relations in social meaning formation.

Maintaining the Participative Impulse

Certainly the experience of the sixties has passed. One fears writing of it for fear the work will be dismissed as romantic. But the issues posed still remain. With the prodemocracy movements in China and Eastern Europe, the human impulse for democratization seems clear. The productiveness of its direction is yet to be worked out. In the sixties, the society had jumped to a new issue, social representation in the nonpolitical aspects of life, even before the various issues of political representation, particularly in light of the growth of mass media and new communication technologies, could be adequately worked out. The attempt to recast and even defuse the sixties experience by granting the eighteen-year-old a vote in the United States was a solution for a different issue. The sixties evidenced the emergence of a social project that continues but remains often superficial and incomplete. Contemporary life can be seen as the continuation of this project in a constantly distorted form. The modern race to individual success is not the endlessness of the attempt to dominate all of nature (as the modern project of science gone astray), but the individual attempt to finally get the promised freedom, the right of self-determination in the postmodern world. The continued failure comes in the incomplete development of a new sense of community. Communication is central to this concept.

The difficulty in developing an adequate conception becomes greater with the continued rapid development of new communication technologies. Most have been developed and assessed primarily through criteria of effectiveness and the advancement of control. This issue requires a considerably different understanding of the nature of the technology. Certainly new technologies can advance either participation or control. The issue of participation is that of how different groups utilize the technologies and what they do to people's capacity to express different kinds of meaning. Each technology, because of its nature and structural place, privileges certain groups of people and certain types of meaning. For example, the presence of large data bases prizes codified, abstract knowledge over intuitive insights. Other than issues regarding access, we know surprisingly little about these relations, however, partly due to the emphasis on effectiveness.

An adequate theory of communication dealing with participation has to be able to assess whether or not people are able to represent their competing interests within the various institutions that compose society. This includes issues such as capacity—are there means available for different groups to participate in the various media of communication? But this is more than simply an access issue. It also has to do with deeper issues of whether or not people are able to openly form their own interests and whether they are able to contribute to the formation of meaning that enables them to represent the interests that they might have. Involved is an attempt to understand the social development of meaning itself and understand the various means by which people participate in the transmission of meaning.

Not only have we experienced a social change in the concept of participation, including who, in what manners, and about what, but we also have a structural change taking place in the nature of society itself. The emergence of the corporate organization as the primary institution in modern society affects any emerging conception of the individual and participation. As we have seen, the primacy of the organization as an institution can be represented both by an increased intrusion into the nonwork aspects of life as well as by an eclipse of the state as the primary means by which social policy is made.

The corporate organization's intrusion into the life world has several possible effects on identity. What was an organic relationship between work and the rest of life developed into a segmented relationship within the development of industrialization. The creation of the worker as a commodity shifted identity and power. The paying of wages rather than paying for a product severed the organic relationship. With the separation, the initial period could be characterized by alienation, loss of identity, and separation from community. In the modern context it turns instead to an intrusion of the workplace into the everyday life world. With this the nonwork aspects of life can be seen as a limit to one's work rather than work being a means to nonwork ends. We see this most clearly in issues of child rearing, illness, love, and friendship, each a calculated cost to professional advancement. While the sixties' worker understood the loss of community and meaning in the life world and sought a new organic relationship in meaningful, fulfilling work, the eighties' worker accepted meaninglessness for the sake of power, excitement, and financial reward and worked longer hours. Thus power and individual control are achieved momentarily but still remain fundamentally unacceptable substitutes for meaninglessness. In education, as discussed earlier, the development of a responsible, enlightened citizen gives way to job and career training. The primary structure of modern education is the development of a labor force, hence the marginalization of the liberal arts education. The emerging centrality of work also in the education context ironically emerged in opposition to the business world. The sixties' students' "radical" claim for curricula relevance, based on a reformation of meaning, quickly became normalized as a call for a relation to the "real world," that is, the world of work. With such a view, enrichment of the life world does not happen in education but through success in an occupation that allows the good life to be bought. As education lines up with the corporate enterprise, the capacity for a critical examination of the nature of work or the corporate form becomes increasingly difficult.

An odd byproduct of the women's movement is that while reform allowed women to enter into the work context, thus to realize themselves in the place of work, it simultaneously denied women the critical outside perspective for considering the life-world consequence of the primacy of the work institution. In some sense the change enabled the workplace to enter even more deeply into the family and community context. How should these changes be considered from a communication perspective?

From a historical context it is easy to see how one might evaluate the effectiveness of communication. Criteria might differ at different historical periods, but the concept of measurement remains consistent. Independent of the complexity of the relationship to audience, the source's intent remained central. The issue of participation poses different problems. If we ask ourselves how to evaluate notion of participation for the Greeks, the Roman's, or in the French and American Revolutions, we appear to be left with a totally historically relative standard. If we accept one conception, such as the freedom of political speech, we find the inadequacy of the concept to highlight central socially defined problems in the contemporary situation.

But these various conceptions do share certain characteristics. Most significant is their application of moral conceptions to guide communicative practice. And these moral conceptions, like systems of morality in general, primarily struggle to account for the inequitable distributions of life's chances. This difference may be conceptualized as based on sin, one's place of birth, or external systems, and the solution to it may be the promise of a glorious afterlife or the ability to transform one's fate. Nonetheless, the very arbitrariness of one's placement has to be accounted for. It seems reasonable to assume that implicitly every human being knows that I could be there and they could be here.

When we look at communication in the social move toward participation in the formation of the life world, we have to ask the basis for the presumption of a right to participate as well as the attempt to do it. What would we use to evaluate the morality of communication systems? Freedom of speech certainly is not socially accepted in all societies, and its philosophical basis in Western thought has long since eroded. But is it still yet a preferable belief even without a foundation? I think not. There are too many new issues in society for which it gives unclear guidance. In particular, it provides little guidance regarding corporate control and the actualization of power in modern society.

Notes

1. I hope that it is clear that I have no desire to glorify any particular democratic model of the past. I have little interest in the specific nature of particular democracies; rather, I am interested in the historical concern with participation. Every democracy has been criticized at a later period of time, and appropriately so. Most of these criticisms, however, have not denied participation as a goal but have demonstrated the inadequacy of participation at earlier times. We need not claim that Greek and enlightenment democracy were unimportant, when we disclose their tragic flaws. In discussing their flaws, we also reclaim their significant, if counterfactual, hope. The tainted history of democracy does not necessarily make democratic participation a sham, but shows the limitations of its concrete historical realizations. It is only on the basis of a more participative model that we disclose the oppressions of past forms.

CHAPTER 5

Language and the Politics of Experience

> The meaning of experience is perhaps the most crucial struggle for meaning since it involves personal, psychic, and emotional investment on the part of the individual.... Subjectivity is produced in a whole range of discursive practices—economic, social and political—the meanings of which are a constant site of struggle over power. Language is not the expression of unique individuality; it constructs the individual's subjectivity in ways which are socially specified.
> (Chris Weedon 1987, 79, 21)

The greatest difficulty in developing a politics of everyday life and more participative communication in the United States is the predominance of particular concepts of experience. The maintenance of a clear split between a subjective and an objective account of experience and the continued tensions between defenders of each position make it difficult to find a discursive space for a position beyond (behind, separate from) them. The difficulty is not from the lack of understandable alternatives. The pragmatists and symbolic interactionists early in this century elaborated a powerful set of alternative conceptions. The phenomenological writings from Europe have long been available, and various Oriental works have been widely understood for some time. But in each case these works have been either ignored or reduced to the subjective or objective pole in the approved tension. Without a stronger account, we cannot demonstrate the particular constituents of experience in everyday life and see the role of corporate life in this constitution.

Concepts of individualism, natural rights, and control form a tight network of essential terms that structure only certain possible concepts of experience. As Henriques et al. (1984) demonstrated, the production of the psychological subject required the separation of the individual and the social as well as a neglect of the social world. The simultaneous support of the personal and psychological with the opposite of objectivity and truth hides the singularity of the two positions together and their privilege over other configurations. Contemporary European works share a denial of this singularity and these pseudotensions, though in different ways. For example, critical theorists tend to take on more directly the problems of individualism and subjectivity, and Foucault, the problem of objectivity and truth. This might be expected, given the traditions out of which they work. Their shared advantage is that each of their traditions was influenced by phenomenology, though each is distanced from it based on the humanistic excesses it produced in their own traditions. I believe that we must first understand the phenomenological account of experience in order to productively utilize recent European works. The most common misunderstandings of the works of Foucault and the critical theorists in the United States, I believe, have come from a lack of understanding of phenomenology rather than from holding on to it too tenaciously.

Starting with phenomenology poses some conceptual dangers. Although the articulation of modern works from there potentially overlooks the careful arguments and counterarguments from the various camps, I think it is necessary. Scholars must differentiate their work from that of others to find a place for a new way of considering central issues. Frequently this means that a great deal of effort is put into distinguishing their works from those that are closest to them, if only to avoid reduction of the work to prior work, but also, perhaps, to distinguish themselves as scholars. Unfortunately, the results of such intercircle positionings are often the exclusion of external audiences and a focus on getting the language of the camp right rather than a public sharing of the issues held in common. In the United States the sharp discussions among the various versions of poststructuralists and critical theorists have been useful in advancing precision, but fail to advance a public understanding of the more fundamental changes that situate these fights. The wider public may at times struggle to develop a politics of everyday life but must do so through a Cartesian discourse. This partially accounted for the reduction of the politics of experience to humanistic psychology and the failure of the sixties to provide an everyday critical practice. Social science is still, by and large, practiced with a nineteenth century concept of experience, and the legal system still operates with a notion of singular, linear cause, with no conception of probability. Sometimes it is useful to return to basics.

This chapter advances five arguments. First, perceptual experience is primary. On the basis of their perceptions, human beings make judgments, decide courses of action, develop feelings, and make claims about the nature of reality. Such a claim is in opposition to the naturalism of empiricists and everyday actors who start with sense data or an objectified world (where constructivist activities are so taken for granted as to be forgotten). It is also in opposition to humanistic phenomenologists and constructivists, who in bracketing the world to examine constructivist activities fail to recall the materiality of the world or the materiality of the subject's placement in it.

Second, perception is formed interactively among subjects and objects. Concepts of the subject and attributes of the object arise together in perception. Neither stands primary, both may be changed in time through further perceptions, and neither may be simply wished away.

Third, perception is directed by institutionalized practices. Perceptions are produced out of a position, point of view, or orientation. Such institutional practices include having particular sense equipment, a manner of comportment, certain material social practices, a particular language that makes certain distinctions and highlights certain aspects, and extensions of sense equipment, such as tools and scientific instruments. Institutionalization enables certain types of perceptions and tends to close off others. The human subject is the subject pole of each unified experience. Institutional practices are not simple and totally coordinated. In each moment there are competing perceptions from competing subject positions.

Fourth, perception is intrinsically political. Due to the sociohistorical development of institutions and the perceptions made possible by them, certain human groups and human interests have greater influence on what is perceived than others, and these interests and groups tend to be advantaged through their influence on what is taken as real. In descriptions of the world, positionality is carried with every assertion, and

every assertion is filled with the power politics of the development of language, institutions, personal identity, and social
practices. No knowledge or reason can escape this.

And finally, certain perceptions become protected as common sense, with social order, legitimate knowledge, and personal identities invested in them. What arises as interactively
formed perception in a practical context becomes built into and
protected by its reproduction in further discourse. Social
arrangements tend to normalize perception and preclude the
continual formation of new perceptions. Past experience, in this
sense, substitutes for possible new experience and dominates it.
Structural arrangement and certain discursive practices actively
protect and reproduce this type of political domination.

The Phenomenological Account of Experience

Phenomenology is critical in providing the concept of the primacy of the perceptual experience. Phenomenology came into
prominence against the background of the narrow naturalistic
and positivistic conception of science and the general skepticism of the late romantic period. Phenomenology was the
attempt to found a rigorous science to break skepticism and yet
avoid the inadequacies of the natural sciences, particularly
when applied to the study of people and their products. As is
well known, Husserl (1962) proposed phenomenology as a science of experience. This was not to be a science of a particular
domain, but the essential basis for any science. The term experience, is not intended to describe a psychological phenomenon but the consciousness of a structured world as we
engage in life activities. The experienced world serves as the
ultimate ground for all knowledge and understanding, and it is
to there that all conflicting claims appeal. Whether in science
or in everyday life, there is no route to the world or other persons except through the experience of them.

The Critique of Naturalism

Typically the scientist, as well as the everyday actor, assumes the
"natural attitude," thereby accepting the "objects" of experience
as they appear as "real," without reflecting on their constitution
in experience (Husserl 1962, 74ff.). Thus, the empirical sciences
are often based uncritically on the world as constructed through

theories, methods, and instruments rather than on the objects they presumed to be real beyond experience. By operating as if their own language and procedures were "transparent," they could claim objectivity, but in doing so they failed to investigate the constitution of their objects of investigation. Thus, the major inadequacy of the natural-science model that phenomenology hoped to overcome was that of "objectivism," that is, the faith in "naturalistic" observation that kept science and everyday people from understanding their own subjectivity in observation. Hence, contrary to the popular misunderstanding, it was not the objectivity of science and everyday accounts that phenomenology criticized but rather their subjectivity, the treatment of a historically perceived world as *the* world. The natural-science model implicitly accepts Cartesian dualism, which suggested that the subject and object were two distinct realms of the world that could be methodically separated. Naturalistic science hoped to free itself from the bias of everyday conceptions by privileging its methods and observations. In effect, then, a particular shared subjectivity became privileged rather than subjectivity being eliminated.

In the attempt to eliminate human subjectivity from science, naturalistic science naively sought to restrict study to the physical and empirical—the objects assumed constant and given for all. Husserl demonstrated several difficulties with this attempt. First, in his critique of the natural attitude, he demonstrated that, to be consistent, naturalism must also find support for itself and its methods "out-there" in the empirical world. This it could not do. As Habermas (1984) put it: "Like traditionalism, logical empiricism has to have recourse to self-evident first principles; only it is the scientific method, the foundations of which remain unclarified, that the later absolutizes in the place of God, Nature, or Being. Positivism is unwilling to ground the identity of science and truth that it asserts. It limits itself to analyzing the procedures of established scientific practice. This may be an expression of reverence for institutionalized science; but why certain procedures may be recognized as scientific is something that requires normative justification" (375).

Further, the scientific positing of a given quality of nature is preceded by and based upon the prescientific claim of constancy, a claim that is in as much need of support and clarification as the first. The natural-science claim to be derived from nature, separate from a historical situation that is the ground of its validity, thus could not be supported. Natural science, like the phenomenology being developed, must be grounded in human consciousness, in human life experience, in a human community. As Merleau-Ponty (1962) later demonstrated: "All my knowledge of the world, even my scientific knowledge, is gained from my own particular point of view, or from experience of the world without which the symbols of science would be meaningless. The whole universe of science is built on the world as directly experienced, and if we want to subject science itself to rigorous scrutiny and arrive at a precise assessment of its meaning and scope, we must begin by reawakening the basic experience of the world of which science is the second-order expression" (viii).

In addition, naturalism could not give an adequate account of experience or understanding. Starting with the notion that experience is caused by objects and events of the empirical world, much of our experience was left unexplained. As Husserl argued, if experience is simply the sum of sense impressions—sensory excitation by stimuli from the outside—how is it that we experience a complete chair while our sense impressions are only from one side? Or how is it that we experience groupness even after all empirical characteristics of the group have changed, or experience a melody as the same when played by different instruments in a different key? Or how could the same empirical object be experienced differently depending on the setting or the person's prior activity? The various naturalistic explanations, that images or concepts form in the head or that memory traces are left, appeal yet to a socially shared experience and language system but cannot be independently "observed" except as themselves holistic and complete. This does not undermine these as interesting claims or science as being productive, but reclaims the experiential base for science against its claims to escape it. The natural attitude is even more problematic in its presumption of naturalism in the observation of human behavior. To maintain the claim of "givenness," the natural scientist has to assume that the behavior can be objectified as an empirical thing in the physical world and given a physical description without loss. As such the behavior cannot be understood in itself as a human product, work, or expression. Abstract metaphysical categories and psychological theories then become necessary to explain what was already understood about the behavior (its unity and directedness) and to reconnect the behavior to the human actor. In addition, the understanding of historical events was a constant problem for natural-science models, since the historical events were not subject to observation. Only the artifacts remain, and their meaning cannot be separated from their connection to human producers, hence their empirical status must always be supplemented.

A final problem the phenomenologists found with the natural attitude was that of relevance. If the scientific observer was outside of the current historical society, so that objectivity would not be threatened by the community's values and practical interests, how could she or he decide which questions to ask, and how was "objective" knowledge to be reported in ways understood by everyday actors? And what happened to objectivity when scientific results were translated back into the natural language of the human community in which human problems are asked and human decisions reached? In practice the scientist became bifurcated—having one life as a supposedly value-neutral scientist, and one as a human subject. Perhaps more importantly the scientist was not as value-neutral as claimed, because values and prejudices were contained in historically developed scientific methods and concepts. The very assumed possibility of purity of method and language kept the scientist unaware of the biases and commitments contained in science itself and precluded their successful evaluation. Concepts like social good or representation for different groups could only be thought outside of science rather than being understood as intrinsic to it.

It can well be argued that this analysis is unnecessary because scientists are no longer so naïve as to make such naturalist claims. Certainly this is partly true. Yet most social science in the United States today is practiced *as if* such naturalist assumptions were true, and many appear to forget the "as if." More importantly, as we shall see, the privilege of certain knowledge claims in corporate organizations, and the lack of their critical examination, are based on precisely this rejected logic of science. The acceptance of a representational conception of understanding and good language use, the privileging of "facts" in data storage and retrieval systems, and the glorification of expertise, all extend different aspects of the natural-science model. The politics of everyday knowledge is better fought along these lines than in argument with the more sophisticated philosophies of science of the day. The maintenance of such a view, despite the critique, suggests the possibility of motives and advantage.

The Structure of Experience

Phenomenology proposed a science of the experienced world rather than of the presumed natural world. In so doing it showed the separation between "objective" world and "subjective" persons to be an abstraction from the more direct experience of subject and object combined in an "intelligible world." Nothing is lost from science, or the everyday usefulness of it, in this move, except for the pretense of fixed, independently structured objects of the world. The insistence of primacy for the world in itself transcendent to the human subject makes objects no more "real" or real in their consequences. The very heart of the phenomenological position is that the holistic, socioexperiential world is more basic and real than the posited elementalistic natural world *or* subjective feelings. The transcendent natural world was not denied as existing; rather, for the purposes of describing the experience of this world, belief in the natural world as a necessary reality was suspended. This suspension allowed the exploration and explication of the implicit structures of consciousness that constitute the world as experienced but that were normally hidden or overlooked in paying attention to the structured world as an independent entity.

In phenomenology, experience is described as being composed of two simultaneous "movements:" (1) an intending act (*noesis,* the consciousness of) and (2) an intended object (*noema,* that which the consciousness is of). The critical phenomenological insight is that neither can stand alone. Consciousness is not directed toward a void, and without an intended unity an object could never be collected from a string of sense impressions. The abstraction of a preexisting object linked in some way to an internal psychological state as if each existed and could be studied separately is given up to the unity as the subject matter. The phenomenological goal is the description of the constitution of the structured world, that is, the preconditions for objects to appear as they appear.

The dualism and resulting problems of naturalism were thus broken by showing that prior to the separation of the person as a psychological being from the world as an objectified entity, experience is consciously structured as more than simple sense impressions or empty mental states. An intelligible, understood world is collected in each individual perception. As Mickunas and Oastler (1972) explained: "For the phenomenologist, the manner in which the thing is seen constitutes the basis for one kind of definition of the thing. His understanding is that the meaning of the thing is defined in terms of the use to which the thing is put.... There can be no universal or ulti- mate definition of a thing; the meaning of a thing reflects the goals and objectives of the perceiver-agent" (244). Adequate knowledge that avoids the theoretical prejudices of naturalism but that is the result of a rigorous science can be founded on the description of consciousness itself.

Husserl initially attempted to develop an absolute, tran- scendent science. As a rigorous science, transcendental phe- nomenology suspended all presuppositions, theories, or other abstractions regarding the existence or nature of the external world or of an internal psyche that might be imposed over and against experience. What remained after these suspensions were the necessary structures of conscious experience itself, which Husserl attempted to make explicit in the phenomeno- logical description. Perceptual experience for the phenomenol- ogist could not be reduced to the sum of sense impressions. As experienced, perception is not impressions from one side; it is integrated, and our perceptions are filled out—we see a com- plete chair, not simply the side facing us.

For example, we perceive a room as a room even though each impression is only from a side and we have never seen it from all sides at once. We can even recognize the room when presented with a floor plan drawn from the top—a perspective from which we have never seen the room. All this is possible because what is understood is an intended "room"—as an implicit structure of consciousness—seen from nowhere, rather than a perspective or learned mental concept of the room. Only on the basis of this "a-perspectival," understood room can the judgment be made that the present view is a perspective, that impressions are only being received from one side, or even that the notion of a side becomes meaningful. The "room" and all interconnections thereof exist independently of each impres- sion but are perceived in each impression. Although the struc- tures of consciousness are temporally constituted, they are not simply the mental re-collection of past impressions or experi- ences. The "room" as an implicit conscious structure is a pas- sive synthesis of all perspectives, prior experiences, and future anticipation. This synthesis is a process not in the head but on the transcendental level. The "room" is beyond the individual yet is manifested in individual experiences. Each side, each impression, gathers and witnesses for the total room and presents the room as a constructed object in human experience in such a way that what is in front of the individual is not understood as separate from the room itself. Each side is not experienced in-itself but as remembering and manifesting the total room and an open ended horizon of action possibilities implied with a room. It is on the basis of this constructed experience, rather than on what might be abstracted as the side in front of the perceiver, that humans act. Understanding the action requires understanding the experience, not describing the natural world in-itself or the individual perspective.

Experience to the phenomenologist, thus, is not an atomistic collection of sense impressions or of independent objects. To focus on an *object* (the italics are to remember the suspension of construction) to engage in phenomenological reduction and investigate its constitution, momentarily suspends but is not forgetful of its interconnection to the whole experience and the horizon of other background experiences. For example, if one were to make color thematic, the quality of redness appearing with the *object* is understood as a point of view or manner of paying attention, rather than simply an attribute of the *object*. The claim that it is a quality of the *object* must presume a structural intention making color of interest. Perhaps this is easier following the example from chapter 3. If presented with a *cat, dog, tree,* and *squirrel* and asked which one is different, we can strike the difference along multiple thematic lines, such as plant/animal, wild/domestic, like/not like, in my yard/not in my yard, and so forth. As a thematic line becomes a focus, it can be extended into an endless horizon of other applications, other moments of decision, considerations of what can be done with it, questions like whether it feels pain and excludes other experiences and considerations. The thematic line can be said to be an articulation (to foreshadow a more recent term) of that experience, a particular way experience is centered and put together. Every experience can be thematized in multiple ways. Certain thematic structures are used over and over again and can be said to become sedimented and thus make it difficult to see the multiple thematic opportunities. For example, amateur thieves will struggle to pick a lock or break down a door for entrance even when an easily broken window is available. In the "natural attitude" of everyday life and science, sedimented thematizations become treated as properties of the objects, and the necessity of a constituting intention is forgotten.

The Social Construction of Experience

Husserl's early quest for a pure or transcendental phenomenology, where all presuppositions are suspended in the description of essences—the necessary intentional structures of consciousness—proved impossible. The phenomenologist is a historical being existing in a particular language and cultural world—a *Lebenswelt*. The background of consciousness could not be reduced to a transcendental ego, but was an embodied experiencer already in a life world. This reconception did not change the basic phenomenological formulation of direct experience as the foundation of knowledge, but rather the object of the phenomenological description. From a reflective analysis and description of the pure structures of consciousness, the aim changed to a descriptive explication of modes of living or styles of being in the world—from a pure to an existential or social phenomenological description.

In a sense, most of recent European social theory can be seen as an interpretation of, though not reduced to, Husserl's description of experience. Whether "existential project," "body," "language," or "discursive formation," each conception tries to show the "intending act" as thoroughly social and historical. The human subject is neither singular nor a manifestation of the essential, but a motion that finds its subjectivity already inscribed as it takes its place in the already socially, historically structured world. It is precisely in that, that the world appears given and objective and that the subject feels able to be separated. The illusion of independent subject and world protects the constitutive activities from examination and obscures the understanding of social and historical construction. Since each of the modern philosophies is a different attempt to unpack this illusion, it is useful to suggest their commonalities.

All share an interest in the constitution of the structured world that entails an interest in the structure of subjects as well as objects of the world. The claiming of the subject as an identity and the world as filled with knowable objects takes place against the backdrop of the already structured world and competitive constitutive practices. All accept the structured world as holistic and thematically organized, though all such unities are surrounded by a horizon of uncertainty and of that not yet unified and held against other competing unities. All thematic unities are historical and can be sedimented and taken for granted. A diachronic understanding of history is itself a historical pro-

duction and becomes one of thematic unities, one characterized by a quest for origins. It is history in experience, rather
than experience in history, that is of concern. And finally, as an
extension, every causal structure is only one possible thematization. Each of these issues is worked out in different and often
competing manners.

The Social Subject

As in Husserl's time, the primary problem today in understanding the construction of experience is the common treatment of
it as subjective, or psychological. It is partly for this reason that
communication so often focuses on speakers' meanings rather
than that which is spoken about. The historical arising of such
a position is not surprising. If, as it is commonly formulated, a
structured objective world is out-there, its understanding and
differences in understanding must arise in-here. The nineteenth-century preoccupation with the relation of the in-here
to the out-there and culturally different experiences led to a
twentieth-century concern with language representation and
procedures for an undistorted understanding of the out-there.
Such a position allowed for individualism and privacy at the
same time that it supported a collective truth, each separate
and in its place. The phenomenological demonstration of the
inadequacy of such a separation was important for the development of critical European thought.

Unfortunately, in the United States phenomenology was
co-opted by humanistic psychologists who used only certain
aspects of phenomenological thought to critique the presumed
"objectivity" of science without understanding the implications
for their own position. The critical impact of phenomenology
was thus lost. In Europe some of the same took place in the
humanistic and existential writings of the fifties and sixties. In
these works the unified experience in the here-and-now was
given a privilege as authentic and able to overcome the sedimented experience of the "they." Such a position would hold
out for a singular unified self as the origin of experience against
historical construction and the material conditions thereof. In
Europe the structuralists would offer a decisive reconsideration,
a move that would only come to America later. The
humanist/behaviorist battle allowed no place for a position
that denied their fight.

Against such a background it is not surprising that the concept of the social construction of reality has been given such a shallow reading in the United States. In many analyses the idea of social construction is treated as individuals with independent experiences coming together to share them and reach a consensus. Such a conception of what is better called a "negotiated order" overlooks the more fundamental issue that shared meaning arises out of a background set of constitutive practices. The most central consensus consists in perceiving the same rather than in coming to share our perceptions. Even in cultural studies the term *culture* is often used to simply stand for these background practices rather than elicit their investigation. Culture is often seen as a kind of social contract consensually entered into rather than as descriptive of the conditions of subjectivity. The term *culture* often is used to denote the subjective experience of world rather than the objective one. And culture is often objectified as one of the many things that a person has. Each of these positions would have to be avoided if the term *culture* were to become useful in the description of the person and experience. Consequently, it is difficult to maintain a critical conception of cultural studies in the United States. I think we will get farther if we focus on the notion of the person in experience.

In phenomenology the "subject" or intending act is not a "real" person or psychological state, but rather is a structuring possibility that precedes the individual who takes it on as her or his own. Only on the basis of the structuring possibility can an individual have the experience at all. The structuring possibility is shared and thoroughly social before the individual actualizes it in a particular experience. Understanding the constitution of reality thus leads not to investigating the "insides" of the individual but to the social possibilities that are neither inside nor outside alone, but that produce among other things the possibility of thinking about the inside and outside. Since thinking about the self with a particular identity is one of our possibilities, the self as an object can be abstracted. And like any other object it can be thematically drawn out of the flow of experience. But this identity is a constituted rather than constituting subject, and we can become interested in its social origin. As a unity it can be either temporarily held as a point of view or sedimented to be reproduced *or* returned to its temporary state. Once the constitutive acts are separated from the individual and psychological states, a variety of analyses become available.

The Institutionalization of Experience

Constituting possibilities are retained in society and made available to members of the society. New members are not so much socialized and taught what to think, see, and believe; rather they follow what can be called "institutional practices," so that thoughts, perceptions, and beliefs arise spontaneously as individuals follow common practices and routines in the accomplishment of everyday life. Following Berger and Luckmann (1967), I use the word *institution* to draw attention to the variety of ways particular thematizations are sedimented. The term is elastic enough to cover buildings and technologies, particular social arrangements, as well as language and various discursive practices and in each case to remind us that they are socially created *and* material. Ultimately the understanding of corporations within the politics of everyday life will require this full range of meanings. Certainly alternative, and potentially richer, conceptions are available, such as Bourdieu's (1977) *habitus*. But *institutions* carries well the combination of material and social and does not commit the analysis to a single theory preference.

An institution can be thought of as the social equivalent of a personal habit (Berger and Luckmann 1967, 53). It arises as a choice within a set of existing institutional arrangements. Over time the practical reasons for the choice are forgotten, and in place of choice the routine takes on a life of its own, both precluding options in thoughtlessness and building a set of secondary justifications for why it is done this way. Other habits at the personal level or institutions at the social level spin off from the initial one. Social arrangements and practices develop that depend on the initial habit and reproduce it. For example, a shy person may form relationships with others that speak for him or her, and they may enforce his or her shyness. Consequently, the continued habitualization and institutionalization are not carried by psychological investment but by the interrelated web of support and dependence that makes any single change difficult. In this we see less causality than forces, hence powerful but not deterministic systems. Marx treated this process in terms of "reifications," and he, like Berger and Luckmann, focused almost exclusively on origins and the politics of formation. Here the concern will be on the structural interrelation of institutional forces, the processes by which they are sustained and changed, and the processes by which their arbitrary nature is concealed and hence closed to discourse. The origin of the institutional form is less important than its continuation.

Experience and meaning arise from the subject positioned in routines and standard practices. Each routine or practice structures a point of view and implements certain value preferences. For a simple example, people frequently stand in line at banks, for auto registration, for concert tickets, and for a variety of other goods. As an institutionalized practice, standing in line structures a particular type of subject with ways of valuing and understanding events. The line and the repetitive standing in line produce and reproduce a type of order, civility, and decorum. Certainly these are not intentional productions by the people, for they stand in line to achieve some other ends, but the person takes the place of a constituted/constituting subject for which the line thematizes a way of being and experiencing in the world. The institutional values implemented and reproduced by standing in line may differ from people's unreflected psychological experience. For example, rarely do they attend to or critically assess the line's implemented value of "first come, first served." If people are asked why they stand in line, they respond that it is fair, efficient, or right. But fair to whom, efficient toward whose ends, and right from what standpoint? Should a person who has time to camp in line to get concert tickets get better tickets than someone with children or who must work?

In fact, in some respects the idea "first come, first served" doesn't strike me as a lot better than the old idea that was "the bigger you are, the quicker you get service." The line system is orderly and we fight less; it is disciplined, as is most modern control. But conflict is hidden and advantage invisible. If people had to fight to get the first ticket, at least it would be clear that the people who were bigger were getting the tickets and the people who were little weren't. It is more honest and also hard to say that the value system involved is less desirable. But my point is not to get involved with the argument but to give a simple version of the common force of order. And in important contexts, people follow the principle, which is represented in this example as enforcing the line order, even when they are in the back and maintaining the line order is to their disadvantage. Understanding such practices is essential to understanding the politics of the workplace. Such issues are reclaimed as language and communication issues when we look at the reasons given for them, the discursive practices that preclude their examination, and the possibility of opening value conflict through discursive means. This will be the primary issue later. Here the concern is only with an initial establishment of how the subject and constitutive activities are embedded in the social world.

Experience as a Political Formation

Institutional practices are historically produced and as such are imbued with and reproduce power differences and advantages. Everyday experience in that sense is thoroughly political. The politics is not in the competition of experiences but already *in* the experience at hand, the person and perception produced. Every building, every sidewalk, institutionalizes a point of view, a point of view sedimented out of the politics of the moment of production; each user reproduces the view of the "winner" of that decision process. It's not that the user must do so, though sanctions and rewards may encourage it. It is in the habit, the routine, and the thoughtlessness that it is reproduced. But this is not to say that it is neutral or innocent. The configuration of routines and other practices leave it inevitable and necessary. And the thoughtlessness and routine are actively protected from thought and alternatives. Understanding how this works requires an understanding of power and how power both advantages and hides advantage. But first I need to expand the concept of institution to make clearer its material and textual character.

Language as a Social Institution

Language is a, if not the, principal institution in modern society. Not only is it a major constitutive condition of experience itself, but it serves as the medium through which other institutions are brought to conception, both in production and understanding. Further, language is intrinsic to second-order legitimations of institutions. As Berger and Luckmann (1967) argued, language is the principal medium through which social reality is produced and reproduced: "Language objectivates the shared experiences and makes them available to all within the linguistic community, thus becoming both the basis and the instrument of the collective stock of knowledge. Furthermore, language provides the means for objectifying new experiences, allowing their incorporation into the already existing stock of knowledge, and it is the important means by which the objectivated and objectified sedimentations are transmitted in the tradition of the collectivity in question" (68). Language in their sense becomes the "depository of a large aggregate of collective sedimentation" that can be acquired as a whole "without reconstructing their original process of formation" (Berger and Luckmann 1967, 69). The freedom from the moment of creation allows a number of reconstructed discourses regarding origins that defend the legitimacy and even the necessity of the order. In this sense linguistic discourse is deeply political, reproducing both an order and a disguise for that order. This analysis, like the phenomenology on which it was based, is an important start but does not go far enough. It comes up short in adequately accounting for the nature of language in the constitution of experience, in its neutrality toward unity and totality, and in its account of power relations. The goal here with Giddens (1979) is to "identify the basic structural elements which connect signification and legitimation in such a way as to favour dominant interests" (192). To do so we must begin with an adequate account of the relations among language, experience, and identity. Language is an institutional practice, and as such its constitutive role must be understood.

The Linguistic Politics of Experience

Most people today, whether they are social scientists or other everyday actors, believe language to be primarily a representational system. The idea that words stand for things in the world or in the head seems to be common sense. With such a view everyday people and neopositivist scientists believe that the goal of understanding is served by making language a good, clean tool of representation, thereby rendering it transparent. The argument here is that representational theories of language are neither very interesting nor useful. And further, the faith in the fixed nature of objects and the possibility of linguistic transparency are strategically deployed to obscure the political working in language.

Language does not represent things that already exist. In fact, language is a part of the production of the thing that we treat as being self-evident and natural within the society. To clarify the productive nature of this view, allow me to begin with a fairly simple problem in language acquisition. I begin with language acquisition because I believe that assumptions here serve to produce the basic common sense exemplar and protect the representational view from examination. A common everyday experience in children's language learning is the parent holding out a cup of apple juice and saying the word *cup* loudly with the hope that the child upon enough hearings will repeat the word and be rewarded with smiles, praise, and the juice. As commonsensical as such an association process seems, problems with it can easily be identified. How does the child know that the word *cup* is to refer to the object cup rather than the shape, the color, the texture, the substance inside, or the act of presentation? That is, how is this learning distinguished from the same act with the parent saying "juice," "yellow," or "say 'please'"? The child has to accomplish two tasks rather than the one the parent assumes. The child has to learn the types of human interests and dimensions upon which things are distinguished as carried by the word—that is the language behind the word—as well as attachment of the word to the object seen in this manner. While children certainly do learn a few associations of words and objects in the way a dog comes to salivate at the ringing of the bell, this has virtually nothing to do with language. And it happens enough to lend surface support to representational views. But as Chomsky (1959) showed, learning by association can account neither for the speed of language learning nor the types of mistakes children make. The child is always learning the whole of language, not a piece at a time. For our purposes here, the various interesting metaphysics proposed by Chomsky and the various mediational theories to account for these are not terribly important. The description of the structural nature of language is sufficient.

The child example above reminds us that words do not simply stand for constituted objects but that each word recalls a means of object constitution. Words recall and put into play the possibility of being interested in color, texture, shape, or relational acts. The historical nature of language is not such that a word stands in the place of an absent, to-be-recalled object. Rather, language holds forth the historically developed dimensions of interests, the lines along which things will be distinguished. Language holds the possible ways we will engage in the world and produces objects with particular characteristics. Thus when we consider language from a political point of view within organizations, the interest is not primarily how different groups use language to accomplish goals, or the rationality in language usage, or how the profit motive influences language use. Social groupings and their interests, types of rationality, and the concept of profit are social productions. Each is produced as distinguished from something else. The questions are thus not whether these things exist, have power, or explain organizational behavior, but how they come to exist, coexist, and interrelate in the production and reproduction of corporate organizations and work in the process of inner and outer colonization. Such an analysis is further applied to the attempt at any explanation. Each explanation (e.g., market conditions, class interest, social structure, gender) is produced in a string of larger significations. The display of these interactivities, or in the narrower sense, intertextualities, in a communication analysis becomes the goal. I start by developing such a view of language.

Language as a System of Distinction

Saussure (1974) is most often given credit for the insight that language was primarily a system of distinctions rather than representational. This was accomplished in two arguments. First, signifiers and the signifieds are separate and arbitrarily related. This severed any assumption of natural, ahistorical, or universal connections. Any particular language is a social historical product, developed in social relations and subject to change. And second, the meaning of signs is neither intrinsic nor derived from the signified but derived from their difference from other signs in the language chain. Each word can reference only on the basis of its relation and contrasts with other words, a contrast that is reproduced in objects. For example, a term such as *worker* has meaning only as it distinguishes from *manager, unemployed,* or *lazy* within a particular socially produced linguistic chain. The word, in our earlier terms, thematizes a perspective against a hidden background of what it is not, which is simultaneously articulated.

Saussure's work is essential in the analysis of the politics of experience, though several extensions are important. First, Saussure's notion that the meanings of signs are fixed as conventions of a speech community must be rejected (see Giddens 1979; Derrida 1976). Attention must be given to the historical conditions by which one "arbitrary" set of distinctions is implemented over others and how preferential systems of language use and interpretation create privileges beyond those embedded in the sign system. Every sign system contains the possibility of conflicting meanings; the fixing of signs against the plurality of meaning becomes the significant issue here. As the early pragmatists were fond of saying, "a vocabulary is only a temporary resting place." Such a view is to be reclaimed.

Every linguistic system, because it is an arbitrary system of distinctions, puts into place certain kinds of values—that is, certain things that are worthy of being distinguished from other things—and puts into play what it is that we could utilize to make distinctions. In other words, on the issue of gender, for example, whenever we distinguish between men and women, whenever we make a description that notes gender, what we're doing is saying distinction along the line of gender is important and valuable to this society. *Man* or *woman* does not simply represent something real out-there; the terms put into play a way of paying attention to the out-there. But no specific of special status can be given to the "out-there." As Derrida (1976) described it: "The so-called 'thing itself' is always already a *representamen* shielded from the simplicity of intuitive evidence. The *representamen* functions only by giving rise to an *interpretant* that itself becomes a sign and so on to infinity. The self-identity of the signified conceals itself unceasingly and is always on the move" (49).

No employment of a distinction can be neutral. The distinction values; it says that the difference is worth noting and that we're going to utilize that difference to make a decision. We would never distinguish between women and men if we were not intending to utilize that distinction in treating women and men differently. The distinction performs a production of identity for the subject as a woman or man and of the person as an object with certain rights and characteristics. As the chain of signifiers webs out, the female can be upheld as a mother in a kinship system, a wife in a marital relation, and so forth. In each case each individual so constituted is both advantaged and disadvantaged in the way the institutional arrangements specify opportunities and constraints. But the distinction remains arbitrary. The signifiers are arbitrary in the sense that at the next moment distinction on the basis of gender can be overlooked, irrelevant, or difficult and in the sense that the system of relations among signifiers could be different.

Most of us accept as self-evident that men and women are different and therefore that the distinction is important. But there are lots of potential differences in our world that exist that we do not pay attention to or distinguish at all. In the same way in the earlier example that the child or teacher may distinguish the pictures based on plants and animals, doing so hides different possible distinctions among those things. The preference for one set of distinctions over other distinctions, however, is political. Certain experiences are going to be had at the expense of other experiences. Speaking a language is not representing a world or personal perceptions. The distinctions that will form the world and experience are put into play.

People speaking a language, however, are not necessarily aware of the values that they are putting into play. These values are often at odds with other values held by the person, if such a person could openly assess them. Yet the embedded values can be reproduced in expression without awareness. Taking an obvious example, recently a woman next to me on an airplane referred to the flight attendant as a stewardess. In doing so she expressed values that probably were not her own. It is not as if she said or felt anything negative, nor did she seem to offend the flight attendant. The term *stewardess* is not degrading alone, but enacts gender as a valuational distinction and relevant dimension of occupational classification. In this case it sets into play the socially constructed female role of emotional labor, including nurturing, support, smiling, and so forth, and simultaneously recollects those as female work (Hochschild 1979; Ferguson 1984). Such an example is easy because most corporations have worked, at least in the obvious cases, to remove gender distinction as a part of occupational classification. But the example is interesting because it shows what hasn't been done, including the maintenance of gender-based work-expectation differences in many corporate contexts.

Moreover gender distinction is only one of many critical distinctions in the workplace, including worker/manager, data/not data, private/public information, rational/irrational, and expert/nonexpert. Understanding the importance of the gender issue reminds us of the multitude of classificatory activities having political implications, protected by their seeming self-evidence and otherworldliness. Further, each of these becomes interwoven in a complex of signifiers; for instance, gender becomes tied to forms of understanding and knowledge, private and public become critical to expertise. And further yet, as will be developed below, occupational classification is only one of many signifying practices that have significance for gender, or any other, politics (e.g., stories, jokes, and dress codes all implement distinction and a chain of signifiers). Far less has been done about these things than about gender and occupational classification. If people could work back through the systems of distinctions they implement, they would often find a gap between what they reflectively think and feel and what they unwittingly express. The point is not to determine what they "really" or freely think, but by reworking we can recall the forgetfulness of construction and begin to understand the plurality of equally plausible subject articulations that are momentarily out of reach due to proclaimed "naturalness and self-evidence." It is this self-evidence and presumed transparency of language that must be given up to understand power and the politics of experience.

Linguistic Subjectivity

Issues of the nature of the human subject and of subjectivity have commanded many discussions. Even in the modern period of epistemological domination, where the subjective is transformed into routinized, standard research protocols, the issue returns at every attempt to discuss what science should study. Phenomenology, even with its several difficulties, was the beginning of the break from dualistic pitting of the subjective versus the objective. The move of the twentieth century has been to gradually account for constitutive activities in terms of social practices, hence the interest here in institutions and language. Even with a conception of subjectivity as momentary but social and historical, the politics of the personal continue to need development.

Recent French authors have added great depth to these analyses through their "theories of the subject." While they have created quite an intellectual stir, their impact on understanding corporate experiences and on the thinking of everyday people has been relatively small (see Cooper and Burrell 1988; Burrell 1988). Much of this can be attributed to the psychological domination of thinking about the personal and subjective in the United States (Henriques et al. 1984). The renewed hopes for a science of the subjective grounded in cognitive structures provides a continued energy and resource drain away from understanding the subjective in social terms. Gardner's (1988) polemic account of the primacy of cognitive science provides the best example of the difficulty. The bet is that in the United States psychological reductionism will continue to rule. Communicational explanations are not likely where reductionism can be applied.

Adding to the difficulties are language differences. The double meaning of the French term *assujettir*—"to produce subjectivity" and "to make subject"—enables a complex conception that is difficult in English. Certainly the English term *subject* carries both the sense of the "free autonomous actor who constitutes" and "the person ruled by the king or circumstances"—"*the* subject" and "subject *to*." But rarely are the two ideas thought at once. The problem is much like that of Therborn's "qualification process" discussed in chapter 2. Putting the two ideas together as "subjectivity/subjectification" (*assujettissement,* in French) is awkward and invites complaints. As should be no surprise, ordinary conventional uses of English enforce an ideology of dualism and autonomy. To move beyond this to more sensitive and revealing analysis is itself a linguistic, conceptual, political battle.

Althusser (1971) gave the most commanding treatment of the relation of language to the production of the human subject. In Althusser's analysis, language is the most general ideological mediation. Building on Saussure, language to Althusser is not a systems of signs that represent. Language appears as discourse, a material practice that is produced out of the same conditions that produce the objects of which it speaks. Language as an ideological practice mediates between individuals and the conditions of their existence. But this mediation is not between preformed individuals and objective conditions; it is the means by which the individual becomes a subject, a process called *interpellation.* Quoting Althusser: "I shall then suggest that ideology 'acts' or 'functions' in such a way that it 'recruits' subjects among individuals (it recruits them all), or 'transforms' the individual into subjects (it transforms them all) by that very precise operation which I have called *interpellation* or hailing" (1971, 162–63). The specific relationship between the subject in a particular world and the individual is *imaginary.* That is, the "subject" is always an image or constructed self rather than an individual in a full set of relations to the world. A "real" form of domination or control is unnecessary to the extent that the individual takes the imaginary construction as if it is real. The individual denies the important freedoms that exist in the situation. But these are not freedoms the subject could exercise if reflectively reconstituted. While Althusser equivocates on the point (see Woodiwiss 1987), following such an the analysis, the subject's sense of freedom and agency (only real in the imaginary world treated as real) is produced as part of the imaginary construction. The individual subject misses the mutual construction and treats both the self and experience as intuitively obvious. Thus, ironically, the individual misses the moment of constructive autonomy in proclaiming the already constructed self as autonomous.

It is of little surprise that the individual makes the mistake or "misrecognition," the processes through which this takes place are quite complex. Pêcheux (1982), following Althusser (1971), argued that ideology "interpellates individuals into subjects" through many complex, "forgotten" interdiscourses whereby each subject has a signified, self-evident reality that is "perceived-accepted-submitted to." As Thompson (1984, 236) presented Pêcheux's analysis, the hidden-forgotten discursive formation "creates the illusion that the subject precedes discourse and lies at the origin of meaning. Far from this being the case, it is the subject which is 'produced' or 'called forth' by the discursive sequence; or more precisely, the subject is 'always already produced' by that which is 'preconstructed' in the sequence." But discursive sequences are never singular and closed. The issue to be of concern, however, is not that an illusion or image is produced, but that the politics preferring one type of image over others precludes the conflict and dialogue among them. There is no claim that there is some simple "real" self. But only in the relation among conflicting images is the arbitrary character of each revealed and potentially open to renewed participation in construction. The presumed singularity is critical to the accepted realness of the imaginary.

Althusser describes this ideological subject domination as central to class politics and secured by what he called *ideological state apparatuses*. Schools, the church, the family, the law, the political system, the media, and culture backed by the repressive apparatuses of the police and armed forces reproduce capitalist social relations. The concepts of "ideological apparatuses" and "subject interpellation" are useful to the analysis here and can be connected to Foucault's concept of strategic apparatus to be described later. But I wish to free the analysis from traditional class politics. In the United States such apparatuses can be more easily seen as extending from (though not exhausted by) corporations reproducing a "managerial capitalism" that is subsidized by the state. But as will be developed, the conception of a relatively monolithic, coordinated production of the subject overlooks the diffused and everyday process of subject production. The description of the full complexity of subject formation will require the analytic power of Foucault's work. But here the basic relations can already be seen.

The ideological imaginary relation works primarily because

it is hidden. Quoting Althusser (1971) again: "Like all obvious-nesses, including those that make a word 'name a thing' or 'have a meaning' (therefore including the obviousness of the 'transparency' of language), the obviousness that you and I are subjects—and that that does not cause any problems—is an ide-ological effect, the elementary ideological effect" (161). Or as Weedon (1987) suggested, "The crucial point...is that in taking on a subject position, the individual assumes that she is the author of the ideology or discourse which she is speaking. She speaks or thinks as if she were in control of meaning. She 'imagines' that she is the type of subject which humanism pro-poses—rational, unified, the source rather than the effect of language. It is the imaginary quality of the individual's identifi-cation with a subject position which gives it so much psycho-logical and emotional force" (31). The consideration of alterna-tive meanings and alternative subjectivities thus poses a threat to the individual's claimed identity. The denial of the self-evi-dence through expressions that shows one's world as a con-struction with plausible alternatives are more often seen as political propaganda than the politically founded first mean-ing. The first is taken on as one's own, and the alternative expressions are seen as attempts to control. The personal is for-gotten as already political. The individual is not simply identi-fying with those in power; that power is the subject.

In sum, the subject as mediated through language is always ideologically produced. There is no place out of the formation to claim a simple preexisting independent subject with know-able interests. "Ideology" thus is not the subjective beliefs, val-ues, and presumptions one has or is given by another. Those are part of what Burawoy (1979) properly calls "propaganda" or "manipulation." The concept of ideology proposed here is more akin to systematically distorted communication, the one-sided subject who unknowingly reproduces the self, to be developed in chapter 7. The ideological structure and semiotic field are coextensive, a point best developed by Volosinov (1973): "Whenever a sign is present, ideology is present too. *Everything ideological possesses semiotic value*...without signs there is no ideology" (10).

The individual experiences a particular world, one that is the product of socially inscribed values and distinctions like the sub-ject itself. Only on the basis of this does the individual claim personal beliefs or values or come to share them with others. A particular ideology is a particular way of being in the world, a social sharing prior to any individual taking it on as his or her own. As will be discussed, the unitary (or at least tied together), one-sided perceptual experience is not so much a "bounded rationality" as a *delimited appropriation of discourse.*" The imaginary thus originates neither in the subject nor in a simple misrepresentation of the world, hence ideology does not represent a false relation to either self or world. As Hirst (1979) argued: "The forms of the imaginary should...have the status of *significations,* representations which are reducible neither to a represented which is beyond them, nor to an origin in a subject, but which are effects of the action of means of representation" (63). Ideology represents an arbitrary representational practice rather than a false or class consciousness. It is a moment in the politics of representation. Before group or class politics using discourse, there is a politics in each moment of discourse (see Frow 1985 for a more complete analysis). In this analysis the possibility of studies based on ideological critique based in moral judgment can be usefully supportive of the more detailed descriptive accounts of Foucault to be discussed later.

The politics of subject constitution and representative practice can be conceptualized in a form less monolithic than appears in analyses like those of Althusser. The subject is subject to a range of discourses, some of which conflict. The modern world does not have simply one dominant ideology but many, though organized in interesting and at times strategic ways. This point, of course, has been made most strongly by Derrida (1976). Meaning is not a singularity claimed by an individual or intersection of texts. It is pluralistic and "deferred" in the sense that there can be no final determination. Unitary meaning is temporary and only held in place by force before it drifts away in a never-ending web of other texts. Only on the basis of the appearance of plurality could ideology be identified at all or could the subject be claimed as an agent. There is never one linguistic expression in one institutional arrangement, but many. And further, our interest does not end with the construction of the subject, but extends to the realities in which subjects find themselves. The critical importance is, thus, not to get behind discourse to a subject, but to reclaim the conflicts that keep one ideological formation from ruling or becoming treated as self-evident and natural. It is not a more certain, fair, or accurate consensus, but more meaningful conflict, that is critical. In the next two chapters I will consider the moral foundation for maintaining discursive conflict and the processes by which it is suppressed. But first let me go a bit further describing the "subjects" that are at issue.

In brief, the notion of the psychological subject as an autonomous originator of meaning, which phenomenology first showed to be an abstraction, is now more precisely replaced by competing points of view arising in many simultaneous texts. People thus are not filled with independently existing thoughts, feelings, beliefs, and plans that are brought to expression. As they move about the world, reading books, watching television, or doing work, they take on the subjects of these texts as their own. The self is not independent of texts but always finds itself in them. Western linguistic conventions, however, name a subject, making the "I" a possible object of concern. As this happens, attributes of autonomy, distance, objectivity, control, and possession become extensions of it. The unity of the reflected subject carries with it possibilities and problems and most importantly conceals its own social/cultural origin and an illusion of a certain presence and freedom. The power given to the self to define its own meaning is an unwarranted privilege, conceals the process of construction, and leaves the subject unaware of multiple systems of control.

Institutions as Textual

Everyday life is filled with institutional artifacts, routines, and standard practices. Each implements values and establishes a subject point of view. Institutional practices are concretized (sometimes literally) in the construction of buildings, the laying of sidewalks, the writing of legal codes, the placement of postings and signs, and the development of stories, jokes, and vocabularies. Cultural researchers have long noted the presence of such features. Unfortunately, they are often treated as expressive of the individual or culture, and therein, their constitution of the subject and world is lost. In other words, even when institutional forms and practices are no longer treated as mute objects and events, they fall prey to the same representational account often given to language. Rather, they can be productively analyzed as signifiers along the same lines just proposed for words. Institutional forms are textual.

For example, the change of banking facilities from an imposing, secure site to home-like, dispersed branches and finally automatic teller booths can be seen as expressive of changing images and needs, but more fundamentally produces and continually reproduces a different "subject" with different social relations and different objects, namely "money." Such a reading recognizes that this happens against the backdrop of other possible relations and absences and possible subjects. The old "subject" in the new configuration becomes absent and is difficult to produce even if the person wanted to do so. The American is produced as a consumer even of money. It's not simply the case that attitudes toward saving have changed. The institution itself, the very subject and routine of saving, is different. Interest rates, legal requirements, and tax laws, for example, are among many institutional practices that both make possible these changes and are changed by them.

But the banking and monetary system itself is produced in a particular way of relating other social changes and practices, and it does not singularly produce the modern person even in relation to money. The person is busy, a home owner, a product consumer, a parent, and so forth. The relation among institutional arrangements produces a complex subject, a subject that is at once dispersed among many and competing institutions, and unified as thematized across interrelatable institutions. As we shall see, the modern workplace both evidences such dispersion and provides a set of practices that unify, and therefore suppresses the potential conflicts. The task of working out these relationships at any particular corporate site or for the more general corporate experience is great, but for now it's enough to clarify what's at stake.

Technologies as Political Institutions

Technologies are politically formed institutionalizations of experience. Each technology can be said to create a particular "subject" with an identity and reality as part of a discursive sequence (Gouldner 1976). For example, the telephone as a technology situates a "self" in a definable role as speaker and posits a distinct perspective on communication as having a fixed starting and stopping point, a source and destination; it is not just a medium, it provides a perspective on both the interactants and the process itself. It is an embodied subjectivity which is reclaimed as the identity of the user. In using a telephone I implicitly enact the value preference of certain sensory experiences over others and the desire for convenience over competing needs. The implied concept of communication and standard telephone scripts define rights and responsibilities, structure the identity of self and other, and give preference to certain topics and types of messages. The bodily presence of the other and the use of nonverbal elements might all change the nature and direction of the conversation.

Moreover, the subject formed is not accidental, since the "world" and "identity" arise historically in power-laden discursive structures. I might not choose to use the telephone *if* I reflected on the way I understand communication, the production of meaning, and the values I have regarding human beings. But the significance of this choice is misunderstood if thought of only in terms of convenience, effectiveness, or effect. The inability to reflect and make such choices is the issue. The fundamental issues of the choice are often hidden and not considered, and the choices that are considered are themselves positioned out of the background of the forgotten. Reflection cannot reclaim a genuine choosing agent, since reflection itself is not an open creation.

The Politics of Sensuality

Every technology extends our sensual self in some direction. In this sense, technologies are extensions of subjectivity (see Merleau-Ponty's treatment of body, 1962, 98ff.). A technology is not a simple tool to be picked up and utilized as something apart from the individual user. Its use provides a point of view or a way for the self to be engaged in the world. In watching a television program, the self is extended to another time and place with a particular situated perspective. The camera angle becomes the self's vantage point, highlighting and bringing certain aspects into view and hiding and passing over others (Sobchack 1982; Bellman and Jules-Rosetle 1977). While as a critic I may step back and curse the camera angle, as an engaged subject I strain to see as I would strain to hear the whispers in the back of the room while giving a lecture.

Technology as an extension of the senses positions us in the world through the same processes through which our senses do in the absence of technology. But as different animals are positioned in the world differently owing to different bodies and different sensory acumen, different technologies position differently, as, for example, when the telephone extends the voice and hearing but not sight. In regard to technologies, the politics of experience is first a politics of sensuality. In what ways will our personal and collective subjectivities exist? In what way will our insides be extended out, and in what ways will the external world be allowed in? When a technology is utilized, its particular subjectivity is encountered at the meeting of the inside and outside as the shape of perception and expression, both of which are systematically constructed and alternatives are systematically excluded.

Understanding the fundamental connection of subjectivity and its extensions is useful in keeping the moral character of the issue clear. If someone were to argue that only certain classes of people should be allowed to have glasses or hearing aids or, more radically, that everyone's eyes should be poked out, we would all readily recognize the moral and political issues involved. Yet technologies are developed that privilege one sense over another, that enable only some people to have access to some data, and that make only certain types of data available. These developments are treated as different kinds of issues lacking moral implications. Communication technologies all have their own ways of positing and extending human senses. Modern computer-assisted communication technologies have changed the way human beings are in the world and thus have moral and political consequences regarding democracy.

First, the electronic connection competes directly with the transportation connection as the primary way of being with others. The data is fundamentally different in each case: to walk through the earthquake rubble is different from seeing it on television; to talk with another is different from the most complete dating service data bank; to face the person to be laid-off and to know his or her personal situation is different from reading his or her file. On the surface this looks like a simple gain, since we now have an additional form of contact and have not lost an old one. This gives people advantages in getting in touch with certain types of data. They can access data that were not available before. But with the institutionalization of preferences and the assessment of economic gains without consideration of human costs, the deck is stacked (Fisher 1985). And as long as short-term effectiveness is the measure, the electronic connection can show a marginal advantage without an adequate calculation of social costs, particularly when there is no one in the decision process who represents certain publics and the general public's interests. At times, such costs affect economic revenues. For example, when Johnson and Johnson substituted electronic ordering for its hospital sales force, numerous other sources of social contact had to be implemented to maintain sales. While this appears to be a natural check on the degree of electronic substitution, it leaves out all effects not translatable to the product being sold and all social interests that are distorted in the economic equation.

The relative cost savings of substituting electronic data for physical association easily leads to the substitution of one form of sensually being with others for another. In an analogy to Gresham's law (bad money drives good money out of circulation), cheap data substitutes for expensive data, particularly when cheap forms of data provide additional benefits to power elites. This can be seen in the substitution of multiple choice for essay examinations in universities. The technology makes possible an institutional structure (i.e., large classes) that in turn makes it unthinkable to do anything but use the technology. As long as the discussion sticks to efficiency criteria coupled with a procedural concept of fairness, neither the history of the change nor the manner by which certain forms and expressions of knowledge become preferred can be discovered.

Further, the substitution of the electronic for the transportation connection changes the speed of decision making. Electronic connections make possible and reward spontaneous, action-oriented decisions. In contrast, transportation connections tend to encourage reflective, critical thought. For example, if you are angry at another and a phone is available, the anger can be expressed in a virtually instantaneous manner. If you must travel to express the anger, the time of the journey allows reflection, rehearsal, and reconsideration. In addition, during travel numerous events and competing systems can intrude, thereby contextualizing and recontextualizing the anger. Through these processes the anger may be increased, diminished, or changed in character, and the decision as to when and how to express it can be considered and reconsidered. Electronic connections encourage focus and reaction. Transportation connections encourage holism, connectedness, and proaction. Electronic connectedness makes possible high-speed management as well as exaggerated stock market swings (Cushman 1990). This change in speed is clearly part of the production of the fragmented subjectivity the postmodernists write about. As Clarke (1988) argued, the new communication technologies "structurally reordered (or disordered) the world, collapsing time and space into an instantaneous succession of communicative instants" (384). The identity has no reflection but is jerked and bounced around in the movement of sensations.

Without any center the moral choice is gone. Not because people are less moral but because there is no space for morality. The intuitive public understanding of this difference accounts for the fear in a nuclear age. The electronic connection, rather than the sheer force of the bomb, is the issue. Human beings have always been able to annihilate the species. What has changed is the speed at which an irreversible decision can be communicated and the action carried out without the possibility of rethought and other systems intervening. Annihilation with clubs, arrows, or guns is slow, and both its sensuality and the possibility of environmental and decisional intervention makes completion unlikely. First, the development of a fast transportation system and second the addition of electronic connection make the modern systems different.

Neither a transportation nor an electronic connection is necessarily better, nor is either neutral. They differ in the way they put us sensually in touch with others and in the relation between spontaneous and reflective thought. The trade-off between narrow sensuality, speed and efficiency, *and* disparate sensuality, reflective thought, and intrusion are experienced throughout modern life. This is manifested in the relatively simple choice of using an on-line search rather than going to the library. In each case the trade-off is similar: getting what you think you want fast or having what you want reformed constantly in light of intrusions and unexpected findings. The political questions arise not simply with the trade-off but, especially, when efficiency becomes the sole criterion and one type of connectedness replaces the other without free and informed engagement in the choice. How are different interests represented? To what extent are different human interests and different group interests privileged, with an advantage given to one type of connectedness? And where is the forum for decisions of such public consequence?

CHAPTER 6

Participation as a Normative Ideal for Democracy and Communication

> [I]n any political election, even by universal
> suffrage, the voter is under an absolute moral
> obligation to consider the interests of the
> public, not his private advantage, and give his
> vote to the best of his judgment, exactly as he
> were bound to do if he were the sole voter,
> and the election depended on him alone.
> (John Stuart Mill 1862, 208)

Not surprisingly, Mill sounds oddly anachronistic today. Expressions like "absolute moral obligation" seem to belong to a past age of romance and chauvinism when women were given neither guardianship of the public nor a place in political expression. All radical ideas perhaps mature into liberal thought and are remembered in their conservative legacy. But rereading Mill reminds us too, against the popular emphasis on individual freedom and representation as the defeat of Aristocracy and autocrats, that democracy was to be founded on a conception of the human character and guided by and ultimately answerable to the public good. In this his liberal and perhaps radical voice is partially reclaimed.

The problem Mill addresses continues today, but the solution must be quite different. "Inalienable" rights have often been transformed into an excuse for the public's inability to advance social good; free speech has frequently been cheapened to personal expression and massive efforts to control; and representation is granted to every personal and special interest but not the collective good. For democracy to be viable, the human character and the nature of communication and representation must be rethought. Recognizing the fundamentally political nature of experience, identity, language, and technologies demands a reconsideration of democracy itself. Fundamental moral issues remain, but they must be reformed. They are not simply choices of who will have what or how much, nor are they easily answered by politically charged statements of human rights. They are issues of the collective formation of culture and human identity. The discussion of morality and moral choices takes on a particular form and peculiar difficulty in the modern or perhaps postmodern world.

Democracy was developed as a social solution to the simple politics of might, but it fails if it becomes the means by which might exerts itself. Public democratic participation in decision making must contribute to continuous determination of choices for the public good, rather than being reduced to a vote on who will set the boundaries for someone else's determination of our future. Democracy reduced to a choice of who controls invites a cynical view of the public and an invitation to private gain to the extent of the law. The reduction of moral obligation to private choice reduces moral conduct to martyrdom; the public's gain means the individual's loss. Moral concern is not just to protect the public from the momentary gain of individual self-interest, but to determine a course of action in which the individual and community gain at once. Morality, like democracy, appears reduced to the choice of limits, not the choice of a future. But can democracy be for the public good rather than a civil form of self-interests warfare? Can a communal morality be developed that guides positive action rather than limits negative ones and yet is not simply some group's vision of the good? I believe the answer is yes to both, and that the possibility already resides, though counterfactually, in the social community. The full development of such a position requires a reconsideration of the nature of communication in democracy, morality, personal identity, social knowledge, and power.

Western concepts of political democracy rest on a "natural" right to have one's interests fairly represented in matters that affect one's well-being and pursuit of happiness. Such ideals are, of course, operationalized in election processes, the bill of rights, and the structure of state institutions. With the development of mass and computer-mediated communication networks, these ideas are extended through the principles of free speech and the free marketplace of ideas. Even if we retain the human nature foundation and supplement it with conceptions of equal access to media, such an approach still leaves out essential concerns with the representation of interests within the politics of identity, experience, and consent.

As previously argued, if identity and experience are not freely formed or if they are distorted in expression, free speech does not help. In fact, the concept of free speech helps guide us away from careful examination of the misrepresentation of interests and the constitutive processes. Having a right to expression cannot assure that a variety of interests are possible or have been taken into account. For example, if equal access to television programming means that groups who get air time differ widely in the resources and skills to use the media well, the free marketplace of ideas fails. More significantly, if people have access to a medium and do use it well, yet the medium carries with it certain vested interests, the marketplace fails and its failure is even more deeply hidden. The action-at-a-distance of television and its reliance on the visual image, for example, may undermine the best televised presentation of feminist conceptions of human interconnectedness.

Television as well as other communication technologies have a politics. Certainly they could be used with greater access and variety of message, but both structure and current usage work against that. The possibility of greater openness seems weak given the comparative ease with which most of these media convey particular types of messages. Further, the existence of real comparative economics and real rather than infinite time frames makes greater variety unlikely. Analysis needs to focus on the actual programming rather than on what is theoretically possible. Present advantage rather than the essence of the media is the critical issue. Some general awareness of the problems and social responsibilities of the mass media is evident. This is largely because the mass media are conceptualized, at least partially, as part of the public arena. Far less attention is given to areas conceptually cast into the private realm such as business corporations. Making the public/private distinction is a significant political act in regard to the extensions of democracy.

Foundations for Democracy and Morality

The natural rights foundation for political democracy as well as for communication policy appears inadequate to provide guidance for political issues—for the politics of everyday life. But there appears to be no transcendental grounding for a new democracy or for evaluating accompanying communication practices. With the questioning of any possible transcendental foundation, the hope for universal human rights has faded. Given the analysis reviewed in chapter 5, universal, nonethnocentric guides to moral conduct in general, and specifically the development of political and communication practices, appears impossible.

The Loss of Foundations and Transcendent Moral Conceptions

In proclaiming the death of God, Nietzsche was one of the first to identify the passing of foundations and the significance of this passage for Western society. In the modern context, concepts of human nature, technological determinacy, and segmented or evolutionary history are increasingly seen as rhetorical ploys to privilege certain meanings and gain political advantage. Each "moral fiction," in MacIntyre's (1984) sense, is an attempt to regain a collective identity and a particular basis for certainty. Every attempt to proclaim a foundation is, hence, a disguised political maneuver to advance a particular group's view of the world. This, plus the relegation of religion to the private areas of life, leaves both scholars and everyday people without a clear foundation for public conduct. The partial cause and clear benefactor of the loss of communal grounding are the "positivist" sciences and specific forms of reasoning and expertise. Despite the fact that these hold powerful adherents who believe in some form of immaculate perception, such positions are increasingly seen as philosophically unsound and politically motivated (Rorty 1979). Certainly neither the attempts of Russell (1968) nor those of Popper (1972) to ground democractic society in the empirical sciences have been without substantial problems. The gradual erosion of certainty, derived from either a universal concept of human nature, a motor-of-history metaphor, or empirical science, is both a liberation and a curse. The liberation is that we can make it up as we go, the curse is that *we* have to make it up. Ironically, I believe that the reason and hope for democracy rests in the lack of foundations for it, the lack of a *substantive* foundation for anything. The fear is that the seductive quality of quick fixes and certainty will undermine the more arduous tasks that lie before us.

The lack of any possible nonarbitrary, nonprivileging foundation in nature can easily lead to giving up on moral questions altogether or relinquishing such questions to the private, subjective, or nonrational realms. No *a priori* standard for democracy—for evaluating the effects of certain organizational forms or technologies or the goodness of our collective movement into the future—seems possible. Power seems to be the only possible arbitrator among positions. The loss of a foundation seems to justify those with advantage extending it into further domination. The various nihilist positions emerging from this perspective have provided human disasters in world politics (Hitler) and in the ecology. Clearly such positions are problematic on both practical and theoretical grounds. Faith in technological futurism and in corporations' ability to deliver the goods are more recent results.

The Reduction of the Political to the Economic

The reduction of political battles to economic ones appears as a necessary and rational consequence of pluralistic, separate but equal, value systems. The rationality of economic determinations appears to be a positive replacement of the arbitrary, irrational determination by power relations. In the most extreme argument, Friedman (1962, 1983) proclaimed that profit was the highest value since the promotion of economic automony and freedom of economic choice facilitated political freedom. But even more moderate "voting with the pocket book" arguments have to presume that a rightful basis of monetary (thus democratic) inequality exists, that all values translate equally well into economic terms, and that hidden costs and long-term benefits can be integrated into monetary exchange systems. The monetary answer essentially presents us with a heavily value-laden but presumably rational and neutral system of conflict resolution that distorts expression of values and suppresses awareness of important conflicts (see Simonds 1989, 185). The political advantage and self-interests extended in place of consensual foundations leads to more sophisticated systems of power as the abitrators.

Goldman (1980) has done the most complete analysis of the apparent special moral status given to business with the translation of potential political values conflicts to economic determination. He showed the many flaws in the segmentation of value questions to professional groups—life to medicine, justice to law, profit and goods to business and so forth. Rather than being isolated questions requiring special professional judgment, each of these values issues, Goldman argued, must be based in wider social judgments of life, justice, and universal human interests. Even if an open economic system could represent social interests, modern systems are hardly open, because the noncompetitive nature of much of the economy inhibits freedom of choice and action by workers, consumers, and suppliers. And the creation of needs through mass advertising, especially in the absence of counterconsumerism advertising, hardly leaves a consumer in an open-choice context.

Participatory Democracy

But where can a grounding be found? The untenability of a natural rights foundation creates specific problems for the conception of democracy on theoretical and practical grounds. The theorist has difficulty building any "moral obligation" that can be held on more solid ground than the divine right of kings or other historical belief systems. The practical problem arises in trying to create legitimacy for order and laws when the foundation lacks self-evidence, as often happens with countercultures and defense of other societies' forms of government. Several theoretically guided practical postures have been presented in response to this condition. Barber (1984) summarized them as *authoritative democracy, juridical democracy, pluralist democracy, unitary democracy,* and *strong democracy.* He summarized each as follows:

> *Authoritative Democracy...*democracy in the authoritative modes resolves conflict in the absence of an independent ground through deferring to a representative executive elite that employs authority (power plus wisdom) in pursuit of the aggregate interests of its electoral constituency (p.140)
> *Juridical Democracy...*democracy in the juridical mode resolves conflict in the absence of an independent ground through deferring to a representative judicial elite that, with the guidance of constitutional and preconstitutional norms, arbitrates differences and enforces constitutional rights and duties. (142)
> *Pluralist Democracy...*pluralist democracy resolves public conflicts in the absence of an independent ground through bargaining and exchange among free and equal individuals and groups, which pursue their

private interests in a market setting governed by the social contract. (143)

Unitary Democracy...democracy in the unitary mode resolves conflict in the absence of an independent ground through community consensus as defined by the identification of individuals and their interests with a symbolic collectivity and its interests. (149)

Strong Democracy...strong democracy in the participatory mode resolves conflict in the absence of an independent ground through a participatory process of ongoing, proximate self-legislation and the creation of a political community capable of transforming dependent private individuals into free citizens and partial and private interests into public goods. (151)

Barber well represents the choices that are available and different ones that are used in different sites in contemporary society. For our purposes here, they need to be transformed somewhat, and we need to go farther than Barber in developing the communicative practices identified with each. Initially, I wish to expand the domain of application beyond the political process. This will include bringing moral and value questions back into the public realm and discussing the social bases of democracy that push us toward accepting the "strong democracy" alternative. From this, the communication process itself can be explored. As will become clear, authoritative, juridical, and pluralist democracy depend on a theory of communication driven by effectiveness, while unitary and strong democracy depend on a communication theory concerned with participation. A participatory conception of communication will be critical to a democratic politics of everyday life.

Community, Democracy, and Communication

The crisis in or demise of liberal democracy, especially as practiced in the United States, was a recurring theme in the political theory writings of the eighties (see Entman 1989; Burnham 1981; Nordlinger 1983). Much of this concern arose out of the exceptionally low voter turnout, the emergence of special-interest politics, the focus on media image rather than political positions, the dominance of polling in position formation, and the power of negative campaigns. Each in its own way demonstrates cynicism about the political process, weakens the legitimacy of governmental decision making, cheapens the citizen and politician, and undermines democratic representation. It is small wonder that the eighties were also a time when public affairs were rapidly transferred to the private, often corporate, realm, and public trust in public decisions plummeted. It makes good sense that a congressional representative earning $80,000 a year was considered overpaid and a corporate manager of even a midsize company could earn ten times that and be considered worth every penny. But the economic is a symbol rather than the problem.

Barber (1984) is perhaps the most direct regarding the problem. He argued that the current cynicism, privatization, and growing paralysis of public institutions are not results of our modern condition but are deeply founded on the American conception of liberal democracy. As he claimed, "The major devices by which liberal theory contrives to guarantee liberty while securing democracy—representation, privacy, individualism, and rights, but above all representation—turn out neither to secure democracy nor to guarantee liberty. Representation destroys participation and citizenship even as it serves accountability and private rights" (xiv). I am inclined to agree with him but for somewhat different reasons and with different results. Representation requires no real discussion, action, or responsibility on the part of the public. For example, voting for someone who will vote for a law that allows the death penalty is far different from voting to put someone to death. Or supporting lawmakers who oppose abortion is very different from making one's own personal decision within the family when concrete details are known.

Actual democratic participation is an involved process and evokes involvement. Public, collective decisions that affect oneself and others are tension filled. Unfortunately, the American public's distrust of collective decisions, which mirrors the social conditions giving rise to democracy as a response to governmental tyranny, paradoxically has given decision making to private interests, where the public has little participation, representation, or rights.

The Community: Highest Good or Greatest Fear

The relation of the individual and the social is considered a basic human struggle. The struggle appears in the Western world as structured by an antagonistic dualist conception of the *individual* and the *social* (Henriques et al. 1984). Human beings, of course, are both separate and together. But the dualism produces a tension between the two poles. The modern formulation of democracy cannot escape a position in this produced as polar struggle. In the early American experience the person/social battle became set as between the democrats and federalists. Clearly the constitutional construction and various compromises demonstrate a way of resolving the tension.

A close look at the resolution shows a simultaneous love and fear of democratic processes but not a balanced one. The rights of the person were to be held as sacred and the public good was a necessary (though hardly desired) constraint on the private pursuit of happiness. As Barber (1984) put it, liberal democracy was "concerned more to promote individual liberty than to secure public justice, to advance interests rather than to secure public good, and to keep men safely apart rather than to bring them fruitfully together" (4). Or as he continued, "The aim is not to share in power or to be part of a community but to contain power and community and to judge them by how they affect freedom and private interests" (7). This conception rested partly on the dominant eighteenth-century views of the natures of persons, experience, and communication as well as on political realities of the time. Liberal democracy as instituted and preserved shows little understanding of the social formation of person and experience as shown in a modern theory of communication (McSwain 1985). The political realities of the day were responsible for conceptually distorting the human struggle between the personal and social into a struggle between the individual and the state. Once conceptualized in this way, the social could become evil, and the individual, good. Legal, institutional, and political forces of the current day sustain these views. While the events of the sixties presented a new way out of the antagonism, largely these conceptions were lost to a newly claimed psychological subject situating a new interpretation of the struggle as between the subjective and objective.

Dualist conceptions are still central in arguments that use the failure of planned economic systems such as that of the Soviet Union as evidence of what happens when the collective replaces individual self-determination. Despite the misassociations, such a conception still serves as a central part of popular political choices (Schiller 1989). On closer analysis, such an equation obviously fails. Strong government does not necessarily equal overemphasis on collective decision making, as all fascist governments show, and the Soviet failure in both collective decision making and economic growth can be attributed more to the implementation of a centralized Western corporate model (principally Taylorism) early on and dictatorial rule than any collective decision making. In the United States, the combined fear of government and distrust of individuals making collective decisions is the ideal setting for corporate domination. Hierarchical control assures people will keep in line, and privatism keeps the government off their backs.

As discussed in chapter 4, early Greek models of democracy did not share this dim view of collective decision making. The natural condition for humans (at least for free males, in their restrictive application) was as citizens of the polis. Individualism was considered a deviate state of affairs. The Greek term for the noncitizen, private person—the uprooted and homeless—was *idiot* (to be ruled by the id). Deeply embedded in the Greek view of life given explicit development by the pre Socratics and repeated often in the works of Plato and Aristotle was the separation between opinion (*doxa*)—that which the subject holds—and truth (*alethia*)—that which reveals or announces itself. The individual could not come to knowledge alone but only in relation to others. The practical life of the state depended on commitment to truth and social good rather than expression of opinion and self-interest. Aristotle was perhaps more direct in the *Politics:* "The man who is isolated, who is unable to share in the benefits of political association, or has no need to share because he is already self-sufficient, is not part of the polis, and therefore must be either a beast or a god" (bk. 1, sec. 14). Plato clearly carried such a view in his various attacks on the late sophists of his day. The modern democrats as well as the modern sophists can be identified in different sites in modern life. Such differences are not just conceptual or attitudinal, but are carried in communication practices.

The Greeks had many advantages in the structure of a community-centered participatory democracy. Size was certainly a key one. The ideal state would have a radius no greater than a person could walk in a day. Even the modern telecommunicationally linked global village lacks the familiarity and ability to directly participate in state decisions. Further, the Athenians guarded against the development of an administrative apparatus by random assignments of administrative roles with very short tenures. But the modern limits on participation rest more on conception and distrust than on capacity, or else more effort would be put into participatory teleconnectedness and administrators would be chosen by lot (a system today reserved for ultimate decisions of freedom and life in the courtroom). Clearly there has been a fear of participation equal to or greater than fear of tyranny, whether tyranny by either autocrats or the majority. As Pateman (1970) argued, "Not only has [participation] a minimal role, but a prominent feature of recent theories of democracy is the emphasis placed on the dangers inherent in wide popular participation in politics" (1).

The twin issues of privatism and individualism are natural, though not necessary, outgrowths of liberal enlightenment concepts of democracy. But they miss what the Greek better knew and what we are coming to know again. The natural tension between the individual and the collective has been transposed into an unnecessary opposition. The individual is a social product. The collective is the upper limit of what a person can be rather than the lowest common denominator of the individuals. The capacity and richness of the individual is limited by the collective capacity, not the other way around. The defense of individual rights as privatism and individualism shrinks the individual's power and capacity. The fear of collective decision making based on social good appears to be a way for an elite to keep most individuals powerless because of the decisions they might make if they were to participate. The emphasis has been on the freedom *from* the decisions of others rather than the freedom *to* participate in collective decisions.

In the same way as the individual misrecognizes her or his constitution as subject, the social is rendered as invisible in its self-instituting capacity. As Thompson (1984, 21ff) showed, following Castoriadis's work, the society negates itself as a society by hiding its social/historical/temporal character and its institutional capacity to order and subject. The social is explained by other factors and protected from examination as ephemeral. The imaginary subject as autonomous is coupled with an imaginary society as conventional in an imaginary relation as social contract. The alterity of the social is lost as the unity and completeness of the individual are èxaggerated.

Privatization of Moral Issues

Conceptions of the *private* and *public* have fallen on hard times. Clearly there is no simple *public* space left in the classic sense

(Sennet 1977). And the *private* realm, such as the family, occupies a new what Donzelot (1979) called *social* area that is neither private nor public, but visibly negotiated and invisibly regulated. Without getting into the far larger issues of what changes have actually occurred, the concept of the private continues as a compelling image in the United States. The term initially signified a protection from state intervention, but it is often powerfully used to prohibit collective decision making on value issues, particularly within the corporate site.

The separation of church and state and the conception of due process are the most visible of the numerous attempts to protect a private realm from state intervention. As already indicated, such protections have been limited in their ability to protect major life institutions from corporate intrusion at the meaning and identity level. Such protection is meaningless if the "enemy" is within, that is, if the family itself is largely colonized. We certainly could try to build bigger and better walls, but the result would be to enclose a smaller and less relevant space. The home can be a castle or a casket.

The task looks much different when progressive individualization is seen as a result of, rather than limited by, social processes. With such a view the goal is not to protect values from the public, but to provide a public space where they may be learned and enlarged. The fear is always that when the home and heart are cast into the public realm they will be lost to the political agenda of the moment. We all recall polemic political interpretations of art and literature, and we know the havoc rendered to family and community with the imposition of utopian ideals. But both of these can better be seen as closures of political discussion than the presence of them. The closure to be feared more is that the progressively "rationalized" worldviews will render the private meaningless. Both fears must be met in the same way through risk, but risk that sees the other as friend rather than enemy. Whether the private is being given up or enriched is an empirical question for interaction systems rather than a necessary presumption. For the risk to be meaningful, there must be a meaningful forum.

The instrumental, amoral orientation of modern corporations assumes that moral decision making is a private responsibility of organizational members and leaders. This position is similar to the Roman conception of "the good man speaking well" as a grounding for an effectiveness model of communication. With a *strong* private morality, pressures for productivity and profits without regard for the public good were counterbalanced into a reasonably productive tension. A shrunken private moral base encourages instrumental values at the expense of moral ones and leads to the necessity of internal and external monitoring systems. Certainly in response to this corporations have taken an active interest in values and value training. Much of this so-called ethical concern can be reduced to concern with systems of internal control. For example, Newstrom and Ruch's (1975) popular Managerial Behaviors Questionnaire operationalization of ethics primarily includes items like "divulging confidential information," "doing personal business on company time," and "not reporting others' violations of company policies and rules." Further, the leading reason for concern with values and ethics beyond internal monitoring appears to be fear that legal and governmental monitoring will take place if corporations do not take control.

Despite the desire, the likelihood that corporations can socialize members to an appropriate value system as confirmed and supported as that of prior ones from the family, church, and community is not great. More likely there will be increased surveillance and control systems with neutral-appearing value principles. But more importantly, it is not likely that corporate-developed and -trained value systems will broadly represent the full set of possible human needs and desires, particularly regarding the public good. In this sense, corporate failure at teaching values may be more attractive than its success. From the society's standpoint the concern is that values and ethics have become reduced to company loyalty and the fulfillment and maintenance of company policies rather than loyalty to the outside community and concern that the company policies and products are socially good. These latter questions are the very ones business ethics frequently keep out of the workplace. The social effects of precluding certain value debates are as significant as the effects on the person as a moral being when the workplace disallows moral development beyond rule following. The moral expectation is extraordinarily low, whether seen in terms of "care" as morality, as in Gilligan's (1982) work, or higher moral levels, in Kohlberg's (1989) work.

The alignment of corporate development with private moral systems has long been understood. Corporate legitimacy and productivity have long depended on an interrelated set of values and social practices loosely referred to as the "protestant work ethic" (Weber 1972; Habermas 1975, 1984). Corporate leaders fear the passing of such a system, even as they advance product and leisure consumerism. As indicated in the discussion of deinstitutionalization in chapter 1, the corporate inability to produce a legitimate and motivating value scheme that does not consume itself with self-interest or the burden of constant value training and monitoring presents both a corporate and a social problem. Motivation and legitimacy problems, corporate domination of value systems, and the lack of a conception of the social good all result from the privatization of values and the lack of an appropriate and meaningful public discussion of moral knowledge. As dangerous and frightening as such a discussion might seem, the alternative to corporate definition and domination is not a protected private realm but a renewed public discussion.

Everyday Life Democracy

If collective decision making is to be meaningful, the political process must be seen as larger than voting. Barber is probably right; representational politics inevitably become special-interest politics. But his "strong" democracy must be stretched to include the political issues of experience and identity. To do this, his concept of the individualism and privatization can be largely accepted, but the application must be extended. Failures in democratizing the everyday have derived from the same flaws as the political systems. The problems of everyday-life democracy become a problem of communication systems and a reconsideration of the connection of the person to the community. In examining the process of communication, we can find a foundation for democracy and begin anew the task of examining democracy in the full variety of human institutions and technologies. The concern here is with the corporation, which is the central institution today.

The Moral Foundation for Democracy in Communication

If an external foundation for democracy is lacking, clearly power need not be the only arbitrator. Instead, we can argue for a different type of moral conception—a moral conception that can help us evaluate decision making and social development and outline the form of a new democracy of everyday life. As will be discussed, Habermas and other critical theorists have shown that moral principles are immanent in the communication process. In this conception, the moral issues change from what is good or right to the process by which we will determine the good and the right (Apel 1979a, b; Deetz 1985b, 1990a). The moral imperative for democracy is a communication issue of ethical knowledge formation (for development of this idea see Apel 1979a, 226-40; Deetz 1983; Habermas 1987, 91ff). How can we engage in communication that enables equal participation in our collective formation? From such a position morality need not privilege one stance over another. Instead, morality can denote democratic discourse that is freed from domination. This is not totally new to us. Our conceptions of democracy in election politics demonstrate a partial public commitment to such ideals. Unfortunately, such conceptions have not adequately accounted for the relation of language and technology to experience and identity. Democracy is a moral issue. Democracy involves the collective decision of what we willfully or unwittingly become. It opposes arbitrary privilege or one-sided considerations in that determination. Filling out such a base requires both a concept of democracy and an analysis of communication processes to sustain it. The remainder of this chapter will develop a theory of communication action for use in discourse and institutional analysis.

Participatory Theories of Communication

Chapter 4 presented the historical tension between effectiveness and participation. In the modern period, participation has been recovered as an issue in the everyday social construction of meaning and identity. This is not based simply on a preference any of us might have but can be shown to be an anticipated, but unfulfilled, condition of every act of communication. Current social conditions, however, make it difficult to clearly understand and articulate this in everyday-life situations. Habermas (1979, 1984, 1987) has done much to thematize this everyday-life condition in his analysis of communicative action. While I wish to add to and depart from his analysis at places, I believe he provides a good point of departure. Much has been written on his theory of communicative action, so I will be brief.

As has already been shown, most commonly used theories of communication focus on effective transmission and persuasive effectiveness (Reddy 1979; Axley 1984). The communication goals and difficulties commonly identified by these theories have to do with the distribution of appropriate, high-fidelity information or with processes of influence and control. Communication effectiveness is based primarily on reproductive fidelity. So-called process models may break the linear conception of this reproduction but still set as an ideal the speaker's ability to lead the listener to a predefined thought or action. Recent works have shown the several liabilities of such conceptions through reconceptions of process, dialectics, and more recently the politics of representation (S. Hall 1989). In chapter 5, I reviewed the conceptual alternative. Here I wish to move beyond describing the politics of language and representation to demonstrating a moral grounding for a more participatory communicative practice. This will require a consideration of the *production* of understanding through communication as distinct from the strategic *reproduction* of meaning.

Gadamer (1975) and Habermas (1984, 1987) have shown how strategic use of communication depends on a more basic communicative attempt to reach mutual understanding. Although their conceptions differ regarding the nature of the process, they both emphasize the continual social formation of consensus in interaction beyond the intentions and opinions of the participants. Mutual understanding focuses attention on reaching openly formed agreement regarding the subject matter under discussion, rather than on the agreement of the perspective of the participants (see Deetz 1990a). As Habermas (1984) presented his position:

> Processes of reaching understanding aim at an agreement that meets the conditions of rationally motivated assent [*Zustimmung*] to the content of an utterance. A communicatively achieved agreement has a rational basis; it cannot be imposed by either party, whether instrumentally through intervention in the situation directly or strategically.... This is not a question of the predicates an observer uses when describing processes of reaching understanding, but of the pretheoretical knowledge of competent speakers, who can themselves distinguish situations in which they are causally exerting an influence *upon* others from those where they are coming to an understanding *with* them.... [T]he use of language with an orientation to reaching understanding is the *original mode* of language use, upon which

indirect understanding, giving something to understand or letting something be understood, and the
instrumental use of language in general, are parasitic.
(286–88)

Figure 6.1 describes the key terms and relations in Habermas's analysis. Such an analysis depends on a careful description of the attempt to reach mutual understanding, a socially
based description of morally guided dispute resolution, and a
description of communicative difficulties, that is, communicative processes that preclude mutual understanding. The effec-
tiveness/ineffectiveness issues become recontextualized by a
concern with participation. From a participation perspective,
communication difficulties arise from communication practices
that preclude value debate and conflict, that substitute images
and imaginary relations for self-presentation and truth claims,
that arbitrarily limit access to communication channels and
forums, and that then lead to decisions based on arbitrary
authority relations. Let me start by developing a conception of
participation as a normative standard against which all communicational practices can be judged, and consider objections
to the primacy of this standard.

Figure 6.1

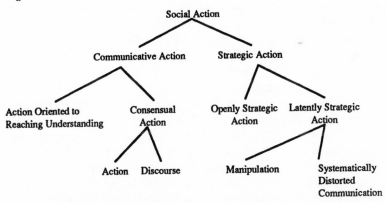

These action types can be distinguished by virtue of their relations to the validity basis of speech:

a) Communicative vs. Strategic Action. In communicative action a basis of
mutually recognised validity claims is presupposed; this is not the case in
strategic action. In the communicative attitude it is possible to reach a direct
understanding oriented to validity claims; in the strategic attitude, by contrast,
only an indirect understanding via determinative indicators is possible.

b) *Action Oriented to Reaching Understanding vs. Consensual Action.* In consensual action agreement about implicitly raised validity claims can be *presupposed* as a background concensus by reason of common definitions of the situations; such agreement is supposed to be *arrived at* in action oriented to reaching understanding.

c) *Action vs. Discourse.* In communicative action it is naively supposed that implicitly raised validity claims can be vindicated (or made immediately plausible by way of question and answer). In discourse, by contrast, the validity claims raised for statements and norms are hypothetically bracketed and thematically examined. As in communicative action, the participants in discourse retain a cooperative attitude.

d) *Manipulative Action vs. Systematically Distorted Communication.* Whereas in systematically distorted communication at least one half of the participants deceives *himself* about the fact that the basis of consensual action is only apparently being maintained, the manipulator deceives at least one of the *other* participants about his own strategic attitude, in which he *deliberately* behaves in a pseudoconsensual manner.

From COMMUNICATION AND EVOLUTION OF SOCIETY. Copyright © 1979 by Beacon Press (Introduction & Translation) German Text © 1976 by Suhrkamp Verlag, Frankfurt am Main. Reprinted by permission of Beacon Press.

Participation as a Shared Ideal

Trying to identify a normative standard for any human enterprise is filled with pitfalls. Most scholars have given up on the attempt to privilege certain forms of communication or social organization on philosophical grounds, though many in the society still argue for certain basic human rights. While most today refuse to articulate normative principles at all, I have not yet seen a work on communication that does not implicitly advance some good/bad, better/worse, healthy/pathological position. In most cases the standard is implicit and not open to debate, though certainly present and operant. A few, however, reject the possibility of any norms not based in opinion and power relations. Foucault in particular has most adamantly rejected the possibility of nonethnocentric, ahistorical normative principles. Nonetheless, even in Foucault one can discern a desire for a type of domination-free "dialogue" where common concerns and conflicting interpretations could be articulated (Waltzer 1986). Even without proclaiming a universal foundation, looking at the attempts to do so can be instructive and useful in guiding fluid and momentary normative choices we make. German philosophical writings in general and critical theory in particular have contributed much.

Following Apel (1979a) a twofold foundation for regulative

communication principles can be advanced: "First, in all actions and omissions, it should be a matter of ensuring the *survival* of the human species *qua real* communication community. Second, it should be a matter of realizing the *ideal* communication community in the real one. The first goal is the necessary condition for the second; and the second goal provides the first with meaning.... [T]he task of realizing the ideal communication community [aims at] the elimination of all socially determined asymmetries of interpersonal dialogue" (282–83). The key issues for us here rest in the relation of the real and ideal communication communities, and the nature of socially determined asymmetries. The significance of the ideal communication community rests in preacceptance by each interactant when engaging in communication. The argument here is not simply that we should believe in and try to create the ideal. Rather each and every interaction assumes the ideal as a background for each communicative act performed. Even the most strategic act of self-interested expression takes place in a language community where presumptions of reciprocity and symmetry exist. For example, lying can only work to one's advantage in a community where honesty is assumed. The act of lying has to present an anticipation of truthfulness. From a participation standpoint, the lie's primary social violation does not come in the deception per se, for the speaker is as much removing him- or herself from representation in the distortion of the decision-making process. The lie, however, functions to undermine the social consensus necessary for the act of communication to function at all. The lie not only is false participation but anticipates and at once denies the social possibility of communication.

The support for participation as a normative ground is thus based on the presumption or anticipation of some ideal communication situation by each real communication community. It is internal to everyday communication (even though implicit and only partly realized) rather than external to it. The anticipation of the ideal community has been demonstrated in two ways. First, Gadamer (1975), in developing an ontology of understanding, demonstrated the social character of the formation of experience that precedes each and every expression of it—the hermeneutic situation. Second, Habermas (1979, 1984) and Apel (1979a) have shown that the illocutionary structure in discourse demonstrates the types of claims presumed as possible in a society and, thus, anticipates the forms of support and dispute in contested claims. In both cases the "hermeneutic" and "ideal speech" situation are counterfactual—that is, rarely fully realized—but each is a necessary anticipation even when violated.

The counterfactual nature of this ideal is frequently bothersome to "empirical" investigators primarily interested in generalization from physical artifacts. They might well ask what is the empirical evidence for such anticipations. Many researchers would only accept a concept of anticipation if it were a testable psychological state such as a goal or attitude. The idea of a structural or implicative relation appropriate to a communication analysis may seem inadequate. There are a number of ways in which most already unproblematically accept such anticipations. In each picture and discussion of even an unexisting entity such as a unicorn, it is counterfactually anticipated as possible or thinkable. True, one may claim that that is based on a real cognitive construction, but such a cognitive construction is never observed but is counterfactually anticipated in every test of constructs. Or for another example, grammar is often counterfactual. As Chomsky (1959) clearly demonstrated, no set of probability models could ever give us grammar. They could only give the likelihood of any word following another in a sentence. No person has to be able to articulate the rules of grammar to speak grammatically. An ungrammatical sentence does not disclaim grammar but is judged ungrammatical or anticipates another grammar that is simply not yet described. In Wittgenstein's sense, to speak a language already anticipates a community of language users. The empirical demonstration of the anticipated ideal requires a careful analysis of empirical events, not a simple empirical generalization.

Further, the claim is not only for the structural anticipation of participation, but also for the preference for participation over effectiveness as an initial normative ground. Neither effectiveness nor participation is fully present in any communication event. Even the best strategies sometimes fail, understanding is rarely complete, and participation is always only partial. Effectiveness and participation are goals that guide the improvement of communicative interaction. Their empirical absence in real situations is in fact what guides conceptions and writings about them. The goal of effectiveness, like participation, is socially developed in communication communities; the concern with social good asks which goals we wish to commit ourselves to. Shall effectiveness be seen within the context of the promotion of participation, or participation out of the context of effectiveness, the dialectic, or marketplace conceptions of democracy? The argument to be advanced in the full development of this volume is the need for stronger social development of the community good. The continued direction of effectiveness-based communication analysis with scant attention to participation will lead to progressively more systems of control by individual and special interests, and consequently, more need for formal external systems of monitoring and control and less explicit exploration of social choice. The preferred hope, I believe, is for more open participation and the evolution of more representative and responsive institutions. This is a change from seeing the individual as more or less effective to seeing the interaction as more or less productive— that is, in the service of further understanding and agreement on the subject matter being determined by the nature of the subject matter itself (Deetz 1990a). The change is from seeing what the individual's point of view is and how it is presented, to determining whether the interaction includes all relevant positions and interests. Interaction cannot be effective in terms of social efficacy without representing the various interests, whether intentionally represented by the participants or not (Habermas 1979).

Conversation and Mutual Understanding

Gadamer (1975) offered much to the development of the concept of participative meaning and interaction as productive in his ontological analysis of understanding. The full significance of his position requires a careful development of a hermeneutic description of language, a development parallel to that of the last chapter (see also Deetz 1978). Central to his theory of language and implicit normative ideal is his description of the "genuine conversation." The genuine conversation is hermeneutically shown to be a special interaction among two persons and the subject matter before them. While most communication studies turn to consider what each person has to say about the subject matter, Gadamer focuses on what the subject matter "says" to each. In other words, the imaginary self and world produced in discourse is challenged by the excess of what the discourse is about over the description of it. The communication question concerns how interaction is to proceed so that this excess is "remembered" or can make its claim. The relationship may become clearer if we look at the experience of a great work of art.

In Gadamer's analysis the great work of art's significance rests more in what it demands of us than in what we say about it or judge it to be. In fact, the great work of art demands from us thoughts, feelings, and the formation of concepts and evaluative criteria that do not precede its presence—it questions the adequacy of what we think and say. If the person with such an experience wishes to bring it to another, it is not one's own feelings and concepts that are at issue, for they are inevitably less than the work has to offer. The attempt is rather to help the other remove limitations to her or his own seeing so that the work may more thoroughly draw on them. Ideally other participants will help reveal aspects of the work that enriches one's own experience. The conversation has the character of progressively opening the prejudicial certainty, the impelled imaginary subject, to question. A truly great work might call one's very way of life into question; it disrupts the totalizing character of the organization of imaginary relations.

The subject matter of most conversations does not have the significance and power of the great work of art, but a productive rather than reproductive conception of communication shows the fundamental process by which mutual understanding arises in regard to the subject matter rather than in the sharing of opinions. Gadamer (1975) argued that the ideal is not "self expression and the successful assertion of one's point of view, but a transformation into communion, in which we do not remain what we were" (341). While the dialectic of the genuine conversation requires a certain commonality of prior understanding, it works more to create and recreate a common language and experience as the tensions of difference question the adequacy of current understandings. More than sharing one's experience or point of view, it is the "art of seeing things in the unity of an aspect, i.e., it is the art of the formation of concepts as the working out of common meaning" (Gadamer 1975, 331). It is not the insides of the other or the self that is to be understood, for either would be covering up the objective demand of the subject matter with one's subjective reaction.

In this brief description it becomes clearer why a "successful" presentation of one's own meaning can limit rather than aid productive communication. For to the extent that the object or other is silenced by the success, the capacity to engage in the reclaiming of difference and conceptual expansion to reach a more open consensus on the subject matter is limited. The "otherness" of the other and of the subject matter before us shows the one-sidedness and suppressed conflict in current perceptions, and forces a surrender of them to the development of consensual thought as a new momentary resting place. The fundamental indeterminancy of the subject matter itself feeds the progressive differentiation and development of experience, but must be conversationally recovered against self-directed perception. Levinas (1969, 75) presented the understanding poetically: "The presence of the Other is equivalent to calling into question my joyous possession of the world." The loss and the growth are critical to human social conduct.

As an ontology of understanding, Gadamer's theory is claiming the genuine conversation as the fundamental way all understanding happens. All reproductions rest on this fundamental production. Conversation is the ongoing process of creating mutual understanding through the open formation of experience. The communicative act should be responsive to the subject matter of the conversation and at the same time help establish the conditions for future unrestrained formation of experience. Such normatively based interaction is not willed or chosen by the individual, nor does it conform to some predefined or routine social practice. Rather, in its natural state the will is produced out of the demand of the subject matter in interaction. But the "conversation" can be blocked or distorted in a variety of fashions. The next chapter will argue that the stoppages maintained in interaction systems constitute unethical communication. The maintenance of a blockage provides an arbitrary restraint on the interaction and prohibits the undistorted expression of human interest and the formation of consensus on the subject matter. The manner of such blockages is critical to assessing the deployment of power in corporations and can be used to evaluate a variety of communication events (Schudson 1978). But Gadamer provides only a beginning for understanding how conversation goes astray.

Even if we wholeheartedly endorse Gadamer's description of the social development of human understanding, and even if we raise his characterization of genuine conversation to a normative ideal for all communicative interaction, we come up short of an adequate view of communication. While it is possible to participate in genuine conversations, such opportunities are relatively rare because of the limitations daily life imposes on both ourselves and others. Rarely is an experience so powerful that the disciplines, routines of life, and ordinary ways of seeing are spontaneously overcome. And where are the experiences to come from that escape routinization and normalcy? There are real power relationships, manifested as institutional arrangements and structures of permissible discourse, that preclude otherness and block conversation. Our shared history carries unexamined beliefs and attitudes that maintain preference for the expression of certain views of reality and of certain social groups. Under such conditions, genuine conversation cannot take place, because there is no "other"; there is no means or forum for "otherness" to be expressed. We gain much from Gadamer's analysis of how new understanding is possible and how we can open to the claims of the subject matter, but how do we construct situations where this is more likely? Gadamer recovers dialectics and understanding from modern epistemological domination, but he has no politics. Such a politics requires a more complete analysis of actual communication processes.

Discourse and Dispute Resolution

In what has been aptly described as a hermeneutics of suspicion, Habermas took head on the issues Gadamer left aside. Systems of domination usually preclude the genuine conversation. What is the nature of interaction where a new consensus does not arise organically out of the interaction? What is the nature of the interaction by which competing claims can be resolved? How can one distinguish consensus reached regarding the subject matter from those knowingly or unknowingly produced by authority or relations of power? Since Habermas's position is well known, I will be brief (see Thompson 1984 for a useful introduction).

Basically, Habermas argued that every speech act can function in communication by virtue of common presumptions made by speaker and listener. Even when these presumptions are not fulfilled in an actual situation, they serve as a base of appeal as failed conversation turns to argumentation regarding the disputed validity claims. The basic presumptions and validity claims arise out of four shared domains of reality: the external world, human relations, the individual's internal world, and language. The claims raised in each are: truth, correctness, sincerity, and intelligibility, respectively. Thus we can claim that each competent, communicative act represents facts, establishes legitimate social relations, discloses the speaker's point of view, and is understandable. Any claim that cannot be brought to open dispute serves as the basis for systematically distorted communication (see again Figure 6.1). The ideal speech situation must be recovered to avoid or overcome such distortions. It should be clear that this conception applies not only to the everyday and ordinary acts of communication but also models the ideal processes by which collective decisions can be made. They can be used in this sense as a guide to defining institutions and practices that advance participation and democracy (see Denhardt 1981; Ulrich 1983; Mingers 1980). Participation modeled in this way is central to our moral responsibility to decide what our society will be and what kind of people we will become. Such principles should be central to corporate design and human interaction within them (see Knights and Willmott 1985). Four basic guiding conditions are necessary for free and open participation in the resolution of claims.

First, the attempt to reach understanding presupposes a symmetrical distribution of the chances to choose and apply speech acts. This would specify the minimal conditions of skills and opportunities for expression, including access to meaningful forums and channels of communication. When we extend these through a consideration of communication technologies, the initial focus needs to be on equal access, distribution of training opportunities, and development of technologies that can be used to express a full variety of human experiences. Such a principle argues against privileged expression forms and routines and rules that advantage certain experiences, identities, and expressions.

Second, the understanding and representation of the external world needs to be freed from privileged preconceptions in the social development of "truth." Ideally, participants have the opportunity to express interpretations and explanations, with conflicts resolved in reciprocal claims and counterclaims without privileging particular epistemologies or forms of data. The freedom from preconception implies an examination of ideologies that would privilege one form of discourse, disqualify certain possible participants, and universalize any particular sectional interest. Communication technologies need to be examined with regard to how they function ideologically to privilege certain perceptions and forms of data and obscure historical processes.

Third, participants need to have the opportunity to establish legitimate social relations and norms for conduct and interaction. The rights and responsibilities of people are not given in advance by nature or by a privileged, universal value structure, but are negotiated through interaction. The reification of organizational structures and their maintenance without possible dispute and the presence of managerial prerogatives are examples of potential immorality in corporate discourse. Acceptance of views because of an individual's privilege or authority or because of the nature of the medium represents a possible illegitimate relation. Authority itself is legitimate only if redeemable by appeal to an open interactional formation of relations freed from the appeal to other authorities. Values and norms legitimately exist in society by the achievement of rational consensus subject to appeals to warrants supporting the assumed social relations. To the extent that particular technologies embody values, hide authority relations, or reify social relations, they participate in domination.

Finally, interactants need to be able to express their own authentic interests, needs, and feelings. This would require freedom from various coercive and hegemonic processes by which the individual is unable to form experience openly, to develop and sustain competing identities, and to form expressions presenting them. Certain communication technologies and structures can produce particular imagistic relations and establish a type of distance that denies the formation of "otherness" and the interrogation of self. In this sense they function immorally. The examination of technology in its structuring of the interior would be important to understanding its effect on the accomplishment of such an ideal.

The most frequent objections to Habermas is that he has overemphasized reason, particularly self-reflection and "mental" activities, and has only a negative view of power, which hampers both the conception of social change and seeing the possible positivity of power. What Habermas does well is to give an arguable standard for normative guidance to communication as a critique of domination, even if his position is distinctly Western and intellectual. I believe that Habermas's description can be transformed from a faith in rational consensus to partial guidance on how conflicting knowledge claims, including those of the body itself, can be expressed to recover conflict from closure. The ideal communication situation is a fiction, but perhaps Habermas is correct that "on this unavoidable fiction rests the humanity of relations among" people.

The Continuing Issue of Moral Communicative Practice

Gadamer and Habermas both offer much to developing communication research grounded in a normative ideal of participation. The participative conception of communication describes the possibility and conditions for the mutual production of meaning, but also provides a description of communication problems and inadequacies. In general most strategic or instrumental communicative acts have the potential of asserting the speaker's opinion over the attempt to reach mutual understanding regarding the subject matter. In such cases an apparent agreement precludes the conflict that could lead to a new position of open mutual assent. In cases where the one-sidedness is apparent, usually the processes of assertion/counterassertion and questions/answers reclaim a situation approximating participation.

In most cases conditions of mutuality are unproblematically temporarily suspended in authority relations such as parent/child, doctor/patient, or teacher/student where we can at least imagine an equable discussion in which the asymmetry could be freely affirmed. Asymmetry and subordination are not themselves the problem. Yet even here we are mindful of the possible arbitrariness of these relations, the power relations that produced as well as are reproduced by them, the need to constantly reassess the possible excessive normalizing and routinizing effects of these relations, and the desire to foster the conflictual as well as consensual aspects of these relations. In general, we understand the moral problems of explicit strategy, manipulation, and instrumental uses of communication, even though such issues are not always taken seriously and the effort to overcome them might be great.

The more serious issues posed by modern analyses are the invisible constraints to richer understanding. Here strategy and manipulation are disguised, and control is exercised through manipulations of the natural, neutral, and self-evident. In a general way these can be described as *discursive closure* and *systematically distorted communication*. The analysis of these will be developed in the next chapter. Both concepts become central when we turn to look at the processes of domination in modern corporations and consider alternative communicative practices. While both Habermas and Gadamer have been criticized as focusing too much on consensus at the expense of conflict and dissension, I hope to have shown that the participatory issues do not depend on this or on the simple critique of false consensus. Implicit in both their analyses is the recovery of conflict as an essential precurser to a new consensus and the perpetual critique of each new consensus as interaction continues.

Lyotard (1984) has perhaps been the most suspicious of the consensus orientation found in Habermas. Essentially he argued that the language of consent is outmoded and incapable of doing justice to the full variety of experience and expression. But he struggled to find his own moral ground for guidance. Lyotard (1984) presented his own "postmodern" project:

> Where, after the metanarratives, can legitimacy reside? The operativity criterion is technological; it has no relevance for judging what is true or just. Is legitimacy to be found in consensus obtained through discussion, as Juergen Habermas thinks? Such consensus does violence to the heterogeneity of language games. And invention is always born of dissension. Postmodern knowledge is not simply a tool of the authorities; it refines our sensitivity to differences and reinforces our ability to tolerate the incommensurable. Its principle is not the expert's homology, but the inventor's paralogy. (xxv)

But Lyotard's "event" in which the inventor's paralogy happens does not differ substantially from the appeal of Gadamer's subject matter in the hermeneutic situation or situations in which Habermas's "discourse" is practiced. The point is that although the motives of different modern philosophies may differ, the need for some normative judgment remains. When such judgments are taken to the practical context, the discursive practices to be preferred are similar. Each makes a necessarily partial attempt to describe a participatory foundation. But this goal is shared in the face of modern forms of domination. The critique of each other's position is a continuing critique of the forms of domination still potential in them. Critique of domination and the advancement of participation are shared twin goals in the analysis of corporations.

CHAPTER 7

Systematically Distorted Communication and Discursive Closure

> Meaning is polysemic in its intrinsic nature;
> it remains inextricably context bound. It is
> caught in and constituted by the struggle to
> "pre-fer" one among many meanings as the
> dominant. That dominance is not already
> inscribed in structures and events but is con-
> structed through the continuous struggle
> over a specific type of practice—representa-
> tional practices.
> (Stuart Hall 1989, 47)

Communication is *distorted* whenever *genuine conversation* is precluded or, more specifically, any of the conditions of the *ideal speech situation* are not upheld. In a general sense, all communication is distorted to some degree. Symmetry conditions are partially violated, because at each moment there is a primary speaker, and every expression is inevitably one-sided and imaginary. Many of these distortions are overcome in the to-and-fro character of interaction. And following a participatory motive, structural conditions and individual ability differences could be overcome to a large extent. In many everyday settings, common distortions could give way to expanded and conflictual meanings in the pursuit of common understanding. Some distortions, however, are *systematic*. In these cases there is a latent strategic *re*production of meaning rather than participatory production of it. *Systematically distorted communication* operates like strategic manipulation, but without overt awareness. The latent prejudice, preconception, predefined personal identity, or object production precludes open formation. The one-sidedness becomes reproduced rather than opened by conflicting representations.

The most familiar cases of this exist when the interactant is self-deceived. The psychoanalytic analogue of this describes when an individual has repressed certain experience and consequently the psychological experience and the expression of it become displaced or projected. In this sense an individual is out of touch with self-interests, needs and feelings and may well substitute other socially derived experiences and expressions for his or her own—an ideological expression or false consciousness. Strategic social forms dominate the individual or group consciousness. In the extreme model, only through a "talking cure" can the code be broken so that the disguised expression of the repressed state can be read and the individual can reconnect with self-experience. In this view, society and organizations can be seen as filled with "social neurosis." While instances of such distortion are at times present and the analysis is useful, such an analysis is too simple and creates difficulties. With the simple view, the role of social therapist, which can be attributed to the theorist, is elitist, and leads to everybody and everything being viewed with suspicion. The search for "real" motives, needs, and interests creates a new domination and another privileged discourse. And the implicit assumption that linguistic expression should represent a fixed, knowable interior provides a weak understanding of language and experience. But we can learn from the intuitive conception.

We know that we respond to unknown socially derived elements of experience, if only in using a particular historical language. We see people unwittingly act in opposition to their own values and needs. And we hear and participate in discourses that feel restrictive, like trying to express a sunset on canvas when you don't know how to paint. These are significant to the communication process. Here, systematic distortion is based not on a simple mismatch of fixed interests with a fixed expression, but on an interactionally determined reduction of certain experiences to other ones outside the intentional awareness of the interactant. The core issue is the way certain experiences and identities are preemptively preferred over equally plausible ones.

A simple example may help display the important complexities. Young boys and girls often tease each other a lot and often profess and probably feel a degree of animosity. Yet an adult watching a young boy tell a young girl that she is "fat and ugly" would understand the expression to mean that he likes her and wants her attention. If confronted, the boy would probably deny it. I doubt that most of us would consider the adult egocentric if he or she thought that the male was only partly in touch with his feelings and that his most explicit expression was a distortion. We seem to accept this because we know that sorting out feelings at transitional points in life is difficult, that what are considered appropriate, even thinkable, feelings are socially developed, and that expression is constrained by group norms and expectations. If we pay careful attention, we will see that the early adolescent male is not experiencing false consciousness, but rather is actually making a fairly clear expression of confusion and mixed feelings, but ones that are "forgotten" or "misrecognized" by both speaker and recipient. The explicit message conceals the full variety of messages, affects both the speaker and listeners, and can elicit responses and counterresponses that perpetuate the one-sided development of feelings and expression rather than foster perceptual and expressive options. The distortion is not the tease (though some freeze that as a response option to the demise of later work relations) but the centering of the variety of experiences in one discourse. If the explicit message changed but was still singular, the distortion would still be present—for example, if in the wake of the television show "The Wonder Years," a twelve-year old male were to say to the female, "I want to go to bed with you," we could determine how such a discourse arose as privileged over other potentially competing relational statements—what it includes and what it leaves out, what kind of imaginary relation it is.

In a more technical sense, what is happening here is one type of self-deception. In this deception the individuals believe that they are engaging in communication action—pursuing mutual understanding—but are actually engaged in a concealed strategic action, even concealed from themselves. As Habermas (1984) described it: "Such communication pathologies [systematic distortion] can be conceived of as the result of a confusion between actions oriented to reaching understanding [communicative action] and actions oriented to success [strategic action]. In situations of concealed strategic action [manipulation], at least one of the parties operates with an orientation to success, but leaves others to believe that all the presuppositions of communicative action are satisfied. On the other hand, [in systematically distorted communication] at least one of the parties is deceiving himself [sic] about the fact that he is acting with an attitude oriented toward success and is only keeping up the appearance of communicative action" (332). When the people acting strategically know they are, we have a clear case of morally reprehensible manipulation. But in the case of systematically distorted communication the individual is self-deceived. A moral violation of participation is present but hidden. The conditions of discourse in pursuit of a legitimate consensus cannot proceed, since an unknown false consensus is already in place. Manipulation is clearly present in organizations, but systematically distorted communication is of more interest. Methods of corporate control perpetuate a false consensus without the members understanding them as a violation of basic moral rights or misrepresentation of interests. Understanding the latent strategic character of the apparently transparent is a step toward reopening the exploration of the private, social, and external world.

I believe that Habermas (1984, 70ff) is right in his analysis of the nature of this reformation. What is involved is a learning process rather than therapy. We can participate in the development of distinctions and articulation. This involvement is certainly not neutral, for our involvement partially determines the direction of development. But we can determine when we participate with the other in development, versus when we try to teach them how to think and express. And we can become aware of when even subtle authority relations change enabling power relations into disqualification and discursive privilege. Such a learning process, however, is not one of putting people in touch with themselves or learning to articulate their insides clearly (hidden effectiveness issues) but one that reopens engagement in the development of differentiated feelings and discursive possibilities, to participate in the affective and expressive development of self and other.

Systematic distortion is a common property of human communication rather than something that occasionally arises during periods of transition. Human thought, feelings, actions, and expressions are often skewed. Certain dominant forms of reasoning and articulations stand in the stead of other valuational schemes. If career development exhausts the expression of personal development, if control drives the forms of human association, or if statements about the external world preclude those about affective states, we have a certain one-sidedness or systematic distortion. Such expressions can and should be examined for possible suppressions of alternative voices, not to implement alternative values, but as part of ongoing community development.

The Pathologies of Systematic Distortion

Processes of systematically distorted communication can be said to be pathological. Following the normative foundation presented in the last chapter, we can say that communication is pathological to the extent that it (1) endangers the survival of the human and other species by limiting important adaptation to a changing environment, (2) violates normative standards already freely shared by members of a community, and (3) poses arbitrary limits on the development of individualization and the realization of collective good. Clearly each of these is true of most instances of systematically distorted communication: To the extent that the communication system precludes responsiveness to an exterior, adaptation is limited; to the extent that the ideal speech situation is denied, freely shared normative standards are violated; and to the extent that the self and experience are reproduced, concept formation cannot occur in regard to otherness. Although the details of this need to be clearly specified, the modern corporation is filled with pathological interaction in each of these senses.

We already know a fair amount about pathological interpersonal systems. Interaction process analysis (Watzlawick, Beavin, and Jackson 1967; Pearce and Cronen 1980) initiated careful research into the way family systems can develop internal logics and rules which structure frozen identities for the participants, which preclude the meeting of critical needs in their production of other needs, and finally strip participants of responsibility and responsiveness (see Laing 1971 for the most extreme examples). Such systems, because of their closure and fixed interpretive processes, properly have no outside, no natural checks and balances, and few moments of escape to see the system as it works. Yet they grow; they become supported by external structures and engulf others in their peculiar logics. The theoretical base of these studies, particularly in regard to the social structure of identity and reality, is too weak to show their political character or to demonstrate the workings of the modern organization, but their descriptions are useful in showing how pathological systems work. Corporate images and career paths, dependent and codependent processes internal to corporations, and reality production operate in organizations much like these interpersonal systems, and thus, provide for particular corporate pathologies.

Systematic Distortion in Decision Making

From a participatory communication perspective, many of the issues of good decision making look much the same as those from an effectiveness perspective. Good decisions require appropriately distributed information, openness to alternative perspectives, and reasoning based on personal insights and data rather than on authority relations. Implicit in these analyses, however, is the acceptance of priorities, goals, and authority relations that are not necessarily warranted or freely selected. When difficulties arise, then, the appeal is rarely to *discourse* along the model of the ideal speech situation. In most decisional effectiveness analyses, problems in the process are often conceptualized as individual or technical, thus requiring technical structural adjustments or personnel training. In cases of conflict, rather than reinvolving the community, higher order privilege is evoked, backed by symbolic control and expertise. The problem is "solved" rather than addressed. Based on the privileged situation, better information is gotten to the "right" people rather than asking who the right people are (based on the full variety of community needs) or what is the nature of the information presumptively included or excluded.

Forester (1989) provided a typology both of inevitable distortions that arise in communication processes and of systematic distortion related to decision making. This is shown in figure 7.1. Distortions in categories 1 and 2 are inevitably given limitations in communication processes and the human use of them. To the extent that they reflect limitations present in legitimate systems that pursue communicative understanding, generally they become remediable over time in question asking, providing warrants, and conflicting interpretations. In these processes meaningful changes are made and the decisional process claims a renewed legitimacy as openly derived asymmetries are reassessed and reaffirmed.

Distortions in categories 3 and 4 are of a different sort. In each of these cases there is either a known or an unknown strategic quality of the interaction that drives the interaction, thus providing a systematic distortion that is protected from assessment. For example, forgetting is a natural human limitation that can be overcome in part by social relations. Selective memory is a produced condition that works against the social attempt to recall. Correction is difficult because the strategic interactant creates both false conflicts and/or a false lack of conflict. Hence, the decisions are distorted, but neither the distortion nor the conditions for it are known. Further, the interactant is less willing to be corrected, since strategic gain is an issue. And perhaps even more importantly, the strategy can remain disguised, because it can be presented as a natural category 1 problem. Systematic distortions thus can be blamed on individuals and inevitable system weakness rather than strategic interaction.

Figure 7.1 Communicative Distortions as Bounds to the Rationality of Action

Autonomy of the Source of Distortion

Contingency of Distortion	Socially Ad Hoc	Socially Systematic/ Structural
Inevitable distortions	**1** Idiosyncratic personal traits affecting communication Random noise (cognitive limits)	**2** Information inequalities resulting from legitimate division of labor Transmission/content losses across organizational boundaries (division of labor)
Socially unnecessary distortions	**3** Willful unresponsiveness Interpersonal deception Interpersonal bargaining behavior; e.g., bluffing (interpersonal manipulation)	**4** Monopolistic distortions of exchange Monopolistic creation of needs Ideological rationalization of class or power structure (structural legitimation)

From *Planning in the Faces of Power,* 1989, 34. Reprinted by permission of the Regents of the University of California and the University of California Press.

Of greatest interest in analyzing corporations, are the distortions in category 4. These distortions are produced by the structural configurations institutionalized in the organization.

To the extent that these institutional arrangements are taken as natural and self-evident, their political derivation is forgotten and their existence is noncontestable. For example, arbitrary authority relations may be disguised as legitimate divisions of labor, thus producing a strategic skewing of decisions, but contestion can only take place within the structural confines, rather than be about them. Pathological, rather than just bad, decisions are made. They are pathological not because they do not effectively meet "organizational" goals, but because of the monopoly of the opportunities to define the organization and its goals as well as the strategic processes of reaching them. For example, the economic property interest can pathologically be reproduced as privileged over the variety of competing interests in a democratic society. The nature of such privileges will be developed later. Here the concern is in providing a general description of the type of distortions that are to be examined. Figure 7.2 provides an adaptation of Forester's (1989) work that described communication distortions in public planning following Habermas's contestable claims in his universal pragmatics. The organizational examples are illustrative of the more extended analysis to be developed later.

Self-Referential Systems

Forester's work is instructive but only takes us part of the way. Forester, like Habermas, operated primarily from a linear model of communication and focused on the speech act within a structural context. Communication researchers are and have been concerned with these relations, but we also know that human interaction takes place within multimessage, multilevel systems that are more complex than the segmented and largely intentional (even if hidden) communicative context described here. Communication systems as suggested by interaction process analysis and in chapter 5 are multitextual and produce the intentions of the participants. Rationality and intentionality are only partially descriptive of operating systems, and not only because they are sometimes distorted. Rather than taking an overtly intentional direction, both an orientation to reaching mutual understanding and strategic interaction can be defined in nonpersonal terms as systemic outcomes owing to internal system logics. The ideal speech situation must be understood in systemic as well as structural and intentional terms.

In organizations the most important systemic forms of sys-

Figure 7.2 The Management of Comprehension, Trust, Consent, and Knowledge

Forms of Misinformation

Modes Through Which Power May Be Exercised	Managing Comprehension (problem framing)	Managing Trust (false assurance)	Managing Consent (illegitimacy)	Managing Knowledge (misrepresentation)
Decision making	Resolutions passed with deliberate ambiguity; confusing rhetoric, e.g., "the truly needy"	"Symbolic" decisions (false promises)	Decisions reached without legitimate representation of public interests but appealing to public consent as if this were not the case	Decisions that misrepresent actual possibilities to the public (e.g., the effectiveness of insufficiently tested medications)
Agenda setting	Obfuscating issues through jargon or quantity of "information"	Marshaling respectable personages to gain trust (independent of substance)	Arguing, e.g., that a political issue is actually a technical issue best left to experts	Before decisions are made, misrepresenting costs, benefits, risks, true options
Shaping felt needs	Diagnosis, definition of problem or solution through ideological language	Ritualistic appeals to "openness," "public interest," and "responsiveness"; encouraging dependence on benign apolitical others	Appeals to the adequacy and efficacy of formal "participatory" processes or market mechanisms without addressing their systematic failures	Ideological or deceptive presentation of needs, requirements, or sources of satisfaction (false advertising, "analysis for hire")

From *Planning in the Face of Power*, Reprinted by permission of the Regents of the University of California and the University of California Press.

tematic distortion can exist in "self-producing," "self-referential" systems. Many recent organizational theorists (Faucheux and Makridakis 1979; Ulrich and Probst 1984; Morgan 1986; Mingers 1989) have used Maturana and Varela's (1980) conception of *autopoietic systems* to describe the *self-producing, self-referential* character of corporate systems. The intent here is to avoid many of the systems' assumptions and terminology, but to use their descriptions to draw attention to practices by which organizations can become distorted in their self-production, cut off from anything other than their own products (be they workers, consumers or the environment), and thus unknowingly engage in systematically distorted communication as they try to operate rationally.

In saying that organizations are self-producing and self-referential, attention is drawn to the way in which corporations, like all human systems, produce themselves in an environment (as signified) that they have enacted from their own internal signifying system, and evaluate their success through the use of criteria developed internal to the processes being evaluated. They do not simply adapt to an external environment, they enact the environment to which they react. The environment in which the corporation exists is "autobiographic" as well as an external reality to which it shapes itself. Maturana and Varela's (1980) work thus denies a simple distinction between the system and environment in much the same way that Althusser denied a person/world separation. There can be no open system, nor fixed external environment to get right or adjust to. The identity of the subject and world arise imaginarily in a chain of signifers. Parallel to the "subjected subject," systems attempt to reproduce themselves by subordinating all changes into a maintenance of their own set of imaginary relations. Corporations attempt to recreate and maintain their imaginary identity by projecting themselves outward, producing a boundary between themselves and an environment, and monitoring that environment for things that reflect their interest and concerns. The corporation and environment are enacted as the same imaginary move. The relations within this large complex "closed" system are central to the analysis here.

The patterns of relations are thus of more interest than the particular substantive character, for substantive elements are products of the system itself. The process, rather than either the initial structure or the "external" conditions, produces the outcome. No action or structure can be good in itself. In Weick's

(1979) work, the various relations internal and external to the system can thus be mapped by a series of causal lines and loops. Some of these produce systems that are "charmed." In a "charmed" loop the enacted environment is produced in regard to a relatively full set of needs and interests facilitating an internal development that enacts a richer environment and increased system differentiation and autonomy (see Pearce and Cronen 1980; Morgan 1986). Others map what Morgan (1986) called "egocentric" organizations, where the attempt to maintain and reproduce existing identities and world relations drive a vicious deviation-amplifying loop. Charmed loops thus describe the systems equivalent of democratic participation, where one-sidedness is overcome as differentiation and autonomy drive enlarged produced identities, whereas "ego- (or any-) centric" forms are latent strategic systems of control. The choice is between a dynamic relation between a self-producing system and an open world, and a system that struggles to reproduce itself by control of the insides and outsides.

A couple of examples may clarify. Recall that identities are always imaginary in the sense of their inevitable partiality and one-sided representation. They momentarily provide a unity, temporarily suppressing conflict among alternative identities and objective relations. In nonpathological systems the illusion of completion and objectivity is temporary and gives way in process to the perpetual antagonisms and resolutions in response to successive life events. In the pathological version the individuals in the system maintain particular identities and object relations as they are reproduced in continued action within the system. Self-fulfilling prophecies are the best examples of this at the individual level, though such systems become quite complex in social organizations.

Control-oriented, self-referential systems exist in many aspects of everyday life. In a system of assumed equality, one individual perceives a control move on the part of the other and thus responds with defensiveness and control, which evokes a countermove of defensiveness and control from the other which evokes a greater move to control by the first, and so on. No one has to desire control for the cycle to work. If the logic of the system demands reciprocity, even a mistaken initial perception sets into play a cycle that feeds on itself. Once in motion, even claims that one or the other does not desire control can be interpreted as a more sophisticated control strategy. And ultimately both may regretfully assume that control is a central part of dealing with others. A relation to the excess of the outside over existing conceptions is lacking, hence the cycle cannot be put in perspective (i.e., Gadamer's "demand" of the subject matter).

Within work life and between work and nonwork life, similar cycles can develop for individuals. Weick has provided a clear example of such self-referentiality when an individual develops a system of reasoning that follows Linder's (1970) rule that people try to equalize the yield of their work and nonwork time. Quoting Weick (1979):

> Suppose that in my work one hour of writing produces one-third of an article. Now suppose that by using a dictating machine I increase my production to one-half of an article per hour. Each of those hours has increased in value. Linder argues that two hours of recreation have to count for more. To accomplish this I add expensive consumer goods to amplify the yield from my consumption time. I trade in my Instamatic for a Hasselblad so that I'll get more return from my two hours of photography. But I have to pay a great deal for the Hasselblad, which tightens the screws on me to become more productive and to earn even more, which in turn makes me try to squeeze even more out of my photography. I then become one more member of the "harried leisure class." (31)

Such deviation amplification often happens within organizations. Most agree that organizations demonstrate bounded rationality whereby members attempt to maximize certain utilities in ways limited by available information, costs, and capacities. In the clearest cases of systematic distortion and system pathology, the normally bounded rationality takes on strange forms. Schulman (1989) demonstrated such processes in a variety of organizational "blunders" owing to a kind of decisional "tunneling" or "traps." Watergate is perhaps the most widely known. In these cases member decisions "interact progressively to circumscribe one another—distorting processes of search and calculation, and narrowing the scope of available options. Under such circumstances, the pursuit of rational self-interest can actually be displaced by 'pathology,' that is, by behavior that is logically self-defeating, both from an individual stand point and from the stand point of the organization as a whole" (32). The primary logic of such systems is fairly common. Individuals overweigh the certainty of winning, hence they will accept assured small successes over more risky but potentially larger gains, and conversely they will attempt to avoid a sure loss even when they have to risk an even larger loss. To worsen the effect, most technical design features account for the successful functioning of a system but not its failure. Often the same features that assure integration in complex working processes create a geometrically expanding system collapse once a portion of the system breaks down. Consequently, there is an unavoidable trade-off between designs for effective functioning and those preventing and containing error. The one-sided emphasis on effectiveness aligns with individual logics in creating pathology in these cases. These are often visible pathologies, because they affect the narrow, but defined as significant, context of self-interest and organizational (read managerial) goals.

Bounded rationality—or in terms of the language here, a *delimited appropriation of discourse*—itself is already political and potentially pathological in a broader sense. The defense industry has grown to great magnitudes through a more complex and invisible, but similar, cycle. Defense is needed, which creates jobs; jobs are needed or feared lost, which creates a need for a claim of outside threat to increase defense, which creates a threatening situation, which creates an environment where defense is needed, which creates greater job dependency.... And some of the clearest examples of egocentric corporations come from the defense industries. Kurtz (1988) provided a useful description of how complex weapons systems become a goal in themselves, threatening world order rather than being a means to the goal of security:

> Because of the way bureaucratic institutions are structured, individuals who work in the military-industrial complex expand the arms race by simply pursuing their own careers. In the day-to-day decision making, in order to justify their job responsibilities, they must provide reports and strategies of action that enhance their work status as well as that of their superiors and the institutions for which they work.... Cooperation in these tasks leads to a final hard-to-resist outcome— career security and organizational expansion. (66–67)

Of course the system has a larger sway than just the internal reports and action. Major media organizations have their own layer of career-minded individuals as well as local communities wanting jobs and congressional representatives wanting to assure them. In the course of events of 1990 prior to the Iraq "crisis," the demise of the "Soviet block" presence was quickly offset in the media with promotion of the fear of a unified Germany. But the self-referential defense system is only the more obvious. The example would run much the same if we substituted in the pharmaceutical, cosmetic, fashion, or auto industries.

In the terms of this volume, the imaginary image is reproduced by the system that it both initiated and is a response to. A communicational analysis of self-referential systems draws attention to the textual nature of the interplay of various produced identities and events. Every linguistic description is a distortion, in that it is partial and imaginary. In open discourse, partiality becomes displayed and partly overcome as further descriptions are advanced. In the continued interplay the outside (the "otherness") initiates concept formation and enrichment of the natural language. Distortion becomes systematic when the process becomes one of *in-formational* repetition rather than conversation. The manner by which this works in larger social systems has been described by Baudrillard (1975). He refers to this as *the monopoly of the code*. In such a situation the signifier changes. Rather than signifying an outside, it becomes signified itself. As Baudrillard (1975) described the relation:

> The form-sign [present in a monopolistic code] describes an entirely different organization: the signified and the referent are now abolished to the sole profit of the play of signifiers, of a generalized formalization in which the code no longer refers back to any subjective or objective "reality," but to its own logic. The signifier becomes its own referent and the use value of the sign disappears to the benefit of its commutation and exchange value alone. The sign no longer designates anything at all. It approaches its true structural limit which is to refer back only to other signs. All reality then becomes the place of semi-urgical manipulation, of a structural simulation. (127–28)

As will be developed in detail later, corporations today operate more and more as systems of *simulations* in Baudrillard's sense. Despite their claim to "real" worldliness, they operate as images reflected upon each other, developing a thickness of images that appears grounded on something solid but that is simply another layer of production. Or as Lefebvre

(1968) showed, "There is *nothing*—whether object, individual or social group—that is *valued* apart from its double, the image that advertises and sanctifies it...imparting an ideological theme to the object...endowing it with a dual real and make believe existence" (105–6). Such simulations run with strange constructed rules, strategically designed to assure power-laden reproductions.

Systematically distorted communication, then, is an ongoing process within particular systems as they strategically (though latently) work to reproduce, rather than produce, themselves. It is shown in systems that respond to themselves and are unable to form a relation to the outside on the outside's own terms; they respond to shadows of themselves cast on the events around them. In this form they translate all back to their own conceptual relations, thus precluding alternative discourses or conflicts with contrary institutional interpretive schemes. Such systems largely fool themselves in presuming themselves to be referential and purposively directed to an actual outside. In order for this to happen and be sustained, active processes of discursive closure occur in the internal discourses.

Discursive Closure

Discursive closure exists whenever potential conflict is suppressed. This might derive from several processes, several of which will be discussed below. One of the most common is the disqualification of certain groups or participants. Disqualification can occur through the denial of the right of expression, denying access to speaking forums, the assertion of the need for certain expertise in order to speak, or through rendering the other unable to speak adequately, including through processes of deskilling. Closure is also possible through the privileging of certain discourses and the marginalization of others. For example, Habermas (1984) and other critical theorists have extensively detailed the domination of technical-instrumental reasoning over other forms in the Western world (see Fischer 1990). Foucault in his many works has shown how certain discourses historically arise as normal and preferred. Organizational studies clearly show how managerial groups and technical reasoning become privileged. Further, closure is present in each move to determine origins and demonstrate unity. In each case the multiple motivations and conflict-filled nature of experience become suppressed by a dominant aspect. Later this will be shown in analyses of organizational narratives, language, and standard practices. With unity the continued production of experience is constrained, since the tension of difference is lost.

Chapter 5 describes the processes of construction of knowledge and identity. Each individual is "subjected" in a variety of competing discourses. The basic political questions concern the interrelation of these competing discourses. In a purely participatory context, the conflict among the alternatives would undermine the necessity felt of any particular concept and open a measure of freedom to choose. In this way particular imaginary relations would be given up in the practical demands of the events and expression of others—in Gadamer's sense, the demand of the subject matter. If this were the case, the particular forms of distorted communication extending from the imaginary relation would be replaced in dialogue with a move toward concept formation and individuation in Habermas's sense. This is of course not to say that the perception would be freed from its imaginary quality or suddenly become a truthful discourse. Rather the formation of experience would be less routinized, less dominated by subjectivity or at least a particular fixed historical subjectivity, and while still socially constrained, it would be more responsible to events and others outside of the socially produced self-centered totality of which each particular experience is a part. In short, the formation of self and experience would more closely match the participative ideal.

Discursive practices, however, can either lead to such open formation by further exploration of the subject matter or divert, distort, or block the open development of understanding. When discussion is thwarted, a particular view of reality is maintained at the expense of equally plausible ones, usually to someone's advantage. It should not be surprising that systems of domination are protected from careful exploration and political advantage is protected and extended. Their continuation provides both security and advantage. The particular alignment between various systems of subject and world production, along with the discursive means by which the politics of production are concealed, will be discussed later as the "strategic power apparatus." Here I only wish to introduce basic discursive moves that conceal the production of subjects and world that we have discussed (see also Pateman 1980).

The primary effect of these moves is to suppress insight into the conflictual nature of experience and preclude careful discussion of and decision making regarding the values implicit in experience, identity, and representation. These are not themselves major value claims or organized strategies. Rarely are they seen in regard to dominating ideologies or the politics of identity and experience. They are rather quiet, repetitive micropractices, done for innumerable reasons, which function to maintain normalized, conflict-free experience and social relations. Allow me to review a few of the more common processes of discursive closure.

Disqualification

As we have discussed, Habermas demonstrated that central to every communication community is an assumption (though not always fulfilled) of equal opportunity to select and employ different speech acts for the representation of one's interests. Many have discussed this principle in regard to access to various forums and media, but it applies fundamentally to the determination of who has a right to have a genuine say. Disqualification is the discursive process by which individuals are excluded (Bavelas 1983; Bavelas and Chovil 1986). For example, statements such as "You're just saying that because you are a woman [manager, lover, angry...]" function within certain systems to exclude the expressed view from the discussion. Such an activity skews the development of mutual understanding.

Socially produced notions of expertise, professional qualification, and specialization are central to qualification and to the imposition of the opposite, the disqualification process. Specialization has always fostered control, whether through deskilling or through loss of understanding of the function and effects of one's own actions. Although such effects can be overcome by integrative activities, they are often precluded. As Jehenson (1984) argued, expertise clearly functions as an ideological fiction, an imaginary relation, but further it reproduces itself by proclaiming who has the capacity to determine and question it. As will be described, the creation of managerial expertise (and management science to certify, institutionalize, and finally signify it) centers management capacity in certain locations and outside certain groups. Such a placement is, even if diffused in more participatory management, retained as a prerogative by its own assertion of placement. The often subtle processes of deferring, calling in, and studying for, operate like the more explicit forms of dismissal and ignorance in protecting powerful groups' inserted realities and denying the implicit values on which they are based.

Naturalization

One the most compelling observations of Marx, and perhaps one of the most shared outside the various Marxists groups, is that of reification. Lukács (1971) in particular has developed how social relationships and subjective constructions become made into objects that are treated as fixed and external, that is, reified. Rather than introducing the commodity theory on which this is based, I wish to focus on one aspect of it—the treatment of the socially produced as given in nature. I call this naturalization. In a naturalizing discourse, the social historical processes (whether in the actual production of objects and institutions or in the production of the subject and structures of experience) are removed from view. Not only is this an occurrence in everyday life of communities, but it is fostered by the operating philosophy of the social sciences. In treating their perceptions as transparent renderings of the external world, the concepts, methods, and practices of perception production are made invisible, especially as abstracted and presented in manuals, textbooks, and training sessions. The constituting subjectivity of science is thus hidden behind the claim of objectivity. Social scientists, news reporters, and other experts help institutionalize a discourse through "the projection of an 'imaginary community' by means of which 'real' distinctions are portrayed as 'natural', the particular is disguised in the universal, the historical is effaced in the atemporality of essence" (Thompson 1984, 25).

In open discourse, the subject matter is a constituted/constituting object in relation to interactants. Every perception has a social historical dimension. In naturalization, one view of the subject matter is frozen as the way the thing is. In this process, the constitution process is closed to inspection and discussion. In a sense, the subject matter has been "silenced" by the claim that someone's conception is what it is. As will be developed, the corporation itself is often treated as a simple existing relational form. On reflection, most know that modern organizations are particular historical constructions, constructed toward certain ends. But in everyday talk, in the naming of the corporation as an object, and in the research treatment of it as an entity, its production is forgotten. Naturalization frequently stops discussion—at the determination of what is—at precisely the place where it should be started—how is it that.

Naturalism always plays in the privileging and marginalizing of discourses. For example, perceived differences between female and male emotional reactions in organizations are frequently treated as naturally occurring, as if women and men were different in some fixed manner. In such a claim, such reactions are depicted as natural and self-evident, thus justifying the necessity of their presence to the advantage or disadvantage of either group. When male aggressiveness or female tears are treated as natural and necessary, we can either adjust to them or use emotional expression to exclude one or the other from certain jobs. But quite apart from the descriptive adequacy of such differences, the claim of being natural often places the value of emotional expression beyond discussion. Aristotle's ancient view of natural laws is overlooked (the fact that people are usually "naturally" right-handed does not keep the left from being developed as well). And the presentation of the perceived differences as a truth claim obscures how the claim of truth works politically to preclude discussion and development.

Neutralization

Neutralization refers to the process by which value positions become hidden and value-laden activities are treated as if they were value-free. Not only are socially constructed objects and processes treated as natural objects, but the values in the construction process are forgotten as arbitrary and chosen as well. Such a process is significant because it is key to the universalization of sectional interests (Giddens 1979). Different groups in a society perceive and interpret events using different values. In Saussure's sense every linguistic distinction is an attention, a valuing. In the neutralization of language, language does not lose its valuing, rather one system of valuing is treated as the only possible one. *A possible world is treated as *the* world.* Weedon (1987) developed this position as one of the presumptions of representational transparency, a presumption that hides the need for examining the arbitrary nature of distinction. The transparency presumption suggests that language, research methods, and other constitutive activities can be seen through to a world as it *really* is. This is neutralization.

Presumed "objective" claims hide both the activities that produced the claim and the values carried with them. For example, just giving the "data" or the "facts" hides the criteria used to choose certain observations rather than others and the conceptual frame that produced the "facts" and "data" in the first place. In the same sense that the documentary film is often the most difficult film to critique since the politics in it are hidden by the proclamation of the "real," judgments disguised as descriptions often effectively block the open construction of the "facts." Recent works in accounting (Ansari and Euske 1987; Hopwood 1987) and data collection forms (Sless 1988) have reclaimed corporate data production from presumed neutrality, showing not only the existence and use of value claims in accounting but also their relation to systems of advantage (see chapter 10). Technologies are often granted the same type of transparency granted to other constitutive activities. As I have argued, technologies as institutions carry a point of view, a way of being in contact with particular aspects of the world. Neutralizing practices hide and forget constitution and thus suppress potential conflict between different constitutive practices.

Topical Avoidance

Every social group prohibits or discourages the discussion of some events and feelings. Often these surround significant areas of potential conflict, such as prohibitions against discussing religion or politics at family gatherings. These prohibitions may be motivated to enhance propriety and order, but they often function to preclude a discussion of the values that define propriety and order and the benefits that certain groups acquire from them. Foucault (1980b, 1977) demonstrated this well in terms of sexual discourse and the hiding away of the insane. Gilligan (Gilligan, Ward, and Taylor 1988) documents much of the same in her treatment of adolescent girls' struggles with their relational attachments and the forces against these attachments in contemporary society, a tension that renders them mute. Males can be muted in a different way. In the most bold way that Wolfe (1987) described, *"masters of the universe* don't cry." From teamsterville to *he-man,* places of expression and topics of talk are highly constrained and constrained to certain ends (Philipsen 1975). The corporate prohibition against expression of personal doubts and problems at home essentially hides the home and removes the corporation from having to change or account for these problems. Their hidden quality makes them the employee's problem even if they result from work-related experiences.

All topical avoidance leads to systematically distorted communication and not only because the interaction must be structured to go around and leave out. The internal state of the person can already experience the exclusion. Bodily states are fundamentally ambiguous. The focus and channeling of physiological excitation is socially constructed (see Harré 1986). Males in a corporate environment may not "feel" betrayal or hurt but may directly feel anger or the drive to control. Only in reflection can the same state in the same context be seen as feeling "betrayal" or "hurt," feelings that more "spontaneously" arise in some females. Who has or does not have certain feelings is a political question. The systematic exclusion of humanly experienceable emotions avoids certain "topics" and thus the concealment of conflict—the conflict over what this physiological state "is."

Organizational researchers have understood the power of omission. Bachrach and Baratz's (1962) familiar work is an example in point. As they argued, pluralist conceptions of power emphasize "the importance of initiating, deciding, and voting and, as a result, take no account of the fact that power may be, and often is, exercised by confining the scope of decision making to relatively 'safe' issues" (6). This point is made even more clearly by Wolfinger (1971) in his study of how routines produce nondecisions. What cannot be talked about and what cannot be brought to decision making are significant in organizations. Their analysis, however, is only a surface reading of the larger issue in the politics of experience and how this politics is concealed.

Subjectification of Experience

A focus on personal experience and the embracing of relativism are common features of today's society (Adorno 1973; MacIntyre 1984). Many communication writings still begin with the claim that meaning is in people, even though the theories on which such an idea were based have been largely dismissed as inadequate and misleading. More sophisticated reader-response theories that focus on subjective interpretation processes might on the surface appear to be concerned with alternative value systems but often have the opposite effect. Private decisionalism and relativism often appear as being open to others but usually function to preclude questioning of normal routines and assure closure of experience. The produced identity is taken as a given rather than a social formation, and the acceptance of the privilege of the personal precludes the examination of that social formation. The proclamation in interaction that the issue is "a matter of opinion" is a frequent casual move used to end the discussion. From the standpoint of participation, this proclamation is where discussion should begin. The difference between different people's opinions represents the opportunity to escape from self-blinders (from opinion) and indicates that more is to be learned about the issue. In fact it represents a major reason to seriously talk at all.

The micropolitics of opinion protection is important. When meaning is personalized, difference of opinion can be resolved only in power politics rather than in examining the politics of opinion formation—an activity that forms opinion as something to be had and a particular opinion. When democracy becomes opinion polls, participative interaction has no place. It is always too late and precluded. Further, the individual is blamed for effects of social institutions. In the same sense that televised violence could be excused since viewing prohibition is a family issue and interpretations of violent acts are individual, both the television production of meaning and responsibility can be precluded at once. Democracy falls to a false assumption of private interpretive processes.

Meaning Denial and Plausible Deniability

Every expression has several possible meanings; such is inevitable in the structure of interaction. Meaning denial happens when one possible interpretation of a statement is both placed in the interaction and denied as meant. The most obvious interpersonal example of this is when someone shouts at you and then proclaims that they are not angry. A similar process is nearly always present with inappropriate sexual innuendo in corporate talk. A message is present and disclaimed, said and not said. The effect is to shift meaning production to a positioned listener, thus enabling the produced speaker control without responsibility and precluding the critical examination of what was said (because it was not said). The listeners respond to the "message" based only on their own produced meanings, but in a context where, if they do not respond to it, the message can be re-evoked as if it were clearly said (i.e., "I don't care what I said, you knew I was angry"). Consent and unowned control are built into such practices.

Eisenberg (1984) affirmed the significance of multiple meaning in corporations in his treatment of the strategic use of ambiguity. He argued that ambiguous messages and the deniability of formal messages are extremely effective means of control. Especially since he intended this positively, his evidence is particularly useful in exemplifying the possibilities of conflict suppression and discursive closure. Eisenberg did not miss the ethical issues involved, but his treatment of them is clearly worth quoting:

> It is easy to imagine the ethical problems that might result from the misuse of ambiguity. In the final analysis, however, both the effectiveness and ethics of any particular communication strategy are relative to the goals and values of the communicators in the situation. The use of more or less ambiguity is in itself not good or bad, effective or ineffective; whether a strategy is ethical depends upon the ends to which it is used, and whether it is effective depends upon the goals of the individual communicators. (239)

Obviously Eisenberg does not see open participation as a value in itself, nor strategy itself as a concern. Clearly his own study had values including the preservation of privileged positions. One wonders how to read his position if strategic ambiguity advances some ends and goals over others, and these same goals are the sole remaining ones used to determine ethics and effectiveness. The neutralization of means is significant and will be discussed later as an important part in the maintenance of managerial advantage.

The logic of ambiguity and meaning denial is institutionalized with new legal rules creating a defense of plausible deniability. Here the test of product liability or plant safety is determined not by critical investigation of adequate testing and appropriate participation in decisions, but rather by the claim that one might not have reasonably known of such a danger. Such a position produces hidden talk, avoidance of exploration, disowned expression and knowledge, and sets in motion a web of concealments. We have orders without orders, knowledge without knowing, practice without intention. The responsible subject disappears but not in the sense of pluralistic subjectivity. Rather the subject hides behind its own shadow.

Legitimation

Legitimation appears in the rationalization of decisions and practices through the invocation of higher order explanatory devices. Such devices make sense out of difficult-to-interpret activities and conceal contradictions and conflict. They attach a higher order value where one's own values might lead to different choices. Habermas (1975), following Weber, has shown that motivation and relatively high productivity have been sustained in the Western world more by the supportive existence of the Protestant work ethic than by intrinsic qualities of the work experience. The invocation of values of hard work, long hours, and stress as evidence of salvation covers up inadequacies in the reward structure and qualities of the work experience. A largely irrational work experience is rationalized through discursively reproduced value principles based on a nearly forgotten and rarely critically examined religious doctrine. As the power of these principles wane, motivation and productivity appear more directly related to the actual work relations. The same analysis could of course be applied to the Japanese. Here concepts of authority, tradition, and honor perform much the same function.

As these grander master values and historical narratives lose their command, newer and more specific ones take their place. Jehenson (1984) demonstrated how effectiveness, excellence, and expertise become new "moral fictions" used in much the same way as the older ones to stop value clarification and lead to commitments and actions that are beneficial to certain dominant groups. Even more specifically, Hannan and Freeman (1977, 128), among others, have concurred that corporate goal statements are more often used to make decisions appear acceptable and legitimate than to guide decisions and action. The reasons for decisions are often different from the reasons given for them. Obviously this gap is political. Here we are interested not simply in how the person giving the reason may gain, but in its effects on the construction of meaning and open choice making.

Pacification

Democracy in the participative sense requires the capacity to mutually solve problems through exploration of different points of view and alternative actions. Pacification describes the process by which conflictual discussion is diverted or subverted through an apparently reasonable attempt to engage in it. In this sense it is a fooler like a pacifier. Messages that pacify tend to discount the significance of the issue, the solvability of the issue, or the ability of the participant to do anything about the issue. Thus discussion is made either trivial, implying that the issues are not worth the effort, or futile, implying that the magnitude of the issue exceeds the limits of capacity. We can all recall how effective such a strategy was in initially avoiding the problems of gender-linked job-classification labels. The jokes said that gender-linked terms were trivial, the opposition said that they were too pervasive. The same is of course occurring with the campaigns for equal pay for equivalent work. The process is not limited to major issues, but is a significant daily practice—what will be called a "micropractice" of power. For example, if an employee requests a raise because of personal need and quality of work, the supervisor could potentially pacify at least temporarily by talking about how many people are out of work and the poor salaries others are receiving. While the employee's claim may now seem trivial in contrast, the minimization has subverted the conflict conception and discussion. Or on the contrary, the supervisor can expand the issue by discussing the company's financial situation, uncertainties in the economy, and effects of the matrix of other salaries. These of course are not irrelevant issues. They work precisely because they are relevant, but they divert attention away from the things that the interactants can change (e.g., the allocation of resources within a unit) to the things that cannot be changed (the state of the general economy).

In complex social settings, both types of claims have a plausible appeal—what is "really so bad" and how could we possibly deal with the size and complexity of most problems confronting us? The debilitating effect of recurring pacification is great. The development and strength of the individual are stripped away along with the possibility of mutual decision making—that is, in the loss of democracy and individual freedom.

Argyris (1986) demonstrated how this type of conflict and solution avoidance can become systemic in corporations in what he called a *defensive routine*. His analysis utilizes concepts similar to the topical avoidance and meaning denial discussed earlier, now placed in a "skilled" strategy of "chaos" production. He suggests four steps in this routine: (1) Design an obviously ambiguous statement that the receiver recognizes as ambiguous but does not question, (2) ignore any inconsistencies in the message, (3) make the ambiguity and inconsistencies undiscussable, and (4) make the undiscussability undiscussable. The culture of chaos and inability to deal with significant problems can become routinized. Systems are then created so that members confront chaos production as the norm for appropriate behavior; in fact, they become practiced and skilled at it. The strategic quality thus becomes doubled. The unowned, routinized strategy of chaos production protects the corporation from examination, discussion, and possible change. And the individual use of the strategy becomes part of the individual's strategy for advancement. In the logic of the distorted system, the individual must produce chaos to be advanced as he or she works hard to solve problems.

CHAPTER 8

The Rise of the
Modern Corporate Form

> The centralization of power in the hands of
> management that organisational giants
> make possible...poses a challenge to democ-
> racies. An efficient admininistrative machin-
> ery vests tremendous power in the hands of
> a few—be they corporate managers, govern-
> mental officials, military officers, party boss-
> es or union leaders—and thereby undermine
> the sovereignty of the many to whom the
> few in a democracy are expected to be
> responsible. Acquiring knowledge about
> bureaucratic organisations is an important
> first step in meeting the threat they pose for
> democratic institutions.
> (Peter Blau and W. Richard Scott 1963, 15)

Work is a central human activity, not only in terms of the total
amount of time spent in it, but also in its relation to social and
personal identity. The workplace and its organization is not just
a human product for the accomplishment of certain functions;
it produces people as well as information, goods, and services. I
have argued that the workplace is a potential site of conflict
over experience and personal identity as well as products, the
environment, and our collective good. The material and discursive structure of the workplace must be understood in order to
understand corporate conflicts and their resolution or suppression. The modern workplace is a historical construction. Investigating the condition in which it could be constructed helps in
understanding the processes of its communicational reproduc-

tion. Many organizational configurations for work and the workplace exist today; none is as important as the publicly capitalized, dispersed ownership, multiunit corporation. Most of the analysis here will focus on this form, owing to the number of people who actually work within them, their effects on competitive work organizations, and the consequences of their decisions for the society as a whole. Clearly this form of organization did not have to exist. Certain conditions made it possible, but human actions and choices both produced and continually reproduce these organizations. But as they have developed, they have also created their own conditions supporting and even necessitating their continuation. The interest here is in the nature of this form, partly as distinguishable from forms that preceded it (and that at times provide the grounds for justification), and the internal configuration of control.

Who holds control, how and on what basis do they hold control, and to what ends is this control directed, are all central questions. Organizational research often treats the modern corporation and the managerial control of them as a naturally occurring, rather than a politically created, form. Consequently, the questions of power and control become narrowed and understood often only from a presumed neutral managerial point of view. In this chapter I will first consider accounts of the effects of organizational forms on human identity and development through a reexamination of Marx's treatment of industrialization and later analyses of the structure of work and control. Second, I will examine the historical development of the modern corporate form to show the forces that shaped it, the historical emergence of the roles and consciousness given in it, and the development of managerial interests as dominant.

Exploitation and Coercion

The works of Marx on the historical development of industrialization and capitalism still provide the most complete treatment of power and control in organizations and the relation of work to human identity. Marx's conceptions changed in his own writings and have continued to be reinterpreted. Despite the changes, however, a core legacy continues to drive applications and interpretations. There are many ways to present this legacy. Since Marx's formulations as well as many of the disputes thereafter are quite familiar, we will not belabor them here. Rather let me briefly sketch what Marx would tell us of the workplace.

Essentially, the workplace is composed of both means and mode of production. The means of production are the processes of work itself, including available technologies, job design, raw materials, and the skills of workers. In Marx's view, industrialization as a new means of production had brought with it dehumanization and alienation from work and work products. Human identity is concretized in the making of a product. Identity cannot be situated in mass production. Further, with capitalist industrialization, workers no longer sold a produced product, but sold themselves as product producers. Hence, the division of labor, the treatment of labor as a commodity, and the separation of the individual from her or his product produced a fragmented, lost person, estranged from her or his own production activities (Marx 1964).

The mode of production is the complex economic and social relationships that exist among parties of the production process. Economically the capitalist mode of production expropriated surplus labor from the owners of that labor. The amount of this surplus could be calculated by determining the difference between the value of the product and what was actually paid for the labor used to produce it (including the labor embodied in making the equipment used in the production process and so forth). Such calculation makes sense if you start from a labor theory of value. To Marx, the surplus value of labor was hidden from both workers and capitalists. The capitalist would understand the realization of profit as coming from the investment in the plant and equipment, with the amount of profit determined by market conditions rather than from unpaid labor. The worker being paid a wage would not be in a position to determine the portion of the value of the product that was a result of his or her labor, and hence could not recognize unpaid labor. Labor was a commodity like other commodities having an exchange value on the market rather than being the source of all product value.

The capitalist mode of production also fixed social relations. The owners of their own labor and the owners of capital entered into the contract differently. Essentially, the worker was placed at a great disadvantage by her or his historical situation. The lack of means of production and the bodily necessity for subsistence during the time of production meant that the worker always bargained and worked under duress (Marx 1906, 80). Hence, exploitation and coercion characterized the work process. The roles of owners and workers were not of their own creation but were produced and reproduced out of historical forms of domination. The means and mode of production at each historical moment form an infrastructure determining other aspects of social relations.

Although it was hidden, the historical situation created continued conflict between the interests of workers and capitalists. These tensions were largely kept in check by the production of a superstructure. The superstructure consisted of the values, laws, rules, ideology, and institutions that both hid the actual conditions under which people worked and governed people's conduct according to capitalist needs. Such a position has been greatly strengthened and essentially rewritten by Gramsci and later Althusser, as has already been discussed.

Marx believed that with the continuing accumulation of capital and the growing gap between the living conditions of capitalists and workers, ultimately workers would realize their true interest and revolt, thus transforming the economic order. Explanations for why this did not take place range from the identification of flaws in Marx's analysis, to descriptions of the manner in which the development of the welfare state has kept the workers' condition tolerable, to the examination of the production of powerful ideological structures obscuring the conditions of exploitation. Unfortunately this preoccupation with a determinist and political reading of Marx has led most to either overlook or distort Marx's useful analysis of control of the labor process and its consequences for human identity formation.

Braverman has been the most significant figure in reclaiming this aspect of Marx's analysis. In *Labor and Monopoly Capital* (1974) he rehabilitated Marx's theory of the labor process through an insightful analysis of the contemporary work situation. Because his work is also familiar to most, I will highlight only a few central points here.

First, the labor process is largely similar in all industrial nations,including the United States and the Soviet Union, with regard to job design and relations among different segments of the work force. Capitalist work relations hold independently of political ideologies.

Second, technological developments, the rise of the service sector, and the increased portion of the economy given to management have not created a new distinct class structure or class identity. In many respects these expanded occupational areas structurally reproduced familiar characteristics of the production labor processes.

Third, and most significantly, degradation of work is ongoing across occupational areas. Contrary to the popular perception that industrial nations are producing a more highly educated and skilled labor force and that continued technological development will require even greater skill on the part of the worker, Braverman demonstrated that "deskilling" was evident in all economic sectors. Essentially, the separation of *conception* from *execution* in production processes and increased division of labor removes knowledge from work and creates a degraded, alienated workforce. With "rationalization" (the application of science to work) all modern office work becomes increasingly clerical, and service occupations become laboring activities outside a physical plant. Others (see Heydebrand 1977) have documented similar changes in the professions. The existence of standard rules of decision and effort initially adds uniformity and efficiency to the work process. But the inability to conceptualize and discuss rule alternatives creates a disciplinary structure whereby identity and experience are singular and imaginary.

To Braverman, the degradation of work and workers is an expected outcome of the drive for capital accumulation. However, while his extensive descriptions of the changes in the nature of work are compelling, his brief analysis of how these changes are carried out are not. Viewing managerial control as motivated and accomplished by a desire for capital accumulation leaves much unanswered. In this regard, his analysis of the control by owners and the linking of upper management with monied interests is particularly strained. It is only partially true that upper levels of management come from wealthy families and probably not true that managerial decisions can be explained by family of origin. Several questions remain. Why do members of the society willingly or unwillingly participate in such a system? What are the mechanisms by which continued participation by workers is insured? And why, if the processes of degradation and alienation are ongoing, does the reported experience of the work force only occasionally recognize this fate? Consent rather than coercion appears to better represent the modern worker's relation to the production apparatus.

Ideology and Manufactured Consent

Such questions as these have driven the work of Burawoy. In *Manufacturing Consent* (1979), Burawoy explored two essential

issues. First, how are the social relations of the capitalist enterprise produced and reproduced? As he argued, organizations are
not simply given in their current form, and they do not simply
persist through time; they have to be continually produced and
reproduced. The capitalist system cannot autonomously and
anonymously accomplish these tasks; they are done by some-
body, somehow. What is of interest is the political relations at
the "point of production," rather than how a capitalist economy produces specific work relations.

Second, the worker, both in Marx's time and even more
clearly today, freely participates in the labor process, giving
support and consent to existing forms of control. What are the
mechanisms of organizing this consent in the activity of work?
How can the experience of the workers themselves be accounted for? This issue is organized for Burawoy around a rather
unique question: quoting Lynd, "Why do workers work as hard
as they do?"

Burawoy argued that both management/worker conflict
and worker consent are organized in the work process itself—
the relations *in* production. Understanding how this relationship occurs in the workplace requires an understanding of the
political and ideological realms of the organization of production. The central issue is how people represent and try to fulfill
their interests in the organization. Representation and fulfillment of interests requires choices arrived at by some reasoning
process. To Burawoy (1979), workers, in making their choices,
can be seen neither as simply irrational nor as economically
rational. Rationality itself is "a product of the specific organization of production and is part and parcel of the factory 'culture'" (4). The fact that workers participate in making choices
generates consent. To the extent that their choices and reasoning processes are not of their own making or in their own best
interest, we have domination.

The key issue is that of reasoning and "consent." In most
organizational theory, consent has been assumed to derive
from something else but has not itself been subject to analysis.
Burawoy, quoting Gouldner (1954), argued: "For Weber, therefore, authority was given consent because it was legitimate,
rather than being legitimate because it evoked consent. For
Weber, therefore, consent is always a datum to be taken for
granted rather than a problem whose sources had to be traced.
In consequence, he never systematically analyzed the actual
social processes which either generated or thwarted the emer-

gence of consent" (223). Consent is a far more effective means of control than coercion. How does it emerge? The answer for Burawoy rests in a conception of ideology and experience developed in the work process itself.

Burawoy, following Gramsci (1971), argued that the experience of a people, and not just their actual situation, is an active force in decision making. Experience is not a personal or subjective thing but arises out of the concrete material situation, one's position. However, the conditions for the production of experience are hidden, and hence it appears personal, natural, and inevitable. In this sense, as shown in chapter 5, experience can be said to be ideological. The conditions of experience production cannot be assessed. Ideology is not imposed on people as a disguise for their true interests but both expresses and is produced out of their life activities. As Burawoy (1979) argued: "Ideology is, therefore, not something manipulated at will by agencies of socialization—schools, family, church, and so on— in the interests of a dominant class. On the contrary, these institutions elaborate and systematize lived experience and only in this way become centers of ideological dissemination. Moreover, dominant classes are shaped by ideology more than they shape it. To the extent that they engage in active deception, they disseminate propaganda, not ideology" (17–18). Ideology is outside what is in one's head. It serves as an organizing force for theories, attitudes, values, and so forth. Individuals' and groups' realizations of their interests and the reasoning process for accomplishing their interests emerge out of ideology. In this sense, interests, choices, and the giving of consent are produced out of the concrete relations in the work process held in place by a capitalist mode of production.

For Burawoy, the modern workplace differs from early industrial ones in that the worker has acquired a type of decisional autonomy and limits have been placed on the coercive power of owners and management. But this situation does not enable the worker to recognize the exploitation through unpaid labor. Workers are less constrained in the pursuit of their interests, but the ideological structure of interests leads them to spontaneously constrain the pursuit of their own interests to the benefit of profit, perhaps to an extent greater than management could ever require. As Burawoy (1979) argued, the changes in the relations in production "have offered workers a very limited but nevertheless critical freedom in their adaptation to the labor process. The rise of rules and, with them, constraints on managerial intervention, have opened up an area of choice within which workers can constitute work as a game. Workers are sucked into the game as a way of reducing the level of deprivation. But participation has the consequence of generating consent to the rules, which define both the conditions of choice and the limits of managerial discretion. Thus, it is not the rules themselves but the activities they circumscribe that generate consent" (199).

Moving Out of the Marxist Tradition

Burawoy and Braverman provide an essential theoretical context from which we can develop and interpret further analyses, but their works have limitations. First, both authors remain preoccupied with a certain category of workers. Without a doubt, Burawoy (1979) produced a penetrating analysis of piece-rate laborers. While this population is significant, the nature of their work is hardly representative of either the work relations or production activities of the modern work force. The demographics of the modern work force virtually demand that an adequate theory incorporate an accounting of the activities and situations of managerial and professional groups as well as laborers. Certainly analogies can be drawn between different groups, but each occupies a different structural place in the organization, with distinct interests. Further, class division does not exhaust the concern with group differences in power, and conditions of domination and class distinction are as much produced by the modern organization as class interest is a critique of it. The modern concern with gender and women's struggle to achieve significant roles in organizations cannot be trivialized or simply reduced to salary differences and conditions of employment, even as significant as those are.

Second, Burawoy's and Braverman's taken-for-granted conception of the management group does not match well with the empirical nature of modern organizations. In both their analyses, management is treated as an extension of owners, administering and making decisions in owners' interests. Conceiving of such a unity hides distinct interest differences between the two groups and misleads the examination of the motivational foundation for many corporate decisions.

Third, both the means and relations of production have a significantly different character from that suggested in even a revisionist Marxist analysis. If we expand the focus of our attention to workers outside the traditional production process, we find different constraints on the nature of the work activity. Although Braverman (1974) may be partially right that the service and information labor force is "deskilled" and economically exploited, the technological infrastructure that supports this condition is different from that supporting the traditional labor process. As shall be developed later, such exploitation may be better explained by the domination of a particular cognitive interest than by a class interest, and hence might restrict everyone to no one's benefit.

Finally, even a weakened notion of economic determinism supplemented by an expanded conception of ideology does not account well for the decisional structure of most modern organizations. The image of modern corporations as driven by a desire for profit benefiting a capitalist group does not match empirical analyses of modern corporate life. Organizations must be understood in a complex fashion. Economic conditions cannot be seen as an independent external force, but become one of several competing logics or discursive practices within organizations. To understand and utilize such a conception and to gather the full benefit of Braverman's and Burawoy's analyses, we must rethink the nature of organizations and the relations of production in modern society.

The Rise of Managerial Capitalism

Without a doubt the nature of the modern organization is protected from rational assessment. But its nature is not only or primarily hidden from the worker for the sake of the production of surplus value. For all groups—owners, managers, workers, and even the Marxist—the concept that ownership equals control organizes both thought and action and obscures the actual relations of production. Historically, such an equation was probably accurate, but many theorists have long argued that management has usurped most practical owner power (Berle and Means 1932; Burnham 1972); yet the continued belief in the equation undoubtedly serves important functions for each group. An adequate discussion of organizations today, however, requires rethinking the relations of production.

Chandler (1977) has presented the most complete and detailed analysis of the historical development of the modern corporation in the United States. Others have duplicated this analysis in other industrial nations (Chandler and Daems 1980). As Chandler (1977) summarized his analysis:

> The institution [modern business organizations] appeared where managerial hierarchies were able to monitor and coordinate the activities of a number of business units more efficiently than did market mechanisms. It continued to grow so that these hierarchies of increasingly professional managers might remain fully employed. It emerged and spread, however, only in those industries and sectors whose technology and markets permitted administrative coordination to be more profitable than market coordination. Because these areas were at the center of the American economy and because professional managers replaced families, financiers, or their representatives as decision makers in these areas, modern American capitalism became managerial capitalism. (11)

Several portions of Chandler's analysis are significant to understanding the internal relations of corporations today and to informing a critical analysis of them. Four points are key here: (1) the conditions enabling the continued corporate expansion, (2) the development of the professional manager, (3) the separation of management and ownership, and (4) the focus on long-term stability and growth rather than profit maximization.

Expansion of the Corporate Form

The corporate form developed and grew in those areas where the combination of technologically driven increases in production and expanded markets, based on population growth, transportation improvements, and new communication systems, increased the advantage of administrative over market coordination. As the multiunit organization freed itself partially from market demand, the ability to administer became the primary limit to size and expansion of control. Communication systems, thus, became a central determinant of the spread of control. The more sophisticated the communication technology, the less central the market conditions in determining the nature and scope of the enterprise. We see here the first step of the move from an economically driven capitalism to a communication-driven one.

Both communication technologies and corporate form have continued to develop since Chandler's analysis and have largely followed suggested lines. New technologies have enabled the development of massive transnational corporations with numerous satellite operations. Key to this has been the continued development of the coordination and control capacities of computer-assisted telecommunications. With the development of "high-speed management," coordination capacity far exceeds the market as the constraint on expansion (Cushman 1990). Companies such as General Electric primarily escape classical market forces by quickly entering and exiting different markets. Pricing in these contexts is more determined by the speed of entering a new market than by cost or competition, since exit takes place at the point of competitive pricing. Such systems place far higher demands on shared values and codified information and tend to eliminate human mediation in the form of middle management. The substitution of decisional/execution rules for conception and decision brings "deskilling" to the heart of the management process.

The Career Manager

Chandler emphasized the increased reliance on managerial training, skills, and movement up the corporate ladder. But certainly more was at stake than this. The development of educational programs and a professional identity transformed the character of managerial knowledge and helped foster a unique managerial ideology. As Merkle (1980) showed in her tracing of the legacy of the scientific management movement, such an ideology did not spontaneously arise out of the society or as a representation of a natural class interest but arose as a result of a massive and systematic attempt to create a form of organization. Even in the Soviet Union, Lenin argued strongly for utilizing scientific management as a means for progress (Merkle 1980, pp.105-9). Taylorism was largely accepted in the industrial world as a material practice and an ideology. Despite the many criticisms of rational models of organizations, scientific management still exists as the primary explicit system of decision making, the primary legitimation for decisions, and the primary defense of managerial decision making. This is seen most clearly in areas like operations research, but it is importantly reproduced in micropractices such as data collection and accounting procedures. This will be developed later.

As Weber (1978) showed more generally in his analysis of bureacratic rationality, the impulse and initial effect of Taylor's work and the professionalization of management was emancipating. "Rational" grounds for decisions replaced traditional practices and values. The codification of procedures offered protection to workers as well as stability and control to managers. As membership in the management group and promotions became, at least partially, based on training and skill, upward mobility became possible for working-class individuals. The corporate organization was opened for a new kind of discourse, one based on reason and consensual rules. But as happens often in society, capricious decision making, discrimination, and privilege are overcome by fixed procedures and rational processes, which in turn contain their own hidden values that generate new forms of domination.

The actual micropractice of this new form of domination is the subject of later sections, but let me sum up here by saying that as management is transformed into administration the product/by-product relation in their work effort is transformed. Initially, bureaucratic rules are produced as a means to better goal accomplishment, with professional advancement and ease of management as by-products. In professionalization, procedures are evoked for control and efficiency in themselves, with the ends for which they are evoked becoming both taken for granted and obscured. The desire for control because it will produce increased profit becomes transformed into a desire for control that might fortuitously increase profits. The change is much like the professionalized student who changes from seeking learning with grades as a by-product to seeking grades with learning as a potential by-product.

The Separation of Ownership and Management

Not only does administration replace aspects of the marketplace in production decisions, but the control of the organizations shifts from profit-centered owners to career-centered managers. Structurally owners have the potential for control through a board of directors; this potential is real even in cases where no group of shareholders holds a large number of shares (Pitelis and Sugden 1986; Vance 1983). But in practice nearly all decision making is in the hands of career managers. There are a number of reasons for this. Most importantly, as will be developed later, control is widely dispersed in the complex modern business unit. Most control takes place through standard local practices, and much of the fact production happens in small decisions of how to word data-collection forms and invisible accounting practices. In fact, boards may well serve more as a way for managers to monitor and affect the external environment than as a means of control over the internal working of the corporation. Thus, boards often extend managerial control more often than they limit it (Tricker 1984, 103).

Further, stockholders tend to be disinclined and/or unable to influence corporate decisions of the companies they "own." Most owner representatives on boards of directors are part-time, with primary obligations elsewhere. Their ability and desire to exercise control is at most occasional. Management through proxy frequently controls a majority of the votes. And most shareholders find it far easier to sell their interest in a company than to try to exercise control in it. As Vogel (1978) argued regarding the Security and Exchange Act of 1934, "The paucity of proxy challenges proposed during the Act's first thirty-five years suggests that the floor of the stock exchange rather than that of the annual meeting is the arena most frequently employed to define the relationship between management and shareholders" (76). But even if they wished to influence major decisions, the vast number of owners have limited power. Necessary information is frequently not available or is greatly influenced in its construction by the management group. Institutional stockholders in most cases have far more potential to influence corporate decisions. But significantly, most board members even representing these groups are themselves managers of other corporate units with many of the same prevailing logics of decision making as those of management. The boards of subsidiary companies are even in a weaker position. As Tricker (1984) demonstrated, "Whilst the boards of directors of the subsidiary companies carry out a de jure accountability function and are the focus of regulatory activity, the reality of the business decision stream and the exercise of executive power flows through different channels" (65).

Shareholders' attempts to influence corporate policy during significant events have usually been failures, particularly when they concerned noneconomic issues. The famed "Campaign to Make General Motors Responsible" in the early seventies, for example, met with both legal and practical difficulties. The legal issues resulted from the SEC exclusion of several of the proxy proposals based on Rule 14a-8 of the SEC: "Those which

by state law are not proper subject for action by security holders; those related to the conduct of the ordinary business operation of the user; and promotions of political, social or similar
causes" (Vance 1983, 145–46). While the rules individually prohibit abuses and shareholder actions that violate legal constraints on corporate activity, collectively they assure that corporate managers' values and practices are only challenged in
narrowly prescribed areas. Further, even when challenged,
management has many advantages. Such movements have to
confront the managerial group's ability to publish and distribute glossy "position papers" filled with selective proprietary
data developed and distributed at corporate expense. And most
importantly, there is no widely-shared shareholder sense that
they should or would want to be involved in even basic policy
decisions. Actually, "Campaign GM" succeeded better than
most. Even though they solidly lost in the voting on even the
two proposals that were allowed, GM did implement the major
aspects of each.

Thus, management's decisional prerogatives may be legitimized through the conception of management as an extension
of ownership, but more often managers actually function as an
independent group actualizing particular interests of their own.
The differences between the interests of management and those
of owners, for example, is vivid in analysis of takeover initiative
difference between managers with significant company stock
holdings and those without. As Friend and Lang (1988)
showed, managers with significant holdings were far more
financially prudent than those without. In takeover battles,
shareholders nearly always lose (Weidenbaum 1988) (as do
lower level managers, workers, and the community). The clean-
est read of the data says that owner interests *may* constrain the
upper managerial desire for size, control, and self-advancement.
Unfortunately, little can be said with confidence about the
amount and effect of managerial self-interest. Large amounts of
personal political activity are casually mentioned in regard to
organizations, but studying the effects of self-interest politics is
largely taboo (Ralston 1985), or they are discussed as inherent
attributes of corporate life (Culbert and McDonough 1980;
Morgan 1986, 148ff.). Rarely are moral issues raised in these
discussions, or their relation to larger social political issues.

A critical analysis based on a labor theory of value fails here,
too, since the primary structure is not capitalist exploitation of
surplus labor for profit. In some respects, modern diffused own-

ership through public stock holding partly meets Marx's ideal. Significantly, even if stock ownership were equitably distributed in the society, domination and exploitation would still prevail through administration. Worker buyouts have rarely affected basic management practice or means of control (Estrin, Geroski, and Stewart 1988). Owner interests are as difficult to represent as those of workers. Such is, of course, also vividly clear in industrialized communist countries where, although ownership may be public, workplace relations are much the same as in all other industrial nations. The Yugoslavian example was as unique to Eastern-bloc countries as the Scandinavian experiments were to the Western world. Managerial interests compete with and dominate the interests of other interested parties, including workers and owners, and do so by evoking accepted, but no longer relevant, social values. Ownership is certainly not irrelevant, but it is not the central issue of the day.

The severing of management from owners (and others) historically developed most completely in the United States. Clearly both structural issues and cultural ones are responsible. Attempts to change these basic relations have only occasionally been successful. The Corporate Democracy Act of 1980, if it had passed, would have been a significant legislative change. This legislation, proposed out of the Senate Subcommittee on Citizens' and Shareholders' Rights and Remedies, would have opened the federal courts to shareholders and other stakeholders for redress for injury by nonperformance to standard and would have developed a constituency board of directors for major corporations. It failed.

Even more fully developed legislation has been in place in Europe for some time. Owing to overseas subsidiaries, many U.S. corporations have been involved with alternative governance forms—the most well known being the German *Mitbestimmung*, which assures some worker participation in corporate governance. Except for the Nazi's dismantlement of it, the concept has been in place for over 150 years. U.S. corporations fully borrowed the Prussian concept of order and bureaucracy but not of participation and democracy. The European societies generally share a cultural understanding that production is for social good and that all stakeholders should have some "voice." This is not to say that managers are not still structurally privileged, but the different kinds of "owners" (owners of labor, needs, and supplies rather than simply of capital) do enjoy more rights and opportunity to direct decisions.

In significant cases of corporate board restructuring in the United States which are usually motived by economic conditions, as in the Chrysler case, boards have been recomposed, but board/management relations have been only partially modified. Labor members on boards are frequently unclear about their role regarding "labor issues" (Vance 1983, 219ff). Boards are frequently prohibited from being involved in "relations at the point of production," which are central to everyday-life democracy. In worker buyouts, the owner/manager separation is retained along with the worker/manager one, leading more often to strikes against themselves than increased owner or worker participation. In most of the new board models, the owners do not have more say but become part of an expanded board that stands in a reasonably weak position regarding management, especially with respect to the actual micropractices of power, which we will examine in the next chapter. In common evaluations of the success of changes, managerial criteria of continuity and efficiency are often used rather than more return on investment or socially better products and services (see Pierce and Furo 1990 for development).

The Corporation as an End in Itself and Managerial Control

A new form of workplace identity and knowledge was formed as the practical interest of the entrepreneur and capitalist became transformed into a technical interest of the manager. For the owner the corporation is a means to profit; professional managers are interested in the long-term stability and growth of the enterprise (or at least their portion of it). Certainly such a change in the basis for decisions is significant. Many have documented the move away from profit as a central focus of decision making, most notably Galbraith (1967), March and Simon (1958), and Cyert and March (1963). In this view, since business decisions are made under conditions of uncertainty and constraint, the driving force of decisions is not "a single profit goal to be optimised in the long term but a process of satisfying a range of, potentially conflicting, interests, including a comfortable life for the decision maker" (Tricker 1984, 101). Pfeffer (1981) would even more strongly argue that managers have very little control over the factors influencing profitability, but far more over internal relations and symbolic events.

There is a modern shift in logic in the organization that has significant implications for the people who work there. In

Marx, as well as in Braverman and Chandler, the focus on economic issues leads to an underemphasis on control for its own sake and on the significance of symbolic manipulation in the drive for control in strange self-referential systems. As Prokesch wrote dramatically for the *New York Times* (cited in Schaef and Fassel 1988, 3): "The new order eschews loyalty to workers, products, corporate structure, business, factories, communities, even the nation. All such allegiances are viewed as expendable under the new rules. With survival at stake, only market leadership, strong profits and a high stock price can be allowed to matter." Like the self-referential system in defense, fear of loss of survival creates the instability that produces the control that creates the instability.... The fear of loss of survival can appear to justify much, but the system itself defines what is at stake in corporate survival (the company, the manager, or meaningful work) and creates the conditions out of its own working form where survival is threatened. The apparent economic rationale hides much about managerial interest and the justification of such extreme reactions.

The reported focus on profits and stock prices, as well as the emergent focus on long-term growth and stability, may obscure the extent to which managers make decisions based primarily on managerial ideology, including emphasis on efficiency for its own sake and personal career gains rather than wider social interests. As Selznick (1957) argued, the pursuit of profit often becomes subordinated to the attainment of efficiency in the bureaucratic organization. Or more vividly, as Bagehot (cited in Tricker 1984, 101) proclaimed, "Bureaucrats will care more for the routine than for results." The uncertainty of the business choice leaves the manager in a precarious position. What is controllable is making sure that one is oneself covered. Therefore standard practices, routine solutions, short-term gains in efficiency, and the utilization of presumed shared values become ends in themselves, since they are rational in the manager's life even if not economically rational for the corporation. What can be known are the effects on self and career; what often cannot be known is the effects on the company's profitability. The recent wave of corporate buy-back of stocks not only assures higher stock prices (including shares owned by managers) and freedom from potential Board of Director scrunity, but creates a corporation with, in the extreme case, a life totally its own, that is management's own. The short-term character of such decisions, since the investment is not in new products or production processes but rather self-purchase, hurts nearly every stakeholder except upper management.

Weick (1979) and Jehenson (1984), among others, clearly distinguish between the reasons *for* managerial decisions and the reasons *given for* them. Numerous values direct decisions, though they are often hidden by avowed economic ones. They range from interest in increased organizational size and control and implementation of state-of-the-art technologies despite mixed balance sheets, to daily preference for easily justified decisions (owing to common practices) over situationally better ones. The existence of a managerial prerogative means that the "extrarational" values of managers have an effect on corporate decision making while those of other groups are excluded based on "rational" criteria of efficiency and profitability. For example, the managerial efforts to monitor and control through new communication technologies can cost considerably more than the "waste" and "inefficiency" that they are designed to control. Diseconomies and of social costs of scale are rarely taken as seriously as promised economies of scale.

Thus structurally, the manager's identity and interests differ from those of owners and workers. As Marx demonstrated, with the rise of industrial capitalism, the worker's identity became fragmented as they were separated from their product, and their labor, rather than their products, became the commodity they sold. A parallel but more extreme fragmentation happens to the manager with the rise of managerial capitalism. In an idealized version, the managers' primary product is themselves. Their subjectivity is embodied more in a position than in a product. The measure of accomplishment is not the self reflected in the product, but in the advancement it achieves. The produced corporate image and self-marketing become central activities of work itself and extend into nonwork areas of life. Corporate and personal identities merge. While the worker seeks freedom——from necessity and for self-fulfillment—and the owner seeks profit, the manager seeks control. Changes in the market, environment, or others pose a threat to the managers identity and need to be brought under administrative control. Stability and growth thus best characterize the optimal conditions under which a manager works. No mission or product can be as important as the survival of self, which often means saving the corporation itself. Both surplus labor and what might be called "surplus capital" are necessary to sustain the career identity of management, the costs of self-marketing, as well as extraordinarily high management salaries.

The managerial interest in control often becomes an end in its own right, even though it is frequently expressed in terms of the outcomes it is to produce. As will be developed, control is the management product and most clearly the one on which individual advancement rests. For a self-referential system, this control is internal, and the external environment itself is made internal. The modern multinational corporation is the most extreme example. As Morgan (1986) argued:

> Of all organizations they come closest to realizing Max Weber's worst fears with regard to how bureaucratic organizations can become totalitarian regimes servicing the interests of elites, where those in control are able to exercise power that is 'practically unshatterable.' Simply put, the name of the multinational game frequently becomes control, control, control. The multinationals readily engage in forms of vertical integration to acquire ownership or control of raw materials and other supplies, and engage in extensive research and marketing to shape consumer preferences. In doing so they make their source of supplies and the markets for their goods a kind of internally administered domain. They also often engage in official and unofficial collusion, developing informal cartels that regulate relations between affiliated organizations, thereby helping stabilize and control aspects of their environment that would otherwise prove uncertain and threatening. (303)

Morgan would rightfully claim that the "degree of social planning and direction appears to have closer links with soviet-style planned economies than with competitive free enterprise" (302). Unfortunately, he contrasts this with the relatively looser controls that rely on familiarity with shared values and norms in Japanese firms. In fact, the control is neither less nor less directed but different in form—it feels like less, it is more sophisticated and effective control (see Parker and Slaughter 1988). Predictably U.S. corporations moved from Prussian forms of control to equally autocratic Japanese forms rather than to an open participatory democracy.

What is gained in these controls is primarily managerial interests in corporate survival rather than other interests. Does this control give better products? Would societies be hurt if multinational corporations failed and were replaced by local ones? Would workers lose jobs if they failed, or would workers have the opportunity for more skilled and stable jobs in emerging corporations? Have investors or society as a whole gained with this control or have only a small segment of them gained? These are of course rhetorical questions. While the fear of a corporation's demise is presented as a jointly held fear, only one group has a clear stake in its maintenance in itself.

The newer issues of competitiveness appear to be used to suggest this managerial interest. The logic of the competitiveness argument suggests a freer hand for management owing to the need to make up for the negative effect of low worker productivity, expensive labor, and federal regulations. The argument misses much in its self-referential logic. The managerial interest in support of particular existing corporations is universalized as everyone's, or at least a national, interest. It overlooks the extent to which the high cost of United States management ("Where U.S. CEOs Have Foreign Rivals Beat." 1990), managerial lack of productivity, and managerial inability to "listen" to the environment has directly contributed to the loss of competitiveness. It also overlooks the indirect effects of managerial control practices in producing a type of labor and laborer (and manager), particularly ones who are deskilled and underutilized. And further, it overlooks the managerial decisions requiring federal intervention in health and safety, environmental protection, and employment practices, *and* the continuation of organizational forms that foster unethical behavior, psychological disorders, and social dislocations that might well necessitate legal intervention. The answer of further (and better) and more autonomous managerial control would appear to be the problem. And perhaps, most importantly, if the real cost of management decisions in the areas of the environment, public health, and worker development were assessed and charged, such corporations might well fail and be replaced by more competitive ones.

This description is, of course, an exaggeration to show the structural force of the managerial condition. Individual managers do make decisions against their careers, and the owner/manager/worker division is never totally clear. For example, many managerial groups have stock-ownership options and profit-sharing plans that partially structure their interests as ownership. But given the rather uncertain predictive relation between particular decisions and the realization of profit and the relatively more direct effects of decisions on career moves, this owner interest remains quite weak.

Management and Interest Representation

Just as Marx could document the significant changes in work life based on industrialization, it is important today to understand such changes based on communication and managerial coordination. With the emergence of managerial capitalism, the modern organization is not well conceived as a site of illegitimate (or legitimate) domination of laborers by owners through managerial coordination. Neither market conditions nor the desire for capital accumulation well explain the process of decision making. In the modern (what has been called "deindustrialized") society, the value of labor and nature of the production process are not as significant as having information and the opportunity to engage in meaningful discourse regarding decisions. Analysis of the tension between capital and labor is less significant than that of the tension within systems allocating opportunities for expression. The modern problem is not monopoly capital but a monopoly of information and dialogue chances, or what Baudrillard (1975) called the "monopoly of the code" (127). Marx's concept of false consciousness gives over naturally to Habermas's concept of systematically distorted communication. The development and implementation of new communication technologies for extended control supports the maintenance and reproduction of a systematically distorted managerial point of view.

The modern organization is potentially a site of struggle by numerous competing needs, perceptions, and identities. Such competition is rarely observed. The conservative position is, of course, that the potential variety of experiences have come to align in the modern corporation, and while each group may have different motives for their actions, they are integrated in modern structures (Parsons 1956; Bell 1960). Rather than pretend that anyone is in a good position to know what anyone's (let alone everyone's) true experiences are, the questions here are different. They might be summarized in this way: Are the structures of discourse such that competing experiential structures can be understood and articulated? Do decision-making processes include competitive experiences? Are there processes that suppress conflict among potentially competing interests? If conditions of inequality exist, how are they justified? When and in what ways are these justifications simple disguises hiding and perpetuating certain identities and experiences at the expense of others?

What is needed is a detailed analysis of how conflict and consent are organized in modern corporate life. The problem is similar to but perhaps more complex than Burawoy's (1979) shop floor. The focus thus far has been general descriptions of the managerial centrality in corporate decisions. This centrality is not simply here once and for all but is actively produced and reproduced. The concern is with how this centrality is maintained at the "point of production"—in the everyday process of working. In order to begin this process I wish to bring prior ideas on the fundamental conflictual nature of experience into the modern corporate context, describing the issues of competing identities, the routinization of conflict, and the motives for its suppression. In the next chapter I will show that a peculiar concept of managerial authority and expertise is key to understanding the centered nature of the managerial reasoning. This will be called "managerialism." The following chapters will show the specific practices by which power operates in the modern corporation, with managerialism being one interesting ideological manifestation.

CHAPTER 9

The "Subject" and Discourse of Managerialism

> What matters at this stage is the construc-
> tion of local forms of community within
> which civility and the intellectual and moral
> life can be sustained through the new dark
> ages which are already upon us. And if the
> tradition of the virtues was able to survive
> the horrors of the last dark ages, we are not
> entirely without grounds for hope. This time
> however the barbarians are not waiting
> beyond some frontiers; they have already
> been governing us for quite some time. And
> it is our lack of consciousness of this that
> constitutes part of our predicament. We are
> waiting not for a Godot, but for another—
> doubtless very different—St. Benedict.
> (Alasdair MacIntyre 1984, 263)

What Chandler (1977) called "the rise of managerial capitalism" is not merely an abstract shifting of control, but more
importantly the development of a new logic and daily practice
of corporations. To distinguish this practice, which "interpellates" managers as a particular type of subject, from the empirical individuals who hold managerial positions, I will call this
new logic and practice "managerialism." In this way I wish to
initially distinguish the practice of managers from "managerial
practice." Later I will take up the complex interrelationship
between them, but first let me turn to managerialism.

The term *managerialism* has been used to differentiate features of the modern organization. Most commonly it has been

used to describe the extent to which managers have usurped owner control of corporations. Certainly this has created much debate, some of which has been reproduced in the past chapter (for review, see Pitelis and Sugden 1986). The debate, which identifies a group or even class supremacy, has several difficulties and can lead us to overlook several features of the modern situation. I wish to suggest that managerialism is a kind of systemic logic, a set of routine practices, and an ideology, rather than the emergence of control by a particular group. In fact, evidence that management groups have gained more control is better explained by widespread managerialism than is defined by it. Scott (1985) defined managerialism as a kind of "orthodoxy," a significant and pathological one. In Scott's words: "Managerialism is one of the main philosophical issues of our time. Its orthodox values trivialize the human essence, diminish human dignity, and widen the gap between a privileged class of managers and the rest of the people" (149).

Managerialism is present as a "discursive genre"—a way of conceptualizing, reasoning through, and discussing events that can be distinguished from potential competitive manners. But it is more than an expressive system; it entails a set of routine practices, real structures of rewards, and a code of representation. It is a way of doing and being in corporations that partially structures all groups and conflicts with, and at times suppresses, each group's other modes of thinking. The logic of managerialism can be articulated by anyone—owners, workers, or society—and defines a place for each of these groups. Labor unions both produce and are produced by a conception of management and the ways of its deployment. Worker ownership changes little in actual corporate thinking and decision making, as long as managerialism as an ideology and practice continues to be reproduced. I hope that it is clear by this point that managerialism exists in relation to actual historical changes that both have produced it and have been produced by it. But managerialism is not necessary, in that the structure and modern corporations could work with other models or logics. The rise of large corporations per se, while fostered by managerialism, do not require it.

Managerialism, as the term is used here, is best seen as a set of discursive moves that interpellates a particular type of subject and produces a particular world. It begins with an imaginary identification where the corporation and management become a unitary identity; its central motif is control; its primary mode of reasoning is cognitive-instrumental; its favored expressive modality is money; and its favored site of reproduction is the *formal* organization. The misrecognition of managerialism as a group or class interest has arisen from inadequate conceptions of interest and power. Ingersoll and Adams (1986) described the pervasive quality of managerialism by describing its presence in the macroculture, the academic subculture, and the managerial subculture as a kind of metamyth. To Ingersoll and Adams (1986) the metamyth has three core elements:

> (1) Eventually all work processes can and should be rationalized, that is, broken into their constitutive parts and so thoroughly understood that they can be completely controlled, (2) the means for attaining organizational objectives deserves maximum attention, with the result that the objectives quickly be subordinated to the means, even to the extent that the objectives become lost or forgotten, and (3) efficiency and predictability are more important than any other consideration. (366)

While different aspects may be more or less popular at any given time, and different groups may invest in each, the three elements have an enduring quality to the extent that it is hard to think of modern management without thinking in these terms. To the extent that the second and third can be actualized, the first becomes more subtle and perhaps less important.

To understand managerialism, I think it is useful to first separate the role of "manager" from the person who holds or is held by the role, and then look at how the role is reenacted or reembodied in daily activities. Since a role is a "sign" in a representational system, we can consider it communicationally as something that produces a distinction and functions to put into play a particular set of discursive sequences. In doing so, we can discuss a type of "subject" with discursively specifiable interests that, while embodied by someone, does not exhaust the potential interests of the empirical actor. This is not to suggest that the person-as-manager has false interest in that role, but he or she has "real" *produced* interests that may at times compete with or suppress other discursively produced interests. This will be developed further in the next chapter. Importantly, no claim is being made for "real" fixed empirical "interests" with which to compare manifest interests. The term *interest* thus refers to a way of thinking about the structure of needs and desires, on the one hand, and the structure (intention, motif) of action, on the other, within particular discursive sequences. The managerial is one such interest. In this sense, an interest is not a property of someone, but a structure that anyone could take on as her or his own to her or his benefit or detriment. Of course, not just anyone can take on a particular position, since our historical context gives a particular one to particular people and not to others.

It should be emphasized that initially these are *positional* rather than *personal* interests. Any individual potentially holds several positional interests—for example, as investor and worker. To the extent that these are conceptualized simultaneously, tension is experienced. The interests of a group of people holding a position are advanced to the extent that the group both realizes and actualizes its interests. The interests of a group of individuals might at times be represented by a dominant interest such as profit for owners or control for managers, but interests of individuals are more complex than this representation. The interests of the individual exceed those resulting from one's structural position. A manager, driven by career advancement and fearing the least inefficiency owing to inconveniences from his or her body, family, co-workers, and friends, can succeed *and* have missed fulfilling other critical needs. The question asked here is not what a person's real needs are, but how does a system of one-sidedness and domination get created and sustained so that other needs are denied or dismissed by either an individual or a group? Ultimately, we are interested in the effects this domination has on the type of products produced, the treatment of the environment, and the development of the citizenry. Finally, although interests are not developed from the psyches of individuals but from historically derived structural positions, it is real people who embody them. The people who get to fill each do not arrive there through nature but out of their chance historical placement. Nevertheless, it is through the concrete expression and action of individuals that such structures are reproduced *or* changed. Let me begin by discussing the characterization of management that becomes the produced and reproduced.

Conflict and the Managerial Interest

The development of the manager in organizations (or better, the organization in managers) was a way to organize conflict.

The manager is "subjected" or positioned in a unique way by the institutionalized organization. Both the coordination and the control functions of the manager centralize potential conflicts between and among individuals and groups carrying out different activities, needing particular resources, wanting limited rewards, and seeking alternative activities and products. In this sense the manager does not so much reduce conflict as locate (and cummulate) it and translate it into resoluble forms. For example, in a simple setting the manager becomes the daily site of the conflict between workers for pay and owners for profit. The idea of contract and fair pay is a translation of the potential daily problem into a routine solution. The conflict is organized and put in its appropriate time and place, it changes from constant to recurring or episodic. In such a model the manager has no particular interest of his or her own but is a pure "medium."

But in this simple form, we see the beginning of a genuine if peculiar managerial interest—an interest in efficiency, rationality, and significantly no visible conflict—all of which are *means* that become *ends* in themselves. In managerialism this motive subdues alternative ones. What was a route to goal accomplishment symbolizes the goal accomplished, and in a self-referential system the symbol becomes the thing sought. In a pure sense the manager need not be concerned with whose or what interests are being mediated—they could be the society's as well as owner's. The primary concern is with translating them into a form of mediation. Pricing becomes a highly effective medium for that, even though it translates some things far better than others. The organizing themes of "making a deal" and "everything went smooth" would appear central to the managerial mythos. The manager and managerial language, like the scientist and scientific language, seek the transparency discussed and denied in chapter 5. But the illusion of transparency is achieved at considerable cost; it requires denial and control. It is neither the power nor the descriptive accuracy that keeps scientific management alive, but scientific management spontaneously arises anew as the managers attempt to articulate the fundamental role of management. As with science, it is not as if management does not know that its activities are value-laden and most often local. But the drive to normalize, generalize, and universalize keeps managerial knowledge abstract and away from a richer understanding of the particular, the individual, and the concrete. Such abstraction leads to reactions along the lines of decisional rules rather than con-textual responsiveness. Ironically, given the linguistic origins of the concepts, professionalization fosters such normalization and reactiveness, taking greater care to not make a mistake than to make a creative decision.

The managerial move efficiently coordinates but often does so by distorting or suppressing some conflicts. For example, conflicts over principles are difficult to mediate, therefore value conflict tends to be suppressed through naturalization, neutralization, or subjectification or distorted through com-modification and translation of "principled" interests to eco-nomic ones. Many conflicts, such as that between home and work, have elements beyond managerial control and tend to be avoided or pushed off to the home for resolution. Emotional expressions always mess up the calculus and thus (unless used as calculable strategic ploys) are to be eliminated. While the account here is all too simple, I believe that within it lies the key to issues of control and conflict as they arise in modern corporations.

The manager is produced as a special actor in the potential battle of the stakeholders—one with a different kind of struc-tural stake, a stake in the process rather than the outcome, not unlike a lawyer in the modern judiciary system. This motive is shared by the union leader, who has an interest in routinizing and centralizing conflict rather than making daily decisions; an interest that is also shared by many in the state political process who prefer representational to direct democratic processes. In such a position, managers do not perceive special interests of their own, but see their own desired processes as in the best interest of everyone. In order for this to be maintained, not only must a number of conflicts be suppressed, but this must be done invisibly so that it seems that there was no conflict at all or that if conflict is visible it is because someone is being unreasonable. The most central of the suppressed conflicts are those internal to the individual manager, those among alterna-tive forms of rationality, and those that defy routinization.

Although normalized, *socially approved* conflicts exist, a conflict-free environment is presented as for the good of every-one. This can be seen both in the nature of *approved* conflicts and in organizational discourse itself. Normalized conflict can be between members regarding the distribution of money and power within the system but rarely about the system of distri-bution itself. Approved conflicts tend to be produced as individual-centered and situational, rather than group based and structural. These are precisely the conflicts that can be conceptualized as episodic rather than perpetual and that do not threaten the normal process of managing conflict. And finally, approved conflicts tend to be produced as technical difficulties, such as lack of information or poor training, that admit of technical solutions and application of existing agencies for solution. The presentation of more fundamental conflicts is considered inefficient, wasteful, and damaging to all stakeholders.

The "managed conflict" image, however, has significant costs. The modern organization is filled with largely unproductive, though approved, conflict. The modern workplace is filled with strategies, competition for advancement, and the dedication of considerable time to internal competition and justification. These are often one-sided expressions of conflicts that cannot be adequately formulated or expressed. For example, the desire for freedom and autonomy is often expressed as a need for money and control. When it is expressed in this form, systems are established that deny freedom and autonomy both to the one seeking them and to others involved, thus setting in process a self-initiating regressive cycle. The hoped-for conflict-free environment is not accomplished but rather produces conflicts of particular types.

Chaos theories and contingency models all remind us that decisions in modern organizations are largely reactive. Decisions are not usually theoretically guided, nor are they in any simple sense goal directed. In situations of uncertainty, imbalance, and disorder, decisions are usually remedial. In most cases they serve as automatic responses to perceived crises or threats (Hirschman and Lindblom 1962). In Mayntz's (1976) analysis, managerial decision "appears to be touched off by preconceived goals or purposes.... [But] organizational activity in general and policy-making in particular is primarily triggered by situational factors which constitute a *pressure to act,* rather than being generated by deliberations on how certain abstract values can be achieved" (119). But there is obviously a self-referential quality about this. The very things that are perceived to be disturbances or situational *pressures to act* are "automatically" recognized using the same conceptual and valuational schemes that produce the action choices. The transparency of management as "system corrective," "putting out fires," and "remediation" overlooks the existence and reproduction of values and goals that, although not deliberated, define both problem and solution.

In a fundamental sense this is linked to a dilemma embedded in the nature of *management as medium*. Managerial success is strangely invisible. To the extent that normalization and decisional rules are effective, the managerial function becomes the background of practice rather than the figure. Effective managers can become invisible and apparently unnecessary. In Braverman's sense, they have deskilled themselves. The process of conceptualizing decisional rules is severed from the daily practice of application of them. Judgment is replaced by reaction. This is not unlike the modern social scientist who deskills the practice of science to the point that anyone can do their science. They can only reclaim themselves in their extrascientific process of preparing for the next study. Similarly, to the extent that the decision rules and reactions are unproblematic, the manager is successful and not needed (just as a lawyer who successfully writes contracts never needs to go to court). The demise of middle management with the introduction of computer technologies resulted in middle management's codification of their "activity," thus eliminating the need for direct human interpretation and judgment. They sucessfully managed themselves, but as in the original *manége,* the trained horse needs no trainer.

While the force of modern management is the normalization of conflict, the upwardly mobile manager needs crises to be managed and unique and special events to display a presence. Only at the top of the organization can the clean desk and freedom to chose activities signify having successfully put things in order. Generally management must demonstrate the need for themselves and their unique capacities. As Scott (1985) argued, this is accomplished through a tie to *entrepreneurship.* The structural placement in the reproduction of bureaucracy renders the manager invisible; however, the manager is symbolically reproduced in association to an age of personal venture capital and entrepreneurs of the past. Institutionalized entrepreneurship as a source of innovation and progress is a key element of the discourse of managerialism. The manager is conceptualized as special in terms of commitment and drive. Phenomenal leadership qualities and dedication to work above all else provide a visible personal quality to the "invisible" function. Managerialism "subjects" the individual manager with a "boom" mentality and great identity investment in advancement. As a young manager explained to me when asked about his "balloon" mortgage: "Hey, if I can't be making over a hundred grand in five years, I haven't got the right stuff, they might just as well plant me tomorrow." The production of figures like Donald Trump as a masterstrategist (if unethical and temporary) and hero to some (though he was finally felled by his nonwork behavior) fails to remind all that thousands of gutsy, talented people have tried Trump's "imaginary" game and not made it. The odds of one in thousands are often a better explanation for an individual's success than superior gift. But more importantly, the actual work experience neither requires nor often allows such a lofty creature. The empirical support for the imaginary gift and relational right to rule must be produced in the ordinary context.

Workers are constituted *as needing to be controlled* in the constitution of the manager as *needed for control*. Unusual events are constituted as crises not so much because of their crisis potential, but because crises are unusual and require actual judgment. This partially accounts for the "skilled incompetence" and chaos production discussed in Argyris's (1986) work (see chapter 7). Managers can become highly skilled communicators in systematically distorted systems who work hard (even too hard), are highly committed (perhaps too committed), seek places to display control (even where control is not needed), and yet use their skills to cover up real problems and avoid upsets and conflicts. They spend the majority of their time praising each other, discussing the difficulties of their jobs, making endless agenda lists, inventing elaborate strategies, and trying to decide what to do, and yet they communicate in ways that inhibit resolution of key problems and they rarely say what they mean. Strategic closure rather than consensus formation becomes common. Such a routine of "skilled incompetency" becomes systemic and creates the chaos that skilled managers appear needed to control. Created problems self-referenced in the system are far easier to manage than the intrusion of the outside environment.

Instrumental Reasoning and Managerial Domination

Managerialism has been characterized by the desire for control, a "will to power" that operates to normalize conflict and enhance efficiency, which makes *managerial* success a means to *everyone's* ends. As Edwards (1979, 148) argued, the "we" comes to express the "we-ness" of the firm defined in managerial terms rather than "we" as workers, as a group with an interest or point of view. If such a conception is useful in lending insight into organizational processes, it should also help describe the preference for certain reasoning processes. Many in organizational studies have followed Habermas (1971) in distinguishing different cognitive or knowledge-producing interests (see Stablein and Nord 1985; Fischer 1990). As is well known, Habermas distinguished between the "technical," "practical," and "emancipatory" as three central forms of human thought. The contrast between technical and practical reasoning has been used most widely in studies of corporations. Technical reasoning is instrumental: it tends to be governed by the theoretical and hypothetical as in modeling and strategic planning, it focuses on the means by which ends will be reached rather than on the ends themselves, and it claims that values are in ends and that means which are neutral. Practical reasoning, in contrast, is end centered; it is governed by the practical and immediate in terms of their goodness as ends in themselves, and means are seen as value laden. Technical reasoning aims at control, mastery, growth, and material gain. Its origin rests in biological survival, but the move for control can greatly exceed that necessary for survival. Practical reasoning is a natural complement to the technical. Human beings seek more than survival but also a meaningful existence and satisfaction of social and symbolic needs. Within the participatory model of communication, the technical interest was described as communication guided by the desire for mastery and control, and the practical interest, as communication guided by the attempt to reach understanding (Habermas 1984).

In Habermas's sense, no universal priority or preference can be given to either of these interests. During particular historical periods, a society may be dominated by one or the other. In more "traditional" societies, the technical interest is subordinated to the practical one. There is little question that many traditional societies had, or could have produced, the technologies for "development" and greater environmental control. They chose not to and instead focused on their "practical" interests. The critical theorists (e.g., Habermas 1975, 1984, 1987) have done much to document the manner in which scientific-technical (instrumental) reasoning has come to dominate modern society. The pursuit of control and economic goals has become the dominant valued (but value-neutral) means to some futuristic (better, though rarely specified in what ways) society. Studies of organizations have documented the manifestations of this domination in corporations (Mumby 1988; Alvesson 1987a). In managerial thought, control and domination of people and nature are critical aspects of the positive societal move to the future (Adorno and Horkheimer 1972; Fischer 1990). Lasch (1978) demonstrated the shift in legitimation to the technical realm. Quoting him: "One of the most important developments of recent years is that the ruling class in advanced societies has largely outgrown its earlier dependence on general culture and a unified world view and relies instead on an instrumental culture resting its claim to legitimacy, not on the elaboration of a world view that purports to explain the meaning of life, but purely on its capacity to solve technical problems and thereby to enlarge the supply of material goods" (45)

In periods like these of interest domination, the productive conflict between the two interests and forms of reasoning becomes suppressed by the reduction of one to the other, and consequently, development becomes systematically skewed. In corporations the long-term conflicts between various versions of scientific and human-relations approaches to management are legitimate offsprings of this interest struggle. But the technical reasoning—disguised often as objective reasoning—has nearly always prevailed. Reasoning itself is often reduced to technical reasoning. Concerns with economic growth, organizational survival, profit, and productivity have become the central criteria. Meaningful work, participation in decision making, and the enhancement of the autonomy of personnel have rarely been treated as goods in themselves. They are goods if they are strategic means to technical control. The apparent concern with culture, quality of life, meaning of life, and empowerment often become new means to tap into a reservoir of unutilized human talent and energies as easier and more effective means of managerial control. Weber's "iron cage" developed by bureaucracy's rationalization (which we read here as technical reasoning) process has a new twist. It is not felt as entanglement in bureaucratic rules but embraced as clarity, self-protection, and an easing of the tensions of work.

In this new logic both the manager and the corporation become pure instrumentalities. The commonly observed moral neutrality of managers was expressed well by a successful and "good" CEO on the popular television program "thirtysomething." In answer to questions regarding the morality of using "moles" and the violation of interpersonal trust, he could only sympathetically emphasize that it was "just business." And his "business is not to do good, but to do good business." The CEO's sense of a higher responsibility to society (or to someone), rather than to the normative community/communicative practice, was expressed with pain *and* mostly honor; he had the *strength* to place his business responsibilities over morality and personal feelings. The moral issues of the practice in this sense are deferred to determination in the marketplace by investors and consumers, but the marketplace only expresses preferences for the ends, not the means. The discussion of the morality of the strategy, in fact of instrumental reasoning itself, is thereby suppressed by the higher duty of efficiency. It is a nondiscussable issue. Efficiency remains above moral reproach. The outcome of such a logic has significant practical moral implications.

To make this clearer, allow me to complete an analogy begun in the last chapter. Students in an educational context might well see learning as *instrumental* and *practical*. Instrumentally, learning helps them succeed in a job and in life at some later point. But practically, learning also can be enjoyment, a fulfillment of understanding things around them, and ways of responding to everyday life problems. In an optimal sense we might see these in a conflictual (though not incompatible) relation with a balance between them. As technical reasoning comes to dominate, the "practical" may be seen as a useful by-product of the "instrumental" learning and even an aid to it. As the technical interest becomes further codified by grades, the learning as means to future success, and the representation of the means, become sought in their own right even if they no longer have anything other than an imaginary—chain of signifiers—relation to the future success. Once this is made into discourse and practices—teaching to the tests, use of grades as carrot and stick—the "practical" aspect of learning is a cost. Efficiency makes learning less pleasurable, and since it is not pleasurable, it must be made more efficient. As the dysfunction of a cycle like this is known, our managerial analogue does not recognize the imbalance, but rather seeks to elicit pleasure in the service of the instrumental, to further the reduction. The constant decline in the system evokes more control, more clearly articulated objectives, more motivational devices—more technical solutions—to the problems technical solutions created. Productivity and pleasure both fail. Unfortunately the reasoning system can not escape from itself to reclaim the balance. The *expert* cannot understand why the less orchestrated system plays better. The potential self-correcting maneuvers in the system are suppressed by control mechanisms. The analogue describes the essential reasoning flaw in corporations. Simply substitute the pleasure of the work experience for the practical, a promise of affluent, leisurely existence for the instrumental end, and power and money for grades. But of course this is not simply an analogy, this is the training ground.

Left out of the analysis thus far is Habermas's "emancipatory" interest. The emancipatory interest represents the human desire for freedom, autonomy, and collective self-determination of the future. None of these terms are usefully read from a simple enlightenment perspective. This is not about individualism, but a realization that most human limitations are arbitrary, hence were, and must continue to be, chosen. The traditional society as well as the modern society do not represent ultimate ends of history, but moments of determination. Human beings desire material well-being *and* a meaningful existence. One need not destroy the other. Emancipation is to reclaim the choices against all forms of domination or privileging of any arbitrary social formation. Managerialism operates actively against emancipation. Its move is control, preservation, and self-reproduction. The modern corporation does little to foster autonomy and choice making, whether it be in decisions, working standard hours, or determination of what one wants to do. The major concern here is how it accomplishes its control and reproduction, and later how emancipation as democracy is still possible. Central to this is the use of power and money as representational practices (communicational logics, the code) within technical-instrumental reasoning domination.

The Power and Money Code

Habermas (1987) argued that money and power become the primary steering mechanism in the colonization process. The life world emphasis on practical reasoning is translated into instrumental-system terms. While Habermas did not directly apply the conception to corporations, clearly the system of translation in the corporation follows the power and money analysis. The modern managerial corporation would hardly be recognizable or thinkable without these primary modes of representation. Certainly for many in the modern corporations, the reason for working is to make money. What would the modern manager be without discussions of money and power?

Alternative motives of enjoying production, producing a quality product, having a good time, or helping people may, in an "enlightened" way, be ascribed to lower level workers but rarely to management itself. Managers work, are devoid of pleasure, suffer the burden of their power, and get paid for it. In other than monetary terms the actual individuals who hold management positions do not have great lives. They work long hours and commute longer than most groups, they feel constant surveillance and scrutiny, they take relatively few vacation days (particularly in the United States, even though they may be granted considerably more), they have little time with their children and friends, and they die relatively young. And they do it to themselves. But they have money and power. As one manager explained to me "power gives us a paradigm for conducting the rest of our lives." She explains in detail that, if you have power at work, you will walk into a restaurant with an "expectation of how you're going to be treated ...it spills over into everything that you do." Clearly, then, one does not just go home at the end of the game and forget about it; it seems to be all-consuming. Managerialism at its best. Given management's actual ability to make decisions of allocation of resources, it is significant that they give themselves money and symbols of power rather than free time, autonomy, and flexibility. And it is significant how much of the money they earn is spent on further symbols of money and power that are often seen as essential for a corporate image for the sake of....

The Managerial Prerogative

But the power and monetary medium of managerialism runs deeper than management's own produced self-interest. It defines the interests of the corporation and the means of corporation goal accomplishment. This is largely through a "managerial prerogative." A managerial prerogative in decisions in the United States is grounded in management's conceptional, and legal, fiduciary responsibility (a legal definition that is an arbitrarily social production, though that seems often forgotten). Since the prerogative rests in fiduciary responsibilities, the translation into monetary terms is not simply the evoking of an arbitrary medium of exchange, it is a shifting of responsibility. Articulating life world issues in terms of corporate costs shifts the decisional responsibility from other corporate members to the manager. Management becomes responsible for anything that has a potential financial implication. And of course control shifts with the responsibility. The control drive of managerialism seeks the medium of its extension, and money is it. In doing so, everything that cannot be adequately translated into money is implicitly suppressed, and all competing rights of decisions regarding one's life are made marginal. Issues such as working hours have a financial dimension and therefore are of managerial concern, but they also have many other dimensions that become lost in management's drive to control. The fiduciary responsibility lays a ground for a managerial prerogative in all matters of the workplace (and elsewhere if they have financial implications).

Storey (1983, 98ff.) provided an excellent account of how the aggressive manner the managerial prerogative has been defended in the United States. I will be brief here. Many of these so-called rights are not negotiable with the union and protected from owner intrusion. The general and inclusive nature of these rights is noteworthy. Quoting Torrence's (1959) conception: "[W]hen we refer to management rights, we are talking about management's right to decide what is to be done, when, where, and by whom. Such as the right to move operations from one location to another, the right to determine the hours of work and the right to take all other decisions which are normally and traditionally the sole responsibility of management" (1, cited by Storey 1983, 99). One does not have to deny management's fiduciary responsibilities to see the problems here. For example, such a view would argue for management's right to close a plant that is making a profit simply because it wanted to or could make more profit elsewhere. A more balanced view would argue that management desires, as well as the extent of profitability, are part of a complex set of rights needing representation in decisions. But such a balanced view does not exist. In its place, there is managerial prerogative. In my view, Storey (1983) concluded correctly that "the managerial justification for prerogative rests upon property-rights of ownership which must be protected (and upon legal enactment which does in fact make them responsible for the companies activities) and, secondly, upon a series of economic 'efficiency' arguments. Both of these streams of argument are traceable to the same spring: the primary of market rationality" (105). "Market rationality" provides a monetary steering mechanism for strategic managerial technical reasoning, strange grounds for democracy based on the ultimate translatability of all human goals into the money code.

Such a view of management's rights has not always existed. In Sloan's (1963) autobiography of his years at General Motors, he recounts with great relief the establishment and acceptance of managerial rights. He described the early years of General Motors (personified as management's early years) as particularly troubled by the issue: "What made the prospect grim in those early years was the persistent union attempt to invade basic management prerogatives. Our right to determine production schedules, to set work standards and to discipline workers were all suddenly called into question" (406). Clearly most labor unions came to accept the monetary code. Unions in the United States often rejected shared governance almost as strongly as management did. Quoting Meany (1976): "Who are you if you are a labor man on a board of directors? Whom do you represent? Labor does not want to run the shop. In the United States participation is absolutely and completely out" (52). The creation of the union itself may well be seen as contributing to the definition of managerial rights. Unionization in producing a differentiation defined two groups with different and specifiable rights. The production of unions itself in many ways restricts participation and conflict on a daily basis by transforming issues into periodic negotiation and approved conflicts, the most central being money. The strategy of strikes and slowdowns were based on economically coded strategies of withholding labor power, thus workers produced themselves in managerial terms. The socially produced and reproduced conditions made this the proper form of power exertion and conflict. In contrast, unions could have locked management out of the workplace, showing that the work could be done without them. Or they could have voted with the stocks held in their pension funds, enough in most cases to wield considerable influence. The definition of labor in management terms (and the laws that held this in place) were costly in the long run for labor's interests. For example, the definition of a part of the corporation as "labor" sustained by unions is a necessary condition for managerial union breaking such as opening small plants or reclassification of employees. Further, the contemporary decline of unions may be attributed to large segments of employees rejecting the worker/management code rather than the failure to deliver financial rewards; for example, many women will accept less pay, longer working hours, and no union protection to be administrative assistants rather than secretaries, even though they are doing the same work. One of the conditions of employment most often forgotten in labor negotiations is the employee's desire to be understood as something other than a worker. Rather than workers failing to understand their class interest, the definition of class interest in monetary terms may be the greatest obstacles to participation. And without a doubt, the ability to define the manager in regard to the "approved conflict" with labor has enhanced managerialism. As Gallie (1978) carefully demonstrated, management's acceptance of the power of unions played a critical role in the British worker's acceptance of managerial authority (182–84). Defining the terms of conflict acted to suppress many potential conflicts.

Certainly the concept of managerial prerogative as explicitly articulated has waned during the seventies and eighties. Workers and lower level managers have more say in fundamental working conditions than they had in the fifties and sixties. But the issues have shifted rather than disappeared. As the next chapter will show, disciplinary structures have replaced the need for "sovereign" style rights. Practices and routines from an earlier time are now institutionalized in the workplace, producing a particular type of subject. Further, the use of money as the representative practice enables accounting procedures and discursive forms used by various stakeholders to produce the effect of the managerial prerogative with full participatory complicity. *Money, power, and control operate as an invisible steering mechanism encroaching further into each stakeholder's conception of self and world.*

The point here is not a critique of a market-driven society any more than it is a critique of capitalism. Hirschman's (1977) and Berger's (1986) point is critical, capitalism emerged from a market-centered orientation in which its "passion" was monitored and regulated by natural countervailing influences. The balance is lost, and the loss is hidden by the apparent neutrality of instrumental reasoning and money. *Market-driven managerial societies* often privilege instrumental reasoning and behaviors and consequently suppress diversity of interests (Ramos 1981). But the emphasis should be on *managerial* rather than *market driven.* As has been suggested, managerialism in its strongest form tends to work toward control rather than meeting markets, though market pressures are often used to legitimize choices. This control includes creating markets and reducing competition as well as routinizing internal structures. The problem is not just that managerialism undermines the positive force of a market-driven economy. More importantly, the dysfunctions of excessive market-driven decision making, articulated through techno-instrumental reasoning and money, can only be overcome by recovering alternative claimants and modes of representation. The reclaiming of the tension among multiple logics and human interests in corporations is of central importance to democracy.

Ramos's (1981) solution to market domination based on "delimitation" goes a different direction than suggested here, and his analysis of potential conflicting outcomes is useful and provides detail often absent in Habermas. Ramos demonstrated that different social settings (e.g., workplace, family, church) were each used to satisfy different desires (e.g., desires for economic goods, disciplined and innovative thought, group affiliation and interaction, and creative personal detachment). In recognizing the colonizing activities of the corporate (and big government), he argued for reclaiming space for the latter three desires through support of small enclaves of cooperation in the community and in small institutions. I wish to push the recovery to the heart of the work process itself as an alternative and perhaps supplemental solution to Ramos's. The point is the same: There are multiple human needs that are currently being suppressed or distorted in translation, and they need to be recovered with equal legitimacy in a democratic society. The translation of all needs into monetary terms is not a simple distortion, because the presence of reduction was not recognized. It is a strategic, instrumental "mistake"—a systematic distortion. The code establishes control.

Management and the *Formal* Organization

The formal organization has always been a particular type of fiction. It is legally defined as a quasiperson and is presented through its artifacts of places and products of work, but has no particular status outside of its symbolic/communicational production. Such a nonstatus would lead Weick (1979) to argue that "organizing" rather than "organizations" is a better description, and surely the various images that Morgan (1986) described are made possible by its ephemeral nature. But as Cooper and Burrell (1988) argued: "The object of orthodox organizational analysis is *the* organization: a bounded social system, with specific structures and goals which act more or less rationally and more or less coherently" (102). Little is more taken for granted in the talk of everyday people and researchers than the actual existence of the thing called the "organization." We rightly should ask what purposes are served by this "misrecognition."

The Organization as an Entity

Surely the most significant accomplishment of the conception is the suppression of conflicts. Granting it the status of a "natural" existence puts behind us questions of the social production of the corporation. The battles won and lost in the development of these forms rather than others recede into history rather than being understood as continuing operant forces of domination. The privilege of the status quo resides in being forgetful of the arbitrary and capricious, the violence of the initial laying claim. (As the Native Americans perhaps best learned, the first violence claims the property, the subsequent struggle over the property is against the law.) But not just the past conflicts are lost; the present ones are also lost. The corporation is held in place in the extreme by laws supported by the police and other agencies, but it need not be, for the complicity in its support is evoked daily by symbolic means. Even before we get to the processes of reproduction of the corporation at the point of production, the corporation is already legitimate and unquestioned. For all the complaints about the work experience, the first protection against change is that "this is the way it is." The individual may not be able to adjust, some workplaces may be better than others, and this manager may be "hard to work for," but left untouched is the capricious fiction of corporations and their fundamental relations themselves. The focus on the organization as a thing is a central aspect of its reproduction. *The* organization can be seen as a social tool (a transparent one at that) that extends the human capacity to fulfill needs. *It* is controlled by human agents. What is forgotten is that *it* is a produced institution that also "subjects" its human embodiments and specifies the nature of their agency.

The Significance of the Formal

But the emphasis is not just on *the* organization but on the *formal* organization. Despite the various criticisms of it, the organizational chart maintains a certain predominance. The chart represents the lines of authority and command, but most would agree that its function is primarily symbolic. And most clearly it symbolizes hierarchy. While there are many ways to represent the functional relations among producing and coordinating, authority and subordination are the preferred ones in corporations. The formal relations are a reminder lest one forget. But the concern is not just with the arbitrary choice of representing hierarchy over other signifying practices—but there are many potential hierarchies in the work environment. Hierarchy could be based on seniority, popularity, skilledness of the job, loyalty, supportiveness of others, or attractiveness. The selection of authority relations as *the* basis of hierarchy is perhaps obvious, in that it is the only one that assures managerial superiority, but it is nonetheless significant in creating an arbitrary valuing distinction (i.e., the power-and-money code). The conception of the informal organization is not of an equal sort. It is that which also happens within the organization structurally bounded in *formal* terms.

But the formal carries more weight than that. The *formal* inserts a sense of propriety and control unnecessary to the functioning of the organization but of significance. In Cooper and Burrell's (1988) terms: "Ordinarily, the word 'formal' signifies what is proper, methodical, and punctilious. In the context of formal organizations and institutions, the 'formal' is not just the proper and methodical but also the 'official'; it becomes raised to the level of law and public truth. What is formally organized takes on the virtue of a moral order" (108). The formal is well defined and directs a certain reserve and constraint on emotional expression, while the informal retains confusion, familiarity, and intimacy. In the formal the "form," the mind, rules over matter—representationally the "male" rules over the "female" dimensions of the human. The body that makes mistakes, that carries competing desires, that gets tired, and that makes demands becomes the first and most critical site of control, of self-(as subjected)-control of the form. The formal context is heavily normative, and status is clearly marked.

Various scholars interested in the gender politics of the workplace have argued that formal bureaucratic rationality is a particular type of patriarchy. Pringle (1988) summarized the analysis well:

> While the rational-legal or bureaucratic form presents itself as gender-neutral, it actually constitutes a new kind of patriarchal structure. The apparent neutrality of rules and goals disguises the class and gender interests

served by them. *Weber's account of "rationality" can be interpreted as a commentary on the construction of a particular kind of masculinity based on the exclusion of the personal, the sexual, and the feminine from any definition of rationality.* The values of instrumentality rationality are strongly associated with the masculine individual, while the feminine is associated with that "other" world of chaos and disorder. (88)

The formally defined setting not only strongly enforces propriety rules that clearly distinguish along class and gender lines, but establishes a gender preference by the very preference of the form itself. The power is one of both exclusion and valuing what is present. In many different ways the formal organization neuters the body and drives sex and the urges of the body out of the corporation (Burrell 1984). The domination of the masculine suppresses gender conflict and provides a place (and personnel) for the care of the body and emotions to minimize their effect on the "real" work processes. But of course discrimination based on both sex and gender fills the organization (Pringle 1988). The alignment of the masculine and the formal both defines and drives the body, the emotional, and the feminine into the margin of the repressed and unpaid.

Nowhere is the normative pressure and status of the formal felt more strongly than in language use. Thompson (1984), following Bourdieu, demonstrated the pressure of self-correction in formal contexts and argued that "the formal presupposes a *recognition* of the legitimacy of the dominant language or dominant mode of language usage, and hence a *misrecognition* of the fact that this language or mode of language use is imposed *as* dominant. The exercise of symbolic violence is invisible to social actors precisely because it presupposes the complicity of those who suffer most from its effects" (58). Certainly the self-corrective pressure is felt most clearly by workers and women, but they simply manifest the pressure long-since inculcated in managerial men.

Huspek (1987) provided clear evidence for the power of formal language in his ethnography of a lumber yard. The workers there generally misrecognized the imposition of the formal, dominant language of management as proper and felt it to be natural and necessary. Rather than seeing the imposition as a problem, even a moral participatory violation, the workers ascribed the deficiency to themselves and their failure to their inability to express themselves well. As one worker described a grievance session:

> "An' we were goin' ta go an' we were really talk some shit in there. Well nobody said a word in there but me. An' I had ta say it to the Raven [a member of the management group]. An' here I'm sittin' down, the Raven's sittin' down, an' the other guys are just standin' around me, not sayin' a word. Well I felt intense pressure ta where I was chokin'. But look nobody said notin.'" (94)

In the sense of Habermas's discourse claims, the workers felt constrained in their ability to express or contest truth claims, to express or to contest normative claims of rightness, or to express inner ideational or emotional states. The immorality of the situation is clear. Management has not explicitly accomplished this, however, but is complicit in creating a situation where the worker creates it. The formal setting is key to this. Bourdieu described this as the outcome of gentle, surreptitious symbolic violence. A violence that

> is never so manifest as in all the corrections, momentary or longlasting, to which dominated speakers, in a desperate effort towards correction, consciously or unconsciously subject the stigmatized aspects of their pronunciation, their vocabulary (with all the forms of euphemism) and their syntax; in the confusion which makes them 'lose their means', rendering them incapable of 'finding their words', or if they had been suddenly dispossesed of their own language. (Cited in Thompson 1984, 58)

Bourdieu reexpresses the feeling and self-definition that the worker expresses so well in his own description, but the worker understands *and yet* enacts the arbitrary managerial desire for formal language without understanding (or perhaps even in understanding) that its primary effect is to privilege managerialism. Clearly the formal language has not produced a happier work situation or greater efficiency or productivity. It has not represented the worker or a variety of potential social interests. What it has done is accomplish control, situated a peculiar managerial self-definition, and demeaned the worker. The formal setting rewards those with a secretary (or word processor), who can correct spelling and typos, through implicitly asserting that they have a superior command, have clearer insight, and take the job more seriously. Thus the formal qualifies and disqualifies and gives an expressive privilege to a managerial voice. The "formal" supports control and exclusion rather than expression and open consensus.

Further, the organization, bounded by the defining charateristic as formal organization, produces a form/content distinction with emphasis on the form over the content. This will become more important when the idea of a personal and corporate image is discussed in chapter 11. Clearly the formal draws attention to the uniform and the standard. The informal becomes rationalized; the uncertainty of the immediate and local becomes routinized (the uncertain is even defined as the nonroutine). In this sense the formal censors the informal, being privileged as the rational place of sorting out the informal. The formal continues the colonization of the life world.

The image of the faceless, grey-suited manager is too severe even as a metaphor, but the conception is not without ground. Given that the uniformity is often disliked and even ridiculed, what purpose does it serve? In many respects even the dress maps well the managerial ambivalence of invisible (transparency) and personal self-display. The uniformity of dress captures the sameness, the normal, and the routinization. And the formal dress distinguishes the groups and members within the group, reclaiming and reproducing the formal context in which being a manager counts. The upper class dress of the manager in the formal reconnects the imaginary wealthy owner. The exceptions to the formal dress would seem to support the point. In occupational areas such as advertising and in groups such as research and development, the dress code is less formal. Whenever there is a tangible product for self-definition, a clear credentialing process, or the lack of deskilling, dress is informal and often expressive of the individual more than of the corporate position. The enforcement of dress codes on lower level employees both depersonalizes them and creates the formal, managerially advantaged context. The bringing of clothing under managerial control is often justified on economic grounds of professionalism or safety. But not only can both be accomplished with individual expressive dress, but professionalism—(and economic considerations)—are only marked within other managerial groups. The dress issue itself is probably not trivial. The pseudorationality of the defense, the high enforcement, and the conspicuous nature of the choices suggest a clear corporate importance. The importance of the "formal" for managerialism appears captured in this icon.

Has Managerialism Been Worth the Price?

I hope that it has been clear throughout this discussion that the issue is neither the presumption of a simple form of domination by one group over others nor a simple negative reaction to the modern corporation. One could counter the analysis here by saying that managerial domination has been good and has produced significant goods for the society. Would we want to lose that for more open, moral corporations? Clearly the response here must be more than a Paine-like proclamation that "one should be more on guard to protect liberty when oppression appears beneficial." Clearly the modern way of thinking and working, and the corporate form accompanying it, has delivered important benefits. If so, why the concern? The issues of whether the modern corporate form has "produced the goods" is a significant one. The legitimacy of the modern corporate form rest primarily on this issue, and consequently a variety of social concerns get pushed aside because of the fear that change will negatively affect production. As Denhardt (1981) claimed: "The instrumental logic of science and organization is predicated on the value of productivity, a value which now underlies claims to legitimacy by those in positions of power. Previously, the major justifications for elite domination were primarily mythical or religious—for example, kings and queens rules by 'divine right.' However,...in industrial society we increasingly find the dominant group in society (which roughly corresponds to the scientific and organizational elite) justifying its position of dominance in terms of providing needed goods and services" (42–43).

Accepting domination by recanting the values of the American way of life, however, often hides more than it reveals. The nasty trick of systematically distorted communication and discursive closure is the denial of the discussion that could raise fundamental issues. The primary concern here is with creating a place for such discussions within the work process itself, but the need for the internal discussion can be aided by a statement of general perspective. I believe that it is fairly clear that most benefits to the general standard of life have come in spite of managerialism rather than because of it. Managerialism has created important dislocations in human experience and material prosperity. And most importantly, the self-referentiality of the system creates a negative cycle that will become progressively more costly. Allow me to briefly raise a couple of simple external questions and demonstrate the complexity hidden in them, before turning to the dislocations intrinsic to the workplace.

Is life better? Have modern corporations delivered the goods? The answer to both is often, "Of course," even if there are concerns with quality, consumerism, and some of the losses. The self-evident, commonsense answer deserves some scrutiny if only because people get so angry when it is challenged. While issues of the power of common sense and the social construction of "facts" will be considered in greater depth later, some suggestive questioning may be useful here.

Again is life better? Certainly on many scales the "objective" quality of life has increased. People live in bigger housing (though more hours of the family members' work is needed to have it), earn more, have more cars, have more consumer goods, and have more years of education. But they are gradually working more hours, have decreasing leisure time, have less time with their families, pay a higher percentage of their incomes to the maintenance of their jobs, live where crime and drug abuse are rising, and have a more narrow education. Better is a complex issue, when we get beyond arbitrary social "leading indicators." Even further, what is assumed in those statistics? Is more square feet of living space better housing, or should quality of design and construction count? Are consumer goods today of higher quality, do they feel better, are they more aesthetically appealing? To what extent does a corporate definition of what the good life should be determine the objective standard? What is measured and what is not? Should quality and fulfillment be measured, and to what extent is measurement itself supportive of a particular logic of the "good life"? Life is better, but how much?

The so-called subjective measures show greater variability. In the subjective ratings people are asked to make their own judgments about life in general (though rarely to give the qualities they would use to define "objective" measures). Such judgments are always in comparison to some, though usually undisclosed, standard. The presence of media in providing images of what people at other times and in other places had (or have) is critical. Even though subjective measures in the United States are not as high as might be expected, they would probably be lower if comparison groups were more fairly portrayed. One wonders how many societies have low subjective measures, given their comparison to the presumed American standard as revealed in movies and on TV. Even given the probable bias on the affirmative side, "subjective" measures have not kept up with the "objective" ones. We don't feel as good as we are supposed to, yet we feel we have it better than anyone else. How do we construct "at least we have it better than" or the contemporary version of "love it, or leave it?"

The media frequently uses the immigrant story to tell how good life is in the United States. The story contrasts life in the United States with life in the immigrant's home country; however, rarely is it clear in the story that often the referenced immigrant is a member of an oppressed group in an underdeveloped society who clearly has it better now. The feelings about the United States and the quality of life here are much different when the visitor or immigrant is from an educated professional home in another developed society. Such individuals are certainly the more similar comparative group. And often the modern immigrant story stops after the proclamation at the point of leaving the boat. Many do not find the United States to be the land of opportunity they expected. When the immigrant is successful, often it is a result of a public training program and in a small private business. The number of these who make it up the corporate ladder is very small. And why not compare our life to what we can be, rather than what others are? But let's not quibble. The safe answer is okay. Life in the United States is good *and* could be better.

Have *corporations* delivered the goods? Has this form of work organization been productive? Again, the answer is usually a quick yes, even though there is concern that the Japanese have a magic formula (but their success is often attributed to cultural differences, better education, harder work, and copying the United States). The everyday account of the success of American business is bolstered by comparisons to the Soviet Union and communist countries in general. We should note the quick confusion of a particular corporate form with the concept of market economy. But even leaving aside the issue of which is more important, clearly the competition was not and could not have been great. The Soviet Union in particular started generations behind, suffered two massive wars on their own territory that caused an incredible loss of lives and property, had a civil war, developed a totalitarian government, incorporated the most rigid model of centralized bureaucratic scientific management, and attempted to maintain a war machine as large as that of the United States. And it did not have the capacity to sell large parts of its own territory to maintain consumer products. It is hard to believe that a different style of management (i.e., if they had one different from the United States) or corporate form would have pulled them materially equal to us. At best a claimed success in regard to an obvious failure hardly makes sense. But the media and corporate-sponsored images are central. Clearly the problems of economically less developed planned economies, including rationing and standing in line for goods, provides a more vivid media image than high unemployment and the lack of money to purchase goods that characterize economically less developed market economies. But the question is not whether an infused market economy can lead to economic development in Eastern Europe. In some respects it might be said that the Soviet government gave management the power to plan and control the economy that management here has sought with largely negative consequences.

Interestingly, the positive view of management in the U.S. is bolstered by its clearly forced and unexplored association with a form of ownership and a market economy, rather than by demonstration of its superior form of decision making and coordination. Even in highly pro-management studies, the costs of managerialism are clear and have been shown to contribute to declining competitiveness for U.S. products and services. For example, Roach (see Bowen 1986) carefully demonstrated that white-collar productivity has been static or even declining during the past twenty years while blue-collar productivity has continued to increase despite much higher capital investment being made in white-collar work. As Baily (1986) concluded: "It appears as if the administrative bureaucracies of the economy absorbed a large share of the total investment without making corresponding improvements in efficiency" (449). And Drucker even more boldly claimed that U.S. companies have 20% to 30% more managers than they need. Clearly the MBAs of the past decade are poorly equipped to make good business or good social choices. When management becomes conceived as medium, as if the managerial function is without substance and is instrumentally interchangeable, different types of skills are applied. Managers are prepared for takeovers, financial manipulations, and setting up profit centers for quick results before they move on to the next industry. Long term development and the broader social agenda are not part of the routine. Clearly such problems are becoming more well known if only from the financial side. But even with decentralization and the squeeze on middle management, little attempt is made to price management personnel in line with the general economy or to reassess the conception and practice of management that has placed the general economy in a weakened condition. And, the invisible costs to the human character and social welfare are hardly mentioned at all.

Clearly, we as a society have made some very good decisions and some less good ones. The question of how to productively engage in our self-determination starts with open discussions of what is working and what is not. Our continued learning depends on it. To the extent that such a discussion is itself distorted and closed, our learning is partial and skewed. The corporation is a historical development that has accomplished certain ends, one of which is to perpetuate itself by creating an environment favorable to it, and one which has often hidden what it is and what it does. This must be understood, to keep it responsive to our full variety of needs and goals. There is a growing awareness among upper managers themselves that the eighties were a time of conspicuous power displays fostering negative effects on the environment and people's lives (see Dilenschneider, 1990). Corporate excesses have led to a weary public, even if they seem to know little other than a managerial logic. And decentralization continues to offer some hope of meaningful change. Firms like Ben and Jerry's have shown that success and a new-styled organization are possible in some industries. But if reported change is a new instrumental strategy—is merely public relations or new quieter, more gentle, system of control—managerialism will continue, only with a different face. Managerialism is not a debate for the newspapers, but an issue of democracy, a struggle to be worked out among everyday people in the workplace. Guidance for this requires a more expanded analysis of power and control in the work site.

CHAPTER 10

Disciplinary Power and Discursive Formations at Work

> Every act reproduces or subverts a social institution.... If every social institution is an organization of power...then every act is political for it either sustains or subverts a given organization of power.
> (Trevor Pateman 1980, 16)

The analysis up to this point has suggested that corporate organizations are an important force in modern society and that if organizational analysis is to be of social value it must work toward providing greater everyday democracy in the corporate context. This has led to a consideration of the political nature of personal identity and everyday experience and their relations to democracy as specified in participatory communication processes. Thus far I have been working within the framework of a type of modern ideological criticism. Mostly I have worked to specify a theoretically guided analysis of corporate domination in the formation of everyday life experience and of the forms of discourse that sustain, hide, protect, and reproduce that domination. This led in chapters 8 and 9 to focusing on the historical development of the "formal" organization and the presence of managerial domination. Perhaps the expected next move would be to suggest a hoped-for class- or gender-driven revolution or at least a manner of restructuring the modern corporation.

The implicit utopian drive of ideological criticism, which I have made explicit here as a moral basis for participation, can be a practical and theoretical problem. Its concepts of control are too grand and its alternatives for action too rational *and* revolutionary to provide much guidance for daily choice-making. This does not mean we need to throw it out. Rather, it has value in itself as a partial but essential project, and it is important to getting us to a place where we can make an equally critical next move. This is a move to what is best called a "micropolitics," the politics in the moment-by-moment. In making this move, the concern of Abercrombie et al. (1980) with the identification of a monolithic group or force can partially be avoided. The manifestation of managerialism is a complex group of forces pulled together here partially that work to different ends for different people but maintain latent control and particular asymmetries. To describe these forces, we'll shift attention from Althusserian "ideological state apparatus"—formed in the United States as corporate organizations—to Foucault's "specific technologies of the social"—managerialism as one of many daily accomplishments in the workplace. To do this, a microanalysis of power and control is essential.

The concept of ideology and ideological critique can be useful in this move, but it must be transformed in such a way as to free it from a free standing foundation, place it within actual practices, yet recognize the strategic manners by which such invisible valuational structures are utilized. I see this as similar to the move suggested by Frow (1985). He argued that it is possible to rework the concept of ideology so that it depends

> neither on a problematic of truth or error, nor on a division of the world into two parts one which is more real than the other, nor on an expressive relation of subjects to meaning. The political force of the concept can be retained if ideology is thought as a provisional state of discourse (a function of its appropriation and use) rather than as a content or inherent structure. Any discourse system produces a particular configuration of subject-positions which are the conditions of entry of individuals into discourse; but these acquire political significance only through the (historically variable) codification of discourse in terms of a play of relations of power, and the positions available can be refused or underminded. (193)

Foucault's work can provide precisely the basis for accomplishing this. Initially, I wish to develop in brief Foucault's reconception of the nature of power as disciplinary and how it relates to specific discursive formations. Then I will expound upon managerial knowledge/expertise, dominant language preferences, and the construction of fact through forms and accounting as the primary ways management establishes a privileged discourse and precludes entry into the discursive process.

Power and Discursive Formations

Power is frequently discussed by both social scientists and everyday people. In Western societies few issues have commanded the attention that the twin issues of freedom and the exercise of power have. Foucault (1980b, 1977), perhaps better than anyone else, has demonstrated that it is frequently because of these discussions rather than because of inattention to power that we have failed to understand its presence and manners of deployment. So too in corporate organizations the attention to intergroup conflict, coalitions, regulations, and rights has often led us further from understanding power and domination. Democracy cannot be recovered in a new form without a more fundamental understanding of power. The discussions in the last few chapters help by identifying the basic social processes by which experience, knowledge, and identity are formed and sustained as political formations.

Most conceptions and analyses of power in organizations have been derived from political scientists. Each of these conceptions was primarily designed to discuss the power of the state, the influence different people or groups have in political processes, or the rights of individuals in opposition to possible state domination. Discussions of leadership, coalition formation, special interests, and authority in corporations is often only distinguished from similar "public" process by scale and the special applicable rights. Similarly, discussions of loyalty and collective priorities closely parallel conceptions developed for the relation to the state. As discussed in chapter 1, Foucault has shown how each of these conceptions are tied to sovereign rights as expanded in a "juridico" discourse. Since power is conceived as restrictive of individual freedom, the question "by what right or necessity is the rule made" serves as a fundamental issue for the exercise of power.

Following Foucault (1980b, 83ff), I argued in chapter 1 that this is not the predominant form of power today. The state still has such power, but it is limited, if only because in its negative form it is always felt as oppressive. And certainly, a kind of sovereign power exists in corporations and can be described as parallel in character to that of the state. But attention to these is misleading and often conceals the actual procedures of power and the operant sites of its deployment. Most significantly control and influence are dispersed into norms and standard practices as products of moral, medical, sexual, and psychological regulation. Foucault called this "disciplinary" power. Rather than being occasional and restrictive, power resides in every perception, every judgment, every act. In its positive sense it enables and makes possible, and negatively it excludes and marginalizes. Rather than analyzing power in the organization as if the organization were a sovereign state, the conception of power has to be reformed to account for this more massive and invisible structure of control supported by social technologies rather than legal and judicial rules. Administration has to be seen in regard to order and discipline if its power is to be understood. And discussions of rights must be recast as resistance to discipline if it is to have meaning in modern society.

Disciplinary Power

Power for Foucault is not the right of the state or systems of domination. Each of these are the outcomes or terminal forms it takes, they witness the operation of power but are not it. Power is omnipresent as it is manifest and produced in each moment. For example, we often speak of the power of managers or the power of workers, but the privileging of certain values comes not in supporting one or the other but in making the separation, in pitting one against the other, the production of the tension. For from another standpoint, every manager is a worker and every worker is a manager. Extending the analysis from chapter 5, power can be shown in the production of linguistic distinction, in separating the activities or possessions of one from others, and in creating one of the two created objects as desirable. Power is exercised in constituting the relation. This "disciplinary" power operates constantly at innumerable sites and moments. From his initial conception Foucault (1980b, 94ff.) offers five basic propositions regarding power:

1. Power is not an object or force that can be acquired or possessed. The individual is neither the possessor nor the vehicle of power but rather one of its effects. Power is a process that operates constantly in the interplay of nonegalitarian and mobile relations. Power is an advantaging practice, as are all

practices. It exists in the choice to orient attention in one way rather than another, to perceive this rather than that. Every asymmetry, every this and not that, every presence and absence, every look here rather than there, is power.

2. Power relations are not external to other relationships but immanent in them. Power relations are the effects of the divisions, inequalities, and disequilibriums that exist in all relations, and all relations are constituted by these very divisions. In this sense power does not merely prohibit and advantage but is productive of the possibilities of relations at all. Organization superordinates do not create discipline through their actions and strategies, nor do they subject others to them. They are as much disciplined as subordinates. The discipline for each is produced together in day-to-day routines. Discipline is built into the organization in training programs, technologies, buildings, and manufacturing processes (Donzelot 1988).

3. Power is not exercised by the "top" but exists in the reciprocal relations of the haves and have-nots. Major dominations in a society are produced out of differentiations and confrontations running across major social institutions. For example, no management group can control the actions, let alone the thoughts, of other groups. Fear (warranted or not), assumptions of knowledge differences, principles of least effort, wanting rewards, and so forth must be provided by the controlled groups. Controlled groups may do so without self awareness, and such things as fears and rewards are not formed outside of specific power relations often supported by other institutions. But power relations remain unowned and invisible. The explicit and unilateral display of authority more often denotes the breakdown of power relations rather than the presence of them. It is the last resort of normal power relations.

4. Power relations are both intentional and nonsubjective. Power relations arise out of aims, objectives, and strategies, but there is no simple choice-making group or guidance to the network of power. In Foucault's words, "The rationality of power is characterized by tactics that are often quite explicit at the restricted level where they are inscribed..., tactics which, becoming connected to one another, attracting and propagating one another, but finding their base of support and their condition elsewhere, end by forming comprehensive systems: the logic is perfectly clear, the aims decipherable, and yet it is often the case that no one is there to have invented them, and few who can be said to have formulated them." (1980b, 95). In

the corporate example, such things as careerism or Burawoy's (1979) making-out game produce complicity in systems of dominations, and while no one can be said to have made them for this purpose, they clearly advance certain groups, and alternative practices do not survive.

5. Power relations are always met by resistance. Resistance is not external to configurations and its presence does not denote the incompletion or absence of power but its presence—for example ownership creates conflict over possession, division of labor creates different interests and conflict of interests. Resistance is not simply opposition. Every formation holds the presence of "necessary" and appropriate conflicts. Resistance notes that the lines of possible opposition themselves often hide meaningful contrary conflict. For example, pitting the worker against the owner (with management as representative) hides site-specific relations where conflict is better seen as workers and owners opposed to management. Radical resistance is rejection of simple placement in structures. Proclaiming rights in the modern workplace functions as such resistance in that it proposes a discourse outside of that of efficiency and instrumental reason rather than fulfilling a conflict within it. Acts of resistance are as dispersed and innumerable as sites of power. Every positivity of a formation is held present against its opposite, which is produced along with it. Like power it can become centralized in a strategic pulling together of the diffused points of resistance. More often it is diffused in random acts, like being late, cheating, or jokes, that reside in tolerable limits of noncompliance and rebellion.

Disciplinary power has been present in corporations from their outset. Perhaps the clearest case is the development of the assembly line. The assembly line transformed an explicit authority relation between the worker and supervisor into a partially hidden one. Rather than the supervisor having to tell the worker how hard or fast to work and dealing with the question, "by what right," the movement in the line already accomplished it. In doing so the functional relation changed. The assembly line extended and enabled a particular worker capacity—instead of being restrictive of the worker, it facilitated an accomplishment. The assembly line, like the new organization, was a new tool extending collective bodies' capacity to produce. But it was also a new kind of tool. Rather than being subjugated to the body's rule, it subjugated the body into an extension of itself—a docile, useful body. While there was still no doubt that authority and explicit power kept the worker at the line and that it was the company's decision to implement work in this way, the relation to the supervisor could also change as well as the nature of agency and reason.

Donzelot (1988) showed that Taylor understood the new power in discipline from the outset of scientific management and that in the transformation the very site of reason changed. Taylor proposed that in place of "a *surfeit of supervisory discipline*—permanent supervision, punishment by fines and deductions from wages, all costly ways of exercising power because of the resistance they evoke, (412)" energies should focus on the workers *optimum adaptation* to the machine. Donzelot described the disciplinary benefit: "It is a question of rationalization since the machinic system will control work, invisibly as it were, as a result of incorporating into the machine's tempo a rational calculation of the time and movements necessary for completing a task. It is an *economic rationality* since a single and sole preoccupation with time and presides over this new organization of work. As a consequence, supervision can be extended and resistance appears as an irrational symptom rather than as an insurrection against an oppressive order, a repressive hierarchy" (413). The effect is not only to free up relations (i.e., suppress conflict) between workers and managers, but to enable the worker to designate him- or herself as the "human factor." Rather than being rational agents, workers now become susceptible to irrationality according to how well they adapt to the rationally regular work. What is further lost is any sense of *social rationality* that might be used to show the irrationality of simple economic rationality.

In the economically rational system, the worker could, through training, keep up with the line with less effort, thus the supervisor could be on the side of the workers in the workers' complicity with the systems that controlled them. The management's interest in suppressing and routinizing conflict could be realized with the full involvement of the worker (see Knights and Collinson 1985). Worker pay could be higher. And the worker/management relation could be rationalized in "open" contractual terms. While new forms of resistance are made possible, they are also made less likely by the complicity and new form of surveillance. Piece-rate payments on up through the various worker-participation programs merely extend this basic model.

In the modern context, disciplinary power exists largely in

the new "social technologies of control." These include experts and specialists of various sorts who operate to create "*normalized*" knowledge, operating procedures, and methods of inquiry and to suppress competitive practices. As with Gramsci's (1971) organic intellectuals, the outcome of their activities is a hegemonic social cohesion lacking the conflicts and differences that characterize an open world context. But unlike in Gramsci's conception, the effect is not a coherent social order, nor is it primarily accomplished through values and ideological consent. Foucault's conception of hegemony is a free-floating set of conflicts and incompatibilities that yet, maintain asymmetrical relations. And Foucault pays much more attention to the way the body itself, rather than simply the thought processes, is subject to particular experiences and action possibilities. As Smart (1986) described Foucault's conception: "Hegemony contributes to or constitutes a form of social cohesion not through force or coercion, nor necessarily through consent, but most effectively by way of practices, techniques, and methods which infiltrate minds and bodies, cultural practices which cultivate behaviors and beliefs, tastes, desires, and needs as seemingly naturally occuring qualities and properties embodied in the psychic and physical reality (or 'truth') of the subject" (160).

Another key aspect of Foucault's conception of disciplinary power is in the presence of new forms of surveillance. The worker was always watched, but disciplinary control allowed a new form of surveillance, self-surveillance. Self-surveillance uses norms backed by "experts" for areas heretofore in the "amateur" realm. Foucault (1977) developed Bentham's "panoptic" prison design as the root vision of this new self-surveillance. In Bentham's design, a single guardhouse stood with a view into each cell, but the prisoner could never tell when he was being watched. The surveillance, hence, could be more complete than from a number of guards walking the cell block; the prisoner imagined being watched constantly. Certainly this is a feeling enforced in the modern organization, particularly at the managerial levels. Employees feel randomly watched. Employees can never tell who might use what against them or when a statement will come back to them to their detriment. And the wider the group participating in decision making, the fewer people who are safe confidants. Worker-participation programs, for example, can move the work group from interest solidarity to member self-surveillance. No cohort in resistance exists when everyone and anyone can be a member of the "management team." The implicit lawyer-at-one's-side while employee's talk is as effective today as a censor as the fear of eternal damnation was in a past time. Managers feel this more than any other group. Management freely fostered surveillance of itself. Beepers and car phones facilitated productivity but also extended the reaches of the corporation, leaving virtually no private space. One can imagine an earlier time, when leisure was a sign of having made it, now replaced with visible signs that work is so important that the employee can go nowhere without it. Discipline exists in even more subtle forms of self-surveillance.

Surveillance is not just of words and actions. With the battery of psychological (and chemical) tests—administered by experts in attitudes, culture, and bodily fluids—the corporation assesses the purity of one's mind and soul (see Hollway 1984). But more importantly, the employees assess on the corporate's behalf. The fear of someone seeing beneath the surface to detect a doubt or disloyalty, or the fear that one's own gender or belief structure won't cut it, conspire to enforce the norms. The new-age self-manipulations are often far deeper and more extreme than Huxley could dream or that any corporation could explicitly require. The continued development techniques of self-control and self-management, while not different in form from older programs of the "power of positive thinking," nonetheless provide an ever-expanding technology of body and mind control. Their pseudoscientific foundation and the implicit hatred of one's own mind and body for the sake of a perfect imaginary one, beg for control by others in the name of self-control (see Luke 1989, 116ff). In several ways the movement of the "back-stage" into the open in the sixties provided new areas of surveillance, particularly self-surveillance. Performance appraisals, designed to enable employee input into the formation of objectives, turn to open the personal to public appraisal (see Levinson 1970). Along with one's work, one's hopes, dreams, and personal commitments are also being appraised. Most employees learn to bring these under their own prior self-assessment by their own private public eye. The failure of the sixties' movements to promote an understanding the politics of the personal enabled disclosure of a constructed psychological state as freedom rather than promoted a more autonomous self-development. In doing so, the rightness of the insides, rather than the politics of that rightness, became an object of public appraisal.

The concept of self-surveillance and monitoring is deeply based in U.S. social science. Mead's (1934) conception of the development of the self drew primary attention to the function of the "generalized other" and "role playing." As Hamilton and Sutton (1989) argued, Mead showed how "individualism and social control could both be accommodated within American society: social control is internalized to become *self* control when individuals take on the attitudes of others as occupants of roles in organized action settings. By conceptualizing individuals as selves, selves and others as role occupants, and groups as organizations of roles, Mead was able to merge role theory with principles of social control, and treat both as processes of social organization" (13). In developing such conceptions, Mead was mostly concerned with how to maintain meaning and social order in a society without tradition and with a weak state. Anomie and anarchy were far greater fears than normalization and routinization. Mead's concern with the lack of an American authority structure would lead to a careful explication of discipline. The conceptions work well as part of the new social technologies of control.

The complicity of humanistic, cognitive, and behavioral psychology in these processes should not be underestimated. Psychology provided the study of the individual, especially the prediction and control of the individual. Psychology, fostered by the massive research support of the military and the professional drive of therapy, was the ideal provider of the tools of the new "discipline" of corporations (see Driskell and Beckett 1989). As an academic discipline, psychology matches well what Scott (1985, 153) identified as the central beliefs of managerialism: "People are essentially defective," "People are totally malleable." The prospect of a well-integrated worker appropriately matched to the job, and the job matched to the individual, bespoke the harmony of managerial hope. The centered self who knows who she or he is and what she or he wants provides the trustworthy person in control (well subject*ed*/subj*ected*). The testing and training programs provided the mechanism of correction in a self-referential system oriented to control rather than autonomy. And significantly, the view of human self-understanding as malleable, and of values as subjective and learned, discredited competing voices and glorified the secular and modern. The helping profession could define healthiness based on social integration and lack of personal conflict, disqualifying radical voices and the fragmentation within and without. Adjustment and retooling could put problems, or at least the solutions to them, within the person. And all this could be done in the realm of a value-neutral science, a discipline at its best.

Discipline is thus a configuration of power inserted as a way of thinking, acting, and instituting. It is shared by both those who control and are controlled; in fact it defines what control will be in its realm and the parts subjects may play. It has a discourse and a practice—a way each signifies. In the Therborn (1980) sense discussed in chapter 2, discipline is a "qualifying" practice, both enabling and limiting "what is, what is good, and what is possible." The disciplined member of the organization wants on his or her own what the corporation wants. The most powerful and powerless in traditional terms are equally subjected, though there is no doubt who is advantaged. But it is not as if either see this advantage as "rightful." In fact its rightfulness may well be contested. But the contestation itself can follow practices that reposition the actors in terms of their difference and establish the resources of one as the preferred in the struggle. Concepts of ideology and interests are useful in enabling the identification of the difference and the manner of discursive moves, but they now have to be situated in the disciplinary structure itself. They are produced there as well as play a role.

Discursive Formations

To describe how disciplinary power is dispersed and organized in particular corporations, the various members, discourses, and sites of discourse need to be analyzed. Research on these corporate elements has been popular for some time. A large body of research literature has reported on the role of communication processes in organizational maintenance, socialization of new members, legitimation of authority and practices, and the production of social order. Most of these studies arose in response to the demise of the assumptions of organizational rationality. And of course, such studies advanced assumptions of nonrational organizations. In the process they both provided a critique of management science and organizational members' "knowledge" about organization and simultaneously denied critique of self-centered member actions through legitimating the counterrational. In this sense their function has been to limit the power of the rational claim and provide power, through self-evidence and naturalness, to person-centered goals.

Much can be and has been learned from these studies. A substantial body of data exists, but the analysis often comes up short. The production of common-sense interpretations of events that every competent individual in the organization at least implicitly knows is a useful descriptive goal but usually tells us little about the corporate production of that common sense, the identity of the holder, and the power relations embedded in it. Further, the focus on "culture" or "social realities" as unified—or, where there is conflict, as conflict between holders of such unities—often overlooks the micropractices of conflict and the production of unity and the role that proclaiming "culture" has in that. Finally, the inductive philosophy of these research programs and the attempt to produce a kind of objective, generalizable knowledge often justifies the researchers' belief in value neutrality and reduces the productivity of the research (see Taylor 1990). The management of the insides rather than members' behavior appears to be a natural and even necessary consequence even though the researcher's intent may be far from this.

These studies can help us, but they must be transformed and in most cases reanalyzed in order to be of use. Primarily they must be rethought in terms of power relations (see, for example, Mumby 1987). To do that I will put aside terms such as culture, systems of meaning, or world views and begin with Foucault's conception of *discursive formations*. The assumption of unity directed by terms like *culture, meaning system,* and *worldview* will be avoided. Rather, the focus will be on discontinuity as well as continuity, resistance as well as conformity, the equivocal and uncertain as well as the processes of reducing equivocality and uncertainty, the integrated as well as the forces of disintegration. These opposite features are not unknown to cultural researchers, but they are often held as exceptions, deviance, incomplete socialization, displaying a deeper unity, or the origin of group conflict. Here these are considered inevitably interrelated in much the way as Saussure demonstrated regarding features of language. The sign must provide a positivity—what it is—but at the same time the absence—what it is not—in order to work as a sign. The matrix of inclusions and exclusions implemented in discourse becomes of concern.

Discursive formations are composed of discourses that bear a relation. For example, in an organization a manager may have a closer parking space, or a larger office, dress differently, give orders, receive higher pay, and possess more privileged knowledge. Each of these is a discourse, a signifying, representational practice. As should be clear now by the analysis, this is not to say that discourses represent a meaning or culture behind or beneath them; rather, they perform the production of subject and world. My interest is not in whether they are rightful, legitimate, or rational, or whether the particular forms of knowledge are correct or true, better or worse. As with phenomenological bracketing of the "natural attitude," I wish, with Foucault, to set aside all such questions and their apparent answers. The obvious is to be reproblematized. The questions then focus on what must be in place for these "practices" to be taken as true, legitimate, and rational and to be contested in the ways in which they are contested.

For such formations to exist, discursive practices must produce necessary objects and classification and posit a set of relations among them. The large office could be seen as a burdensome space to clean, and the close parking space would be less desired in a group where authority was shown in the public display of walking from one's car. Each of these elements has a value in relation to each of the others—something becomes valued in part because a high-status person has it, and a high-status person acquired it because it is desired. These sequences of discourses thus mutually define and support each other. They become routine, institutionalized, and rest on a set of background practices such as legal codes, ownership rights, and so forth. They thus form normal (approved) conflicts and division of resources, rewards and punishments, objects and identities. As I have already discussed, the concept of bounded rationality can be more adeqautely specified here as a specific delimitation of discourse, the putting into play of a particular discursive formation.

In sum, the following can be said about a discursive formation (see Foucault 1972, 116–117).

1. The discursive formation provides the structural interpretation of each element, but only exists as brought into play by the element.
2. Any particular statement, use of concepts, or action exists correlatively with the formation, as a sentence exists in a larger text. Neither causes nor has existence without the other. The formation thus does not exist like laws of logic or a larger deductive theory, but as a manner of unity with an internal interpretive rule structure.
3. "Discourse" thus can be seen as a group of state-

ments and conceptual configurations brought together in a discursive formation, with each discourse maintaining a relative autonomy. "Managerial discourse," for example, denotes neither who the speaker is, external to the discourse, nor a set of intentions, but a particular construction of the speaker and a specific social historical set of distinctions, interpretive practices, and integrative unities.

4. And, finally, a discursive practice notes not the existence of an individual with plans, reasons, and interests who speaks and acts, but a set of anonymous rules or structural principles that arise in a social/historical/economic/geographic area.

Each different discursive practice establishes the operation of what Foucault called an "enunciative modality." By this he suggested that objects, particular identities, and events are pulled together in various partial totalities. For example, in contemporary society we may designate "religion" as a sphere of concern. Religion is "enunciated" in contemporary society in particular manners, through institutions, practices, concepts, and bodies of knowledge. The contemporary enunciation is both related to and distinguished from that which is separate from religion and other historical enunciations. The corporation is a modern enunciation of working relations to be distinguished from nonwork and other work enunciations. The enunciation sets forth a particular set of human motivations, particular object constructions and means of valuing objects, a means of exchanges, places and processes of exchange, and means of determining worth and elite groups. At the same time, it positions the possibility of the subject being in tension with nonwork subject determinations, competing values, and particular acts of resistance. Academic social science disciplines may be said to be different enunciations of knowledge about human beings. Although many researchers act as if there were sociological, psychological, and economic forces, such entity status is produced in opposition to each as a total description— for instances, in claims that psychology can explain all of sociology or economics, or that economics can explain all of psychology or sociology. The choice is one of enunciations, the world is indifferent to the choice. The concept of enunciation, which will be made more precise as "articulation," works much the same as Weick's (1979) notion of "enactment." An enunication is a moment of *selection* and *retention*. Unlike Weick, we will see these enunciations in larger power configurations. The significant enactment is the deployment of power relations.

The individual is "subjected" in a variety of such modalities. But such formations may be contradictory and competitive in particular sites. Foucault's concept of a *discursive field* helps describe the complex interrelations among various discursive sequences as they exist in various sites. A discursive field consists of alternative ways of structuring the world and organizing social processes. For example, a woman with a young child and a position in a corporation is subject to both family discourses and corporate ones. To the extent that these offer conflicting images and behavioral scripts, she will experience considerable tension, a tension that can productively display each image and script as a construction and hence offer her a choice. But more often the tension remains to be suppressed by various means of "articulating" (or joining) the discourses, as in the "have-it-all script." The male counterpart being subjected in different discourses is likely to feel different tensions, with different articulated unities.

Not all discourses are equal or have the same power. Some justify and coexist well with other dominant discourses. Others contest the current social order and are likely to be marginalized or suppressed in various manners. For example, in many corporations an adult male is supposed to be a family man (e.g., Kanter 1977), a discursive activity that is normalized in particular ways. The man displays his family qualities by working long hours to provide a certain standard of living and quality of home life. Being "subject" in this way benefits the corporation by assuring a surplus of work over that required by the job for the sake of the eventual promotion—managerial surplus labor—and provides a relatively conflict-free identity for the male. A possible competing discourse of doing one's job so that one can spend more time at home with the family meets in certain sites with corporate disapproval and maintains the identity tension (and choice) for the manager. The corporation's interest (specified in managerialism) in a particular type of approach to work thus extends into particular child-rearing practices. Such an interest is further secured by expecting the "comer" to work a particular amount of time beyond regular hours (the popular "show" time) rather than favoring a highly productive absent worker who is "out of control" and surveillance. The long hours reproduce a "hard works gets you ahead" script that becomes self-confirming whether or not anything productive is done in that time. Having the gym at the place of work can be preferred because it creates a social continuation of work, keeps one healthy, and allows for longer hours in the evening at the workplace. Women entering the managerial ranks often point out the arbitrary nature of these practices precisely because they present discursive tension. Women's conflicts, unlike the men's, can be experienced, because the creative "articulations" (joined production) of discourses have not yet been worked out, and thus the conflict is not yet suppressed. The female employee experiences a period of strain, but also relative freedom and a chance for personal and corporate development. In this sense, the woman could be considered more free and as we shall see, more powerful at the same time as she is burdened and relatively powerless in particular discourses.

Analyses that identify such tensions have often treated them as a property of the individual—a personal problem— since the individual cannot produce a unity from which to make decisions. While the individual becomes the site of such tensions, they exist externally and structurally in regard to the person. Enunciations are not caused by external factors, nor do they originate in the person or represent something behind them. They are descriptive of the relations; the subject exists on the surface of them, as does the external world. As Foucault (1972) described it:

> In the proposed analysis, instead of referring back to *the* synthesis or *the* unifying function of *a* subject, the various enunciative modalities manifest his [sic] dispersion. To the various statuses, the various sites, the various positions that he can occupy or be given when making a discourse. To the discontinuity of the planes from · which he speaks. And if these planes are linked by a system of relations, this system is not established by the synthetic activities of a consciousness identical with itself...but by the specificity of a discursive practice. I shall abandon any attempt, therefore, to see discourse as a phenomenon of expression...I shall look for a field of regularity for various positions of subjectivity. Thus conceived, discourse is not the majestically unfolding of a thinking, knowing, speaking subject, but, on the contrary, a totality, in which the dispersion of the subject and his discontinuity with himself may be determined. (54–55)

The regulation of the various enunciations thus is not performed by a transcendental or psychological subject but by the relations of power that produce the subject.

The Strategic Power Apparatus and its Articulation

As an analytic tool to look at power relations, Foucault proposed the concept of "apparatus." This concept will be useful for describing the complex ways power relations operate within corporate organizations. The apparatus is a discursive and nondiscursive formation that shows how power is deployed in various strategic moves. Such a concept allows us to move beyond chapter 5's analysis of experience as sedimented and institutionalized to describing the interrelations among the various institutionalizations as based on strategic power relations. Foucault (1980a) described the apparatus as "a thoroughly heterogeneous ensemble consisting of discourses, institutions, architectural forms, regulative decisions, laws, administrative measures, scientific statements, philosophical, moral, and philanthropic propositions.... The apparatus itself is the system of relations that can be established between these elements" (194). The systems of relations among these elements composes power in organizations. The apparatus is the form of latent strategic action central to systematically distorted communication from a disciplinary perspective. The apparatus describes a context in which both the control strategies and genuine attempts at a common understanding are formed on top of an unexpressed strategy that makes each possible.

The conception of apparatus moves the analysis beyond the discursive formations along to the full set of discursive and nondiscursive relations that work together to produce particular subjects with particular knowledge and realities. The corporation is a produced site of numerous discourses standing in relatively mobile relations with each other. Although arbitrary, they are relatively ordered with expected gaps and conflicts, with ambiguities and discretion, with order and enforcement, with advantaged groups and comparatively deprived ones. Each is secured by a complex web of relations and concealed by discursive practices. This much is obvious and for many unproblematic. But would we chose these if a wider range of experiences were available? At what times and places would such orders be desired? And are experience and development open? Unlike some, there is no claim here that subordination is bad.

We all choose it and choose it appropriately. Asymmetry is present in every interchange of speaker and listener. Oppression—to be subordinated against one's will—is of moral concern, a moral concern that can be expressed in terms of discursive practices. Understanding the apparatus of control within the corporate site is critical to the moment-by-moment choices of the consent to domination or the struggle for freedom.

The apparatus can help describe the strategic nature of power formations that Foucault's earlier work missed. There is an order and advantage to each particular discursive formation. To keep the strategic and power sense of the apparatus distinguished from Foucault's earlier work, I will refer to the specific surface modalities as *articulations* rather than *enunciations*. Further, this allows an extension along the same lines but beyond Foucault into the more recent work of Laclau and Mouffe (1985). *Articulation* will carry the same sense of a particular thematization that *enunciation* did. The term, however, better avoids the notion of speaking or being a product of a person. It also allows a second meaning, that of being segmented and connected by joints, as in an articulation agreement.

Laclau and Mouffe's concept of articulation, like Foucault's concept of apparatus, enables a critique of hegemonic formations freed from the logic of historical determination of the totality. As Angus (in press) described: "Articulation theory is the form hegemony takes when it has ceased to be the thematic concern against a presupposed background of historical logic and has itself become the background against which any historical figures emerge" (5). With Foucault such a conception can recall a theory of conflict and conflictual relations without reduction to class struggle or simple interest domination. Neither power nor resistance is centered. Both are dispersed. Any move toward greater democracy must start there. Class conflict or gender conflict are neither necessary nor essential but tensions produced at moments in particular configurations. Domination must be understood within shifting configurations.

At any time a number of articulations are possible. Each is a specific practice but brings to bear a particular totalization, much as each word dually signifies what is external to it and the entire system of distinctions from which it can make reference. Using the earlier phenomenological example, to describe something as "red" puts into play an interest in color as a point of view potentially extended to everything and discriminates objects within that interest. Competing articulations operate within discursive and nondiscursive fields. Any particular articulation dominates and persists to the extent that it can be rearticulated against competing articulations. All such domination-produced totalities are based in contingent but powerful logics.

For example, if particular social sciences study only measurable objects, the world and relations there become objectified (if it exists, it exists to some extent and can be measured). Such a social science is not dependent on particular researchers making certain assumptions or on the world having certain properties. The researcher does not have to agree or consent, the practice already accomplishes the belief. The practice of the social science posits a researching subject with those assumptions and a world with those properties, even in potential opposition to what the researcher is articulated as in another context (e.g., when talking about the choice of doing research). Such an articulation holds power until a counterarticulation is advanced. Such articulations and counterarticulations take a variety of forms. In understanding them we acquire insight into the microplay of domination, resistance, and mutual formation.

Managerial Knowledge and Expertise

Most fundamentally each strategic apparatus or particular articulation positions an identity for members and a realm of knowledge about both themselves and the world around them. Both identities and knowledge are strategic. This is not to suggest that they are done with foresight, or understanding or for gains. They are rather natural, self-evident, and as discovered by the appropriate experts. Nonetheless, they are clearly to some people's benefit rather than others', and they must be rearticulated in opposition to possible challenges. While this rearticulation may be performed by both those advantaged and those disadvantaged, the rearticulation is done as if motivated and strategic. And if the psychological prejudice is cast aside, the "as if" can be taken away. The constant rearticulation of identity and knowledge is key to understanding control as practiced in corporations and demonstrates far more than any concept of control described as psychologically intended by corporate actors. The role of knowledge and expertise is central. Initially power can be seen as deployed in processes of conception, accounting, data collection, and information technologies, each functioning as a social technology of control. The next chapter will take up the issue of identity and the production of the corporate actor.

Knowledge and Common Sense

With Foucault, it seems clear that there is no deployment of power without a correlative deployment of knowledge. Knowledge is disciplinary. Knowledge is "right" by virtue of the normal procedures and the practice of the expert. The modern corporation reveals a dynamic interplay between common sense and expert knowledge. The two become intertwined in interesting and decisively political ways. Each form of knowledge is intrinsically political and each is enacted in specific, strategic, if unintentional, practices. Researchers have often opted to play in the realm of experts against the myths of common sense (see chapter 3), but as we shall see it is their profession of objective knowledge (the possibility of it), rather than their knowledge, that is most often of interest to corporations.

Since Schutz's (1962) work it has been common to talk about taken-for-granted knowledge as central to social interaction. Taken-for-granted knowledge is clearly political, as it is no more than the sedimented experience of a social group. Everyday actors, less precisely but perhaps more accurately, refer to this knowledge as "common sense." Common sense consists of shared meanings and the implicit acceptance of concepts and activities that produce and confirm these meanings. While these meanings and processes inevitably favor certain groups and interests, common-sense knowledge becomes relatively fixed and widely accepted even when it is to the disadvantage of the user. In this sense it is both naturalized and neutralized. As Hall (1977) described the power and concealment of this knowledge:

> [Its] "spontaneous" quality, its transparency, its "naturalness," its refusal to be made to examine the premises on which it is founded, its resistance to change or to correction, its effect of instant recognition, and the closed circle in which it moves what makes common sense, at one and the same time "spontaneous," ideological, and unconscious. You cannot learn, through common sense, how things are: you can only discover where they fit into the existing scheme of things. In

this way, its very taken for grantedness is what establishes it as a medium in which its own premises and presuppositions are being rendered invisible by its apparent transparency. (332)

Clearly common sense is not monolithic. It often is filled with areas of incompletion and contradiction and is differentially socially distributed. Its power is linked to its self-evidence and the ability to fragment it and produce answers in different contexts that would be contradictory if put together. The forgetfulness of its one-sidedness is often because of its fragmentation and unresolved tensions within it. Common sense is protected from critique because of its pervasiveness and the formation of institutions and practices that extend and confirm its truth. Opposition to it could only be for personal gain or because of disconnection from life (ivory towers), and experience has taught that new ideas, like new management theories, come and go, but basic shared principles stay much the same. "Everything I ever really needed to know I learned in kindergarten."

Modern forms of scientific knowledge and expertise are treated as natural opposites to common sense. Historically, the production of the first lens literally and metaphorically provided the first challenge to the obvious and shared. More is going on than meets the eye, and the one with the lens leads the newly sight impaired. Knowledge could replace wisdom, book smartness could exceed street smartness, and experience could be a flawed teacher. We all grew up knowing that those with common sense would laugh at believers in a flat world, and that Columbus would have the last laugh as belief in a round world would stand in place of every daily perception to the contrary long before the pictures came from the moon. The tension between common sense and codified knowledge, however, still exists—a tension recalled in stories of disdain and respect for the other in both everyday and scientific communities. Despite residual tensions in corporations, science has become everyday practice. Not that art and common sense are absent or ever totally marginalized. But training and marketing reside alongside gut reactions and intuition. Understanding the interplay between these two forms of knowing is essential to understanding the deployment of power.

Common sense in the corporation is not an organic *sensus communis,* as existed in traditional societies. As socialization has gradually become performed by secondary rather than primary institutions, common sense has changed with it. The common understandings growing out of the integrated family, work, community, and church were grounded in tradition and integrated across experiential realms. Their character was wisdom, and their mode of development was experience. They were possessed and passed on by the elders. Modern common sense is fragmented like the modern identity. It is often based on "autonomous" choices lacking history or resonance. Faith is the recent conversion, principles are from the latest book, social position is the latest job, learning is training, contribution is assessed early. Common sense is more a shared opinion than a tradition. The point is not to lament the passing or to contend that this is all there is, but to characterize a difference that changes the relation and possible tension between science and common sense. Not only is common sense a political formation of interest in its own right, but the felt autonomy, the lack of a connection to historical experience, and its fragmentation further protect it from critique and make it easier to control.

"Scientific" knowledge is central to the functioning of modern corporations. The domination of a techno-instrumental reasoning process in corporations, as should be clear from the past chapter, has been well documented for some time. This is not simply the legacy of scientific management theory, though certainly it is an early articulation of it. American corporate leaders as a group prefer implementation of equipment, continue to implement communication technologies even where gains are marginal at best, and believe that more technological development is the ultimate solution for all difficulties, including those created by technology. The loss of competitiveness is far more often attributed to declines in science education than to declines in arts and humanities education. Pay structures that greatly reward "engineering," over human relations or production, interlock well with class and gender differentiations. Business publications are filled with popular discussions of theoretical science in astronomy, medicine, and physics. Modern science, with its control of nature and people aligns well with the corporate transformation of nature through people management.

One could hardly be impressed, however, with the American corporate use of science. Most research and development groups are given remarkably constrained problems. Major advances in new technologies and conceptions have come from the separate institutes and universities. U.S. engineering has often not kept pace with that of other countries, even before U.S. education institutions presumably failed in science preparation. The engineering in Japanese and German cars arises not because labor costs are less or their engineers are better, but from a better utilization of science. Even innovative groups like Bell Laboratories have gradually fallen to marketing people. The development of management science and professional managers, as has been developed, arose in a particular formation, but the use of social science has not kept pace with the apparent belief in it. Without a doubt, corporations collect lots of data, but that data is often used to justify decisions after they are made rather than to guide them. Educational use of case studies and storytelling indicate a commonsensical rather than scientific approach to decision making and human relations. Consulting and training are often done by people with research credentials, but their judgments, not their science, appears to be of concern. Their studies certify them to talk, but what they say is rarely connected in any rigorous way to their studies. By the time the findings and ideas are packaged for corporate use, one could hardly discern the assumptions and constraints of the studies. If social science has an effect on corporations at all, it is through the introduction of new concepts rather than the production of anything approaching a claim to truth, a logic contrary to management science. The endless studies appear largely unused.

How do we put together the respect *and* disuse accorded to science? The privilege given to science and its presumed neutrality are absolutely essential to suppressing the tensions arising from asymmetries in the modern corporation. It is not the knowledge of science that is critical, though it is useful, but the claim of science to produce privileged, apolitical knowledge. The concern is not with epistemological hegemony that produces a certain type of knowledge, but with the assumptions proclaimed by that science. Managers use social-science-generated knowledge less than they use the proclaimed existence of special knowledge and expertise. For example, it should be of no surprise that, since upper level managers make pay decisions, that they pay managers more; they value more what managers are able to do. This could be seen as blatantly self-serving, and owners as well as other groups could raise difficult if not impossible questions. Managerial *expertise* is a critical claim. Not only do managers presumably care more about the corporation, but they have greater expertise and warrant greater pay. But expertise is as complex and difficult as economic conceptions of scarcity and replaceability that often accompany it.

There are many forms of expertise in most corporations besides that claimed by management, and much of this expertise is scarce and essential for the corporation to function, yet it is debased and marginalized, and science plays a part in that. Some of the most impressive human acts require great manual expertise. But rather than paying for it, much corporate energy is put into eliminating any manual task requiring such training and native talent. Science must replace it, presumably to reduce labor costs, but more often the effect is to make labor less interesting and to generate higher costs in the monitoring and maintenance of the replacement. Labor is made ugly and tedious, and science (in the hands of managers) must save us from it. Clearly, not all expertise and scarcity are respected or have high monetary value. A garage mechanic who can quickly identify the origin of a noise is an expert and scarce. A teacher who can enthrall a class is an expert and scarce. A secretary who handles people well, keeps the books, and manages incoming information is an expert and scarce. In the same twist that lets working after hours evoke the logic of "one gets ahead by hard work" even if one isn't working hard but only talking about it, the possibility of a privileged knowledge and access to it defines the possibility of managerial elitism, our modern version of the divine right of kings. Ivy League programs, named and separate professional schools, and highly paid consultants become important parts of the total articulation. It matters not whether the secretary is more competent than the person for whom "she" (usually and significantly) works. She doesn't have the right credential, the "tie" to the right knowledge. She's not the surrogate scientist with a white shirt and computer substituting for the lab coat and instruments. Significantly, "emotional labor" of all kinds, no matter how critical, is debased. The rational and scientific are privileged. And this remains the case even where it is clear that computer-supported decision systems can replace virtually every part of the work decision process except emotional labor.

As suggested in the last chapter, managerialism has a unique identity for managers, derived from their abilities, their expertise, their entrepreneurian spirit, and their leadership qualities. Miller and Form (1964) summed up well what many have observed: Top management is "a highly self-conscious group whose ethnocentrism leads them to believe that they have special gifts and attributes not generally shared by the population. The greatest of these is the ability to manage and organize people.... Top management is an authority-conscious group. Men at the top of the supervisory structure are consumed with decision-making and commanding. Yet they do not like to believe that men obey them because they have power...they want to feel that they command because they are gifted to lead" (186, as cited by Storey 1983, 104). Thus while at another time one's power might have been justified by a connection to a god, or the leader might have delighted openly in raw power, the managerial articulation describes "command by ability." The possession of special knowledge and expertise is essential to the structure. Reclaiming alternative notions of expertise is critical to any democracy of everyday life.

And what of management as an art? Every discourse, as we have seen, establishes its opposite, it positions what is contestable and what is not. Management as art evokes the older formation from which science positioned itself as a contrast. But it is not less elitist. The energy is put into discussion of the different sources of expertise, but the outcome is the concealed reproduction of advantage in each. Again the "approved conflict" suppresses the more essential one. The resolution of management as both art and science can even further conceal the asymmetries each creates.

The earlier formation of art constructed the "genius" in the deep intuitive insight. Prior to the rise of individualism in the nineteenth century, such genius arose out of the *geist* of the tradition itself. The possessor was properly possessed. The early "mad" scientist and tuberculous artist both articulate this formation. The creation of science as methodic both civilized and democratized this image. The *geist* became the socially shared tools and instruments that could now be picked up by anyone. Hard work could now achieve the insight. The conception of management as art and science claims both the rational and the irrational, but not just any rational or irrational. The rationality peculiar to science and the irrationality of one uniquely possessed. Debates over the rationality of organizations miss the point of knowledge in power formations. Corporations have reasons; the interesting questions are what reasons do they have, and how are they deployed and reproduced.

The Transparency of Language in Knowledge

The "communication as transfer of meaning" conception is central to hierarchical systems. I have argued that conceptions of words as representational and of communication as a process of transferring meaning by use of signs are misleading, both because they treat meaning as fixed somewhere and because they assume that language is transparent. Meaning is created in the interactions among people; it is not a commodity possessed and traded. Certainly this has been commonly understood for some time (see Smith 1970 1972). Still, as Axley (1984) has shown, the "communication-as-conduit" metaphor pervades the writing about communication in organizations. The common substitution of the word *communications* for *communication* when describing occupational roles and the process of interacting further evidences this domination. Actually we need little evidence; such a conception is so pervasive that most of us conceptualize our own acts of communicating in this way in common everyday settings (Reddy 1979). Not only is such a conception theoretically weak, it works against useful conceptions of organizational problems and, as Sless (1986) documented, costs money. So why does it remain pervasive?

Such a conception demonstrates power and can be described in numerous articulations. Everyday talk in organizations asks others to be clear, to know what they want to say, to define terms, to use terms for which there is already shared meaning. Such statements in a general way function to conceal power relations in treating words as transparent (or potentially so), to naturalize meaning as existent rather than produced, and to advance personal meaning as unitary and determinable. They enact power in privileging clarity over uncertainty and ambiguity, in producing expression and interaction as controllable objects, and in advancing influence and control rather than participation. The individual is centered as site and controller of meaning. The conception of communication is legitimized in routine, if unstated, enthymematic linguistic sequence connections to efficiency and rationality. In these interconnections, being controlled by your emotions, being carried away by an idea, trying to sort it out in public are marginalized or set aside to specific times and places. Judgments of trust, confidence, and intelligence become "natural" consequences of certain expression styles. And institutional practices further extend the momentary expression. Manuals are written and training sessions offered to add a coat of knowledge and expertise. An organizational hierarchy is established in terms of a linear communication network. Legal codes are written in terms of statement and intent rather than systemic meaning. Ideas are owned and copyrighted. Information is bought and sold. The data base holds past statements waiting to be retrieved and distributed. Responsibility and worth are assessed in terms of knowing. The whole of the American way of life and the enlightenment tradition becomes invested in the instruction "be clear." It's little wonder academic statements of "process" and emergent meanings have so little practical effect.

But the communication conception is powerful not because a manager demands it, but because of the formation. "Clarity" and linear models of communication do not represent a monolithic formation. The "organized society" does not have a reality outside the articulations of it. Each practice, including commands about the practice of communication, has to produce/reproduce the formation. The treatment of the "organization," "culture," or "society" as existing apart and given power to cause the string of interconnections in the formation is a secondary power move like a more ancient pronouncement of "God's will." The power of the conception of communication does not come from the outside. Its power rests in the network of routines, past experiences, and technologies. The complicity of the powerless is essential, a complicity aided by a discourse of large linear causal forces. The telephone and the clock *discipline* toward the linear and efficient in ways no manager could. The conduit view of communication is not felt as oppressive and capable of suppressing mixed feelings and emergent meanings. Rather it is an opportunity for greater efficiency and productivity. But greater efficiency and productivity toward what goals and whose interests? Efficient "communication" at work often means less personal contact and new meaning creation so that there can be more leisure, personal contact, and edification outside of work. But this outside space continues to be reduced by the processes of trying to produce them. The power of the formation is in its channeling.

Lest this seem too deterministic, recall that the formation is power, but does not have power. Even while the "communication as conduit" conception is ubiquitous, the individual's experience is not closed. Rather it is forgetful or, better, does not arise in other ways at this moment. The situation at this moment is foregrounded against potentially competing experiences and formations. We *could* remember productive misunderstandings, recall the many things we wanted to say at once, recall the talk with a friend in which we could not remember who first had the idea we came to share, recall the ambiguity and uncertainty that didn't go into the report, recall the times when we knew what we wanted to say after we talked, recall when we wanted to retrieve a feeling that could not be stored. Although we could remember these things, in most moments we don't. The managerialist command to "be clear" is always a moment of advantage in potential antagonistic relations; it passes over conflicts that don't happen. Conflict, if present, could threaten order and create a different order. The "clear" expression is a moment of not choosing, not recalling, a moment of democratic failure. If each moment of forgetting appears too small and insignificant, recall that these, rather than the armies of the state and revolution, are the manners of control, consent, and resistance that make up the modern democratic struggle. The innumerable sites of power and resistance. It is not the power from above that is the issue but the power that is everywhere. Each moment of recalling and action is a move toward democracy. And again, this is not to say that sloppy thinking and expression are critical to democracy. Rather, the politics of clarity and transmission, and the conception of sloppy and participatory development of meaning, exemplify one site of the many that are of potential concern.

Further, the presumed transparency of language embedded in the managerial formation suppresses important conflicts and provides a measure of systematic distortion as latent strategic action. As is clear in the treatment of language in chapter 5, conception is a practical accomplishment of valuation in corporations. The ethnomethodologies (see Mehan and Wood 1975) have made clear the practical and arbitrary nature of classification. Daft and Wiginton (1979) have shown how concepts and classifications direct corporate experience and reactions. People evoke and use concepts to provide for an orderly existence. We have already seen that the linguistic system of signifiers is intrinsic to the constitution of the objects of experience. And finally I have shown that elements of experience always exceed the moment of their being articulated in a certain way. *Power* exists in the "valuing"—the attending to this not that—and *domination* in the concealment of valuing and freezing of the person/object in a set of articulations. The presumption of transparency completes the cycle by presenting the frozen person/object as naturalized and neutralized, as spontaneously there (see Clegg 1987). The person/object is presented as a real object in the world to be described, rather than its present description/constitution as being in need of exploration. The corporate formation has "real" people with "real" characteristics acting in "real" situations. The imaginary quality of the "realness" is lost, and the power in and implications of their production remains invisible. The potential conflicts over "who" and "what" exists are suppressed. Differentiations of people based on "obvious" and "self-evident" traits in concepts like "worker" and "manager" are taken-for-granted, and remarkably arbitrary, productions. As Hall (1988) put it:

> Ruling or dominant conceptions of the world do not directly prescribe the mental content...of the dominated classes. But the circle of dominant ideas *does* accumulate the symbolic power to map or classify the world for others; its classifications do acquire not only the constraining power of dominance over other modes of thought but also the inertial authority of habit and instinct. It becomes the horizon of the taken-for-granted: what the world is and how it works, for all practical purposes. (44)

The denial of transparency—of such a faith in the naturalness and self-evidence of experience—enables an analysis of language use in corporations based on an interest in power relations and participation.

Accounting as Guardian of the Code

The accounting process is of particular significance in the modern corporation. If money is the primary "code" in managerialism, accounting becomes the primary guardian of that code. It clearly functions as a social technology of control. As would be expected in looking at the corporate apparatus, accountancy carries the familiar qualities of expertise, instrumental reasoning, linear communication models, and transparency. The latent strategic function seen as discipline is deployed in each (see Knights and Collinson 1987).

The accountant report is one of the most basic produced "facts" of the corporation. Particularly as it appears in the annual report, it is one of few public glances at the interworking of the corporation (at the "real," rather than public relation's image). Its "factual" quality enables it to be used strategically to support decision making, especially regarding efficiency, to advance personal political motives, and to support the corporate facade to internal and external audiences (Ansari and

Euske 1987). Whether it advantages or harms a particular management team, accounting adds a quality of "bottom-line," rationality, and legitimacy to corporate decision making. But it is a construction and a constitutive steering mechanism in the social system. Much has been written on these issues (see Armstrong 1987; Hines 1988; Hopwood 1987; Laughlin 1987; March 1987; Penno 1984; Power, in press). Neither these detailed analysis nor their controversies will be repeated here. But I do wish to highlight the conclusion that every aspect of the modern corporation, including the relatively autonomous discourse of accountancy, conjoins in particular ways with the managerial apparatus.

Accounting is usefully understood in communicational terms. It is not simply the recording of data to be distributed in information systems. The accounting report is socially produced through a system of social relations including the privileging of certain interactants and particular distinctions and values. Power (1986) concluded, following Stamp (1981), that accounting is a "social process in which the negotiated relationship between preparers and users of financial information is central. This is less a recognition of the wider political nature of accounting than an injunction against those who would give it a purely technical status, abstracted from the communication processes that are actually fundamental" (393). The communicative dynamic is interesting because of the conflicting needs of the multiple audiences of potential users. And more fundamentally, the outcome of the communication processes is the accountants' constitution of reality itself, a constitution that reappears as neutral and consensual, even though not all groups had an equal say in the construction process.

From a representation standpoint, clearly not all users of financial information have an equal opportunity to determine what assumptions will be built into the statistics themselves. Workers, owners, management, the public, and the Internal Revenue Service can all have quite different interests. Arguments over reporting environmental costs, pension fund payments, and methods of reporting earnings evidence the conflict. While it is unclear whether managerial groups consistently lobby for self-interested accounting standards, it is clear that there is remarkably little public discussion of the accounting process (see McKee et al. 1984). And at a micro level, management has clear control over significant determinations. For example, fixed assets such as cars and buildings can be valued using selling price, replacement cost, or original purchase cost. The choice significantly changes the corporate profile. While the alternative chosen must be disclosed, the potentially discussable value-laden choice rests with management's accountants, who operate with a cloak of expertise. For example, managerial expense accounts and perks, while counted as a cost, have lifestyle and value foundations that are themselves rarely discussed. The lack of public discussion of the various issues gives a hint of the greater significance. The presence of "facts," rather than the content of the facts, is of greatest importance to managerialism. While relatively little discussion takes place regarding the construction of particular facts, even less opens the conflicts suppressed by the existence of facts. The lack of both conflicts is an active production.

Accounting procedures, like scientific method, acquire an important transparency in the corporate context. A central element of this is the production of accountancy as a science and the accountant as an expert. Despite the new discussions of accounting standards arising from Eastern Europe as they become market economies and active discussions in professional publications such as *Accounting, Organizations, and Society,* accountants have maintained their formal, grey image as rational, quiet arbitrators and certifiers of fact. Accountants have achieved the qualities of what Collins (1979) called a "strong" profession: One that "requires a real technical skill that produces demonstrable results and can be taught.... The skill must be difficult enough to require training and reliable enough to produce results. But it cannot be too reliable for then outsiders can judge work by its results and control its practitioners by their judgments" (132–133). As will be shown in the next chapter regarding language use, the exclusion of outsiders as possible discussants suppresses important conflicts. The trick is to both codify the procedures to support neutrality and consensus and maintain enough areas of discretion for the presence of mystique and judgment to sustain the claim of expertise (Power, in press). Although the purpose may be to support and advance accountancy as a profession, the significant benefactor is managerialism. The strategic implications of the apparatus are clear.

The accountant's report, like the scientific finding, rarely carries with it the details of its construction. Standard accounting practices, like scientific methods, remain outside of corporate discussion. In addition, even routine information that would be required for replication is rarely reported. The report, like the scientific finding, stands as a certified fact and invites use but closes off discussion of itself. The greater the consensus on the standards, the less that has to be reported in terms of the "fact production" procedures. The standards assure transparency and suppress the availability of the information that would make the facts contestable and show the standards themselves as arbitrary. Accountancy as a profession has an interest in minimal conflict, an interest that aligns well with the power/knowledge equation in the managerial apparatus. The accountant's report invisibly creates the "visible" organization as a financial entity and provides a language for corporate self-understanding. Accounting is a disciplinary power that colonizes the organization by creating newly internalized facts and vocabularies that are constitutive of organizational reality in a way that suppresses potential conflict over its mission (see Roberts and Scapens 1990; Hines 1988). The constitution of the worker as a cost, for example, can preempt any other articulation and thus hide the cost of the work experience to the worker. The worker, except for the arbitrary representation as a cost, is as much the "visible" corporation as the balance sheet, but the balance sheet, rather than the worker, becomes the public display. The "fact" quality hides the arbitrariness of the monetary code as translation, as well as the assumptions by which the translation works. Occasionally there are discussions of triple-entry bookkeeping, in which costs and benefits to the general society (e.g., environmental costs, product quality, landfill implications, mental health) could be entered along with economic debits and credits. But such efforts are often dismissed out-of-hand, owing to costs (!) or economic (!) repercussions. The monetary code rules.

Clearly power and domination would exist in the corporation without the accounting, but the production and investment choices would be more visibly ideological and contestable. Accounting as a social technology provides a disciplinary intervention and the properties of normalization and self-surveillance that come with it (Tompkins and Groves 1983). Significantly, it suppresses a number of conflicts that are central to managerialism.

Data Collection and Forms of Control

Even more basic than accounting practices are the forms used to collect and construct both financial and nonfinancial data.

Data presented on forms make up a significant part of what is known of the individual in terms of background, health, productivity, and psychological makeup. Forms are usefully thought of as a major mode of discourse in corporations, a communicative practice. To some extent this is widely known. Job applicants fill them out carefully (and even know when they can lie), considerable help is given to particularly favored new members to help them present themselves in a good light, and even a casual look at a form can reveal values expressed (even unknowingly) by the form maker. And like any message, data collected from forms can be interpreted in many ways and utilized for many different ends. Yet it is not uncommon for such data to be treated as an "objective" record, fully naturalized and neutralized. The attention to competing interpretations of the record hides the conflicts suppressed by the first interpretation, the production of the record itself. Legal requirements, grievance rules, and a host of other routine institutionalized practices structure the "discourse of forms" in a unique and powerful manner. When this occurs, forms are treated as transparent in much the same way as language and other institutional practices. The manners in which they constitute the data become invisible; data become an objective reality. Forms-as-medium become simply one more element in a linear communication sequence. Even the fact that they are often "badly" worded and constructed misdirects attention from their serious importance and strategic value. One struggles to become competent in filling them out or to present oneself well, or curse the maker, but misses the significance of the form itself as a normalizing process.

The relation between the form and the person filling it out is not a *means* of communication, but it is communication; it is a production of meaning. In the phenomenologist's terms, forms are a type of *administrative sedimentation,* an intentional practice that became routinized and institutionalized. Forms have their own subjectivity. As in using a camera or walking a sidewalk, the self's subjectivity merges with that of the institutionalized form to see and express the world in a particular manner. The form, like any institution, has a subjectivity; it has values, distinctions, and intentions. As a discourse it "interpellates" a particular subject. But the interaction cannot be participatory. The individuals filling out the form struggle to express themselves in the discourse of the form, but the form is not transformed. The multiple discourses that "subject" the complex individual are reduced to the discourse of the form. The reasons for a gap in the record—the illness or sick child, the time to help someone else, the absence of resources—have no place on the productivity record. The codifiable and the requested are a social technology of normalization—of conflict suppression. As Sless (1988) argued, the form is potentially "a site of intense and direct ideological struggle over meaning—a battleground on which competing and conflicting interests converge" (57). But the struggle is often personal and informal; it has no record; it has no place in corporate memory. Corporate members fight over the meaning of data, the access to the data, and the use of data, but far less over the collection and production of data.

Ironically the attempt to protect the "personal" from formal corporate intrusion (for example, in collecting data about one's family) ultimately denies the personal. The individual must manage it to stay normal in the corporate code. The personal information cannot be used against the person, but it also is denied a place. Making the personal invisible means that the corporation does not have to adjust, as the form does not adjust. The corporate illusion that men and women with children compete equally with those without is formally reproduced. The corporate discourse in this example is protected from value questions regarding how personal factors should be handled (in fact, the discussion is legally precluded), but it is filled with invisible values that advantage and disadvantage regarding personal factors. Various disadvantaged groups have understood this for some time in "objective" educational assessments. As I demonstrated in another place: "The most disadvantaged groups may be those most unfairly treated by the objective and objectified procedures which were developed in the pursuit of accuracy and fairness" (Deetz and McGlone 1983, 81). This is not to fault those who have worked to overcome arbitrary and capricious decision making through hiring and assessment guidelines, but to argue that explicit and objective critieria and procedures can be an even more effective means of control. They are invisible; they suppress a conflict at the site of hiring; but they are not less arbitrary, and they are often capricious in effects. The "form" is the first and most basic deployment of this type of disciplinary power (see Hollway 1984).

The issue of significance is not simply who controls the forms, but what is their discursive character. In his work, Sless (1988) focused on the production of forms. In the bureaucracies he observed: "At any moment a form is a cumulative record of decisions that have been made within a bureaucracy. This is never...a coherent rational process. There are, of course, strong elements of competing rationality between different interests, but the convergence of these on the forms is seldom coherent" (58). In general Sless argued that there are four groups that principally influence form construction; the first two are the most influential. First are the officers who are responsible for interpreting legislation and setting policies. Second, system developers, computer programmers, and systems analysts wield considerable control because their machines must deal with the mass of data collected. Third, some control is exercised by those who administer the filling out of forms, primarily from their desire for efficiency and accuracy. And finally, data processors have some influence because the speed of their operation influences the timeliness of the output. What is of greatest interest is not who these people are but what their interests are. Clearly managers only occasionally explicitly assert their values in form construction; rather, they only try to "collect" what is *necessary, useful,* and *efficient.* They hope to do it with *expertise.* It is not managers that control, but managerialism—a particular perception of what the corporation is, what its goals ought to be, and what codification is possible. Surveillance through forms is conducted in certain areas, and for their own advantage employees self-monitor and report themselves in those areas. But the employee efforts for gain fail to account for their own enactment of managerial control over self-definition and their work effort.

Those working in universities often see clearly the extent to which nontenured faculty structure their lives (often with the full support of others) around the production of the tenure packet rather than their research and teaching. In a sense these individuals (and often departments) feel as if they have beaten an oppressive system for the sake of an eventual freedom. But more often they have enacted the discipline that need not be enforced and will continue to do so as definitions of success are routinized that deny the ever-in-the-future freedom.

Such is the nature of discipline. The production of the facts, the record, deploy a system at a microlevel that webs out across discourses. The great conflict over promotions and reward systems, over levels of productivity and systems designed to increase productivity, frequently draw attention away from the conflicts suppressed in the measure itself, the preference for the measurable, and the production of the measured subject.

Information Technologies and Data Bases

Similar issues arise in a careful exploration of the development of communication technologies and data bases. As developed in chapter 5, every technology extends the "subject" (and subjects/sub*jects*) in particular manner and hence engages in a politics of sensuality. Technologies discipline by normalizing and standardizing the position and movement of the body. By doing so, they enable activities the subject could not otherwise do and enhance coordination while they delimit the subject and his or her experience. Information processing technologies, of course, do this also. Altheide (1985) has shown this to be true of even the use of the keyboard. Most basically, such technologies structure what can be seen, felt, and heard, and not every thing or everybody has an equal opportunity. Each technology privileges, favors, and excludes. New technologies have the capacity to diminish the importance of dominant groups and their knowledge (Barley 1986), but more often they extend control and reproduce dominant values, practices, and forms of knowledge. Such effects are doubled by rules and resources that specify inequality in availability of data and access to communication channels.

Not only do communication technologies shape the body and senses; each is an extension of thinking and memory. Each technology, especially as attached to a data base, embodies a way of thinking and a kind of memory. Each gives preference to certain forms of knowledge and communication. Turkle (1984) has, of course, shown this in regard to female and male students' use of computers, but the issue can be framed in more general ways. Book smartness is easy to store, street smartness is difficult. Codified, classified "knowledge" is easily stored and retrieved in such systems; intuitive, conceptual insights are not. Mitroff (1983), following Jung, demonstrated that in organizations, different individuals have identifiable preferences for different types of data in their decision making. Existing communication technologies give preference to "thinking-sensing." In fact, the concept of data in modern society is often reduced to this single type. What Weber and Habermas have called "rationalized knowledge" holds a certain primacy over potentially competing forms of reason. The data base further institutionalizes this preference.

Structural changes in the use of electronic connections and efficiency evaluations, added to the implementation of specific technologies, privilege a type of data and, hence, people who prefer that form of data. Individuals with other preferences find their data less valued and less available. Some of these data-preference differences may be divided roughly along gender lines, if we apply analyses like Gilligan's (1982; see also Kramarae 1989; Rakow 1988). If it is possible that some thinking styles are more generally used by women and others by men, communication technologies and attendant storage and retrieval systems have implications for gender politics. The difficulties of properly opening up such a discussion are great. The historical development of technologies and the language of the discourses about technology are so completely dominated by male interests that there seems to be no place for a discourse (see Jansen 1989). The emotional labor of women already debased in the "formal" and in managerial expertise appears to be structured as a natural opposite to the information technologies being developed. The potential conflict between these interests becomes suppressed in a medium that has already made up its, and everyone's, "mind."

Continued technological developments in current directions aid some groups over others by reproducing and accentuating existing power differences. Even if preferences change and different groups become equally proficient in the use of the preferred rationalized data form, we are still left to ask what has been lost and in what ways decisions (and ultimately, our collective development) have been altered. Would we have chosen this direction, had we been given the opportunity to participate in the decision?

Further, the current preference given to certain technologies along the lines of the dominant form of rationalization leads to a continuation of the process Braverman (1974) called "deskilling." As developed in chapter 8, Braverman means that the conception of problems and possible responses becomes severed from the execution of the chosen action. Work in this special sense becomes "thoughtless." This does not mean that modern jobs are not frequently quite skilled in an ordinary sense. High-tech jobs may require high degrees of training, but what is learned are rules of execution based on decision chains devised by absent decision makers. Resultant alienation and procedural ideology without responsibility, as shown, have personal and collective costs.

Various technologies have different effects on the expression of human interests, the prevailing form of knowledge, and the structure of decision making. Recent technological developments, particularly those in communication technology, are clearly a micropolitics and are part of, even if unwittingly, a strategic move in a larger apparatus of control. If we understand this politics we have choices to make. This includes the type of technology, and data base and access to them.

Finally, the issue of access to information technologies is extraordinarily important. Limiting access is like denying the eyes, ears, and mouth of the modern world to large segments the public and, in the terms here, to important stakeholders of the corporation (Murdock and Golding 1989; Reinecke 1987). There are key access decisions to be made. Lyotard (1984) summed up the alternative futures well: information technology could become the "dream instrument for controlling and regulating the market system.... [Or] it could also aid groups discussing metaprescriptives by supplying them with the information they usually lack for making knowledgeable decisions. The line to follow for computerization to take the second of these paths is, in principle, quite simple: give the public free access to the memory and data banks.... This sketches the outline of a politics that would respect the desire for justice and the desire of the unknown" (67). The difficulty is the domination of commercial decision making over political ones. The relative superiority of the French information-technology networks has resulted from clear value preferences and social-choice making. The economic model reproduces a managerial control mode of interaction and diminishes the variety of human interests. As the Council on Library Resources argued in 1985: "Ways must be found to assure continuing attention for those aspects of culture and learning that are important, but in a commercial sense, not necessarily in fashion.... Uncritical adherence to the concept of information as commodity will distort the agendas of institutions and disciplines alike.... Public interest in the principle of open access must appropriately influence the structure of the information systems and its components. It is certain that the information need of society cannot be defined by the marketplace alone" (cited in, Schiller 1989, 88). The difference between political and economic decision making in technological implementation is important in process, as well as outcome.

But the issue remains complex. If access is freely granted but the political implications of the nature of the media itself are left unexplored, disciplinary structuring is even more assuredly extended into the everyday experience of heretofore diverse sections of the corporation. Lyytinen and Hirschheim (1988) have shown both the inner colonization potential as well as the democratic issues involved in information systems. Such work must be greatly extended.

CHAPTER 11

The Imaginary World of Work: Reproblematizing the Obvious

> Where the struggle ceases ...the world turns
> away.... Now it is merely found ready made; it
> is datum. The end result is no longer that
> which is pressed into limits (i.e., placed in its
> form); it is merely finished and as such avail-
> able to everyone, already-there, no longer
> embodying and world—now man does as he
> pleases with what is available. The essent
> becomes an object, either to be beheld (view,
> image) or to be acted upon (product and cal-
> culation). The original world-making power,
> *physis*, degenerates into a prototype to be
> copied and imitated.... The original emer-
> gence and standing of energies, the
> *phainesthai*, or appearance in the great sense of
> a world epiphany, becomes a visibility of
> things that are already-there and can be point-
> ed out. The eye, the vision, which originally
> projected the project into potency, becomes a
> mere looking at or looking over or gaping at.
> Vision has degenerated into mere optics.
> (Martin Heidegger 1961, 51–52).

The interest in democracy leads to descriptions and critique of
dominant articulations and to a description of the possibility of
freedom in which a more democratic politics can have meaning. The basic theoretical perspective for the former is developed from modern perspectives on discourse and power. The
analysis is justified by a common moral interest, an interest
that does not advance one interest or group against another but

instead advances the possibility of mutual decision making. Chapter 10 began a demonstration of the moments of corporate articulation that partially unify and totalize experience consequently hiding potentially productive antagonisms. Essentially the routine, obvious, and largely unproblematic ways of *being* in the corporation suppress conflicts that are essential for wider participation in the various constitutive practices. The point of these discussions has been to describe the more central and obvious moments of closure to make the taken-for-granted and obvious problematic.

The point is not to create a less efficient, tension-filled organization, nor is it to reopen dispute over issues properly settled. But the closures *and* conflicts currently in corporations were produced in an asymmetrical power situation, advantage some interests at the expense of equally important ones, and rarely lead to efficiency when wider interests are considered. Displaying the latent strategies provides for a critique based on arbitrary advantage and system pathology. The latent strategies are embedded in even the most routine activities of "collecting" data, technologies of interaction, and language. Bypassing approved conflicts and reopening productive suppressed ones is the critical task.

The goal is not simply description and critique, but simultaneously reclaiming the possibility for conflict. Ideally, a moment of counterarticulation is created to show the possibility of more democratic processes in the moment-to-moment. I should reiterate here that the goal is not to construct a "democratic" corporate form. Democracy is a moment-by-moment, everyday issue. Closure and suppressed conflict happen in producing and filling out the form, in following the routine. The struggle is not against some powerful force out there that directs thought and action, but against the forgotten, hidden, misrecognized, suppressed conflict—the disciplinary power—of the momentary practice. Understanding the micropractices of closure in the corporation, and as they extend out of the corporation, is a first step. The ideal is to engage in corporate discourse in a way that regains significant conflict and reopens experience on critical social issues. Habermas's anticipated ideal here becomes a set of concerns. Are different positions given an opportunity for expression, can the variety of possible interests be realized, are social relations open to mutual choice, do conceptions open the world to new possibilities? The examples are not presented as generalizations about corporate articulatory practices. What is general is the way such practices work, though the content would be different in each work site. Site-specific examples help provide the analytic for each specific analysis or everyday practice. In chapter 10 I described the invisibility of power and the latent strategies of the apparatus, the hidden strategy in the obvious. Here I wish to look at the more obvious explicit strategies for control, to show latent strategies of conflict suppression at work within them.

The Managed Image and Self-Normalization

Images of self, other, and world are formed and used in all interactions. In actual interactions they become invoked, elaborated, reproduced, and/or changed. These images are social historical constructions retained and made available in media and numerous textual forms. Such images are remembered and carried into future interactions as well as used as interpretive principles for past interaction. Human interaction is fundamentally between images or "faces" in Goffman's sense. This is inescapable. Authenticity in the humanist sense is a particular fiction and performs a concealment by naturalization. Such an idea is not foreign to those working with human interaction from a variety of different theoretical perspectives, though usually they work without political sensitivity to the issue. The formation of images is not unethical from a participative standpoint. It cannot be avoided. But when images are protected from examination in interactional systems, often through either invisibility or identity protection, they distort the development of each participant and consensus reached on the subject matter at hand. In participative interaction, these images are utilized improvisationally to provide a moment of articulation that is freely transformed into another, constantly moved by the excess of meaning and possible experience over that which is momentarily present. Domination occurs when a particular moment of articulation of a self-other-world relation is frozen or fixed, when the singular holds sway over the plurality. This is a common possibility in any interaction.

Managerial logic provides an interesting move in these relations. First, as has been shown, the individual is frozen as an identity (as subjected) within the various discourses of the corporation, and both the imaginary and the conflictual qualities of this are forgotten or concealed. But the next piece is more

fantastic. As a move of self-determination, the individual ironically actively participates in producing an image and maintaining its constancy within the corporate context. Three questions
become important in this. First, what are the latent strategic
moves that produce the misrecognition of self-determination,
thus give the individual the self-conception of being able to
engage in strategic action to her or his own benefit? Second,
what are the discourses and conceptions by which the explicit
strategy is employed and thus the latent strategy deployed?
And third, where are the moments of reclaimed conflict that
provide the resistance within the discursive formation?

The Misrecognition of Agency

The first has the quickest answer, since much of this has been
developed in the past several chapters. Any social identity, as
with human character, is imaginary; that is,it is constructed
within particular social historical articulations against other
possible ones. The socially constructed personal identity takes
on a particular form in the modern articulation. In place of
understanding the social-construction process, three basic
imaginary positions are essential to most corporate practices
and are embedded in the managerial discourse. Laclau and
Mouffe (1985) summarized the three positions central to the
modern conception of the individual: "the view of the subject
as an agent both rational and transparent to itself; the supposed unity and homogeneity of the ensemble of its positions;
and the conception of the subject as origin and basis of social
relations" (p.115). The first is necessary for the illusion of freedom that allows the subject to be conceptualized as openly subordinating him- or herself in the social contract of the corporation and having choices based on self-interests there. The second sets out the hope of a well-integrated society where the
work relations fit without conflict into other institutions and
coexist with the democratic processes. The third describes the
individual as the fundamental site of meaning production and
the chooser of relations with others, hence the personal is protected from the examination necessary if it were seen as an
arbitrary social production resulting from certain social
arrangements. Each of these conceptions reproduces domination in producing the rational, consenting individual, and in
eliciting the individual's activity in extending that domination.
As various feminist writers have shown, the individual is not

only a social production but a fragmented, conflictual subject produced out of many social discourses. The recovery of the conflicts from the suppression by dominant, unitary discursive productions is accomplished by showing the connection between exclusion and the apparently coherent discourses (Flax 1990). In modern organizations such a recognition does not happen, and members accept the coherence and take with it both the benefits and the exclusion given to their group.

The Managed Self and Self-Surveillance

From the misrecognition of agency, the "coherent" individual engages in presumed free development of public images and social relations. Central to this practice is both the assumption of a unitary self and the production of one, each prescribed in discursive arrangements. The attempt to produce a unitary self produces closure and is a hidden political issue. This politics can be seen in the gap between the full range of possible personal identities and the images people live. At the most basic level, for example, one can look in a mirror and evaluate the body based on privileged external images while never carefully considering competitive personal feelings and desires or the arbitrariness of the image signifier. The use of the mirror is more than a metaphor here. The image is more controllable than the self, and the image is used to control the self. In the sense that some diet to get the right "mirror" image (and forget what it doesn't reflect), the "as seen by others" is of centrality to the modern corporate subject. The disciplinary self-surveillance is at root an "as seen by others." But the "generalized" other is equally imaginary. The "other" that the self sees from is not a conflict-filled perceiver but normative and normalized. The self is not only controlled, but controlled by a strategic norm that structures the self and other in strategic self-deception.

The strategic corporate "dress for success" clothing, for example, hopes to produce a unitary, norm-alized, image covering up and suppressing the full variety of identities for the purposes of personal success. Ironically, the inability of people to understand the politics of identity construction can lead them to be most powerless at the moment they think they are powerful. For example, an image may be constructed to enable one to succeed. Yet at the moment of success the image rather than the person has the success, a success that means that the individual didn't get expressed at all. Rather than being functional for the individual, the hoped-for personal success reproduces success in the corporate code and supports the managerial drive to further control and sustain particular work relations. The presumption of personal goals hides the real strategy at play, the reproduction of managerialism. Communication is systematically distorted on both the personal and the social level. The individual self-manipulation prohibits self-differentiation and the pursuit of common understanding with co-workers. Rather, it functions to create a false consensus with others and a normalization of self. At the social level the latent strategy suppresses the individual as filled with competing needs and interests and subject in many discourses, positions other individuals in prescripted relations to the person, and creates an arbitrary relationship to the environment. In each case the system denies responsiveness to the actual individual, others, or environment in their competing multiple articulations. Rather, each are reduced to a projection of the system itself as enacted by the individual seeking control.

Debord (1983) described in depth, in his analysis of the society of the "spectacle," how forms of life based on images develop and how they produce and reproduce specific social relations. As he argued, "In societies where modern conditions of production prevail, all of life presents itself as an intense accumulation of *spectacles*. Everything that was directly lived has moved away into a representation" (1). Or in pithy Neil Simon's terms, people come to have a "life style rather than a life." Not only does this include the accumulation of representational commodities for their demonstrative value, but people themselves and their modes of action become representational commodities, themselves a product for sale and display. The general outcome of this is well expressed by Luke (1989): "As people accept this unrelenting colonization of their private and public lives by commodification, many of life's most intimate situations are increasingly experienced passively and contemplatively through these endless circulating and evolving representations. For example, 'love' is actually practiced by many as reenacted advertisements for diamonds, greeting cards, laundry soaps, life insurance, or prepaid funeral plans.... These corporate-designed scripts for personal emotional expression are voluntarily self-imposed on intimate human relations not only to express emotions but also to give closure in cultural practices to corporate marketing plans" (27). The interest here is not primarily with the corporate colonized world of consumer constructed through advertising, but more importantly with the *spectacle* of the person in the place of work. This "spectacular," self-commodified existence is carried into the workplace, further developed by work practices and experience, and carried home, completing the necessary cycle of the self-referential system pathologically reproducing itself.

The modern corporation is filled with specifications of emotional as well as thought and action components. In the managerial and largely male "formal" discourses, emotional expression is constrained and often conspicuous by its absence. Where it exists, it often exists in the form of practiced displays of respect, friendliness, groupness, or strategic anger. For the "informal" and nonmanagerial women, presentation is also carefully prescribed, but usually in regard to support. Ferguson (1984) demonstrated this vividly in her description of the bureaucratic appropriation of emotion in flight attendants: "The flight attendant's smile is like her makeup; it is on her, not of her. The rules about how to feel and how to express feelings are set by management, with the goal of producing passenger contentment. Company manuals give detailed instructions on how to provide a 'sincere' and 'unaffected' facial expression, how to seem 'vivacious but not effervescent' .... Emotional laborers are required to take the arts of emotional management and control that characterize the intimate relations of family and friends...and package them according to the 'feeling rules' laid down by the organization" (53). In self-management such "emotional makeup" is not expressively required (though it might be in its absence) but is accomplished as that which is appropriate and advantageous, even though the person for whom it is advantageous is already imaginary.

Since all representational images as spectacles reside as parts of large discursive formations, they are underdetermined by the practical conditions of their creation and overdetermine responses in each new practical situation. Such images collect around them sets of unexamined beliefs and values that come to be centered in and deployed by a particular display. When these images are held above examination, all communication is systematically distorted. As the talk continues, the response of each participant is interpreted within the context of the image that is not (cannot be) discussed. The participatory normative violation of imagistically based interaction is not to be blamed on the person who forms the image in spite of the great identification they make with it. The responsibility for the maintenance of the image is mutually shared by all participants. The interaction system distorts the systematic expression of each participant. The responsibility for the deconstruction of the image is mutually shared, because neither party alone can work through it.

Images are articulated or produced through spectacle in a variety of ways in the corporation. People are caught between simultaneously fragmented *and* frozen images, providing momentary completions but little development. Private/public person, male/female, career/family are all the most simple and obvious socially articulated moments of conflictual subjectivity (antagonisms) that are carried into the place of work. They coexist with potential tensions over friends/competitors, self/group interest, and the long/short term. Interactional processes at work, as well as outside work, can foster, control, and manage these antagonisms in different manners. As already indicated, one term in these oppositional pairs can be privileged, thus suppressing the conflict. Integrative processes can be developed that conceal the conflict and usually foster advantage. *Or* the tension can be maintained, and every move to unilateral or frozen privilege can be disrupted. The democratic goal is to advance the latter. The managerial corporation provides and protects particular frozen images. Their power comes in the disciplinary structures available, the various social technologies of their production and reproduction, and the individual's active participation.

As is clear to anyone familiar with the modern corporation, the imagistic properties of communication that are identified in different aspects of society often appear to be dominant in this setting. Boorstin's 1961 treatment of the rise of a society based on images and pseudoevents appears as a virtual plan book for modern corporate life. His famous quip—"If you like the baby, just wait until you see the pictures"—could be extended to every new product developed and employee hired. Marketing, public relations, and personal career images have a particular significance in the modern corporation, and this significance is being taught, sometimes with subtlety and sometimes not, throughout society. All of this *could* be seen as a contemporary, everyday "art," bringing to experience dimensions that are hidden in the ordinary view, but instead the image appears to substitute for, rather than direct attention to, the world. Such a substitution wastes resources, distorts personal and social development, leads to ecological harm, and fails to fulfill essential human needs.

Being Real and the New Appropriate of Trust

Given the centrality of images, it is important to describe how they come about and are sustained and reproduced in corporate practices. Most centrally, the movement of identity from "the subject inscribed in the product produced" to "identity from the position held" creates both an absence of identity and a space for ideational rather than material fabrication. The image of the person is strategically deployed and justified (and required) for the sake of reflecting the image of the corporation, a modern fabrication with a market value. The perceived right of control arises out of the monetary code. And significantly, the substance of both the person and the corporation is suppressed. The strategic concern is for choosing the right personal and corporate image out of the conflicting ones, rather than a discourse to discover what each is. Alvesson (in press) has made the change clear: "In a society where the identity of the individuals was clearly based in the substantive activities of the collective, the need to focus on the 'identity' of the corporation as a specific topic would hardly seem necessary. It is the identity problems in our general culture (including the parts of it that exist in corporations) that accounts for the preoccupation with corporate identity" (3). In his sense, then, the issue of personal identity is not to be separated from the issues of corporate identities or the changing relations among institutions in society. Because the quality of work is hidden, position advancement signifies an esteemed identity, but it is grounded symbolically rather than substantively. The formation of a unitary identity in the string of signifiers is posited apart from the world and others—a self walled in by formal definitions and reflections of reflections, rather than extended out to the world and others. This symbolic identity becomes institutionally extended in monetary concepts of worth, legal responsibilities, mobil relations, and isolation from community.

In the terms of this work, the corporate colonization of other social institutions suppresses competing identity formation and defines the context for an inner colonization whereby the individual forms the self intentionally for work relations. The corporation thus less regulates the identity rather than allows the individual to constitute it on the corporate behalf. The individual provides the construction based on limited conceptual alternatives from primarily the corporate-controlled media, in a context of corporate rewards and sanctions, and for representation in the managerial code. In this process, images enable greater systematic control and instrumental action in corporations through normalization than would be possible in simple authority relations.

But the problem is not just that the images are one-sided and perform the latent strategic function of control. They set in play an open context of strategic manipulation that undermines the possibility of productive critiques of the latent strategic function. In the proud (even vain), active manipulation, the very foundation of participative communication is denied. In a sense beyond Wolfe (1987), the "bonfire of the vanities" is not just a destruction of people as they struggle for a moment of success, but is a destruction of the bystanders—the possibility of community—in the process. Images are knowingly and strategically false. Obviously they cannot be too false or they wouldn't work or they would be found out and lose their strategic force (see Alvesson, in press). What is interesting is that the issue of the strategic value of the image takes precedence over aiding a useful insight into actual processes. In saying this I am not trying to evoke an interest in what is real or true, since each is partial and one-sided. What is of interest is the self-conscious one-sidedness and the explicit denial of communication. The process differs little whether the corporation as a produced *entity* or person as a produced *identity* is of issue. The demise of concern with participatory communication in personal and internal marketing must be a social concern greater than that of external images. The expectation of imagistic interaction poses participatory communication as poor imagining rather than as a recovery of conflict, persons, and that which communication is about. The obvious everyday expected use of images easily leads us to forget the unethical, immoral nature of the practice and its effects on the feeble attempts at everyday democracy.

Rather than being the "real" world, the corporation is frequently one of many images playing upon images, artifacts upon artifacts. As developed in chapter 7, the corporation acts as a closed and often systematically distorted system. In Baudrillard's (1983b) conception, corporations are *simulations*. Their languages and images do not attempt to represent an outside, to symbolize or structure a world of distinctions that provides a way of seeing or thinking about empirical events and people; rather, they signal or evoke other images and signifiers. But the un- (or hyper-) real string of signifiers without a signified are not random and arbitrary. Like the accountant's report and data collection, personal images are normalized along specific lines configuring together a "web of power"—the strategic power apparatus (Clegg 1989; Foucault 1980b). They are enforced through real rewards and sanctions, but most centrally they are deployed with the weight of "knowledge." Psychological conceptions, personnel testing, and psychological attributions give a "real" certainty to advantaging preferences (Hollway 1984). The sanctions and rewards thus do not come from authority. If they did so in our "liberal" society, they would clearly be seen as preferences and challenged. When backed by the psychological experts, the proper "subject" merely strings out the "neutral" efficiency drive as managerially prescribed. Control is self-control, with the army of psychologists standing behind the curtains. And importantly, the image must be forgotten as an image. It cannot be a put-on; the unreal must be lived as the real.

Such a reasoning process becomes embedded in self-surveillance, observing others, and personnel decisions. Frequently individuals "objectively" decide that they "don't have what it takes" to be an upper level manager. The "knowledge" of "what it takes" is often an extension of managerialism. The potentially good (nonmanagerial) manager, much like Willis's (1977) British lads, is thus self-excluded through recognition of the managerial game. The acceptance and enactment of their roles in this game precludes the articulation of an alternative, and the fault is held to be one of a personal deficiency.

Kanter (1977) in her classic study of "men and women of the corporation" showed that imagistic relations are related to predictability and, ironically, to trust. Given the ambiguity of personnel decisions, upper level managers will identify "comers" who "look" like themselves and in so doing overlook even the artifactual record of accomplishment. They look for evidence of the "gift" that they themselves assert in playing their hunches, in this case regarding personnel choices. The normalized individual is predictable and, hence, instrumentally trustworthy. The logic, style, and mythos of managerialism is reproduced as proper and trustworthy. In managerialism, individuals who are subject in many competing discourses are complex, less predictable, uncertain, and problematic. All these qualities work against control, but are essential to participation and broad representation of interests. The efficiency argument for the need for predictability hides the inefficiency of the "instrumental advancement" images in meeting other essential goals.

An instance I observed may help make this clearer. A female secretary of a large corporation with a large number of female employees took a leave of absence to acquire a college degree for eventual advancement. When she returned she was placed in a rather large pool of "surplus" (which of course might have been described as "underemployed") workers doing low-level secretarial work. After a short period of time she "bid" on a low-level managerial position. Owing in part to the efforts of her former boss in addition to her relevant training, she was virtually assured the position until the director of the personnel office denied her eligibility to bid based on the lack of adequate qualifications. When the woman raised the issue with the personnel director (who was female), the director argued that she hadn't been around long enough and hadn't "networked" enough. "Networking" was the key to being qualified for advancement. Ironically, networking, which was a means to advancement, now became an end to be achieved for advancement. The "network" that had been an important formation for female advancement in a situation of male domination became imagistically reconstructed as the only appropriate route to advancement, assuring the female network domination. The imaginary means replaces the substance of qualification as the ultimate criteria. Female advancement had been normalized on a basis as arbitrary and unrelated to the nature of the work as the domination it replaced.

And finally, the image works in a further way in the managerial discourse. Despite the emphasis on control and command, managerial managers are slow to take personal responsibilities for failures and problems. The emphatic "The buck stops here" asserts the command, but it usually means "I'm in charge of placing the blame." Both the life of images and the set of formal roles and relations work against personal responsibility; an image playing a role in a simulation is never fully a person making a decision. The claim of "Not me" does not always or even primarily exist in passing the blame to others, but rather appears in the claims of "It's my job" or "Company policy." The site of agency is thus shifted away from the person. While never complete, the conflicts of personal responsibility are themselves suppressed and passed away to "It's just business." As long as the person is not really there, the image makes the decision. The image is suddenly the end rather than a means.

The Linguistic Production of the Work World

Up to this point the concern with language has been primarily with the production of linguistic distinction and thus the development of categories of individuals and events that can be the recipients of certain qualifications. But the concern needs to be extended to the way such groups *use* language in the processes of participation or control. In such usages the initial distinctions are either reproduced or challenged. Disciplinary power resides in the distinction but is (and must be) reproduced in the usage. The interest here, then, is in the existence of linguistic strategies of compliance and control as well as with what has to be in place for them to work. Every persuasive appeal and every compliance-gaining strategy takes place within a set of background practices and institutions and basic conceptual views of the world. A symbolic elite can only arise within a formation that distinguishes and specifies an elite. In Foucault's sense, a particular form of knowledge must arise as dominant, simultaneously empowering those certifying and possessing it, in order for it to be reproduced in new situations. This must be studied not by looking at power differences or powerful and powerless language, but by close analysis of the site-specific play of power.

Such analyses focus on how systems of signifiers are evoked in specific instances of language use. The implementation and overlaying of routine signifying chains gives insight into the web of institutions, conceptual distinctions, practices, and knowledge that is pulled into play. Thus my interest is not in words, symbols, conventions, and knowledge, as if they had meaning or existed, but rather the manner of their deployment, how their evocation constitutes a field of meaning and action. Such an idea is not far from the ethnomethodologist's use of "indexicality" but adds the concern with power relations and the strategic effect. Recall, of course, that power and strategy are systemically intentional but do not imply personal foresight or plans. The organizing capacity of language usage both to provide a realm of specifiable objects and to utilitize such objects in defense of the transparency of language usage is of utmost concern. Here I will consider the usage of categories and metaphors, the linguistic production of the memory of people and events, and narrative accounts as strategic moves in the play of power.

Linguistic Discourse in Organizations

Texts and discourse, in the more ordinary senses of these terms, perform important articulations in corporations. Speaking and writing take place within the fundamental ambiguity of the "elements" of organizational life. Each expression is the attempt to produce a unitary conception over and against the multiple ways the elements could be "valued" (distinguished, or attended to) in signification. Suggesting the unitary drive should not suggest that expressions are simple. Each expression has multiple possible interpretations as it itself becomes an object of concern and functions in multiple realms—for example, the "same" manager's statement can be "read" in terms of legal statutes, in particular interpersonal relations, by an outside public, or in regard to corporate policy. In each of these realms something is affirmed and others things are denied, some meanings are privileged and others are pushed aside. In each case the complex relations among and within these discursive realms is of interest. For example, reprimanding a friend may be followed by claiming that it is necessary to do so because of position or corporate policy. This evokes a routine, claiming a context for privileging positional over interpersonal relations and at the same time claiming an oppositional context for defining and privileging conceptions of how friends should be treated.

The endless everydayness of small, insignificant claims and counterclaims provides the full measure of the functioning of power in corporations. Each of these construct (and reconstruct) complex, interest-dependent social realities. Understanding how they work does not require the collection of a specific number of these innumerable instances for analysis. Rather the point is to provide a rich analysis of any of them to open a way of thinking and feeling that provides an interesting and useful understanding of others. The point of social science research, as developed in chapter 3, is not to find an answer but through careful analysis, to open the indeterminancy of events and objects in a way that stimulates an active fomulative agent. Literatures describing discourse in organizations are plentiful. Rarely do these analyses move beyond descriptions to the analysis of disciplinary power relations. The treatment of power is nearly always understood from an explicitly strategic standpoint.

Van Dijk (1989) has done an excellent job of summarizing the various approaches to looking at discourse and power. From his standpoint, "power is exercised through differential access to various genres, contents, and styles of discourse" (22). In corporations this can be seen in rules limiting access to expression outlets, control of messages in reports and newsletters, determination of who may speak about what, deference in meetings and other forums, control of the expression of criticism, establishment of agendas, control of information distribution, and so forth. Each of the inequalities could be critiqued as in opposition to a participatory ideal. Much of this control may be exerted by what Bourdieu (1977) called "symbolic elites." Management groups, through their extension into choices of technologies and training programs, often determine the genres, contexts, and style of discourse. Management's use of social science experts in such determinations both naturalizes the actual choice and enhances the elitist claim. Pettigrew (1973) and Pfeffer (1981) have detailed the use of interaction forms to enact, display, signal, or legitimate power relations. Even the use of different forms of address, such as first names for subordinates and title and last name for higher management (Slobin, Miller, and Porter 1972), are part of rather obvious instances of politeness and deference that discursively enact power differentials. Their use in specific instances frequently disqualifies or reprimands individuals with a contrary point of view. The enumeration of such activities is possible and important (e.g., see van Dijk 1985, 1989), but it must be extended.

The point of analysis of linguistic practices is to understand each instance. The instances can help a more general view that is not the end but rather an initial cut to further understand the implications of the next instance in such a way that the generality itself is further differentiated or transformed. This is a partial statement of the famous hermeneutic circle, but the intent is not as many ethnographers would have it, to form a tighter unitary description. Here the desire is to show how unity is being developed in the discursive system itself and reveal the moments of freedom, resistance, tension, and choice standing as the hidden opposition to the unity. Allow me to start with some simple principles and examples.

The language used sets in play not simply categories and classifications but the value or interest dimensions along which categories and classifications will be made. There are a number of ways such an analysis might proceed. Hodge and Kress (1983) have offered much in their development of what they called "functional semiotics." While most of their work has been used in the close textual analysis of media (Kress and Hodge 1979), they have shown how it can be applied to organizations. Hodge, Kress, and Jones (1979) performed a reading of a middle manager's description of the category of management. The middle manager's description of the nature of management follows:

But um, it's officered, if you like, by people who form the management team. And most of Mike's [a "figure-head"] management decisions are made amongst that team, you know. And you find that um, some will lead the team from the front, and they all agree, that's the way we're going to go, yeah, others will lead it from the back, but that's the way they go anyway. And Mike normally sounds everybody and takes a—pretty close consensus of opinion before a decision is made, and the decision that's made is usually made amongst us, you know, we each of us decide. (Hodge, Kress, and Jones 1979, 82).

The analysis is too long to be presented here, but the basic conclusion demonstrates processes that we might see in a number of instances. In this case the middle manager simultaneously enacted a tension through expressed certainty *and* constant equivocation in descriptions—an uncertainty of status and function expressed in a style of certainty. By evoking a concept of the *management team* as an entity, he could discuss the things "they" do and "their" action capacity. It remained unclear whether he actually did these things or could have, but on the basis of *their* action and his membership he could confidently describe himself as a manager. His identity remained positioned by the maintenance of the group, yet neither his actions nor his responsibility become part of the signified relation.

The professional report as a corporate genre demonstrates further the way discourse is utilized within disciplinary structures. Both the language of reports and the use of reports in talk perform control. Key to this is the deployment of the expert and the resultant technical language usage. Mehan (1986) demonstrated that "when technical language is used, and embodied in the institutional trappings of a meeting, the grounds for negotiated meaning are removed from under the conversation" (160). The recipient cannot participate in negotiation, because he or she does not understand and is not qualified to understand. The fact that the hearer cannot understand is assumed as a deficiency in the hearer—his or her lack of training and special qualifications. Often, however, the reports themselves are obscure and ambiguous. Although this may evidence bad writing or the lack of concern with clarity, the presence of the "Be clear" dictum would argue for a strategic motive. Mehan argued that such a motive is present. Quoting him:

The authority of the professional report comes from its very incomprehensibility and its obscurity. The psychologist and the nurse [in this setting] gain their authority from the mastery and use of a technical language that others do not understand and do not question. The professional report gains its status and authority by virtue that it is obscure, difficult to understand, and is embedded in the institutional trappings of the formal proceedings of the committee meeting. (161)

One does not have to believe that the professional is trying to be obscure to understand how such reporting, in trying to be clear and complete, accomplishes the suppression of conflict. Its strategic, persuasive force on the surface itself is an attempt at that, even though (and while) it presents itself as neutral information for someone else's decision. But the formal language, like the accountant's report, suppresses more basic conflicts over representation and community responsibility for the claim, a responsibility that would be clear if expressed in everyday language. The report controls with limited responsibility. In "public" settings much effort has been expended to produce more accessible reports as a moral responsibility. The corporate report rarely bears the light of public scrutiny.

Another way to approach this descriptive task is through metaphor analysis. Unfortunately metaphor analysis has often gone the way of cultural indices and word counts. I would suggest a couple of basic conceptions that are necessary for our use here. First, metaphors are not special words to be distinguished from literal representations. Metaphor is a way to describe a particular word/world relation, a relation that can be revealed in any language usage—though this relation does not exhaust our full potential interest in language. This relation is that of "seeing as." An element is *articulated as*, in our current terminology. Metaphor analyses are usually interested in the more obvious cases where the "seeing as" is not concealed, since they reveal a reasonable explicit understanding of constitutive practices; however, some analyses have looked more closely at so-called dead metaphors, because they reveal sedimented constitution (see Deetz 1986; Deetz and Mumby 1985). Our earlier discussion of the conduit metaphor exemplifies this type of sedimentation.

Second, metaphors do not in a simple way represent or reveal a deeper culture or hidden structure. Their use enacts such a structure. Their power comes in the systems deployed, not in something outside or beyond them. The presence of military metaphors in an organization does not reveal militaristic thinking or necessitate centralized control. Rather, the use of metaphors implements a manner of distinguishing people and events, unities and oppositions. The repetitive use of a metaphorical cluster is nothing more or less than that. Counting the number of a particular type of metaphor in a text tells us virtually nothing. Without locating the particular situational deployment, we could not tell whether the same word implemented the same set of distinctions or what the system of control was like. For example, extremely tight conformity can be set in play with team and family metaphors as well as with military ones. The move in the particular system of relations rather than what is external to them is the key to the analysis. Metaphors implement power relations, but they also provide opportunity for elaboration, clarification, and resistance.

The special interest in metaphors in power relations arises from the manner in which equivalencies are constructed that substitute for social differences. As an analogue, recall that imaginary relations are produced in an ongoing fashion in discourse and that they can close discourse. But they also can be deconstructed by the presence of "more," which shows their inevitable one-sidedness. Iconic images, for example, are able to put into play a set of imaginary relations that reference and construct absent events, events that have no external quality to ultimately claim to be more than the moments of articulation. Metaphors, like iconic images, function to signifiy themselves as their own outsides. Whereas words in a simple "seeing as" relation put into play as set of differences—this, not that—and thus articulate the element in a particular way, the metaphor evokes a purely positive logic—this is like or equivalent to that. The equivalence exists in a symbolic space with no outside. In the metaphoric system, the metaphor no longer expresses the part or particular element by use of the system of differences, but references the symbolic totality, which has no proper object. As Angus (in press), following Laclau and Mouffe (1985, 142ff.), argued: "The construction of equivalence is the assembling of a chain of substitutions in which each term stands as a metaphor for the others.... For this reason hegemony is fundamentally metonymical; the metaphorical equivalences, once established, are triggered by any of them. Any part is displaced to, and confirms, the whole." (13)

Social Memory in Corporations

The corporation is a special type of fiction held in place by a set of discourses including legal statutes, contracts, and linguistic production of roles, authority, and meaning. It usually resides at a site and has members, but both the physical site and the members can change without its being lost. Its material character rests on a discursive production and reproduction institutionalized as routines, expectations, payments, deliveries, and so forth. Its constancy has to be produced as a sequence of texts drawing together events and things having a particular meaning regarding the corporation. Much as Mead (1934) claimed that grass became food at the appearance of the first cow, the things associated with the corporation become what they are because of the corporation, including the identity of individuals, resources, and facilities. Unlike the cow, however, the corporation, as a fiction, has no character and must produce its identity and existence. Most important in this is a memory of itself.

Routines and standard practices and their manner of institutionalization are arbitrary, but to continue to suppress conflicts they must be seen as natural, self-evident, and in the interests of all. Their presence arises out of solutions to past problems, historical needs or events, and the presence of particular individuals, but they must survive the passing of each. The construction of the memory justifies not only the presence of corporations and their practices, but also their construction and endurance. Memory recalls, interprets, and makes the events of the past have implication for the future. Memory when shared is textual and posits as much the person who remembers as those who are remembered. Narrative theory has been helpful in giving insight into the politics of the discursive production of memory.

Narrative theory in the broadest sense studies texts, discursive objects. Linguistic accounts, like any historical rendering, are part of a larger group of cultural productions, like art and architecture, that remember a particular account of a people. In its political interest, narrative theory draws attention to the way such accounts are produced and thus retain in themselves the power-laden forces of production as hidden causes. Jameson (1981) claimed the relation in the following way. All the works of history, "as they have survived and been transmitted to people the various museums, canons and 'traditions' of our own time, are all in one way or another profoundly ideological, have all had a vested interest in and a functional relationship to social formations based on violence and exploitation; and that, finally, the restoration of the meaning of the greatest cultural monuments cannot be separated from a passionate and partisan assessment of everything that is oppressive in them and that knows the complicity with privilege" (229). What Jameson offers, however, is not a mere Marxist analysis of the forces of class domination but a deep analysis of the political unconscious present in all discourse, in his case applied to the criticism of literary texts. The "political unconscious" Jameson writes about can be better described as the forgotten formations that articulate a particular consciousness. In this way, his particular approach to analysis can be usefully applied to corporate discourse.

Jameson argues that the discursive text contains a double production. First, a production of a historical narrative—a narrative that structures the perception of past events, mediating social contradictions, and that performs a utopian move to a new continuity of understanding. Second, the text is a repression. It hides its own conditions of production and silences the voices of dialogic opposition. The text's historical speaking forms a new continuity, has a place in the historical dialogue, but is simultaneously a closure—a stopping of the human conversation. The story's freedom from the context of events, separates an "articulation" from its "elements," in Laclau and Mouffe's (1985) terms, or the subject matter, in Gadamer's (1975). This can be seen in more specific terms in the work on social memory.

The concept of "social memory" developed in narrative theory helps reveal processes in organizations by which power is deployed in the production of a corporation' s sense of natural, necessary, and appropriate. Nerone (1989) described social memory in the following way: "A social memory is an artificial recollection of some experiences by some groups, institutions, or individuals in society organized according to recognizable scripts and having a moral dimension" (92). In this sense, social memory need not be identical with any individuals' memories, though it may account for them and gradually remake them. It is not the same as a corporate history, in that it is produced in the course of everyday life, though an explicit history may try to influence it (see Popular Memory Group 1982). It is more an organic account of how a group got where they are, but this in no way reduces its political importance.

This can be seen in its character as developed by Nerone (1989, 92ff.), whose account I will now sketch.

First, social memory is artificial and arbitrary. In this sense it is never a natural and neutral remembering of the past; it is an interested one. People do not generally recount that which is of little concern. Importantly, what is remembered appears as the natural things to have been remembered. There is a sense that "of course" this was remembered. *Second, social memory is a recollection.* Artifacts and records remain, but the past happens in the past and memory in the present. Some artifacts and records are what a past people wanted remembered, but they are not themselves memory. They are the "articulations" of the "elements" that remain to be rearticulated. Memory in this sense always changes as it is articulated in light of new human interests. *Third, social memory is selective.* Only some experiences are included, and not all groups are equally involved as historical subjects or as present constructors of the memory. Memory is constructed in the interests of some but not all. But as Nerone argued, "Social memory universalizes itself—it presents itself as a memory of the total society rather than as property of any segment" (93). *Fourth, social memories are organized according to recognizable scripts.* Dramatic and extraordinary people and events are recalled (or produced). Social memories tend to simplify not because the complex is difficult but because achieving consensus on events is easier with least-common-denominator scripts. Conflict is suppressed in memory even as it is recalled as an event. *Finally, social memory has a moral dimension.* Every recounting produces heros and villians and provides lessons and meaning. The legitimating power of the accounts of the past is impressive primarily in the way it naturalizes current social order and disorder, institutions and resistances. Social memory "disciplines" just as bloodlines produced sovereigns.

The managerial apparatus is significant in the accompanying social memory. The social memory connects the manager with the past owner-entrepreneur. The firm is reproduced in the same line as the family business. Modern control-dominated business is wed with the past free enterprise system. The massive availability of goods and services and production potential is attributed to competitive marketing. The large, powerful corporations are a result of managerial expertise. A few great leaders have made the significant choices and inspired the masses to achieve. Large salaries are appropriate for those with a unique, irreplaceable gift. Loss of international competitiveness is connected to the rising cost of labor, educational failures, and government intervention. Bureaucratic inefficiencies are unique to governments and middle managers who couldn't make it. Pfeffer (1981) made clear that most corporate successes and failures are a result of factors beyond managerial control. At most in his sense, managerial power comes in directing the symbols rather than the events. Nowhere is this clearer than in the production of social memory. But we can see a similar process in the everyday narrative production of events and people.

Narrative Accounts and the Political Organization of Events

Organizational members have long known the value of a good story. Stories structure the perception of events, provide heros and villians, accentuate details, resolve contradictions, teach new members, and legitimate social orders. As "images" become more important in the corporation, story becomes more important with them. The story brings the image to life and action. It imbues the "simulation" with vitality and order. As the instant replay has become a central feature of the corporate sport of football, the story in corporate life can be more significant than the event. The ambiguity of actual events, the difficulty of tolerating ambiguity (at least that which cannot be managed), and the far greater control that is possible over the story than the events, frequently make the story more real than any event. And further, given the particular privilege given to objectified knowledge and the effectiveness of naturalization in concealment, the story that can purport to represent the real—that can be neutral and transparent—would be prized over all others. Hence, the accountant's report, the fact-finding mission, the bottom line, can be *the* reality of the corporation. The story develops a string of signifiers that are more real than any people or events that are discussed.

Storytelling, like memory production in general, inevitably makes choices. The minutes or summaries of meetings record statements made but not the nonverbal reactions, glances, and intensity. And some stories are more tellable than others. Like the construction of any news, complex events with multiple perspectives are not as tellable as those with clear polar conflicts. "Comers" learn quickly which activities have story value. Doing the one right thing well, producing the "spectacle," goes much farther than doing lots of things in a more ordinary or even excellent fashion. Stories inevitably construct images and can contribute to systematically distorted communication. They, like metaphors, work like the rhetorical strategy of synecdoche. The single story references a string of increasingly larger stories, creating a complex with little or no outside. Since the story takes on a life of its own, the events it reports and the practical constraints of its production become forgotten. In this sense the moments of *articulation* are freed from the deconstructive capacity of the *elements* articulated. The excess of the event over any telling of it is lost to the vivid power of the story over any actual event. The stories can come to reference each other in a complex formation that substitutes for actual people and external events. Significantly the issue is not just what stories can do, for stories do not function in the same way in all corporate formations. Corporate size and complexity, for example, contribute to the power of stories generally, thus supporting greater systematic distortion.

Researchers have been active in recording stories and describing their various functions. Martin, et al. (1983) offered one of the best known analyses of this sort. They argued that stories provide an easily understood and remembered "slice of life" that represents important aspects of the corporation's culture. As stories become retold, they develop a quality of realness and self-evidence. In their particular study, the authors were interested in the way stories were used to demonstrate the uniqueness of members' particular organizations. In examining stories from a variety of corporations, they argued that common themes arose across groups, that uniqueness was expressed in much the same manner in different corporations. In general these themes deal with common member concerns: "How will the boss react to mistakes?" "Can the little person rise to the top?" The stories help resolve conflicts that arise from member goals and values and the actual practical context of rewards and decision making. Hence, stories foster motivation and integration.

Most other analyses, like this one, have been rather detailed accounts of the maintenance of organizational/managerial legitimacy, coherence, and order. Managers maintain many advantages in storytelling. First, they have privileged speaking forums, including means of mass distribution such as meetings and newsletters. Their access to relatively closed information sources, private meetings, and more senior executives makes it difficult for lower level employees to check stories and develop alternative ones. Managerial access to a wider range of information allows resequencing events, and filling in holes, and provides a more complete, and integrated, and apparently less one-sided, account. And management's positions of authority allow them to center themselves as the principal actors, defenders, or victims. Such stories are, thus, authorized by both being made official and being claimed as official. Most of the research appeared to enhance this advantage by describing how stories worked and what makes good stories. The managerial metamyth (Ingersoll and Adams 1986) and the "moral fictions" of *excellence, expertise, and effectiveness* (Jehenson 1984), developed earlier, demonstrate the presence of managerialism in the privileged stories of the workplace.

In works like these, researchers have gradually come to understand the political significance of stories through their own applications of narrative theory. According to such works, the role of critical analysis, in what Jameson calls a "negative hermeneutics," is to reclaim the voices silenced—to break the closure of the narrative produced, to recover the silenced conflict. Reports of organizational stories have often failed to break closure in two ways. First, they fail to reflexively examine their own historically developed concepts and methods. Thereby they become masters and victims of their own attempts at continuity through failing to reflect on the closure in their own narrative product, the story of the story. And second, they fail, through their own assumed political neutrality, to examine deeply the power relations in the story production, the conditions necessitating their presence and retelling in the corporation, and the counternarratives that have been silenced. The way some accounts become authorized and others marginalized is significant to any account of corporate stories.

Mumby (1987) showed how such limitations could be overcome, in his reanalysis of a story from the classical article by Martin et al., (1983). He showed that the stories of uniqueness can function to produce domination. First, such stories can represent sectional interest as universal— what I have called "neutralization"—thus obscuring the advantage given to upper management in the integration. Second, the identities produced in the stories take on their own life, growing farther from the complex human being from which they were abstracted, a frozen naturalized image. And finally, the distinction of characters produces a structural arrangement held out as based on natural characteristic of the individual and context and consequently neither humanly produced nor changeable.

Martin in her own more recent work (1990) has become increasingly sensitive to the political function of stories. In one recent analysis she reports on a story about an upper level executive's pregnancy and shows that while the story was intended to demonstrate organizational efforts to help women, the effect was to suppress gender conflict and reify false dichotomies between public and private realms of behavior. Martin claims that stories such as this, as well as many efforts to end discrimination, in fact explain why it has been so difficult to eradicate gender discrimination in organizations. Through deconstruction she is able to reveal conflicts of interest and points of view that are potentially disruptive of existing power relations as well as how these are obscured and silenced. For example, in separating the private from the public, many conflicts experienced by the working mother are defined as personal problems requiring individual solutions, hence reducing the role that organizational policies play in them and making collective action by women difficult. In many of the more "enlightened" corporations, the conflict is suppressed differently. Stories can intermingle the private and public. The following report by a top executive officer in a public meeting demonstrates this story quality.

> We have a young woman who is extraordinarily important to the launching of a major new [product]. We will be talking about it next Tuesday in its first world wide introduction. She has arranged to have her Caesarean yesterday in order to prepare for this event, so you—We have insisted that she stay home and this is going to be televised in a closed circuit television, so we're having this done by TV for her, and she is staying home three months and we are finding ways of filling in to create this void for us because we think it's an important thing for her to do. (339)

In this story the pregnant executive's caesarean operation enabled the employee to match corporate timing, and the corporate concern and efforts to involve the woman during her leave is easily seen as positive. What is hidden is that the "we" making the decisions is not the woman and her spouse and doctor, but the corporate "we," with the woman consenting to the singularity. It can well be asked what values are required to make the timing accommodation to the product-release date an acceptance of the importance of childbearing. And of course, the full implication of the story does not stop with birth. Corporate policies follow the growing child. For example, corporate daycare, in contrast to flextime or bringing the child into the office, provides an extended story with an advantaging collectivity substituting for the individual making choices in terms of job and family.

But stories do not need to be so isolated or provided by upper level management. Everyday descriptions show that workers provide their own accounts that can function to enable power configurations. This can be demonstrated by a further example from Huspek (1987). The story below is a worker's description of a meeting that he and the union shop steward had with a management group regarding a company policy of laying off workers irrespective of their seniority. They fail to win their case, and more importantly, once in the setting they never effectively challenge the management group. As the worker told of his reticence:

> I would of jus' been lettin' off steam y'know. An' they already think I got a bad attitude down there. See they'll tell ya, sure he'd give up his wife to go with the company if the company asked that y'know. That's the kinna guy—well that's what he told me one time. He said if he had ta choose between the company and his wife he'd go with the company. Yeh, an' he's not talkin' money. He's talkin loyalty to the company. [...] An' like he told me I don't know what it's all about. I haven't had it hard. An' I definitely don't need anything yet. See it's all right to get a raise if ya say ya need it. But if ya want it, you'll never get it. An' I went in there askin' for a raise because I wanted it. I didn't need it. I wanted it. So I never got it. Ever since that day I've felt more pressure than I'd like ta have. (94)

The worker clearly describes himself, his choices, and the logic of the story in management terms. If he had challenged the management group, he already self-classifies the act as "lettin' off steam" by one with a "bad attitude." He suggests an inability to self-present an alternative self-description or interpretation of his action. The potential managerial story of his behavior becomes his story for the absence of it. The notion of potential alternative ways of approaching the task that wouldn't be just "lettin' off steam" is never broached, managerial interpretive authority appears unquestioned. This is not to say that he made a poor choice, but he accepted being a loser in their game without devising a game of his own. Once this is set in motion, the differences and conflicts are already established. Any challenge to company policy is read as disloyalty, and the worker's loyalty can not be compared with the manager's. Forgotten is the question of why it should be. While we can always conceptualize three possibilities in corporate opposition—*exit, loyalty,* and *voice*—the worker can only conceptualize the first two (Hirschman 1970).

Further, the discussion of money recalls a past meeting where a similar structure was present. The worker is not able to operate as a fellow person, wanting things, giving reasons, negotiating. Rather, the worker is rewarded for dependency and displays of dependency. To gain any measure of self-determination, he must give up his adult status. Clearly he displays the discouragement of being caught in the contradiction, but he appears to accept the problem as one of him as an individual, not his group, and uses the contradiction as a reason for inaction. He is lost in a discursive trap where any request appears self-serving, since he with management defines it as "he versus company group," rather than "he for worker group" or "he as company." At the point he becomes self-serving in "needing" the money, his loyalty is displayed as he reenacts the hierarchy but not as just the right of management to determine pay but to determine his identity. The full tension of the contradiction is felt by the worker, and he seeks only to not have a "bad attitude"—to be silent and invisible. The evidence of systematically distorted communication is clear. From virtually any standpoint the interaction violates a participatory moral conception.

The worker is "subjected" in a particular way in "his" (though borrowed from management) story. But the full articulation and supportive power apparatus extends far beyond this. The worker does not just tell this story, any more than Martin's manager just tells his. Actual contracts, legal statutes, reward structures, and places of talk are further reproductions of the same relations. Whether the management group intends it or not, this is a strategic exertion of power. The active complicity of the worker is only part of a larger system enabling fear, intimidation, and active coercion to accomplish the same at other moments. But importantly, the conflict that would be displayed if those other means were used remains hidden and inoperant due to the complicity.

Structure, Site, Routine, and Scripts

Until this point articulations have been considered in their discursive forms. Such images and text are material or materializable. Nondiscursive articulations extend and situate these. The power apparatus in Foucault's sense has both discursive and nondiscursive aspects. Decisions in organizations, like the production of experience itself, take place in material relations, sites, and practices. These are historical productions and hence can never in either production, meaning, or maintenance be separated from discursive formations around them. But temporarily pulling these things out allows another angle on the field of relations.

Organization structure has been discussed in depth for years. Like social structure, it, is a fiction in one sense. It is made up and resides only as an abstraction from a set of practices. But it is materialized in pay differences, office spaces, and more recently in technological connections and through material texts such as statements of responsibility, legal accountability, and authority to reward and punish. The hierarchical form as well as its extensions and alternatives are clearly products of interaction but also have the capacity to direct interaction (Ranson, Hinings, and Greenwood 1980). Giddens (1979, 1984) has captured this well in his conception of "structuration." Structures are constituted and constituting. They are an outcome of power relations and play within them (Riley 1983). Despite the research use and corrections, the concept of structure is quite misleading. As a naturalization, even the most careful treatment of it enacts an image of it as object. The deployment of the term is far more interesting than the presumed significance of structure. Like reason and expertise, the significance is the talk of it. Structure is no more and no less than routine practices of who talks to whom about what, who is held responsible in regard to what, who has which legal rights, who gets paid what, and so forth. Certainly the structure is "real" in regard to the individual but not from the standpoint of the collection of individuals. The abstraction draws our attention away from this complex intertextuality to a quasi-casual, naturalized force. The enactment of it as such, as well as the enactment of specific texts in this complex, enhances control. To look at this power deployment analytically, I think we can go further by looking more narrowly at routines in sites.

Routines are standard practices, shared taken-for-granted

scripts for behavior—the simple, repetitive, habitual recipes for accomplishing the practical tasks at hand. Routines are practical matters. They form in regard to real problems and events, even though they survive the conditions of their production. A road is under repair on my way to work, so I go a different way, a way I may thoughtlessly continue to use after the other is open. A corporate routine may begin out of real conditions of reward and sanctions and continue after they are gone. The power present in the formation of routines can be separate from the power in routines once established. And other practices are built around them. No one and everyone enforces the routine. In daily life, structure exists only as routine. Routine posits the place of a restricted specialized knowing. This specialized knowing and doing is not captured well with simply the concept of "bounded rationality" or even by an extended conception of "bounded emotionality" (Mumby and Putnam 1990). Every knowing, reasoning, and feeling is limited, that much is easy, but the politics of this "boundedness" are of far more interest. Routines can be thought of as a *specific delimited appropriation of discourse and normalized, standardized practice keyed to specific produced audiences in specific produced sites.*

Routines both take place in sites and lead to the production of sites for their performance. The modern workplace is a site produced out of industrialization. As the practices of industrialization reconfigured families and communities, their sites become a place for social relations and contacts for career advancement. Through the development of regular hours for the control of production, workers become routinized, making flextime and open scheduling potentially disruptive. The force is the configuration that comes to advantage certain groups, not the power of those groups per se. Sites become important materializations of routines providing their own force of who talks to whom in what ways (see Foucault 1972, 50ff). We often see accounts of office spaces and furniture as expressive of status and as used to one's interaction advantage. The expressive and instrumental aspects rest on a reproduction of a background of configurations that enable them to work as they do. The desk as a barrier can be used to control by demonstrating authority differences, but so too can the team or arm around the shoulder be used to control.

Lindblom (1959) added much to the understanding of routines by arguing against a comprehensive rational model and for a model of "successive limited comparisons." In this sense the routine and bounded nature of reason provides a rationality for reactivity. Reactivity rather than comprehensive rationality is efficient. This was positively summarized by Wildavsky (1962):

> Organizations would find life unbearable if they treated each stimulus requiring action as something new. Every situation would then require an agreed definition of the situation, a frame of reference for interpreting events, a specification of the mixture of values involved, a thorough search for policy alternatives, and much more. In order to avoid the *enormous effort* and intellectual capacities required to accomplish these tasks, organizations normally cut their decision costs and their burden of calculation by developing set patterns of responses to frequently encountered situations. (178, emphasis added)

Certainly this is true and reasonable. But it also *pacifies* in the sense developed in chapter 7. The problem of examining the political advantages hidden and invested in routines is constructed as having "enormous" magnitude; too much is at stake to carefully consider unnecessary routines. The routine represents a battle already won, reconsideration represents risk. In fact routines are reconsidered in organizations but, in the managerial logic, only for the sake of greater efficiency or control. The problem that they control unnecessarily is not raised as an issue. The problem is not just that they are protected except in specified ways, but that they often slip by invisibly as a social technology without realization of the political implications.

In the public political realm, Bachrach and Baratz (1962) showed this clearly in the analysis of nondecisions. In their conception of "mobililization of bias," groups can evoke a "set of predominant values, beliefs, rituals, and institutional procedures ('rules of the game') that operate systematically and consistently to the benefit of certain persons and groups at the expense of others" (43). The concern in this volume is with how corporate procedures do this. Wolfinger (1971) adds to the analysis by elaborating on the forms nondecisions take in routine practices. He defines three: *renunciation, abstention, and nonparticipation. Renunciation* includes those instances where a position is not advanced because the actor already assumes that it will be unacceptable to some group, a form of self-surveillance and self-censorship. *Abstention* is a withdrawal from settings where decision making or even renunciation will take place. Cynicism, frustration, or fear may contribute to its presence. *Nonparticipation* defines those situations where individuals are unaware of their interests and therefore do not press for their accomplishment. Each of these are useful areas of investigation but can be misleading partly because they focus on the individual and on power as a property of particular groups. The routine is a subtle, everyday way that the apparatus is present in the *self*-definition of propriety, the qualification (and disqualification) of participants, and the production of *self*-interests.

Let me work through a relatively simple and obvious example. One of the most recurring features of the American corporation is the use of meetings. The notion of "meetings" seems unproblematic, but it is a complex accomplishment (see Atkinson, Cuff, and Lee 1978). Certain decisions may only be made in meetings. The legitimacy of decisions is often dependent on proper membership, the inclusion or exclusion of certain people may undermine outcome legitimacy. Rules and policies regarding membership, publicness, and availability of data exist in most organizations. One's relative status is often determined by inclusion and exclusion. Training programs for running meetings are common. Committees, task forces, and ad hoc groups nearly all receive meaning in meetings, even if technologically mediated. It is not uncommon to hear complaints about having meetings all day, the difficulty of getting work done around meetings, and the cost of travel associated with meetings. Japanese managers often suggest frustration with the time it takes for U.S. corporate officers to reach decisions, the number of people who must be involved. In the corporate mythos, this is often described as thinking too much rather than acting (Cushman 1990). Such a conception fits better with other dominant conceptions.

With the number of meetings and the composition of those involved, meetings enable important opportunities and pose risks. The meeting may be one of the few contacts with more senior officers and with people outside one's immediate area; it allows the sharing of perceptions and information not usually available, and it allows joint commitment to decisions. But it can also be a place of surprises, public embarrassment, and pressure from powerful figures. It is of little surprise that meetings are greatly routinized. Every choice would have apparent significance. And although meetings would seem to be the corporation's greatest display of a commitment to democracy (and often its best example of why democracy can't work), rarely are meetings participatory, and rarely are critical decisions risked in that context. Meetings are better read as rituals and signifiers than activities. They are most often routines of control, that conceal the control.

For example, in one division of an organization I observed, meetings appeared to be a dominant feature of life. They happened frequently, they were discussed at length, and even those calling them frequently described being overwhelmed by the time commitment. Key administrators, even in the midst of complaints, often lamented a past when they met even more often and knew everyone so much better. Clearly meetings were central to their definition of the group as community or family. Rarely were decisions made in the groups, however. The meetings were usually too large to discuss alternative points of view and reach consensus, and members rarely had adequate information ahead of time to be well informed. If decisions were made, they were by votes, as time was running out, or when a significant new piece of information was suddenly revealed. Meeting leaders usually heavily contextualized issues before discussion, but speaking by all was actively encouraged and expressions (usually confessions) were met with approval as long as they were positive and built on the one that went before. Comments with larger implications or a critical nature were always said to be important and passed to some future discussion, which rarely occurred. Ironically, the sheer number of meetings frequently led to situations where people were not available for critical, timely decisions, and no one seemed to plan ahead, so meetings were frequently at the last minute and under crisis rules.

In my experience there is little that is exceptional about this setting. It represents a common failure of using meetings, and social scientists have worked for years to teach better practices. But it is was very powerful as a means of control and was surely perpetuated, if unwittingly, for its strategic value. Bad administration became powerful administration. It allowed for administrative involvement in every aspect of work, monitoring every decision. It created a place where the top administrators could justifiably be in control and direct others and force public over private expression of interests, disagreements, and alignments. This tended to be confirmed by the lack of private conversation between senior officers and lower level individuals and the consequent absence of any symmetrical interpersonal relations. Particularly more junior individuals were virtuely forced by routine and encouragements to express opinions in front of upper administrators, where they were more vulnerable. The size of meetings made it virtually impossible to pursue disagreements without appearing self-serving or occupying others' created-as-precious time. The structure created particular images as being essential for advancement and disadvantaged more work-centered individuals who had less time for meetings and perhaps resented them more. And it created an impression that administrators had a high level of work effort, since they were so visible, without drawing attention to their lack of task accomplishment. And importantly it was "democratic." A "we" is created as the "we" meet all the time, the "we" decided everything. The subject is articulated here as a funny subject, self-defined in terms of process—routinized as involved, without involvement; committed without anything to commit to; and defined and affirmed by public ritual.

Participation Programs and The Management of Culture

Despite the various "obvious" ways in which control is accomplished and conflict suppressed in the modern corporation, the workplace is rarely directly experienced as a "prison," "iron cage," or place of authority relations. In fact, several of the organizations that would rank high on the managerialist control dimensions discussed in the past three chapters, such as GE or IBM, have high employee-satisfaction ratings. The continued presence of some openly autocratic administrators is often considered to be a problem or embarrassment. Foucault's concept of discipline helps much in understanding this.

The development of social technologies of control has essentially replaced authority in the managerial strategic apparatus. With such a concept we no longer have to contend that the workplace is well integrated and hegemonic to demonstrate domination. The corporation is filled with conflicts, but approved ones. People largely know their own interests, but these interests are produced in standard codes along normalized and one-sided lines. Surveillance is both internal and external to the individual, but for the good of efficiency and all members. The fear is not of an authority oppressor, but that one's own self will not behave and conform. Trust is enacted in images, since the whole person, filled with emotions, urges, and importantly, wasteful conflicts, cannot be trusted. The mind, body, and will are transformed into *means* in a long, strategic, instrumental chain toward some obscure end. But the preoccupation with control of the means leads to a constant overlooking of the distribution and advantages, the marginalization and control, that continue to be produced as the critical outcome of corporations.

Teamwork, worker participation programs, and the management of culture become important modern means of control and conflict suppression. Clearly these are to be preferred over the more authoritarian forms of managerialism, but modern managerialism loses no control even if it fosters involvement. As Foucault argued, disciplinary power enables as well as restricts. New managerial practices encourage a measure of dignity at lower levels of the organization, a reversal of some of the effects of deskilling, higher senses of self-worth in part because of higher quality products, and a site and routine in which presently suppressed conflicts *could* be discussed. But they also form more invisible and potentially, in the long run, more stultifying suppressions. If the enabling potential is to be realized, investigating the function and effects of these programs is essential. Here I only wish to outline the issues in such an investigation.

The Managerial Desire for New Systems of Control

A number of social changes have implications for control in the workplace as well as changes in the work process itself. Many of these grew out of the changes in expectations of participation and attitudes toward big business and management in the sixties. Others result from the growth of information technologies, service industries, and structural configurations. With these changes the managerial logic calls for new strategic means of control. Part of the failure of these modern programs to promote participatory democracy come from their strategic implementation rather than the moral recognition of their social importance. Positive economies and social good need not be contradictory but can be made so. Let me begin by outlining several changes that warranted the managerial response. These are adapted from Alvesson (1987a,b; in press).

First, as indicated in chapter 1, the society is experiencing a period of deinstitutionalization. Importantly this includes a decline in the moral and ethical background necessary to sus-

tain organizational practice in the absence of its ability to justify itself. The work ethic provided an important extraorganiza-
tion motivational form. Basic standards of honesty, belief in
quality and standards, and accurate reporting provided a voluntary conformity to social practices. The general expectation and
support of these has declined. Certainly the work experience
has been partially responsible for this decline. With strategy
and instrumental reasoning as basic processes, should anyone
be suprised that for many individuals ethics becomes reduced
to the calculated risk of getting caught, and motivation is
exchanged for rewards. The current situation is a place for freedom, in that past systems of control have diminished. Organizations could be reformed to at least reduce their own contribution to this decline. Instead, most corporations have implemented explicit strategies of value teaching and loyalty, hence
deepening the negative spiral.

Second, there have been changes in attitudes to authority
itself. Traditional figures of authority have been questioned and
even ridiculed. In the sixties' shifting of the "backstage" into
the "social" arena, authority lost its important mystique and
was seen as arbitrary and negotiated. In an age of the antihero
and the loss of the traditional commanding myths, managerial
authority itself declined. Management could not so easily manage by authority or coercion. As has been shown, managerialism evidences the passing of the authority to the expert. The
prerogative rests in symbols of superior ability and the invisible
good of efficiency for all, rather than in position. But because
of this the manager cannot govern by authority, permanently
installed in the position, but command must be symbolically
reproduced.

Third, the centralization of power itself created legitimation problems for the corporation in a democratic society. It is
difficult for the large centralized corporation to mimic the
characteristic of the family firm and thus to acheive the loyalty and personal identification frequently attributed to it. The
lack of personal and interpersonal contact places greater
demands on reason giving and explicit justifications, but these
become increasingly abstract and hidden from view. Decentralization was efficient due to diseconomies of scale and
reclaimed legitimacy.

Fourth, explicit systems of rewards and sanctions are difficult to administer in the modern organization. The supervisor
frequently lacks the "trade-relevant knowledge" necessary to

assess the worker's effort. The complex processes of production and the nature of managerial work make it difficult to assign fault, or fault is shared at so many levels that "scapegoating" is a common complaint. For example, consider the difficulty of getting a conviction in the publicly investigated Valdez disaster or of identifying a responsible party in the Challenger tragedy. Sanctions in most day-to-day operations are difficult to assign, often have negative side-effects, and usually end up appearing capricious. Rewards in even the more obvious cases of sales commissions are often complicated by the effects of support staffs, engineers, and others traditionally outside the sales process. Monitoring the amount and quality of work in the service industries becomes increasingly difficult. And supervisors often lack the authority to reward meaningfully except in unusual cases.

Fifth, along with the difficulty of using sanctions, the cost of member disruptions and even sabotage are great in highly centralized and interdependent work settings. The computer "virus" and the so-called data crimes (though there are rarely more "criminal" than many standard practices) are modern versions of inappropriate employee exercises of control. Although sometimes, they are motivated as unfocused resistance to the work environment and process, they evoke great fear, because corporations have generally relied on voluntary compliance to rules and internal regulations. Because they involve sophisticated equipment, common data banks, and highly coordinated processes, these acts are considerably more costly and harder to blame on someone. Surveillance through increased monitoring is costly and often fosters an environment where increased disruption is likely. Self-surveillance is obviously a preferable solution for most managerial groups.

Sixth, work itself has often become increasing fragmented, monotonous, and deskilled at the same time that the educational and expectation levels of new workers have increased. The managerial assumption that the problem is in education rather than work design is likely to lead to even more deskilling. Motivation, thus, must often be applied from the outside, because the work experience is not intrinsically motivating. Job enrichment is only a beginning of the massive effort necessary to make products, production, and coordination meaningful. New high school and college graduates may be happy to have a job at all, but the expectations of what will come with it do not disappear easily, especially with a consumer-advocating media pushing the good life.

Finally, the high expectation from new workers buying into managerialism, coupled with slower economic growth and loss of competitiveness, creates a legitimacy problem in the heart of management. The system requires high pay increases, expanding markets, and growth to meet its internally defined criteria of success. Initially periods of recession can be cast in positive Darwinian terms. Cleaning out the deadwood, trimming the fat, and streamlining can lead to seeing the individuals who are not making it as weak and add to the perception that those who do make it must be uniquely gifted, but events as they happen can be cast in alternative articulations that are not easy to suppress. Longer periods of slow growth start to suggest that no one can make it or that those at the top are denying opportunity.

The New Systems of Control

Putting these changes together, it should come as little surprise that a number of changes are occurring in the relations at the point of production. Behavioral control is difficult and costly, and motivational techniques are complex and often ineffective. The management of the "insides" and the routines along the lines of discipline and self-surveillance answer a lot of problems from a managerialist standpoint. The widespread appeal of such approaches has created a new industry and new set of professional experts. Some of these, such as "survival training," are sufficiently extreme as to be considered a type of psychological warfare. I will not discuss these here. Though it should be clear that an extremely large number of managers go through such training, and the constructed orientations to employees, coworker, and families constitute a significant effect. Of more interest are *cultural management and "team participation"* programs. Even though these are primarily co-opted as new control systems, each has democratic potential. There is no lack of significant and interesting alternative processes of managing today. Unfortunately nearly all of them fail to make a real difference, as they are frequently motived by managerial assumptions and nearly always finally dominated by them. The way these very different changes fulfill strategic goals should be explored prior to looking at the moments of democratic potential.

Cultural Studies and Cultural Management.   Smircich and Calás (1987) argued that cultural studies were dominant but dead. By "dead" they meant that the genuine change potential in them was gone. I would certainly agree. Cultural analyses abound, they are reported in both professional and trade publications, and management takes them seriously. The amateur anthropologist has joined the psychologist in providing new normalizations and sources of expertise within the modern managerialist apparatus (Knights and Willmott 1987).

As I argued a while back (Deetz 1985a), despite good individual intentions the potential for control is embedded in the anthropological project. Nineteenth-century anthropologists, who, rather than the more modern critical ones, frequently serve as models for cultural research in organizations, were often torn between their sentimentalist leanings, directing them to a value-neutral recording and preservation of culture, and their clear, if unwitting, complicity with the colonists and missionaries who manipulated and destroyed these same cultures. High-tech organizations may have replaced the sensual South Sea islands as the site, and career-minded executives in search of excellence and competitiveness may have become the modern colonists and missionaries, but the problem remains. Unfortunately, cultural researchers' answers to this dilemma have been similar to those of traditional social science (see Taylor 1990 for treatment of the controversy). Values are extrascientific. Even though the researcher may personally argue against the abusive use of knowledge, the research is treated as value-free. The knowledge is created as if it were politically neutral and open to use by competing groups. The majority of cultural studies and cultural advice has been anything but value-free or politically neutral.

Cultural research has arisen in corporations with an avowed atheoretical, apolitical focus, yet starts with a clear consensual point of view and participates in the internal (and implicitly the external) politics of the corporation. As Alvesson (1987b) argued, what has passed for culture in organizations is better understood as ideology, or, in Foucault's terms, a particular disciplinary practice, since it often represents a symbol system deployed by actors (though not necessarily knowingly) to define as well as secure their sectional interests. This can be seen in a number of characteristics of cultural studies, particularly as they imply value standards for cultural evaluation. In general, cultural studies can be seen to (1) emphasize the managers' picture of successful integration and corporate goals, (2) treat top management's culture as the organizational culture, (3) treat socialization and legitimation practices as positively affecting culture (when they work *right*) and as needed where cultures fail rather than as processes securing advancing domination, (4) judge cultural phenomena (e.g., stories, perceptions, and images) based upon their functional value rather than truth value, and (5) downplay conflict and contradictions in the discovery and presentation of culture (if only to make the concept of "culture" describe something real in the organization) and as problems where they do exist (see Alvesson 1987a, 206–15 for development).

Cultural studies do not have to be pursued in this manner. Research could instead follow the hermeneutic anthropological desire to recall, record and preserve existential-logics that are often lost to "progress," suppressed by dominant cultures, or hidden by dominant interpretations. Such studies could be given a critical turn. If such a position were accepted, cultural analysis would follow the direction suggested by Young (1989): "[O]rganizational culture emerges as sets of meanings constructed and imputed to organizational events by various groups and interests in pursuit of their aims. The analysis shifts from an appraisal of the content of meanings, toward identifying how meanings are constructed and imposed in order to mobilize interest group support" (191). A cultural researcher then would not seek simply the dominant cultural systems for the sake of describing or managing it, but would ask the manner by which it is held in place and utilized to advance self-interest and suppress alternatives. Ideally the researcher would follow the goals of chapter 3 of *insight, critique, and education* (see also Deetz 1982). The point would be to display suppressed conflicts and aid their rearticulation, an articulation contrary to the dominant one. The researcher could aid in developing a more open and productive conflictual environment for the sake of progressive opening of the variety of human interests and the means of their fulfillment. Some recent authors (e.g., Pacanowsky 1988) have worked to display the culture of empowering organizations. In doing so, they provide useful models for implementation elsewhere. Without an adequate account of disciplinary power, it is hard, however, to assess the suppressive and democratic potential, to distinguish between the image and the workings.

Job Enrichment and Team Work. *Quality of life, quality circles,* and *Japanese management* methods are popular terms pulling together a "new" team model of production. These programs often accomplish some job enrichment but mostly enhance control for the hope of increased productivity. The media-aided public relations campaign by management has claimed increased productivity and happy, freely participating workers. The image may be of a democratic workers meeting where jobs are determined and new processes devised, but the reality is often quite different. As argued throughout this volume, democracy is an everyday issue. Parker and Slaughter (1988) share such an evalution: "But team meetings last only a half an hour a week. Ultimately the team concept must be judged on what workers actually do during the eight to 10 hours per day, five to seven days per week, that they spend working" (88).

Many labor representatives are clear that if productivity has increased, it is because of increased work effort by production workers rather than by better management, and worker complicity is rarely free. The most comprehensive and pointed analysis of the everyday nature of the "team concept" has come from Parker and Slaughter (1988). They describe the team concept as "management-by-stress" (MBS). As they described it, after looking at fourteen of the most widely known industrial examples: "Management-by-stress uses stress of all kinds—physical, social, and psychological—to regulate and boost production. It combines a systematic speedup, 'just-in-time' parts delivery, and strict control over how jobs are to be done, to create a production system which has no leeway for errors—and very little breathing room" (14).

Managerial control is frequently enhanced through the team concept with reduced worker resistance. The fact that the worker participates in choice of jobs makes it easy to overlook that discipline is already deployed in the choice of technology, the layout of the work area, and the product and product design. The value of the team concept in enabling open discussions that would help the corporation in meeting its many potential objectives is lost. The worker takes over contestable, and often unpleasant, managerial functions like job assignment, which makes the conflicts become regularized and suppressed. And the creation of the context for decision making becomes increasingly hidden behind the making of decisions within the prescribed context.

The team concept also has implications for surveillance in the workplace. Both group and self-surveillance are enhanced. By making same-level employees responsible for each other's work, the work group becomes invested in reproduction of managerial control disguised as the good of the group. Rather than the work group sharing a site of solidarity and potential resistance, the group members function more like managers in relation to each other. The team concept, like cultural studies, has the potential to aid democracy. The team meeting as a routine provides an accepted site where more important issues might be discussed, and where the greater flexibility of work rules might allow the development of standard procedures that enable the discussion and accomplishment of different goals. The possibility exists for team-supported flexible work hours and a more informal, individual-centered approach to task accomplishment. This is not currently happening in the major corporations.

Neither cultural changes nor team processes offer much when dominated by managerialist precepts and practices. When the motive is narrow and singular, new systems of control and suppression of conflict are almost certain to come about. Some programs have more co-optive potential than others, but as long as strategic actions fostering one-sided goals are in place, all stakeholders of the corporation finally lose.

CHAPTER 12

Workplace Democracy as a Responsive Micropractice

> To escape from barren routine and vain fantasy in order to leaven reality with its possibilities: This is the endless effort of a democratic people.
>
> (Walter Lippmann 1914, 327)

Of course, there are no answers at the end of any modern book on social theory. This one will be no exception. I feel little guilt for that. In fact, solutions exist everywhere from a variety of political persuasions. There are careful critical theories of the organization (e.g., Denhardt 1981; Alvesson 1987a). There are suggestions for greatly enhancing worker participation (e.g., Mason 1982; Rubinstein 1987). There are equally insightful and productive suggestions for restructuring corporate governance (e.g., Tricker 1984). In most respects most of these suggestions need to be applauded. The lesson of this volume is in part to argue that we must say an emphatic yes to many of these. Yes, research must be conducted with a new political sensitivity. Yes, there should be more and broader participation. Yes, the work experience should be enriched. Yes, more women should be in upper management positions. Yes, labor laws should be changed to guarantee greater due process and a say in significant corporate decisions. Yes, decentralization remains a significant concern. Yes, the media should be diversified, ending the corporate stranglehold on public information and entertainment. And yes, the educational experience must emphasize critical decision making and broad development of the individual. But none of this appears very satisifying. All these things could and should make a difference. Yet even with wide agreement on issues like decentralization, the talk has been greater than the actual implementation, and the amount of change has been small and short-term. Something has been missed, or perhaps it is too obvious.

My own experience is better captured by a quote from a female executive in an in-house memo at a Fortune 500 company, cited by Schaef and Fassel (1988):

> What is a productive organization? We have been inundated in the last few years with books, articles, case studies, and news stories that describe the attributes of excellence and successful organizations. As a country of business people we have studied our competitors. At various times with various voices we have touted high tech, robotic, and electronic solutions. From Europe we have accepted a need for cooperation and collaboration with our employees by starting quality-of-life and employee-involvement efforts in major companies like GM, AT&T, and Ford. Unions like the UAW, the Communications Workers of America, and the Steel Workers became leaders in the changes. Yet many of these very hopeful programs have lost their initial charge. We have looked to the East and started Quality Circles, Just in Time delivery programs, Total Quality Control, Statistical Process Control, and Company-Wide Quality Control.
>
> Yet, through all our writing and research, we still seem to be missing something. We are attracted to these demonstrations of excellence; we recognize that there is something that we do not have, yet the majority of executives and managers in the United States are unable to implement significant permanent change incorporating these ideas. What is it that we are attracted to? What is it that eludes us when we try to implement these changes? (2)

While I share in the frustration, I think I better understand the attraction and why change eludes us. The same system produces both. The hope for greater efficiency and productivity through the finding of a new technical solution and strategic intervention is a never-ending and fundamentally destructive project driven by a peculiar logic and faith in an end state. The lesson is important, if the goal is changed to greater social participation, but the means is simply a different strategic innovation—if a new utopia replaces an old one, we may change who is frustrated but not the destructive impact. Let me propose at the outset that the project is endless, hence, the *means* and the *momentary* take on special significance. No new social scientist should replace the manager as the engineer. The concept of the engineer must go. What has eluded us is the fullness of the present, which has been constantly deferred to some fading-away future. The issue is not a new democracy, a new structure and practice, but a micropractice, a democracy of the insides and the everyday perception, conception, and response to events. But how is this to be publicly characterized?

The Approach to Change

Burrell (1990) proposed the clearest statement of three common alternatives for the characterization of change. First, one could argue for a new "utopian" vision from which a more extended critique of the modern workplace could be offered. Second, one could argue for "entryism," in which means could be suggested for the development of a workplace where a broader range of interests were represented. Or third, one could argue for a kind of poststructuralist (decentered) sabotage or resistance that would at least deny the domination and provide for spaces of automony. I do not believe that it is too Pollyannaish to argue for each. The image I have in mind is close to what Jansen (1989) refered to as "commuting." It would include ideals and realistic compromises; protective colonies and entry; interpretive guerrilla warfare and understanding mainstream discourse.

The positions become contradictory in carefully developed philosophies. Each of these philosophies would appear useful in describing an aspect of modern life, but none the totality. As individual actors we often choose contradiction and we live with tension. The essential lesson to be learned is that significant changes more often result from small innovations designed to solve everyday problems than from grand revolutionary projects (Weick 1979, 1984). We do not need a complete philosophy to make significant choices. But the choices we make both facilitate innovations and direct their impact. I will discuss each of these three ways of looking at organizational change briefly before putting them together in a conception of the responsive agent.

A Hopeful Vision of the Future

I think a vision of a more participatory future is important in the modern context, a vision can help guide our conceptions and practices. The vision I have in mind is more like a Rortian (Rorty 1982) social hope than a utopian ideal, more a touchstone than a definitive conception. Such a morally-guided "hope" is a critical aspect of the position taken here. In the past thirty years, where the public has actively discussed the social construction issues, and the faith in truth and authority have waned, corporate control has increased. While increased freedom was the intent of those who brought the "backstage" to negotiation, the result has been different from this. With the misrecognition of these works through humanistic psychology and relativism, only power would appear to remain as the final arbitrator. Nihilism is often the alibi of fascism. Individuals sought self-initiated power, and no one was equal to the corporate organization of power. With the loss of the "real," images appeared to be all that was left anyway, so why not manage them. Deep cyncism could lead a generation to struggle to book first class on their own self-described Titanic. The social technologies of control were fostered by the opening. The private realm was no longer competing institutions and authorities but merely the insides of the individual that themselves eventually came to be controlled.

But we gave up on a moral community too early. And we mistakenly believed that the choice was between either an authoritarian, traditional, totalizing morality or individual freedom and autonomy. Individual development *and* autonomy can be fostered by the moral community. I believe that Habermas offers much in his ideal speech situation. The community already accepts his conceptions of open discourse, at least in everyday action (if counterfactually). Our commitment to them has to be "remembered," and we must be willing to act morally. Immoral actions in the modern corporations may be powerfully determined, but they are neither outside member control nor possible without active complicity. Such a vision is helpful in the critique of unethical practices and the ideologies that support them. But for such a critique to be productive, the investigation must focus on the routines and everyday practices that form the subtle deployment of the suppression of conflicts and democratic participation itself. If such goals are kept in the foreground, it does not take an expert to see strategy and suppression or to devise systems where there is effort to realize conflict *and* move to common understanding. But it has to be done by someone. Stated in the visionary Kennedy cadence: "If not us, who; if not now, when." But it is no longer a liberal social planning project, as the prophet became the priest. Creativity is present in all groups. Perhaps it is greatest in the concrete and specific response to a real need. If worker efforts to find a space of control, or manager efforts at imagining, could be put to reformed communication, much could be done immediately, and progressively each would get better at it.

Such a vision is not antimanagement, antiefficiency, or antiprofit. It is antimanagerialism, and it is supported by recalling that the corporation is about more than economic efficiency and profit. There are no necessary contradictions, only tensions among the various stakeholders of the corporation. Managerialism produces approved conflicts and contradictions that help sustain its force. There are conflicts and tensions among stakeholders that, if fostered, can enable greater balance in the meeting of the various goals and probably even greater productivity as a by-product. Managerialism works against such a vision, the teaching of it, and the practice of it. And managerialism is shared by nearly all. New visions can replace those of managerialism. Until then life is "dominated by a self-defeating preoccupation with effecting social closure upon world-openness through the control of nature, self, and social relations" (Knights and Willmott 1985, 26).

The Possibilities in Entryism

Managerialism is a white, middle-class, male system (see Gilligan 1982; Pringle 1988). As it suppresses the conflicts within even white, middle-class males, it transforms the interests and identities of groups in the society who initially were produced as its opposite. Many women have left the corporate ranks owing to the lack of equal advancement and nonchanging cultures (Jacobs and Hardesty 1986). But there is a second serious fear. A fear of advocating corporate entry for women and minorities has arisen from the observation that they, as they try to succeed, no longer embody "the different" and the tension but become "normalized" in the system. Certainly both women and different minority groups have often had transformed identities as they succeed. Their possible group interest becomes undermined by individualism, system problems are quickly taken on as the deficiency of the person, and "success" is frequently achieved by giving up one's own "voice." The "trip to the foot binder" may be disguised as "dress for success," but the structural relation is only different in the way authority gives way to discipline as a means of control. Women may learn to "talk like a man" and succeed, but the corporation (in nonmanagerial terms) suffers until she can "talk like a woman" (with all the ambiguities such an idea leaves). The same is true for each ethnic, racial, and class distinction in the United States. Normalization and standard usage can be morally justified by efficiency only when all groups have openly determined the norms and standards that efficiency helps accomplish. Gender and group distinction may be essential until the complexity in each individual is recovered. Until then, such distinctions may uphold rather than suppress conflict, and may produce a space for difference.

But nothing is gained by holding out hope for revolution or vast national reforms, and the victims cannot suffer for us all. All groups have a right to desire something of the "good life" and broader representation in existing organizations without simple co-optation and loss of responsiveness to larger issues. Greater entry by traditionally excluded groups is critical and must be supported by internal corporate struggles to make it a meaningful entry. They must become financial equals and critically equals in the construction of identity, meaning, and knowledge. Genuine financial equality cannot be sustained without identity equality. The task is one shared by all, but the affected groups have the key role. Entry is a beginning rather than the end of a struggle.

The Place of Resistance

Disciplinary structures as codes "interpellate" subjects, stop their speaking, and formally call them. But as will be developed later, a space remains for agency. The "agent" will not be an actor free from structure, but one who recovers the tensions of the various discursive fields. With every "positive" move in disciplinary practices, there is an oppositional one. Managerialism has carefully constructed the actors and their approved conflicts. Metaphorically, the choice proposed here is to choose the "game" rather than choose a "move" from the set prescribed by the game. Everyday men and women resist managerialism. They do so by "choosing," sometimes explicitly, to reject the desire to win at it. They choose balanced lives, and they pay for it primarily in the financial code favored by management. But many are happier people; the simple life can be the better life. They are heros of one kind. And many have chosen to be direct and honest, struggling to express their best guess as to what is real, rather than operating strategically and working at images. And they have done this without becoming crass and antisocial. They are often mistrusted and confused people, but they are heros of another kind. And some members of corporations have approached their jobs and other people with an ethic of care and facilitation rather than control and competition. They are heros of another kind yet.

Resistance can also be more systematic. Women could end all inequalities in the workplace tomorrow, but they have to want to and feel that they deserve it. They must demand it from others, and most importantly from themselves. This is developing not simply a group or class consciousness but an organized resistance, a resistance to discipline rather than as disciplined. Workers could change the financial structure of the corporations for which they work by voting with the stock held in their pension plans. But even in companies that they own, they have rarely trusted themselves. Clearly there are important signs that groups are becoming more clever. Union members in some plants are working without contracts rather than striking (Parker and Slaughter 1988, 76). In the daily contract-free negotiations of work rules, they sometimes develop more satisfactory informal working relations, some of which will survive the contract. There are dangers in such a move. Without solidarity, workers can lose formal rules that have protected them, but the present system contains a long sustained systemic danger. The union and its "victories" have reproduced the worker as worker and established one basis for managerial control (R. Harris 1987, 61). Productive resistance denies the discipline rather than plays its role in it. Careful analysis can provide new actions with potential large effects without condemning significant portions of the population to mere reactivity.

The Concept of Balanced Responsiveness

The opposite of domination in the disciplinary mode is not personal autonomy, but *balanced responsiveness*. In responsiveness lies the hope for differentiation and individualization, an autonomy that differs greatly from controlled images and individualism. Against either rational or reactive decision making, the argument is made for responsive decision making. Responsiveness is to seize the moment with care and moral direction, rather than with instrumentality and decisional rules. If commitment to a vision is not to be a new domination, if entryism is to be saved from co-optation or cynical exit, and if resistance is to be more than reactive expressions of violation, we need a sense of balance in this responsiveness.

The enlightenment project became oppressive primarily because it structured a hope for a centered, unitary answer to life's difficulties that autonomous human individuals would come to see and choose. Enlightenment held out the hope of a new, conflict-free answer based on reason and science. Democracy was seen as a one-time achievement to henceforth be defended from darkness and evil. In opposition to such a view, I believe that every new vision or program can become a new form of domination and control. The point is not to give up on meaningful changes, but to understand that what is an important response to a moment is itself open to analysis and critique at the next. Democracy is an ongoing accomplishment. Difference, conflict, and balancing demands are to be embraced as human rather than answered by systems and idealized images.

Balance does not mean having it all, any more than it means replacing all of being human with one aspect of it. It means giving up part of all things so that the whole can be bigger. Gilligan's (1982) descriptions of young girls playing games is not a bad model. She described their play as a balance of competition and facilitation. They played to win as part of the logic of the game itself. But they also played to learn and help the other learn, and importantly to keep the game going and interesting. If the rules disadvantaged one player, they changed the rules. The game even became more fun to play.

The game balance is accomplished by periodic, momentary responsiveness. The attempt is not to find the ideal system (or game) and freeze it. Rather, there are moments of perceiving imbalance and rectifying them through responsive action. We have here an imperfect model of a self-referential system that has autonomy by staying in relation to its environment rather than being dominated by a control model. This is an odd contingency model—not one driven by the strategic success of the particular corporation, but one that attempts to balance the various needs of the insides and outsides using multiple semiotic systems.

To be responsive requires taking responsibility for one's complicity as well as one's action, identifying contexts of responsive action, and responding. For this to happen, responsiveness requires productive antagonism. The reclaiming of suppressed conflict identifies the places of complicity in control, establishes a choice context, and requires a new choice. In their game, the young girls feel the conflict of wanting to win, wanting the game to be fun, and wanting self and other to play well. They must in each instance choose. When the game is played simply to win, the choices are made—the emotions are prescribed for each turn of events, the winner dominates but is already dominated. I wish to claim momentary balanced responsiveness to recovered antagonisms as the basis for a political micropractice.

Reclaiming the Responsive Agent

Resistance, entryism, and visions, the balanced responsiveness, must be grounded in a conception of the person in relation to disciplinary power. Otherwise the phrases of hope and new reform become a new jargon adding to ever more sophisticated social control. But given the analysis in the previous chapter, how can we find a space for hope? How can freedom and democracy be possible without the disciplinary co-optation that makes them neither? Following the analysis here, it may appear that the subject has no place of freedom, especially since most common conceptions of freedom are written in opposition to power. Certainly others have come to this place, and "agency" is one of the biggest issues of this decade (see Reed 1988; Westley 1990). The space of freedom and choice must be reconceptualized outside of its present disciplinary articulation if it is to have meaning and form a ground for new choices.

The Space of Agency

The free subject, an agent, is not a thinking, choosing, or reflecting one. The illusionary "free" subject as a part of the disciplinary practice of managerialism discussed in chapter 11 must be rejected. But neither is the subject determined by any condition of *necessity* in the disciplinary formation. The subject may be forgetful of the constitutive process, and there may be active conditions of concealment, but each is partial and incomplete. The recovery of the subject as agent is in recovering the subject not as unitary and rational but as responsive. Agency is dependent not on a new-found internal will but on a recovery of the demand on the outside, of "otherness," or "subject matter" in Gadamer's participative sense developed in chapter 6. It is fostered by communicative processes that perpetually recover a space for exceeding personal and systemic restraints and distortions, communicative practice as outlined in Habermas's many works. Such ideas need yet to be related to the issues of discipline.

The political character and open formation of experience are always left a space, a space experienced as conflict and fostered by appropriate analysis. Debord (1981) has added much to the finding of such spaces, with his analysis of *situations,* or *passageways.* In Debord's argument, "The life of a person is a succession of fortuitous situations, and even if none of them is exactly the same as another the immense majority of them are so undifferentiated and so dull that they give a perfect impression of similitude. The corollary of this state of things is that the rare intensely engaging situations found in this life strictly confine and limit this life" (24). Such chance events make possible reclaimed conflicts and transformations, and importantly, their effect is directed by the alternatives available in the moment. The production of alternative social memories and counternarratives demonstrates the possibility of new articulations of the elements of experience and opens them to a new political understanding. The openness of personal identity is deeply involved in these processes. While openness may not be able to be intentionally produced, the potential in the "crisis" moment is realized by the availability of intellectual resources and significant communication processes.

Otherness as Reclaiming Process Subjectivity

The presence of a space does not assure its actualization. In fact, as I have shown there are active processes of closure that protect current articulations against the possibility of competing ones. Fundamentally, as I have argued, we must reclaim a conception of the communicative process powerful enough to give liberatory guidance to communicative practice while demonstrating places of communication failure. Chapters 5, 6, and 7 developed the argument for this. It remains here to reassert the possibility in the face of corporations as communication systems of control. I wish to begin with the explicit and ordinary sense of communication and gradually move to the latent strategic level.

The contemporary everyday conceptions of interacting with others through effective communication are conceptually flawed as a basis for participatory democracy. This we have seen, as well as the managerial motive for deploying such a conception. The everyday conception focused attention on the act of self-expression and the processes by which personal meaning is transferred to others. With such a view the self is held as fixed and knowable, and language and information technologies are rendered invisible. The constitutive conditions of self-production cannot be seen as politically charged. In practice this gives a false sense of the individual as the originator of meaning and leads to self-expressionism and strategic control of others through expressive acts. The stage is set for control of self and control of others, but strategically positioned outside of the illusionary self. The growth, differentiation, and progressive individualization of the self require giving up the unitary self and its control. Only in the development of the "other" can the self develop.

Identity is fixed in distorted communication systems even before it is fixed again as an explicit image. I have attempted to show how such fixings work in corporations. The point here is to describe the possibility of regained conflict and open self-formation. Weedon (1987) developed this as *process subjectivity*. In her sense, the freedom from the domination of any particular identity fixed in a discourse is the presence of alternative discourses, discourses, in the sense used here, that have not been articulated with the dominant one. Deconstruction and the providing of alternative accounts is essential to this. Her conception has been useful in the exploration of how managerial discourse is part of a strategic deployment of control. Here I believe we can fill this concept out to give it greater life in an everyday sense.

In opposition to the common-sense view, I will argue that communication is not for self-expression but for self-destruction. The point of communication as a social act is to overcome one's fixed subjectivity, one's conceptions, one's strategies, to be opened to the indeterminacy of people and the external environment. Communication in its democratic form is productive rather than reproductive. It produces what self and other can experience, rather than reproduces what either has.

Self-expression is misleading not because people don't or should try to express their experiences but because such expressions are the raw material for the production of something new rather than the product of self-interests. We have seen this in Gadamer's (1975) description of the genuine conversation; its critical potential is great. The self cannot simply choose to be open, for that would presume that it has already determined what it is to be open to. Rather, process subjectivity happens in the responsiveness to the pull from the outside. The "elements" must be allowed to exceed each "moment of articulation," in Laclau and Mouffe's (1985) terms.

Despite the misleading humanist uses of his work, Buber (1970) provided one of the most compelling descriptions of discursive identity closure and the manner of open participation with his ontology of "thouness." In Buber's work, "I–it" relationships are not unethical because they objectify the other through conceptualization *per se,* but they can become unethical in certain interaction processes. When the I–it relationship is held above examination, when the other is held as a common object unable to ob-ject outside of its conceptualized character, both the I and the other have been violated. Buber is not suggesting by thouness that every relationship should move toward intimacy and the disclosure/realization of the other's real self, but that the "realness" of the other is the resistance to fixation. The problem is not I–it relationships, but the forgetting of thouness, the closing of communication. The recognition of "the otherness of the other" breaks a discursive stoppage by posing questions to any "it" conception. The "other" exceeds every possible conception of it. In modern terminology, thouness is an act of deconstruction.

By removing the mystical term *thou,* we can hold on to what is critical in Buber. "Otherness" is property of people, but also of things and events. The excess of the element over its articulation represents its pull of otherness. The fundamental otherness suggests that any possible label or conception of self, other, and world is capable of being questioned. Perception, as well as conception, is the end product of a conflict—a struggle between one's fixed identity and conceptual scheme and the excess of the "other" over that. The remembrance of this struggle leaves each and every attempt to form an object potentially available to be questioned. Otherness in this sense is critical to the formation of self and other and leads to a type of conceptual sabotage. "Itness" inevitably leads to imagistic interaction and a limitation to the free and open formative discourse, whether the "it" is held as one's real self or conceptualized by the other. Every interaction thus holds both the possibility of closure or new meaning, either a reproduction of the dominant socially produced subjectivity or responsivness to the excess of external events over these conceptions. Developing a sense of *care*, as an appreciation of *otherness*, is central to reclaiming a form of democracy appropriate to the modern age.

Beginning the Micropractice of Democracy

The efficiency of the managerial corporation works against the claim of otherness as it works to suppress conflict. The suppression works against the development of self, other, and the corporation. We do not need a corporate policy of more open communication or a new structure approaching the ideal speech situation to begin the practice of democratic communication. The goal is not to persuade upper management that a different ideology or value system would be beneficial. Managerialism is in place as a practice. Identities and massive systems of rewards are not likely to be changed by arguments. Managerial managers will not give up significant control. They believe that they alone have the corporate interest in mind. Management will not distribute income more reasonably. The system spawns a web of needs including perks, oversized house payments, and cars that "must" be cared for. One would even be properly suspicious if upper-level management were to actively become involved. But one can begin to work on behalf of the corporation (in its fuller sense) through enacting processes that subvert managerialism. I believe this requires responsiveness by the various types of "owners" of the corporation. And it requires the modern intellectual as a representative of the public, whether in the guise of teacher, consultant, or researcher. First let's look at the direct stakeholders, starting with those in production jobs and "lower" paid services

First, practices rejecting managerialism will focus primarily on the nonmonetary issues and explicit control. Power and money are the favored codes of managerialism and the place of its normal, "approved" (and advantaged) conflicts. Many critical labor issues have been lost for the sake of a pay increase. More change potential exists in focusing on how the accounts are kept than on the amount of corporate profit or managerial pay. Balance sheets that represent more than profits and losses through explicit accounts of environmental and social impact and long-term effects on worker development legitimize equally important corporate concerns. Job design, choice of equipment, and flextime arrangements are all significant issues. At a more macro level, work rules are significant. As Parker and Slaughter (1988, 77) argued, "Work rule changes can go deeper and last longer than monetary" ones. Labor can foster democracy by focusing on the routines and relations at the point of production. Unnecessary rules and regulations can often be eliminated. They are rarely followed, and they are usually evoked for control or punishment. Democracy is aided by making the supervisor take responsibility for controlling action, the use of rules too often removes that responsibility. Recalling forgotten questions and avoidance of routines are daily acts of freedom that can have significant effects. In self-referential systems, small changes can have massive effects (Weick 1979, 81–82). Make small changes because they are practically (in Habermas's sense) better, rather than because larger effects can be anticipated. The effect is always a by-product.

While "lower" level employees must look for more productive conflict sites, individuals in "managerial" positions need to reclaim the conflicts within themselves. This is particularly true for men. Managerialism is a power-filled apparatus stretching into most aspects of life. The discourses are most carefully articulated regarding males. The routines, identity, and language are felt most to be "natural" there. The tension of the insides can be fostered by extended vacations, going home on time, attending community rather than company gyms, and developing nonwork friendships. Managerialism works to the extent that the manager's primary identity lies there. When a manager feels indispensable or fears that others will find out what he or she really does, managerialism is at its worst. Only real people and actual other events are likely to have the power to reclaim productive conflicts.

The external relations follow in a similar line. Democratic potential exists in treating people, including the self, as human beings. When people are cared for in the sense of being appreciated for their differences, their feelings, and their competing needs, images are seen as distractions and represent fears rather than being powerful and trustworthy. Democratic managers experience legitimate pain, including facing laid-off people and the hard questions and insecurities that come with being explicit about values and criteria used in decision making.

Managers can foster democracy by directly confronting immoral practices. Games and imagining need not be tolerated, and unethical communicative behavior (in the broad sense outlined in chapters 6 and 7) should not be accepted, any more than false expense reports. People in the corporation are more important than the books. Informal environments and more flexible working hours enhance democratic participation. Routines and standard practices can often be avoided, thereby minimizing rules and increasing judgment. Alternative means of presentation and reasoning processes can be encouraged in most corporate contexts by paying more attention to the adequacy of the expression rather than controlling the person doing the expressing. If individuals do not express themselves well, different means of expression are often appropriate rather than judgments of expression deficiency.

The cycle of silence regarding "unapproved" conflicts and the suspicion and surveillance among managers in many corporations are often self-generated and supported. People often think everyone has to dress, act, and respond in certain fashions because everyone thinks you have to. Such managerial groupthink, coupled with the ideological effect of corporate stories and disciplinary practices, leads to self-control and self-surveillance that have no basis other than their own thickness and the silence of alternative voices.

The Intellectual's Task

Rethinking the role of the modern intellectual as researcher, consultant, and teacher is another significant task. This volume is written primarily for this group, and I hope much of a new agenda is present. Despite the extent of public funding, the public responsibility of organizational scholars has come up short. Fischer (1984) may have gone too far when he declared that, "As unabashed students of industrial efficiency and stable work relations, its first theorists laid the groundwork for a discipline designed to supplement and support the bureaucratic mode of authority and control. Since then the study of organizational behavior has never swung far from narrowly defined objectives of corporate organizations" (172). But his point is well taken. The goals, topical issues, and study methods conspire together to provide a remarkably narrow and politically loaded analysis of corporations. In opposition to this, I initially proposed a research agenda with three goals, *insight, critique, and education.* The acceptance of such goals has rather immediate practical implications.

The role of the intellectual is socially important, but anti-intellectualism is a feature of contemporary discourse in the United States. Part of this is well deserved. The smugness and elitism practiced by many groups is deplorable even when it is unknowingly committed. And surely parts of this work can be criticized for inaccessibility. I am not always sure how to separate sophisticated theoretical analysis from mere elitism. But in the same way that we can identify the difference between strategic communication and communicating to reach a common understanding, I think we often know the difference. I believe that we are morally obligated to try to create a discourse that invites participation and that crosses community lines. But much of the anti-intellectualism today is based on political prejudices. The claim for practicality is more often a call for managerialism than practicality. Our work and our applications cannot favor a particular segment of society based on money and power. The intellectual needs to be reclaimed as one who reflects critically on life. If the intellectual in contemporary society becomes simply a lower paid trainer or R&D personnel for corporations, that role is lost.

The modern intellectual can make a difference by helping to prepare students for their democratic role in corporations. Clearly intellectuals have often lost faith in education. Yet the classroom, seminars, and community programs probably have far more potential effect than books and treatises. The university experience is still a powerful one for students. When I hear reform-oriented faculty lamenting the conservatism of students today, I wonder how much time they spend with them. Students still gravitate to action and excitement. If it is not in ideas, it surely is elsewhere. The hope for a spontaneous liberalism fails to account for the managerial encroachment, and the fact is that it probably never happened that way. Instructional practice and instructional contact has changed as much as students. And those changes definitely influence what students become. It is the responsibility of university faculty to take back the university, to become involved in education and student's development. This may mean fewer publications and less career focus. This is not a call for a radical change in students or the university, but a micropractice of democracy in the education industry.

As was made clear in chapter 1, instructional practices and textbooks establish a managerial bias, but so does the content of education. Managerialist education is frequently present. Perhaps the worst cases exist in instructional use of simulation exercises and case studies that basically teach survival skills for the worst organization you could imagine. Equally important are dress-up days and "image" assignments that teach adjustment to the corporation as if it were an existing, natural object rather than an arbitrary construction. At the least, instruction should make clear the oppressive character of these corporate practices and more importantly invent and teach alternative forms. The constructive capacity of individuals as well as the breaking of the naturalized, neutralized organization teaches the places where freedom is possible. In the enlightenment the university transformed itself to teach science and a "rational" way of thinking against superstition and traditional ideologies. Such a project has partially gone awry. The university has a role again to teach reason in place of narrow rationality and participation in identity and knowledge construction against managerialism.

The role of consulting is also important. Many performing a consulting role forget that it is the corporation who hires and pays for the help, not the manager (except in those rare cases where the manager pays out of his or her own pocket). All too frequently, the would-be intellectual in the consultant role acts like a low-paid junior executive who loves dressing up for a day and acting like an affluent powerful executive. In their role such consultants actively support managerialism, though their own values would never let them take a job in a place like that. The consultant should represent the various stakeholders—the total corporation. Any report should be publicly available. If increased efficiency is to remain the issue, efficiency should be calculated on the basis of human and environmental cost and the meeting of many goals. Process reforms and the elimination of control mechanisms should accompany more focused problem solutions.

The research function has been a focus throughout this work. The need for detailed, theoretically guided empirical analysis is constant. But "empirical" analysis cannot mean simply more fieldwork, observations, surveys, or interviews. The insight and critique possible by the researcher are not matched by others within most corporations. The researcher alone often has the outside, multi-interested, long-term perspective. This needs to be brought to the corporate context. Most research conducted with categorization, linear models, and generalization as guiding elements has little potential for anything else but furthering control (see Hamnett et al. 1984 and Deetz 1985a for development). Little of the research on corporations has aimed at fostering disciplinary resistance or wider interest representation, even when its focus is on "participation" and "democracy." Efficiency criteria defined in narrow terms have dominated most research efforts. Most studies of participation programs have looked at traditional issues of efficiency, productivity, and satisfaction (Miller and Monge 1986; Wagner and Gooding 1987). But do such programs give rise to conflicts that have been suppressed? Do they shift control with decision making? Is a wider set of interests produced and represented? Studies of information systems and new communication technologies continue in the same line. Frequently the professed "neutrality" of these technologies is displayed by contending that they largely support existing values and practices rather than change them. This of course assumes these values were politically neutral in the first place. The issue is not just the changes with new technologies, or their continuity, but their effects on daily democracy.

Research always functions to give some voice to those things that were hidden or not immediately visible. That voicing needs to be fostered. Often the voicing is immediately silenced by translation into favored codes, particularly those that are objectifying and control centered. The political choice of what gets voiced and how it is represented are central to research in corporations today. I hope some of the conceptions presented in this work aid the continued development of research of this sort.

Bounded Democracy in the New Public Sphere

Corporations are the new public sphere. First, they are clearly public in their structure and effects. They are the site where human and material resources are managed; they are the site where major social policy decisions are made; they are the site where decisions influencing the public welfare are made; and they are the site where the lives and identities of a vast number of citizens are constructed and directed. Second, they are public in their nature. They are a social creation for the social good; they are owned (especially if we remove the reduction to the monetary code) by numerous stakeholders for and by whom they are created; and they differ in significant ways from any ownable private property or the private sphere. The point of this work has been to show the significance of organizations in contemporary society and corporate encroachment into all other aspects of life. Most significantly, this new public form controls and colonizes modern life, especially at the level of identity, in ways no government or public body thought possible.

Proclaiming the corporation as a public sphere is not a new call for greater governmental ownership or regulation. The managerial logic that dominates corporations is actively present in government as well. Hopefully, greater democratic participation in worklife will lessen the amount of governmental activity. This is clear when one considers the amount of governance devoted to upholding autocratic corporate control, requiring corporations to operate with basic socially shared values, monitoring legal abuses, and providing social support for those hurt by corporate policies. We all pay for the inefficiencies of modern managerial practice through bearing the cost for social welfare, environmental impact, and resource usage. At the least, these costs should be recorded at the site where they were produced. A competitive market situation should lead to competition, with full statement of cost, rather than it being shifted to another public group or subsidized by the government. With such calculations, wider interest representation would already be present in economic decisions. But beyond that, greater shareholder involvement in corporate design, practices, and production decisions creates a value base more closely aligned with the general public and the goals that governmental bureaucracies only weakly represent. We all also pay for monitoring corporations from the outside. This is also infrequently recorded as a cost of the modern corporation. If we monitor from the inside, would any possible loss in efficiency be as great as the current cost?

Our shared beliefs mandate that communication within corporations, as a new public sphere, ought to be democratic. We must stand vigorously opposed to the saw: "Autocracy at work is the price we pay for democracy after hours." Meaningful democracy happens at the sites where meaningful decisions are made. I concur with Golembiewski (1990) when he argues that the concept of organizational autocracy in the service of representative democracy can no longer be sustained. In his words: "This convenience may have been tolerable in earlier days, but it poorly suits our 'organizational society' in its progressive forms and it increasingly generates unanticipated consequences that undercut the liberal state and political citizenship" (494). Clearly we must reverse the question that Wolin (1960) denied in his classical response to Selznick's (1957) conception of organizations as polities: "The modern question is how much democracy can organization endure?—never the reverse." We need to ask, how much organization can democracy survive? And more importantly, we must ask how to make our organizations more democratic.

Many have come to these issues at various times and along various paths. Concepts of workplace democracy have a long and varied history. The number of recent full-length volumes devoted to the issue is impressive (for example, Bernstein 1980; Ewing 1977; Mason 1982; Greenberg 1986; Nightingale 1982; Rubinstein 1987). Clearly these often share little in common with the so-called participation programs in place in many organizations today. What is key to their difference is not always the actual practices involved but the motive. While many participation programs are dominated by economic rationality and a strategic technical interest in control, workplace democracy has focused on the political issues involved. This work has clearly been in the latter tradition. Workplace democracy is a moral political issue, not one of greater productivity and satisfaction, though these usually result. If there is a new public sphere, there is the need for a new "corporate citizen." Such a term may appear misleading to some (see Stivers 1989), but it opens a connection to things we already partially understand and struggle to work with. We know something of civic responsibilities, and we need to take them to work. We know something of democratic public participation in public agencies (Golembiewski 1989; Gormley 1986), and we need to incorporate something of that in corporate organizations. Much of it is immediately applicable. We know something of the right to be informed and have a say on issues of public importance, and we must not lose this to a new privileged realm.

Much can be said for the careful writings on workplace democracy, and each of us gains new options for our own workplace as we read them. To begin even a review of them here would be to start another book. Rather I wish to recall the argument of this work to focus the contributions to these literatures. In contrast to much of the workplace democracy work, the present one does not ground the issue of democracy in a basic human right or set of external values. The moral foundation for democracy is in the daily practices of communication, the presumptions that each of us make as we talk with each other. As a moral political practice is grounded in the everyday, so too is the violation. Democracy is denied by neither armies nor powerful figures, but in the moment-to-moment. This denial is misrecognized at the start and actively concealed by discursive practices. These are not necessarily done for the purpose of control, but they enact a web of strategic moves of asymmetrical power relations. The recovery of democracy must start in these practices.

Further, most works on workplace democracy have focused primarily on representation in decision making. They begin by assuming that different groups (differentiated by stake, class, or gender) have different interests and that the goal is to create new structures in which these groups may express their interests. This work has reversed the issue. The first issue must concern how such groups are produced within or in relation to the closed, self-referential system of the corporation. Such a production creates particular interests, sites and forms of articulation, and the produced conflict among them. Such conflicts reproduce the configuration that put them in play. The point here, then, has not been to create forums for the expression and resolution of conflicts among stakeholders over and against domination but to understand the domination present in these interests and conflicts, with the hope of recovering conflicts that have been suppressed through latent strategic normalization and routinization. This led to a focus on language, experience, knowledge, and identity as principle sites of the move of disciplinary power. They are also the sites of resistance and member-generated alternative practices. The issue is thus not oppressed groups per se, but the skewedness of all development and the active complicity of even disadvantaged groups in it. The plan here is not to suggest what these groups should do but to offer a mode of analysis and insight into the corporate process so that they can be more responsive.

The argument here has been for a new form of participatory democracy fundamentally rooted in corporate citizenship and moral communicative practice. While both terms may be problematic, they offer a way of putting together a variety of images that can give guidance to a new everyday practice. The type of balanced responsiveness might be conceived along the lines of a kind of "bounded democracy." Even though all attempts at democracy may be partial at best and the vision of the outcome incomplete, each moment calls for our best attempt to utilize what we have. A new moral order cannot be conceived of as a "Sunday" democracy. Continuing to choose anew is painful and hopeful and requires a constant rekindling of suppressed conflicts in everyday life at work.

BIBLIOGRAPHY

Abercrombie, N., S. Hill, and B. S. Turner, 1980. *The dominant ideology thesis.* London: Allen & Unwin.

Abrahamsson, B. 1977. *Bureaucracy or participation: The logic of organization.* Beverly Hills, Calif.: Sage.

Adorno, T., E. Frenkel-Brunswik, D. Levinson, and R. N. Sanford. 1950. *The authoritarian personality.* New York: Harper.

Adorno, T. 1973. *The jargon of authenticity.* Translated by K. Tarnowski and F. Will. Evanston, Ill.: Northwestern University Press.

Adorno, T., and M. Horkheimer. 1972. *Dialectic of enlightenment.* New York: Herder & Herder.

Agor, W. H., ed. 1989. *Intuition in organizations: Leading and managing productively.* Newbury Park, Calif.: Sage.

Albert, M., L. Cagan, N. Chomsky, R. Hahnel, M. King, L. Sargent, and H. Sklar, eds. 1986. *Liberating theory.* Boston: South End Press.

Algarotti, F. 1742. *Sir Isaac Newton's theory of light and colours, and his principle of attraction, made familiar to the ladies in several entertainments,* vol. II. London: G. Hawkins.

Altheide, D. 1985. Keyboarding as a social form. *Computers and the Social Sciences* 1:97–106.

Althusser, L. 1971. Ideology and ideological state apparatuses. In *Lenin and Philosophy and Other Essays,* trans. Ben Brewster. London: New Left Books.

Alvesson, M. 1987a. *Organization theory and technocratic consciousness: Rationality, ideology, and quality of work.* New York: de Gruyter.

Alvesson, M. 1987b. Organizations, culture, and ideology. *International Studies of Management and Organizations* 17:4–18.

Alvesson, M. 1989. The culture perspective on organizations: Instrumental values and basic features of culture. *Scandinavian Journal of Management* 5:123–36.

Alvesson, M. In press. Organization: From substance to image? *Organization Studies.*

Alvesson, M. In press. Organizational symbolism and ideology. *Journal of Management Studies* 28.

Alvesson, M., and H. Willmott. 1990. *Making sense of management: A critical analysis.* London: Sage.

Angus, I. 1992. The politics of common sense: Articulation theory and critical communication studies. In *Communication Yearbook 15,* ed. S.Deetz. Newbury Park, Calif.: Sage.

Ansari, S., and K. Euske. 1987. Rational, rationalizing, and reifying uses of accounting data in organizations. *Accounting, Organizations, and Society* 12:549–70.

Apel, K. O. 1972. The *a priori* of the communication community and the foundation of the humanities. *Man and World* 5:3–37.

Apel, K. O. 1979a. The *a priori* of the communication community and the foundation of ethics: The problem of a rational foundation of ethics in the scientific age. In *Towards a Transformation of Philosophy,* trans. Glyn Adey and David Frisby. London: Routledge & Kegan Paul.

Apel, K. O. 1979b. Types of rationality today: The continuum of reason between science and ethics. In *Rationality Today,* ed. T. Gelusd, 307–40. Ottawa: University of Ottawa Press.

Aram, J., and P. Salipante. 1981. An evaluation of organizational due process in the resolution of employee/employer conflict. *Academy of Management Review* 6:197–204.

Argyris, C. 1986. Skilled incompetence. *Harvard Business Review,* Sept.–Oct., 74–79.

Aristotle. 1966. *The politics,* translated by T. Sinclair. Baltimore: Penquin Books.

Armstrong, P. 1987. The rise of accounting controls in British capitalist enterprises. *Accounting, Organizations, and Society* 12:415–36.

Arterton, F. C. 1987. *Teledemocracy: Can technology protect democracy?* Newbury Park, Calif.: Sage.

Atkinson, M., E. Cuff, and J. Lee. 1978. The recommencement of a meeting as a member's accomplishment. In *Studies in the Organiza-*

tion of Conversation Interaction, ed. J. Schenkein. New York: Academic.

Austin, J. 1961. Philosophical papers. Edited by J. O. Urmson and G. J. Warnock. Oxford: Clarendon Press.

Axley, S. 1984. Managerial and organizational communication in terms of the conduit metaphor. Academy of Management Review 9:428–37.

Bachrach, P., and M. S. Baratz. 1962. Two faces of power. American Political Science Review 56:947–52.

Bagdikian, B. 1990. The media monopoly. 3d ed. Boston: Beacon Press.

Baily, M. (1986, October 24). What has happened to productivity growth? Science, 443–451.

Bakhtin, M. 1981. The dialogic imagination. Edited by M. Holquist and translated by C. Emerson and M. Holquist. Austin: University of Texas Press.

Barbalet, J. M. 1985. Power and resistance. British Journal of Sociology 36:521–48.

Barbalet, J. M. 1987. Power, structural resources, and agency. Perspectives in Social Theory 8:1–24.

Barber, B. 1984. Strong democracy. Berkeley: University of California Press.

Barley, S. 1986. Technology as an occasion for structuring: Evidence from observations of CT scanners and the social order of radiology departments. Administrative Science Quarterly 31:78–108.

Barnard, C. 1938. The function of the executive. Cambridge: Harvard University Press.

Bateson, G. 1972. Steps to an ecology of mind. New York: Ballantine Books.

Baudrillard, J. 1975. The mirror of production. Translated by M. Poster. St. Louis: Telos Press.

Baudrillard, J. 1981. For a critique of the political economy of the sign. St. Louis: Telos Press.

Baudrillard, J. 1983a. The ecstasy of communication. In The anti-aesthetic: Essays on postmodern culture. Port Townshend: Bay Press.

Baudrillard, J. 1983b. Simulations. New York: Semiotext(e).

Bavelas, J. 1983. Situations that lead to disqualification. Human Communication Research 9:130–45.

Bavelas, J, and N. Chovil. 1986. How people disqualify: Experimental studies of spontaneous written disqualification. *Communication Monographs* 53:70–74.

Becker, L., J. Fruit, and S. Caudill. 1987. *The training and hiring of journalists.* Norwood, N.J.: Ablex.

Belenky, M, B. M. Clinchy, N. R. Goldberger, and J. M. Tarule. 1986. *Women's ways of knowing: Development of self, voice, and mind.* New York: Basic Books.

Bell, D. 1960. *The end of ideology.* New York: Free Press.

Bellah, R., R. Madsen, W. Sullivan, A. Swidler, and S. Tipton. 1985. *Habits of the heart: Individualism and communication in American life.* New York: Harper & Row.

Bellman, B., and B. Jules-Rosetle. 1977. *A paradigm for looking.* Norwood, N.J.: Ablex.

Beniger, J. 1988. Information and communication. The new convergence. *Communication Research* 15:198–218.

Ben-ner, A. 1988. Comparative empirical observations on worker-owned and capitalist firms. *International Journal of Industrial Organization* 6:7–31.

Benson. J., ed. 1977. *Organizational analysis: Critique and innovation.* Beverly Hills, Calif.: Sage.

Berger, C., and S. Chaffee, eds. 1987. *Handbook of communication science.* Newbury Park, Calif.: Sage.

Berger, P. 1986. *The capitalist revolution: Fifty propositions about prosperity, equality, and liberty.* New York: Basic Books.

Berger, P., and B. Berger. 1983. *The war over the family.* Garden City, N.Y.: Anchor Doubleday.

Berger, P., B. Berger, and H. Kellner. 1973. *The homeless mind: Modernization and consciousness.* New York: Random House.

Berger, P., and H. Kellner. 1965. Arnold Gehlen and the theory of institutions. *Social Research* 32:110–15.

Berger, P., and T. Luckmann. 1967. *The social construction of reality.* Garden City, N.Y.: Doubleday.

Berle, A., and G. Means.1932. *The modern corporation and private property.* New York: Macmillan.

Bernstein, D. 1984. *Company image and reality. A critique of corporate communications.* Eastbourne, Great Britain: Holt, Rinehart & Winston.

Bernstein, P. 1980. *Workplace democratization.* New Brunswick, N.J.: Transaction Books.

Bernstein, R. 1984. *Beyond objectivism and relativism.* Philadelphia: University of Pennsylvania Press.

Bineham, J. 1988. A historical account of the hypodermic model in mass communication. *Communication Monographs* 55:230–49.

Blau, P. M., and W. R. Scott. 1963. *Formal organizations.* London: Routledge & Kegan Paul.

Blum, L., and V. Smith. 1988. Women's mobility in the corporation: A critique of the politics of optimism. *Journal of Women in Culture and Society* 13:528–45.

Bobbio, N. 1987. *Which socialism? Marxism, socialism, and democracy.* Minneapolis: University of Minnesota Press.

Bollinger, L. C. 1984. The press and the public interest: An essay on the relationship between social behavior and the language of first amendment theory. *Michigan Law Review* 82:1447–58.

Boorstin, D. 1961. *The image.* New York: Atheneum.

Bourdieu, P. 1977. *Outline of a theory of practice.* Cambridge: Cambridge University Press.

Bourdieu, P. 1984. *Distinction: A social critique of the judgement of taste.* Translated by R. Nice. Cambridge: Harvard Universtiy Press.

Bourdieu, P. 1986. The production of belief: Contribution to an economy of symbolic goods. In *Media, Culture, and Society: A Critical Reader,* ed. R. Collins, et al., 131–63. Newbury Park, Calif.: Sage.

Bourdieu, P., and J. Passeron. 1977. *Reproduction in education, society, and culture.* Beverly Hills, Calif: Sage.

Bowen, W. (1986, May 26). The puny payoff from office computers. *Fortune,* 20–24

Bowles, S., and H. Gintis. 1976. *Schooling in capitalist America.* London: Routlege & Kegan Paul.

Braman, S. 1989. Vulnerabilities: Information and the changing state." Unpublished paper available from the author.

Braverman, H. 1974. *Labor and monopoly capital: The degradation of work in the twentieth century.* New York: Monthly Review Press.

Buber, M. 1970. *I and thou.* Translated by F. Kaufmann. New York: Charles Scribner's Sons.

Burawoy, M. 1979. *Manufacturing consent: Changes in the labor process under monopoly capitalism.* Chicago: University of Chicago Press.

Burnham, J. 1972. *The managerial revolution.* John Day, 1941. Reprint. Westport, Conn.: Greenwood Press.

Burnham, W. 1981. The 1980 earthquake. In *The Hidden Election,* ed. J. Rogers and T. Ferguson. New York: Pantheon.

Burnheim, J. 1985. *Is democracy possible?* Cambridge: Polity Press.

Burrell, G. 1984. Sex and organizational analysis. *Organization Studies* 5:97–118.

Burrell, G. 1988. Modernism, post modernism, and organizational analysis 2: The contribution of Michel Foucault. *Organization Studies* 9:221–35.

Burrell, G. 1990. Response to Deetz. Unpublished paper presented at the Critical Theory and Management Science Colloquium, Shewsburg, England.

Callinicos, A. 1988. *Making history: Agency, structure, and change in social theory.* Ithaca, N.Y.: Cornell Univeristy Press.

Callon, M. 1980. Struggles and negotiations to define what is problematic and what is not: The socio-logic of translation. In *Sociology of the Sciences Yearbook 4: The Social Processes of Scientific Investigation,* ed. K. D. Knorr-Cetina, R. Krohn, and R. D. Whitley, 197–219. Dordrecht: Reidel.

Callon, M. 1986. Some elements of a sociology of translation: Domestication of the scallops and the fishermen of St. Brieuc bay. In *Power, Action, and Belief: A New Sociology of Knowlege? Sociological Review Monograph No. 32,* ed. J. Law. London: Routledge & Kegan Paul.

Cameron, K., and D. Whetten. eds. 1983. *Organizational effectiveness: A comparison of multiple models.* New York: Academic.

Carbaugh, D. 1988. *Talking American: Cultural discourses on Donahue.* Norwood, N.J.: Ablex.

Carey, A. 1987. The ideological management industry. In *Communications and the Media in Australia,* ed. T. Wheelwright and K. Buckley. Sydney: Allen & Unwin.

Carter, P., and N. Jackson. 1987. Management, myth, and metatheory—from scarcity to post scarcity. *International Studies of Management and Organizations* 17:64–89.

Caulkin, S. 1988. Faceless corridors of power. *Management Today (UK).* 62–68.

Caygill, H. 1988. Postmodernism and judgement. *Economy and Society* 17:1–20.

Certeau, M. de 1984. *The practice of everyday life.* Berkeley: University of California Press.

Certeau, M. de 1986. *Heterologies: Discourses on the other.* Minneapolis: University of Minnesota Press.

Chandler, A. 1977. *The visible hand: The managerial revolution in American business.* Cambridge: Harvard University Press.

Chandler, A., and H. Daems, eds. 1980. *Managerial hierarchies: Comparative perspectives on the rise of the modern industrial enterprise.* Cambridge: Harvard University Press.

Chesebro, J. 1984. The media reality: Epistemological functions of media in cultural systems. *Critical Studies in Mass Communication* 1:111–30.

Chomsky, N. 1959. A review of B. F. Skinner's *Verbal Behavior. Language* 35:28–57.

Clark, G. 1989. *Dialogue, dialectic, and conversation: A social perspective on the function of writing.* Carbondale: Southern Illinois University Press Press.

Clarke, J. 1988. Enter the cybernauts: Problems in post-modernism. *Communication* 10:383–401.

Clegg, S. R. 1983. Organizational democracy, power, and participation. In *The International Yearbook of Organizational Democracy,* ed. C. Crouch and F. Hellar, 1–34. London: John Wiley.

Clegg, S. R. 1987. The power of language, the language of power. *Organization Studies* 8:60–70.

Clegg, S. 1989. *Frameworks of power.* Newbury Park, Calif.: Sage.

Clift, E. 1990. They're crying in the capital: Washington discovers its gobal irrelevance. *Newsweek,* 19 Mar., 23.

Collins, R. 1979. *The credential society.* New York: Academic Press.

Cooper, R., and G. Burrell. 1988. Modernism, postmodernism, and organizational analysis. *Organization Studies* 9:91–112.

Coward, R., and J. Ellis. 1977. *Language and materialism: Developments in semiology and the theory of the subject.* London: Routledge & Kegan Paul.

Crystal, G. 1990. Cracking the Tax Whip on C.E.O.'s. *The New York Times Magazine, The Business World,* Part II., September 23; 48–57.

Culbert, S., and J. McDonough. 1980. *The invisible war: Pursuing self-interest at work.* Toronto: John Wiley.

Culler, J. 1983. *On deconstruction.* London: Routledge & Kegan Paul.

Cushman, D. 1990. *High-speed management.* Albany: State University of New York Press.

Cyert, R., and J. March. 1963. *A behavioral theory of the firm.* Englewood Cliffs, N.J.: Prentice Hall.

Daft, R., and J. Wiginton. 1979. Language and organization. *The Academy of Management Review* 4:179–92.

Dahl, R. A. 1957. The concept of power. *Behavioral Science* 2:201–15.

Dahrendorf, R. 1959. *Class and class conflict in industrial society.* Stanford, Calif.: Stanford University Press.

Dallmayr, F. 1984a. *Polis and praxis: Exercises in contemporary political theory.* Cambridge: MIT Press.

Dallmayr, F. 1984b. *Language and politics: Why does language matter to political philosophy?* Notre Dame, Ind.: Universtiy of Notre Dame Press.

Debord, G. 1981. Report on the construction of situations and on the international situationalist tendency's conditions of organization and action. In *Situationist International Anthology,* ed. and trans. K. Knabb. Berkeley, Calif.: Bureau of Public Secrets.

Debord, G. 1983. *The society of the spectacle.* Detroit: Red & Black.

Deetz, S. 1973. An understanding of science and a hermeneutic science of understanding. *Journal of Communication* 23:139–59.

Deetz, S. 1978. Conceptualizing human understanding: Gadamer's hermeneutics and American communication research. *Communication Quarterly* 26:12–23.

Deetz, S. 1979. Social well-being and the development of an appropriate organizational response to de-institutionalization and legitimation crisis, *Journal of Applied Communication Research* 7:45–54.

Deetz, S. 1982. Critical-interpretive research in organizational communication. *Western Journal of Speech Communication* 46:131–49.

Deetz, S. 1983. Keeping the conversation going: The principle of dialectic ethics. *Communication* 7:263–88.

Deetz, S. 1985a. Critical-cultural research: New sensibilities and old realities. *Journal of Management* 11:121–36.

Deetz, S. 1985b. Ethical considerations in cultural research in organizations. In *Organizational Culture,* ed. P. Frost, L. Moore, M. Louis, C. Lundberg, and J. Martin (Eds.), 251–69. Newbury Park, Calif.: Sage.

Deetz, S. 1986. Metaphors and the discursive production and repro-
duction of organization. In *Organizations and Communication:
Emerging Perspectives 1*, ed. L. Thayer, 168–82. Norwood, N.J.:
Ablex.

Deetz, S. 1990a. Reclaiming the subject matter as a guide to mutual
understanding: Effectiveness and ethics in interpersonal interaction. *Communication Quarterly* 38:226–43.

Deetz, S. 1990b. Representation of interests and the new communication technologies. In *Communication and the Culture of Technology*,
ed. M. Medhurst, T. Peterson, and A. Gonzalez, 43–62. Pullman:
Washington State University Press.

Deetz, S., and E. McGlone. 1983. An interpretive perspective on testing
and measurement. In *Qualitative Methodology, Theory and Application*, ed. J. Murphy and J. Pilotta, 81–100. Dubuque, Iowa:
Kendall/Hunt.

Deetz, S., and D. Mumby. 1985. Metaphors, information, and power.
Information and Behavior 1:369–86.

Deetz S., and D. Mumby. 1990. Power, discourse, and the workplace:
Reclaiming the critical tradition in communication studies in
organizations. In *Communication Yearbook 13*, ed. J. Anderson,
18–47. Newbury Park, Calif.: Sage.

Deetz, S., and S. Stevenson. 1986. *Managing interpersonal communication*. New York: Harper & Row.

Dégot, V. 1987. Corporate culture and the concept of rationality in
corporate models. *International Studies of Management and Organizations* 17:19–39.

Denhardt, R. B. 1981. *In the shadow of organization*. Lawrence, Kans.:
Regents Press.

Dennis, E., D. Gilmore, and T. Glasser. 1989. *Media freedom and
accountability*. Westport, Conn.: Greenwood Press.

Derrida, J. 1976. *Of grammatology*. Baltimore: John Hopkins University
Press.

Dewey, J. 1916. *Democracy and education*. New York: Macmillian.

Dewey, J. 1927. *The public and its problems*. New York: Henry Holt.

Dilenschneider, R. 1990. A new understated kind of power. *New York
Times*, 3 June, sect. F, 13.

Donzelot, J. 1979. *The policing of families*. New York: Pantheon.

Donzelot, J. 1988. The promotion of the social. *Economy and Society* 17:395–427.

Dreyfus, H., and P. Rabinow. 1986. What is maturity? Habermas and Foucault on "What is enlightenment." In *Foucault: A Reader,* ed. D. Hoy, 109–22. Oxford: Basil Blackwell.

Driskell, J., and O. Beckett. 1989. Psychology and the military. *American Psychologist* 44:43–54.

Edwards, R. 1979. *Contested terrain: The transformation of the workplace in the twentieth century.* New York: Basic Books.

Eisenberg, E. 1984. Ambiguity as strategy in organizational communication. *Communication Monographs* 51:227–42.

Elden, M. 1981. Political efficacy at work: The connection between more autonomous forms of workplace organization and a more participatory politics. *American Political Science Review* 75:43–58.

Elias, N. 1973. *La civilisation des moeurs.* Paris: Calmann-Lévy. Cited in Dégot, 1987.

Eliasoph, N. 1988. Routines and the making of oppositional news. *Critical Studies in Mass Communication* 5:313–34.

Elliott, P. 1986. Intellectuals, the "information society," and the disapperance of the public sphere. In *Media, Culture, and Society: A Critical Reader,* ed. R. Collins, et al., 105–15. Newbury Park, Calif.: Sage.

Entman, R. 1989. *Democracy without citizens: Media and the decay of American politics.* New York: Oxford University Press.

Estrin, S., P. Geroski., and G. Stewart. 1988. Employee share ownership, profit-sharing, and participation: An introduction. *International Journal of Industrial Organization* 6:1–6.

Eurich, N., and E. Boyer. 1985. *Corporate classrooms: The learning business.* Princeton, N.J.: The Carnegie Foundation for the Advancement of Teaching.

Evangelauf, J. 1985. Academe and business tighten ties: Corporate giving nears 1.5 billion. *Chronicle of Higher Education* 21 (Nov.):1.

Evangelauf, J. 1987. Line between public and private institutions is blurring in nations around the world. *Chronicle of Higher Education* 23 (July):25.

Evans, P. 1989. Declining hegemony and assertive industrialization: U.S.—Brazil conflicts in the computer industry. *International Organization* 43:207–38.

Ewen, S. 1976. *Captains of consciousness: Advertising and the roots of the consumer culture*. New York: McGraw-Hill.

Ewing, D. 1977. *Freedom inside the organization*. New York: Dutton.

Ewing, D. 1983. *Do it my way or you're fired: Employee rights and the changing role of management prerogatives*. New York: Wiley.

Ezorsky, G., ed. 1987. *Moral rights in the workplace*. Albany: State University of New York Press.

Faucheux, C., and S. Makridakis. 1979. Automation or autonomy in organizational design. *International Journal of General Systems* 5:213–20.

Ferguson, K. 1984. *The feminist case against bureaucracy*. Philadelphia: Temple University Press.

Ferment in the field. 1983. *Journal of Communication* 33:4–362.

Ferrarotti, F. 1988. *The end of conversation: The impact of mass media on modern society*. Westport, Conn.: Greenwood Press.

Fischer, F. 1990. *Technocracy and the politics of expertise*. Newbury Park, Calif.: Sage.

Fischer, F., and C. Sirianni, eds. 1984. *Critical studies in organization and bureaucracy*. Philadelphia: Temple University Press.

Fisher, C. 1985. Studying technology and social life. In *High Technology, Space, and Society*, ed. M. Castells, 284–300). Beverly Hills, Calif: Sage.

Flax, J. 1990. *Thinking fragments: Psychoanalysis, feminism, and postmodernism in the contemporary west*. Berkeley: University of California Press.

Flood, R. L. 1990. Liberating systems theory: Toward critical systems thinking. *Human Relations* 43:1, 49–75.

Forester, J. 1982a. Know your organizations: Planning and the reproduction of social and political relations. *Plan Canada* 23:3–13.

Forester, J. 1982b. Planning in the face of power. *Journal of the American Planning Association* 48:67–80.

Forester, J. 1983. Critical theory and organizational analysis. In *Beyond method: Strategies for social research*, ed. G. Morgan, 234–46. Beverly Hills, Calif.: Sage.

Forester, J. 1989. *Planning in the face of power*. Berkeley: University of California Press.

Foster, H., ed. 1983. *Postmodern culture*. London: Pluto Press.

Foucault, M. 1970. *The order of things*. New York: Random House.

Foucault, M. 1972. *The archaeology of knowledge*. Translated by A. Sheridan Smith. New York: Pantheon.

Foucault, M. 1977. *Discipline and punish: The birth of the prison*. Translated by A. Sheridan Smith. New York: Random House.

Foucault, M. 1980a. *Power/knowledge: Selected interviews and other writings, 1972–1977*. Edited by C. Gordon. New York: Pantheon.

Foucault, M. 1980b. *The history of sexuality*. Translated by R. Hurley. New York: Vintage.

Foucault, M. 1982. The subject and power. In *Michel Foucault: Beyond Structuralism and Hermenuetics*, ed. H. Dreyfus and P. Rabinow, 208–26. Sussex, England: Harvester.

Foucault, M. 1986. Disciplinary power and subjection. In *Power*, ed. S. Lukes 229–41. Oxford: Blackwell.

Fowler, R., B. Hodge, G. Kress, and T. Trew. 1979. *Language and control*. London: Routledge & Kegan Paul.

Freire, P. 1970. *Pedagogy of the oppressed*. New York: Herder & Herder.

Friedman, M. 1962. *Capitalism and freedom*. Chicago: University of Chicago Press.

Friedman, M. 1983. The social responsibility of business is to increase its profits. In *Business Ethics*, ed. M. Snoeyenbos, R. Almeder, and J. Humber, 73–79. Buffalo, N.Y.: Prometheus Books.

Friend, I., and L. Lang. 1988. An empirical test of the impact of managerial self-interest on corporate capital structure. *The Journal of Finance* 43:271–81.

Freud, S. 1975. *The psychopathology of everyday life*. Harmondsworth, England: Pelican.

Frost, P. 1980. Toward a radical framework for practicing organization science. *The Academy of Management Review* 5:501–8.

Frost, P. 1987. Power, politics, and influence. In *Handbook of Organizational Communication*, ed. F. Jablin, L. Putnam, K. Roberts, and L. Porter, 228–63. Newbury Park, Calif.: Sage.

Frow, J. 1985. Discourse and power. *Economy and Society* 14:193–214.

Gadamer, H. G. 1975. *Truth and method*. Edited and translated by G. Barden and J. Cumming. New York: Seabury Press.

Galbraith, K. 1967. *The new industrial state.* Boston: Houghton Mifflin.

Gallie, D. 1978. *In search of the new working class: Automation and social integration within the capitalist enterprise.* Cambridge: Cambridge University Press.

Gallie, W. 1955–56. Essentially contested terms. *Proceedings of the Aristotelian Society* 56:167–98.

Gandy, O. 1982. *Beyond agenda setting.* Norwood, N.J.: Ablex.

Ganley, O., and G. Ganley. 1989. *To inform or to control: The new communications networks.* 2d. ed. Norwood, N.J.: Ablex.

Gans, H. 1979. *Deciding what's news: A study of CBS evening news, NBC nightly news.* New York: Pantheon.

Gardner, H. 1988. *The mind's new science.* New York: Basic Books.

Garnham, N., and R. Williams. 1986. Pierre Bourdieu and sociology of culture: An introduction. In *Media, Culture, and Society: A Critical Reader,* ed. R. Collins, et al., 116–30. Newbury Park, Calif.: Sage.

Gatlin, H. 1977. Private lives and public order: A critical view of the history of intimate relations in the United States. In *Close Relationships,* ed. G. Levinger and H. Raush, 33–72. Amherst: University of Massachusetts Press.

Gaunt, P. 1990. *Choosing the news: The profit factor in news selection.* New York: Greenwood Press.

Geber, B. 1987. The forgotten factor in merger mania. *Training* 24:28–37.

Gebser, J. 1985. *The ever-present origin.* Translated by N. Barstad and A. Mickunas. Athens: Ohio University Press.

Geiger, R. 1980. *The college curriculum and the marketplace: Academic disciplines and the trend toward vocationalism in the 1970s.* New Haven, Conn.: Institute for Social and Policy Studies, Yale University.

Gergen, K. 1978. Toward generative theory. *Journal of Personality and Social Psychology* 31:1344–60.

Gergen, K., and K. Davis, eds. 1985. *The social construction of the person.* New York: Springer-Verlag.

Giddens, A. 1979. *Central problems in social theory.* Berkeley: University of California Press.

Giddens, A. 1984. *The constitution of society.* Berkeley, Calif.: Campus.

Giddens, A. 1989. The orthodox consensus and the emerging synthesis. In *Rethinking communication 1: Paradigm dialogues,* ed. B. Dervin, E. Wartella, and L. Grossberg, 53–65. Newbury Park, Calif.: Sage.

Gilligan, C. 1982. *In a different voice: Psychological theory and women's development.* Cambridge: Harvard University Press.

Gilligan, C., J. V. Ward, and J. M. Taylor. 1988. *Mapping the moral domain: A contribution of women's thinking to psychological theory and education.* Cambridge: Center for the Study of Gender, Education, and Human Development (distributed by Harvard University Press).

Gitlin, T. 1980. *The whole world is watching.* Berkeley: University of California Press.

Goffman, E. 1959. *The presentation of self in everyday life.* Garden City, N.J.: Doubleday.

Goldman, A. 1980. *The moral foundations of professional ethics.* Totowa, N.J.: Rowman & Littlefield.

Golembiewski, R. 1989. Toward a positive and practical public management: Organizational research supporting a fourth critical citizenship. *Administration and Society* 21:200–27.

Golembiewski, R. 1990. A bit further toward "A positive and practical public management." *Administration and Society* 21:493–500.

Gonzalez, H. 1988. The evolution of communication as a field. *Communication Research* 15:302–8.

Gooding, D., T. Pinch, and S. Schaffer. 1989. *The uses of experiment.* New York: Cambridge University Press.

Gormley, W., Jr. 1986. The representation revolution: Reforming state regulation through public representation. *Administration and Society* 18:179–96.

Gouldner, A. 1954. *Patterns of industrial bureaucracy.* New York: Free Press.

Gouldner, A. 1976. *The dialectic of ideology and technology.* New York: Seabury Press.

Gramsci, A. 1971. *Selections from the prison notebooks.* Translated by Q. Hoare and G. Nowell Smith. New York: International.

Greenberg, E. S. 1986. *Workplace democracy: The political effects of participation.* Ithaca, N.Y.: Cornell University Press.

Grossberg, L. 1984. Strategies of Marxist cultural interpretation. *Critical Studies in Mass Communication* 1:391–421.

Grossberg, L. 1987. Critical theory and the politics of empirical research. In *Mass Communication Review Yearbook, Volume 6,* ed. M. Gurevitch and M. Levy, 86–106. Newbury Park, Calif.: Sage.

Guth, W., and I. MacMillan. 1986. Strategy implementation versus middle-management self-interest. *Strategic Management Journal* 7:313–27.

Habermas, J. 1970. On systematically distorted communication. *Inquiry* 13:205–18.

Habermas, J. 1971. *Knowledge and human interests.* Translated by J. Shapiro. Boston: Beacon Press.

Habermas, J. 1973. *Theory and practice.* Translated by T. McCarthy. Boston: Beacon Press.

Habermas, J. 1974. The public sphere. *New German Critique* 3:49–55.

Habermas, J. 1975. *Legitimation crisis.* Translated by T. McCarthy. Boston: Beacon Press.

Habermas, J. 1979. *Communication and the evolution of society.* Translated by T. McCarthy. Boston: Beacon Press.

Habermas, J. 1984. *The theory of communicative action, volume 1: Reason and the rationalization of society.* Translated by T. McCarthy. Boston: Beacon Press.

Habermas, J. 1986. *Philosophical discourse of modernity.* Translated by F. Lawrence. Cambridge: MIT Press.

Habermas, J. 1986. Taking aim at the heart of the present. In *Foucault: A critical reader,* ed. D. C. Hoy, 123–48. Oxford: Basil Blackwell.

Habermas, J. 1987. *The theory of communicative action, volume 2: Lifeworld and system.* Translated by T. McCarthy,. Boston: Beacon Press.

Haggard, S. 1988. The institutional foundations of hegemony: Explaining the Reciprocal Trade Agreements Act of 1934. *International Organization* 42:1.

Hall, D. 1990. Promoting work/family balance: An organization-change approach. *Organizational Dynamics* 18:5–17.

Hall, S. 1977. Culture, the media, and the "ideological effect." In *Mass Communication and society,* ed. Curran, et al. London: Edward Arnold.

Hall, S. 1982. The rediscovery of ideology: Return of the repressed in media studies. In *Culture, Society, and the Media,* ed M. Gurevitch, T. Bennett, J. Curran, and J. Woollacott. London: Metheun.

Hall, S. 1985. Signification, representation, ideology: Althusser and the post-structuralist debates. *Critical Studies in Mass Communication* 2:91–114.

Hall, S. 1988. The toad in the garden: Thatcherism among the theorists. In *Marxism and the Interpretation of Culture,* ed. C. Nelson and L. Grossberg, 35–57. Urbana: University of Illinois Press.

Hall, S. 1989. Ideology and communication theory. In *Rethinking communication 1: Paradigm dialogues,* ed. B. Dervin, L. Grossberg, B. O'Keefe, and E. Wartella. Newbury Park, Calif.: Sage.

Hamilton, G., and J. Sutton. 1989. The problem of control in the weak state: Domination in the United States, 1880–1920. *Theory and Society* 18:11–38.

Hamnett, M., D. Porter, A. Singh, and K. Kumar. 1984. *Ethics, politics, and international social science research.* Honolou, Hawaii: East-West Center and University of Hawaii Press.

Hannan, M. T., and F. Freeman. 1977. Obstacles to comparative studies. In *New perspectives in organizational effectiveness,* ed. P. S. Goodman, J. M. Penning, and Associates, 106–31. San Francisco: Jossey-Bass.

Hanson, N. 1965. *Patterns of discovery.* Cambridge: Cambridge University Press.

Hardt, H. 1989. The return of the "critical" and the challenge of radical dissent: Critical theory, cultural studies, and American mass communication research. *Communication Yearbook* 12:558–600.

Harré, R., ed. 1986. *The social construction of emotions.* Oxford: Basil Blackwell.

Harré, R. 1989. Language games and the texts of identity. In *Texts of Identity,* ed. J. Shotter and K. Gergen, 20–35. Newbury Park, Calif.: Sage.

Harris, L. 1987. *Inside America.* New York: Vintage/Random House.

Harris, R. 1987. *Power and powerlessness in industry: An analysis of the social relations of production.* London: Tavistock.

Hatano, D. 1984. Should corporations exercise their freedom of speech rights? *American Business Law Journal* 22:165–87.

Heidegger, M. 1961. *An introduction to metaphysics.* Translated by R. Manheim. Garden City, N.Y.: Doubleday.

Heidegger, M. 1962. *Being and time.* Translated by J. MacQuarrie and E. Robinson. New York: Harper & Row.

Hein, C. 1989. *New York Times Magazine,* 17 Dec., 77.

Held, D. 1987. *Models of democracy.* Stanford, Calif.: Stanford University Press.

Henriques, J., W. Hollway, C. Urwin, C. Venn, and V. Walkerdine, eds. 1984. *Changing the subject.* New York: Methuen.

Heydebrand, W. V. 1977. Organizational contradictions in public bureaucracies. In *Organizational analysis: Critique and innovations,* ed. T. Benson, 85–109. Beverly Hills, Calif.: Sage.

Heydebrand, W. V. 1983. Organization and praxis. In *Beyond method,* ed. G. Morgan, 306–20. Beverly Hills, Calif.: Sage.

Hines, R. 1988. Financial accounting: In communicating reality we construct reality. *Accounting, Organizations, and Society* 13:251–61.

Hirschman, A. 1977. *The passions and the interests.* Princeton, N.J.: Princeton University Press.

Hirschman, A., and C. Lindblom. 1962. Economic development, research and development, policy making: Some converging views. *Behavioral Science* 7:211–22.

Hirschman, P. 1970. *Loyalty, exit, and voice.* Cambridge: Harvard University Press.

Hirst, P. 1979. *On law and ideology.* London: Macmillan.

Hochschild, A. 1979. Emotion work, feeling rules, and social structure. *American Journal of Sociology* 85:551–75.

Hodge, R., and G. Kress. 1983. Functional semiotics. *Australian Journal of Cultural Studies* 1:1–17.

Hodge, R., G. Kress, and G. Jones. 1979. The ideology of middle management. In *Language and Control,* ed. R. Fowler, B. Hodge, G. Kress, and T. Trew, 81–93). London: Routledge & Kegan Paul.

Hohendahl, P. 1986. Philosophical discourse of modernity. *Telos: Quarterly Journal of Critical Thought* 69:49–65.

Hollway, W. 1984. Fitting work: Psychological assessment in organizations. In *Changing the subject,* ed. J. Henriques, W. Hollway, C. Urwin, C. Venn, and V. Walkerdine, 26–59). New York: Methuen.

Hopwood, A. 1987. The archaeology of accounting systems. *Accounting, Organizations, and Society* 12:207–34.

Horowitz, I. 1983. New technology, scientific information, and democratic choices. *Information Age* 5:67–73.

Hoy, D. C. 1986. Power, repression, progress: Foucault, Lukes, and the Frankfurt school. In *Foucault: A critical reader,* ed. D. C. Hoy, 123–48. Oxford: Basil Blackwell.

Hume, E. 1990. Why the press blew the S & L scandal. *New York Times,* 24 May.

Huspek, M. 1987. A language of powerlessness: Class, context, and competence among lumber industrial workers. Ph.D. diss., University of Washington.

Husserl, E. 1962. *Ideas: General introduction to pure phenomenology.* Translated by W. R. B. Gibson. London: Collier-MacMillan.

Ingersoll, V., and G. Adams. 1986. Beyond organizational boundaries. Exploring the managerial myth. *Administration and Society* 18:360–81.

Jacobs, N., and S. Hardesty. 1986. *Success and betrayal: The crisis of women in corporate America.* Danbury, Conn.: Franklin Watts.

Jameson, F. 1981. *The political unconscious: Narrative as a social symbolic act.* Ithaca, N.Y.: Cornell University Press.

Jameson, F. 1983. Postmodernism and consumer society. In *Postmodernism culture,* ed. H. Foster. London: Pluto Press.

Jamieson, K. 1984. *Packaging the presidency: A History and criticism of presidential campaign advertising.* New York: Oxford.

Jansen, S. C. 1989. Gender and the information society: A socially structured silence. *Journal of Communication* 39:196–215.

Jehenson, R. 1984. Effectiveness, expertise, and excellence as ideological fictions: A contribution to a critical phenomenology of the formal organization. *Human Studies* 7:3–21.

Jocoby, R. 1975) *Social amnesia.* Boston: Beacon Press.

Kant, I. 1965. What is enlightenment? In *Conjectures and refutations,* ed. K. Popper. (Original German publication, 1785). New York: Harper.

Kanter, R. 1977. *Men and women of the corporation.* New York: Basic Books.

Karasek, R. 1981. Job socialization and stress. In *Working life,* ed. B. Gardell and G. Johansson. New York: Wiley.

Katz, D., and R. L. Kahn. 1978. *The social psychology of organizations.* New York: Wiley.

Keane, J. 1984. *Public life and late capitalism. Toward a socialist theory of democracy.* Cambridge: Cambridge University Press.

Keeley, M. 1984. Impartiality and participant interests theories of organizational effectiveness. *Administrative Science Quarterly* 29:1–25.

Kelly, G. 1955. *Psychology of personal constructs.* New York: Norton.

Knapp, M., and G. Miller, eds. 1985. *Handbook of interpersonal communication.* Newbury Park, Calif.: Sage.

Knights, D., and D. Collinson. 1985. Redesigning work on the shopfloor: A questions of control or consent? In *Job redesign: Critical perspectives on the labour process,* ed. D. Knights, H. Willmott, and D. Collinson, 197–226. Aldershot, England: Gower.

Knights, D., and D. Collinson. 1987. Disciplining the shopfloor: A comparison of the disciplinary effects of managerial psychology and financial accounting. *Accounting, Organizations, and Society* 12:457–77.

Knights, D., and H. Willmott. 1985. Power and identity in theory and practice. *The Sociological Review* 33:22–46.

Knights, D., and H. Willmott. 1987. Organizational culture as management strategy: A critique and illustration from the financial service industry. *International Studies of Management and Organization* 17:40–63.

Kohlberg, L. 1989. *Child psychology and childhood education: A cognitive developmental view.* New York: Longman.

Kramarae, C., ed. 1989. *Technology and women's voices: Keeping in touch.* London: Routledge & Kegan Paul.

Kramer, R. 1989. In the shadow of death: Robert Denhardt's theology of organizational life. *Administration and Society* 21:357–79.

Kratochwil, F., and J. G. Ruggie. 1986. International organization: A state of the art on an art of the state. *International Organization* 40:753–75.

Kress, G., and B. Hodge. 1979. *Language and ideology.* London: Routledge & Kegan Paul.

Kristeva, J. 1984. *Revolution in poetic language.* New York: Columbia University Press.

Kuhn, T. S. 1962. *The structure of scientific revolutions.* Chicago: University of Chicago Press.

Kurtz, L. R. 1988. Military organizations. In *Handbook of organizations,* ed. James G. March, 838–78. Chicago: Rand McNally.

Lacan, J. 1968. *The language of the self.* Baltimore: Johns Hopkins University Press.

Laclau, E., and C. Mouffe. 1985. *Hegemony and socialist strategy.* Translated by W. Moore and P. Cammack. London: Verso.

Laing, R. D. 1967. *The politics of experience.* New York: Ballantine Books.

Laing, R. D. 1971. *The politics of the family.* New York: Vintage.

Lambert, S. J. 1990. Processes linking work and family: A critical review and research agenda. *Human Relations* 43:5, 239–57.

Landy, F., and J. Farr. 1980. Performance rating. *Psychological Bulletin* 87:72–107.

Lannamann, J. In press. Interpersonal communication reasearch as ideological practice. *Communication Theory.*

Lasch, C. 1978. *The culture of narcissism.* New York: Warner Books.

Lasch, C. 1984. *The minimal self: Psychic survival in troubled times.* London: Picador.

Lash, S., and J. Urry. 1987. *Disorganized capitalism.* Cambridge: Polity Press.

Lasswell, H. D., and A. Kaplan. 1950. *Power and society.* New Haven, Conn.: Yale University Press.

Laughlin, R. C. 1987. Accounting systems in organizational contexts: A case for critical theory. *Accounting, Organizations, and Society* 12:479–502.

Lazarsfeld, P. F. 1941. Remarks on administrative and critical communications research. *Studies in Philosophy and Social Science* 9:2–16.

Lazarsfeld, P. F. 1969. An episode in the history of social research: A memoir. In *The intellectual migration: Europe and America, 1930–1960,* ed. D. Fleming and B. Bailyn. Cambridge: Harvard University.

Lefebvre, H. 1968. *Everyday life in the modern world.* New York: Harper & Row.

Levin, D. M. 1988. *The opening of vision: Nihilism and the postmodern situation.* New York: Routledge & Kegan Paul.

Levinas, E. 1969. *Totality and infinity.* Translated by A. Lingis. Pittsburgh: Duquesne University Press.

Levinson, H. 1970. Management by whose objectives? *Harvard Business Review,* Jul–Aug, 125–34.

Levitt, T. 1981. Marketing intangible products and product intangibles. *Harvard Business Review,* May–June, 94–102.

Lindblom, C. 1959. The science of "muddling through." *Public Administration Review* 19:79–88.

Lindblom, C. 1977. *Politics and markets.* New York: Basic Books.

Linder, S. B. 1970. *The harried leisure class.* New York: Columbia University Press.

Lippmann, W. 1914. *Drift and mastery: An attempt to diagnose the current unrest.* New York: Mitchell Kennerly.

Lukács, G. 1971. *History and class consciousnes.* Translated by R. Livingstone. Cambridge: MIT Press.

Luke, T. 1989. *Screens of power: Ideology, domination, and resistance in information society.* Urbana: University of Illinois Press.

Luke, T., and S. White. 1985. Critical theory, the information revolution, and an ecological path to modernity. In *Critical theory and public life,* ed. J. Forester, 22–53. Cambridge: MIT Press.

Lukes, S. 1974. *Power: A radical view.* London: Macmillan.

Lyotard, J. 1984. *The postmodern condition.* Minneapolis: University of Minnesota Press.

Lyytinen, K., and R. Hirschheim. 1988. Information systems as rational discourse: An application of Habermas's theory of communicative action. *Scandinavian Journal of Management* 4:19–30.

Machlowitz, M. 1978. *Workaholics.* Reading, Mass.: Addison-Wesley.

MacIntyre, A. 1984. *After virtue: A study in moral theory.* 2d ed. Notre Dame, Ind.: University of Notre Dame Press.

Maier, C. S., ed. 1987. *Changing boundaries of the political: Essays on the evolving balance between the state and society, public and private in Europe.* Cambridge: Cambridge University Press.

Mansbridge, J. 1980. *Beyond adversary democracy.* New York: Basic Books.

March, J. 1987. Ambiguity and accounting: The elusive link between information and decision making. *Accounting, Organizations and Society* 12:153–68.

March, J., and H. Simon. 1958. *Organizations.* New York: Wiley.

Marcuse, H. 1964. *One-dimensional man.* Boston: Beacon Press.

Markoff, J. 1989. Here comes the fiber-optic home. *New York Times,* 5 Nov., sect. 3.

Martin, J. 1990. Deconstructing organizational taboos: The suppression of gender conflict in organizations. *Organization Science* 1:339–59.

Martin, J., M. Feldman, M. Hatch, and S. Sitkin. 1983. The uniqueness paradox in organizational stories. *Administrative Science Quarterly* 28:438–53.

Maruyama, M. 1963. The second cybernetics: Deviation-amplifying mutual causal processes. *American Scientist* 51:164–79.

Marx, K. 1906. *Capital: A critique of political economy.* Translated by S. Moore and E. Aveling. New York: Modern Library.

Marx, K. 1964. *Economic and political manuscripts of 1844.* Translated by M. Miligan. New York: International.

Mason, R. 1982. *Participatory and workplace democracy.* Carbondale: Southern Illinois University Press.

Maturana, H. 1988. Reality: The search for objectivity or the quest for a compelling argument. *The Irish Journal of Psychology* 9:25–82.

Maturana, H., and F. Varela. 1980. *Autopoiesis and cognition: The realization of the living.* London: Reidl.

Mayntz, R. 1976. Conceptual models of organizational decision-making and their application to the policy process. In *European contributions to organizational theory,* ed. G. Hofstede and M. Kassem, 114–25. Amsterdam: Van Gorcum.

McHoul, A. W. 1986. Writing, sexism, and schooling: A discourse-analytic investigation of some recent documents on sexism and education in Queensland. In *Discourse and institutional authority: Medicine, education, and law,* ed. S. Fisher and A. D. Todd, 187–202. Norwood, N.J.: Ablex.

McKee, J. A., Jr., T. B. Bell, and J. R. Boatsman. 1984. Management preferences over accounting standards: A replication and additional tests. *The Accounting Review* 59:647–59.

McKerrow, R. 1989. Critical rhetoric: Theory and praxis. *Communication Monographs* 56:91–111.

McSwain, C. 1985. Adminstrators and citizenship: The liberalist legacy of the constitution. *Administration and Society* 17:131–48.

Mead, G. H. 1934. *Mind, self, and society.* Chicago: University of Chicago Press.

Meany, G. 1976. Workers on boards of directors. *Nation's Business,* Feb., 52.

Mehan, H. 1986. The role of language and the language of role in institutional decision making. In *Discourse and institutional authority: Medicine, education, and law*, ed. S. Fisher and A. D. Todd. Norwood, N.J.: Ablex.

Mehan, H., and H. Wood. 1975. *The reality of ethnomethodology.* New York: Wiley.

Merkle, J. 1980. *Management and ideology: The legacy of the international scientific management movement.* Berkeley: University of California Press.

Merleau-Ponty, M. 1962. *Phenomenology of perception.* Translated by C. Smith. London: Routledge & Kegan Paul.

Meyer, J., and B. Rowan. 1977. Institutionalized organizations: Formal structures as a myth and ceremony. *American Journal of Sociology* 83:340–63.

Meyrowitz, J. 1985. *No sense of place: The impact of electronic media on social behavior.* New York: Oxford University Press.

Mickunas, A., and J. Oastler. 1972. Toward a rapprochment. *Philosophy and Phenomenological Research* 33:241–48.

Mill, J. S. 1862. *Considerations on representative government.* New York: Harper.

Miller, A. 1981. On politics, democracy, and the first amendment: A commentary on *First National Bank v. Bellotti. Washington and Lee Law Review* 38:25.

Miller, D. C., and W. H. Form. 1964. *Industrial sociology.* New York: Harper.

Miller, K. I., and P. R. Monge. 1985. Participation, satisfaction, and productivity: A meta-analytic review. *Academy of Management Journal* 29:727–53.

Mingers, J. 1980. Towards an appropriate social theory for applied systems thinking: Critical theory and soft systems methodology. *Journal of Applied System Analysis* 7:41–49.

Mingers, J. 1989. An introduction to autopoiesis—implications and applications. *Systems Practice* 2:159–80.

Mintzberg, H. 1973. *The nature of managerial work.* New York: Harper & Row.

Mintzberg, H. 1983. *Power in and around the organizations.* Englewood Cliffs, N.J.: Prentice Hall.

Mirow, K. R., and H. Maurer. 1982. *Webs of power: International cartels and the world economy*. Boston: Houghton Mifflin.

Misgeld, D. 1985. Education and cultural invasion: Critical social theory, education as instruction, and the "pedagogy of the oppressed." In *Critical theory and public life*, ed. J. Forester, 77–118. Cambridge: MIT Press.

Mitroff, L. 1983. *Stakeholders of the organizational mind*. San Francisco: Jossey-Bass.

Moi, T., ed. 1986. *The Kristeva reader*. Oxford: Blackwell.

Montagna, P. 1986. Accounting rationality and financial legitimation. *Theory and Society* 15:103–38.

Morgan, G., ed. 1983. *Beyond method: Strategies for social research*. Beverly Hills, Calif.: Sage.

Morgan, G. 1986. *Images of organization*. Newbury Park, Calif.: Sage.

Moulin, H., and J. Roemer. 1989. Public ownership of the external world and private ownership of self. *Journal of Political Economy* 97:347–67.

Mumby, D. K. 1987. The political function of narrative in organizations. *Communication Monographs* 54:113–27.

Mumby, D. K. 1988. *Communication and power in organizations: Discourse, ideology, and domination*. Norwood, N.J.: Ablex.

Mumby, D. K., and L. Putnam. 1990, August. Bounded rationality as an organizational construct: A feminist critique. Unpublished paper presented at the Academy of Management Association, Aug., San Francisco.

Murdock, G., and P. Golding. 1989. Information poverty and political inequality: Citizenship in the age of privatized communications. *Journal of Communication* 39:180–95.

Nerone, J. 1989. Professional history and social memory. *Communication* 11:89–104.

Newstrom, J., and W. Ruch. 1975. The ethics of management and the management of ethics. *MSU Business Topics* 23:29–37.

Nightingale, D. V. 1982. *Workplace democracy*. Toronto: Univeristy of Toronto Press.

Nord, W. 1978. Dreams of humanization and the realities of power. *Academy of Management Review* 3:674–79.

Nordlinger, E. 1983. *On the autonomy of the democratic state*. Cambridge: Harvard University Press.

Offe, C. 1985. *Disorganized capitalism. Contemporary transformation of work and politics.* Oxford: Polity Press.

Oye, K. A., ed. 1986. *Cooperation under anarchy.* Princeton, N.J.: Princeton University Press.

Pacanowsky, M. 1988. Communication in an empowering organization. In *Communication Yearbook 13*, ed. J. Anderson. Newbury Park, Calif.: Sage

Pace, L., and W. Suojanen. 1988. Addictive type A behavior undermines employee involvement. *Personnel Journal* 67:36

Parker, M., and J. Slaughter. 1988. *Choosing sides: Unions and the team concept.* Boston: South End Press.

Parsons, T. 1956. *Economy and society.* Glencoe, Ill: Free Press.

Pateman, C. 1970. *Participation and democratic theory.* Cambridge: Oxford University Press.

Pateman, T. 1980. *Language, truth, and politics,* rev. ed. Newton Poppleford, Great Britain: Trevor Pateman and Jean Stroud.

Pearce, W. B. 1989. *Communication and the human condition.* Carbondale: Southern Illinois University Press.

Pearce, W. B., and V. Cronen. 1980. *Communication, action, and meaning.* New York: Prather.

Pêcheux, M. 1982. *Language, semantics, and ideology: Stating the obvious.* Translated by H. Nagpal. London: Macmillian.

Penno, M. 1984. Asymmetry of pre-decision information and managerial accounting. *Journal of Accounting Research* 22:177–91.

Perrow, C. 1979. *Complex organizations: A critical essay.* New York: Random House.

Peters, J. 1986. Institutional sources of intellectual poverty in communication research. *Communication Research* 13:527–59.

Peterson, S. 1990. *Political behavior: Patterns in everyday life.* Newbury Park, Calif.: Sage.

Pettigrew, A. M. 1973. *The politics of organizational decision making.* London: Tavistock.

Pfeffer, J. 1981. *Power in organizations.* Marshfield, Mass.: Pitman.

Philipsen, J. 1975) Speaking "like a man" in teamsterville: Cultural patterns of role enactment in an urban neighborhood. *Quarterly Journal of Speech* 61:13–22.

Pierce, J. and C. Furo. 1990. Employee ownership: Implications for management, *Organizational Dynamics* 18:32–43.

Pitelis, C., and R. Sugden. 1986. The separation of ownership and control in the theory of the firm. *International Journal of Industrial Organization* 4:71–86.

Popper, K. 1972. *Objective knowledge.* Oxford: Oxford University Press.

Popular Memory Group. 1982. Popular memory: Theory, politics, method. In *Making histories: Studies in history-writing and politics,* ed. R. Johnson, et al. Minneapolis: University of Minnesota Press.

Poster, M. 1980. *The critical theory of the family.* New York: Seabury Press.

Power, M. 1986. Taking stock: Philosophy and accountancy. *Philosophy* 61:387–94.

Power, M. In press. Educating accountants: Towards a critical ethnography. *Accounting, Organizations, and Society.*

Presnell, M., and S. Deetz. 1982. Interpersonal icons: Myth and ideology in remembered images of an other. Unpublished paper presented at the Myth and Society Conference, Apr., New Concord, Ohio.

Pringle, R. 1988. *Secretaries talk.* London: Verso.

Productivity worse near the top, study finds. 1983. *Chicago Tribune,* 1 Mar., sect. 4, 9.

Przeworski, A. 1980. Material bases of consent: Economics and politics in a hegemonic system. *Political Power and Social Theory* 1:21–66.

Przeworski, A. 1985. *Capitalism and social democracy.* Cambridge: Cambridge University Press.

Rachlin, A. 1988. *News as hegemonic reality: American political culture and the framing of news accounts.* Westport, Conn.: Greenwood Press.

Radford, G. 1990. The subliminal discourse: A Foucaultian analysis of a controversy in psychology. Ph.D. diss., Rutgers University.

Rakow, L. 1986. Rethinking gender research in communication. *Journal of Communication* 36:11–26.

Rakow, L. 1988. Gendered technology, gendered practice. *Critical Studies in Mass Communication* 5:57–70.

Ralston, D. 1985. Employee ingratiation: The role of management. *Academy of Management Review* 10:477–87.

Ramos, A. G. 1981. *The new science of organizations.* Toronto: University of Toronto Press.

Ranson, S., B. Hinings, and R. Greenwood. 1980. The structuring of organizational structures. *Administrative Science Quarterly* 25:1–17.

Reddy, M. J. 1979. The conduit metaphor. In *Metaphor and Thought,* ed. A. Ortony. Cambridge: MIT Press.

Reed, M. 1988. The problem of human agency in organizational analysis. *Organization Studies* 9:33–46.

Reilly, B. J., and J. A. DiAngelo. 1985. From ideology to pragmatism: Management's growth and development. *Advanced Management Journal* 50:28–33.

Reinecke, I. 1987. Information and the poverty of technology. In *Communications and the media in Australia,* ed. T. Wheelwright and K. Buckley. Sydney: Allen & Unwin.

Riley, P. 1983. A structurationist account of political cultures. *Administrative Science Quarterly* 28:414–38.

Roberts, J., and R. Scapens. 1990. Accounting as disipline. In *Critical accounts,* ed. D. J. Cooper and T. M. Hopper. London: Macmillan.

Robinson, G. 1988. "Here be dragons": Problems in charting the U.S. history of communication studies. *Communication* 10:97–119.

Rogers, T. G. P. 1987. Partnership with society: The social responsibility of business. *Management Decision* 25:2, 76–80.

Rorty, R. 1979. *Philosophy and the mirror of nature.* Princeton, N.J.: Princeton University Press.

Rorty, R. 1981. Hermeneutics and the social sciences. Unpublished paper presented at the annual conference of the Society for Phenomenology and Existential Philosophy, St. Louis.

Rorty, R. 1982. *Consequences of pragmaticism.* Minneapolis: University of Minnesota Press.

Rose, N. 1989. Individualizing Psychology. In *Texts of identity,* ed. J. Shotter and K. Gergen. 119–32. Newbury Park, Calif.: Sage.

Rowland, W. 1988. Recreating the past: Dilemmas in rewriting the history of communication research. *Communication* 10:121–40.

Rubinstein, S. P. 1987. *Participative systems at work. Creating quality and employment security.* New York: Human Sciences Press.

Russell, B. 1968. Philosophy and politics. In *Unpopular essays.* London: Unwin

Salaman, G. 1979. *Work organizations: Resistance and control.* New York: Longman.

Sampson, E. 1989. The deconstruction of the self. In *Texts of Identity,* ed. J. Shotter and K. Gergen, 1–19. Newbury Park, Calif.: Sage.

Sashkin, M. 1984. Participative management is an ethical imperative. *Organizational Dynamics* 13:5–22.

Sashkin, M. 1986. *A manager's guide to performance management.* New York: American Management Association.

Saussure, F. de 1974. *Course in general linguistics.* London: Fontana.

Schaef, A., and D. Fassel. 1988. *The addictive organization.* New York: Harper & Row.

Schaffer, S. 1989. Realities in the eighteenth century: Nature's representatives and their cultural resources. Unpublished paper presented at the Realism and Representation Conference, Rutgers University.

Schiller, H. 1986. The erosion of the national sovereignty by the world business system. In *The Myth of the information revolution: Social and cultural implication of communication technology,* ed. M. Traber, 21–34. Newbury Park, Calif.: Sage.

Schiller, H. 1989. *Culture, inc.: The corporate takeover of public expression.* Oxford: Oxford University Press.

Schudson, M. 1978. The ideal of conversation in the study of mass media. *Communication Research* 5:320–29.

Schudson, M. 1989. The present in the past versus the past in the present. *Communication* 11:105–13.

Schulman, P. 1989. The "logic" of organizational irrationality. *Administration and Society* 21:31–53.

Schutz, A. 1962. *Collected papers: Vol. I, The problem of social reality.* Edited with an Introduction by Maurice NataMson. The Hague: Martinus Nijhoff.

Schwartz, F. 1989. Managment women and the new facts of life. *Harvard Business Review,* Jan.–Feb., 65–76.

Scott, G. 1987. A perception of managerial practice in Australia in the 80s. *Practising Manager* (Australia) 8:29–32.

Scott, W. G. 1985. Organizational revolution: An end to managerial orthodoxy. *Administration and Society* 17:149–70.

Scott, W. G., and D. K. Hart. 1979. *Organizational America.* Boston: Houghton Mifflin.

Scott, W. R. 1987. The adolescence of institutional theory. *Administrative Science Quarterly* 32 (October):493–511.

Selznick, P. 1949. *TVA and grass roots.* Berkeley: University of California Press.

Selznick, P. 1957. *Leadership in administration.* New York: Harper & Row.

Sennet, R. 1977. *The fall of public man.* New York: Knopf.

Shapiro, M. 1981. *Language and political understanding: The politics of discursive practices.* New Haven, Conn.: Yale University Press.

Shotter, J., and K. Gergen, eds. 1989. *Texts of identity.* Newbury Park, Calif.: Sage Publications.

Shreve, A. 1987. *Remaking motherhood.* New York: Ballantine.

Simmons, J., and G. Blitzman. 1986. Training for self-managing work teams. *Quality Circles Journal* 9:18–21.

Simonds, A. 1989. Ideological domination and the political information market. *Theory and Society* 18:181–211.

Sklar, M. 1988. *The corporate reconstruction of American capitalism, 1890–1916: The market, the law, and politics.* Cambridge: Cambridge University Press.

Sless, D. 1986. Repairing messages: The hidden cost of inappropriate theory. *Australian Journal of Communication,* 10:82–93.

Sless, D. 1988. Forms of control. *Australian Journal of Communication* 14:57–69.

Sless, D. In press. Equity and efficiency in corporate communication: The emerging challenge. *Australian Journal of Communication.*

Sloan, A. P. 1963. *My years with General Motors.* London: Sidgwick & Jackson.

Slobin, D. I., S. H. Miller, and L. W. Porter. 1972. Forms of address and social relations in a business organization. In *The psychosociology of language,* ed. S. Moscovici, 263–72. Chicago: Markham Pub. Co.

Smart, B. 1986. The politics of truth and the problem of hegemony. In *Foucault: A Critical Reader,* ed. D. Hoy. Oxford: Basil Blackwell.

Smircich, L., and M. Calás. 1987. Organizational culture: A critical assessment. In *Handbook of organizational communication,* ed. F. Jablin, L. Putnam, K. Roberts, and L. Porter, 228–63. Newbury Park, Calif.: Sage.

Smith, D. 1970. The fallacy of the communication breakdown. *Quarterly Journal of Speech* 567:343–46.

Smith, D. 1972. Communication research and the idea of process. *Speech Monographs* 39:174–82.

Sobchack, V. 1982. Towards inhabited space: The semiotic structure of camera movement in the cinema. *Semiotica* 42:317–35.

Stablein, R., and W. Nord. 1985. Practical and emancipatory interests in organizational sysmbolism: A review and evaluation. *Journal of Management* 11:13–28.

Stamp, E. 1981. Accounting standards and the conceptual framwork: A plan for their evolution. *The Accountant's Magazine*, July, 216–22.

Steiner, L. 1988. Opositional decoding as an act of resistance. *Critical Studies in Mass Communication* 5:1–15.

Stivers, C. 1989. Organizational citizenship—a problematic metaphor: Comment on Golembiewski. *Administration and Society* 21:228–33.

Stivers, C. 1990. The public agency as polis. Active citizenship in the administrative state. *Administration and Society* 22:86–105.

Storey, J. 1983. *Managerial prerogative and the question of control.* London: Routledge & Kegan Paul.

Streeter, T. 1989. The dependence of the commercial broadcasting on government and the limits of the private/public distinction. Unpublished paper presented at the Culture and Communication Conference, Philadelphia.

Tannenbaum, A. S. 1986. Controversies about control and democracy in organizations. In *The organizational practice of democracy*, ed. R. N. Stern and S. McCarthy, 281–83. New York: Wiley.

Taylor, J. 1990. The great debate as to the relative merits of ethnography and critical theory, considered as alternative approaches to the conduct of non-positivist organizational communication research. In *Organizations—Communication: Emerging perspectives, volume 3*, ed. L. Thayer. Norwood, N.J.: Ablex.

The payoff from the teamwork. The gains in quality are substantial—so why isn't it spreading faster? 1989. *Business Week*, 10 July, 56–61.

Therborn, G. 1980. *The ideology of power and the power of ideology.* London: Verso.

Thompson, J. 1984. *Studies in the theory of ideology.* Berkeley: University of California Press.

Tomaselli, K., and P. Louw. 1989. Communication models and struggle: From authoritarian determinism to a theory of communication as social relations. Unpublished paper presented at the Conference on Culture and Communication, Philadelphia.

Tomkins, C., and R. Groves. 1983. The everyday accountant and researching his reality. *Accounting, Organizations, and Society* 8:361–74.

Torrence, G. W. 1959. *Management's right to manage*. Washington, D.C.: Bureau of National Affairs.

Touraine, A. 1977. *The self-production of society*. Chicago: University of Chicago Press.

Trachtenberg, A. 1983. *The incorporation of America*. New York: Hill & Wang.

Tricker, R. I. 1984. *Corporate governance*. Brookfield, Vt.: Gower.

Tuchman, G. 1978. *Making news*. New York: Free Press.

Turkle, S. 1984. *The second self: Computers and the human spirit*. New York: Simon & Schuster.

Turow, J. 1984. Media industries: *The production of news and entertainment*. New York: Longman.

Turow, J. 1989. Television and institutional power. In *Rethinking communication, volume 2: Paradigm exemplars*, ed. B. Dervin, L. Grossberg, B. O'Keefe, and E. Wartella. Newbury Park, Calif.: Sage.

Ulrich, W. 1983. *Critical heuristics of social planning a new approach to practical philosophy*. Bern: Haupt.

Ulrich, H., and G. J. B. Probst, eds. 1984. *Self-organization and management of social systems*. New York: Springer-Verlag.

Urwin, C. 1984. Power relations and the emergence of language. In *Changing the subject*, ed. J. Henriques, W. Hollway, C. Urwin, C. Venn, and V. Walkerdine, 264–322. New York: Methuen.

Valesio, P. 1980. *Novantiqua: Rhetorics as a contemporary theory*. Bloomington: Indiana University Press.

Vance, S. 1983. *Corporate leadership: Boards, directors, and strategy*. New York: McGraw-Hill.

van Dijk, T., ed. 1985. *Discourse and communication: New approaches to the analysis of mass media discourse and communication*. Berlin: de Gruyter.

van Dijk, T. 1989. Structures of discourse and structures of power. *Communication Yearbook* 12:18–59.

Vibbert, C. B. 1990. Freedom of speech and corporations: Supreme court strategies for the extension of the first amendment. *Communication* 12:19–34.

Victor, B., and J. Cullen. 1988. The organizational bases of ethical work climates. *Administrative Science Quarterly* 33:101–25.

Vogel, D. 1978. *Lobbying the corporation.* New York: Basic Books.

Volosinov, V. N. 1973. *Marxism and the philosophy of language.* Translated by L. Matejka and I. Titunik. Cambridge: Harvard University Press.

Votaw, D., and P. Sethi. 1973. Do we need a new corporate social response to a changing social environment? In *The corporate dilemma: Traditional values versus contemporary problems,* ed. D. Votaw and P. Sethi. Englewood Cliffs, N.J.: Prentice Hall.

Wagner, J., III, and R. Gooding. 1987. Effects of societal trends on participation research. *Administrative Science Quarterly* 32:241–62.

Wallerstein, I. 1980. The withering away of the state. *International Journal of the Sociology of Law* 8:369–78.

Wallerstein, I. 1989. 1968, revolution in the world-system: Theses and queries. *Theory and Society* 18:431–49.

Waltzer, M. 1986. The politics of Foucault. *In Foucault: A reader,* ed. D. Hoy, 151–68. Oxford: Basil Blackwell.

Waltzer, M. 1987. *Interpretation and social criticism.* Cambridge: Harvard University Press.

Watzlawick, P., J. Beavin, and D. Jackson. 1967. *Pragmatics of human communication.* New York: Norton.

Weber, M. 1947. *The theory of social and economic organization.* London: Oxford University Press.

Weber, M. 1972. *The protestant ethic and the spirit of capitalism.* New York: Scribners.

Weber, M. 1978. *Economy and society.* Translated by G. Roth and C Wittich. Berkeley: University of California Press.

Webster, F., and K. Robins. 1989. Plan and control: Towards a cultural history of the information society. *Theory and Society* 18:323–51.

Weedon, C. 1987. *Feminist practice and poststructuralist theory.* Oxford: Basil Blackwell.

Weick, K. 1979. *The social psychology of organizing.* 2d ed. Reading, Mass.: Addison-Wesley.

Weick, K. 1984. Small wins: Redefining the scale of social problems. *American Psychologist* 39:40–49.

Weidenbaum, M. 1988. The economic effects of corporate takeovers. *Executive Speeches*, May, 33–36.

Werhane, P. 1985. *Persons, rights, and corporations*. Englewood Cliffs,N.J.: Prentice Hall.

Westley, F. R. 1990. The eye of the needle: Cultural and personal transformation in a traditional organization. *Human Relations* 43:3, 273–93.

Where U.S. CEOs have foreign rivals beat: Paychecks. *Business Week*, Economic Trends. 1990. Sect., 5 Feb.

Whitfield, C. 1987. *Healing the child within*. Deerfield Beach, Fla: Health Communications.

Wickham, G. 1990. The political possibilities of postmodernism. *Economy and Society* 19:121–49.

Wildavsky, A. 1962. The analysis of issue-contexts in the study of decision making. *Journal of Politics* 24:718.

Williams, R. 1977. *Television: Technology and cultural form*. New York: Schocken.

Williams, R. 1982. *The sociology of culture*. New York: Shocken.

Williams, R. 1983. *Toward 2000*. New York: Pantheon.

Willis, P. 1977. *Learning to labor*. New York: Columbia University Press.

Willmott, H. 1983. Paradigms for accounting research. *Accounting, Organizations and Society* 8:389–405.

Willmott, H. 1989. O.R. as a problem situation: From soft systems methodology to critical science. In *Operational research and the social sciences*, ed. M. Jackson, P. Keys, and S. Cropper. New York: Plenum Press.

Winch, P. 1972. Understanding a primitive society. In *Ethics and action*, ed. P. Winch, 8–49. London: Routledge & Kegan Paul.

Winograd, T., and F. Flores. 1986. *Computers and cognition: A new foundation for computer system design*. New York: Ablex.

Wolfe, T. 1987. *The bonfire of the vanities*. New York: Bantam.

Wolfinger, R. E. 1971. Nondecisions and the study of local politics. *American Political Science Review* 65:1063–80.

Wolin, S. 1960. *Politics and vision: Continuity and innovation in western political thought.* Boston: Little, Brown.

Wood, J., and W. B. Pearce. 1980. Sexists, racists, and other classes of classifiers: Form and function of "ist" accusations. *Quarterly Journal of Speech* 66:239–50.

Woodiwiss, A. 1987. The discourses of production (part 1): Law, industrial relations, and the theory of ideology. *Economy and Society* 16:275–316.

Woodman, R. W., S. J. Payne, and D. Rubinstein. 1985. Personality correlates of a propensity to engage in political behavior in organizations. *Proceedings, Southwest Academy of Management*, 131–35.

Young, E. 1989. On the naming of the rose: Interests and multiple meanings as elements of organizational culture. *Organization Studies* 10:187–206.

Ziehe, T., and H. Stubenrauch. 1982. *Plädoyer für ungewöhnliches Lernen: Ideen zur Jugendstituation.* Reinbek bei Hamburg: Rowohlt, Taschenbuch Verlag. Cited by Alvesson.

NAME INDEX

Celeste Hodges

SUBJECT INDEX

Celeste Hodges